PANDORA'S GAMBLE

LAB LEAKS, PANDEMICS, AND A WORLD AT RISK

ALISON YOUNG

CENTER
STREET

NASHVILLE   NEW YORK

Center Street
Hachette Book Group
1290 Avenue of the Americas, New York, NY 10104
centerstreet.com
twitter.com/centerstreet

First Edition: April 2023

Center Street is a division of Hachette Book Group, Inc. The Center Street name and logo are trademarks of Hachette Book Group, Inc.

The publisher is not responsible for websites (or their content) that are not owned by the publisher.

Center Street books may be purchased in bulk for business, educational, or promotional use. For information, please contact your local bookseller or the Hachette Book Group Special Markets Department at special.markets@hbgusa.com.

Library of Congress Cataloging-in-Publication Data

Names: Young, Alison (Journalist), author.
Title: Pandora's gamble : lab leaks, pandemics, and a world at risk /
    Alison Young.
Description: First edition. | Nashville : Center Street, 2023. | Includes
    bibliographical references and index.
Identifiers: LCCN 2022053082 | ISBN 9781546002932 (hardcover) | ISBN
    9781546002956 (ebook)
Subjects: LCSH: Laboratory infections—History—Popular works. | Laboratory
    infections—Prevention—Popular works. | Microbiological
    laboratories—Safety measures—Popular works. | Microbiological
    laboratories—Security measures—Popular works. |
    Epidemics—Prevention—Popular works.
Classification: LCC QR64.7 .Y68 2023 | DDC 579.0289—dc23/eng/20221223
LC record available at https://lccn.loc.gov/2022053082

ISBNs: 9781546002932 (hardcover), 9781546002956 (ebook)

Printed in Canada

MRQ-T

10   9   8   7   6   5   4   3   2   1

CONTENTS

Covid-19, a Wuhan Lab— and a Horrifying Possibility

THE CABLE SENT from the U.S. embassy in Beijing[1] in January 2018 flagged a concerning safety issue to officials in Washington.

The Wuhan Institute of Virology's state-of-the-art biosafety level 4 laboratory facility—the first in China—had recently become operational, enabling scientists to conduct experiments with far more dangerous pathogens than they had previously. Even some of the lab's own scientists were concerned.

During a U.S. embassy team visit to the facility and conversations with staff, it was "noted that the new lab has a serious shortage of appropriately trained technicians and investigators needed to safely operate this high-containment laboratory," the cable said.

The embassy's cable briefly discussed the institute's ongoing research involving SARS-like coronaviruses from bats that have the potential to cause disease in humans and said the lab's scientists would welcome more help with biosafety.

Two years later, when every country in the world started to be ravaged by an unusual and new kind of coronavirus that claimed its first known victims in Wuhan, a haunting question emerged: Did the Covid-19 pandemic come from a lab?

It was an obvious question.

Wuhan, an industrial metropolis larger than New York City, is about 1,000 miles north of the caves where bats are known to carry coronaviruses that are similar to the virus that causes Covid-19.

But the city was the location of several major coronavirus research laboratories, most notably the Wuhan Institute of Virology. The WIV had a history of collaborating on controversial experiments[2] and had amassed a collection of specimens through years of virus hunting trips to China's southern provinces.[3,4]

Yet almost immediately, there was an extraordinary effort by government officials in China—and also by leading scientific experts in the United States and around the world—to shut down any investigation of a possible laboratory accident.

As the death toll mounted and the virus spread at the speed of jet travel, the idea that this disaster could have come from a laboratory was derided by many scientists and journalists who publicly branded it as a conspiracy theory.

Legitimate questions about the origin of Covid-19 became entangled with then president Donald Trump's China-bashing rhetoric. In the toxic atmosphere of the nation's capital and a country divided, the lab leak theory became politically and racially weaponized in ugly ways.

During the first year of the pandemic, it seemed that anyone who raised questions about whether SARS-CoV-2, the virus that causes Covid-19, could have come from a lab in Wuhan was accused of peddling conspiracies.

In private, however, some of the world's elite scientists saw a lab accident as a very real and horrifying possibility.

They knew what the public didn't: Lab accidents happen with shocking frequency, even at the world's best-run labs.

Most of the time, nobody becomes infected. And even when infections happen, the workers inside the labs are usually the only people at risk. The chances are smaller still that any infection will spread outside a facility. In fact, many pathogens studied in labs aren't capable of spreading easily from person to person, or they are effectively stopped by vaccines.

Yet there are some kinds of pathogens—especially those that spread through invisible airborne particles—that pose an increased potential for escape and the capability to ignite an outbreak or, worse, a global pandemic.

Coronaviruses are among those pathogens.

All it would take for such a virus to get out of a lab is simple human error, a lapse in judgment, a failure to fully follow a safety protocol or wear appropriate protective gear. Equipment failures and malfunctions can also play a role.

Just one slip-up and a lab worker could unknowingly become infected, then go about life at home and in public unaware they were spreading contagion—especially if symptoms were mild or nonexistent.

Dangerous pathogens also have the potential to escape through infectious laboratory waste, something that has happened with deadly consequences. Another long-standing concern is the insider threat posed by a lab worker seeking to deliberately misuse their access to biological agents—a risk made apparent in the United States when the FBI accused a senior U.S. Army scientist of perpetrating the deadly anthrax attacks that took place in 2001.

This wasn't the stuff of crazy, politically driven conspiracy theories—even if there may have been some seeking to use the situation to serve political purposes.

For more than a decade, staid, non-political groups like the U.S. Government Accountability Office had warned[5] that a worldwide building boom of high-containment laboratories was increasing the risk of a catastrophic lab accident. The more labs, workers, and experiments, the greater the chances something could go terribly wrong.

The implications of the virus first appearing in Wuhan were potentially enormous.

It was getting late on a Sunday afternoon in the first few weeks of the growing Covid-19 outbreak when James Le Duc finally hit send on a difficult email to a friend and scientific colleague at the Wuhan Institute of Virology.

The message broached a disquieting subject and had the potential to harm a relationship carefully nurtured over several years. Each sentence was written with great care.

"I am devastated to see the evolving nCoV epidemic unfolding in Wuhan and I just hope that you, your family and the larger Institute colleagues are well and surviving this very difficult time," Le Duc's email began,[6] referring to the novel, or new, coronavirus by its abbreviation nCoV.

Le Duc[7] was the director of the University of Texas Medical Branch's Galveston National Laboratory, one of the world's top biological research facilities and one of just eight in the United States registered with federal officials to operate labs at biosafety level 4,[8] the maximum level of containment. He also was a respected international leader on laboratory safety issues who had spent years building relationships with lab operators around the world in an effort to improve safety and security through the sharing of best practices.

That was how Le Duc had come to know Yuan Zhiming,[9] director of the Wuhan Institute of Virology's biosafety level 4 lab. As the Chinese lab prepared to open, their two institutions had participated in personnel exchanges,[10] allowing the long-established Texas laboratory to share its experience with providing biosafety training and managing the complex operations of a maximum containment laboratory.

Together, Le Duc and Yuan had been advocating for the creation of an international network of maximum containment laboratories to grow similar collaborations and improve the safety of labs worldwide.[11]

But now the Wuhan Institute of Virology seemed to be at the epicenter of a deadly emerging outbreak of a new kind of coronavirus.

"I want to suggest that you conduct a thorough review of the laboratory activities associated with research on coronaviruses so that you are fully prepared to answer questions dealing with the origin of the virus," Le Duc wrote in his email to Yuan.

The email was dated February 9, 2020.

The outbreak had first surfaced in Wuhan, catching the attention of local doctors[12] in the final days of December 2019. Although the Chinese government had initially tried to conceal and censor information[13] about the rapidly spreading disease, as Le Duc wrote his email, the danger posed to the world by the new virus was becoming alarmingly clear.

More than 37,000 cases, including more than 800 deaths,[14] had been confirmed in China at that point. And this disease, which caused deadly pneumonia, was jumping across international borders, with more than 300 cases detected in 24 countries. In the United States, 12 cases had been identified.

Chinese authorities had initially linked early cases of the outbreak to the Huanan Seafood Wholesale Market[15] in Wuhan, which they had closed down for disinfection on January 1.

The market, which traded in live animals, was a likely suspect. Wildlife markets in China were deemed the culprit back in 2003[16] during an earlier epidemic of a different kind of SARS coronavirus.

When new diseases emerge, they typically are the result of people coming into close contact with animals that are carrying new types of pathogens that have the ability to infect humans.

But in recent days, the Huanan seafood market in Wuhan was looking less certain as the source of the outbreak.

Researchers in China had just published a paper in the *Lancet* describing some of the first cases[17] of the new disease. Of these initial forty-one cases, only twenty-seven had a history of exposure to the Huanan market. And the earliest of these known cases, a patient who became ill on December 1, 2019, had no link to the market.

As the wider world started to become aware that Wuhan was a major center of coronavirus research, the first speculative questions emerged about the Wuhan Institute of Virology.[18]

"This coronavirus is a catastrophe on the scale of Chernobyl for China,"[19] U.S. Senator Tom Cotton, a Republican from Arkansas, said during a January 30, 2020, hearing of the Senate Armed Services Committee.[20] "But actually, it's probably worse than Chernobyl, which was localized in its effect."

Cotton, in comments shared on Twitter, stated that the virus's origin was still unknown—and that it could have come from a market, a farm, or a food processing company, adding: "I would note that Wuhan has China's only biosafety level 4 super laboratory that works with the world's most deadly pathogens to include—yes—coronavirus."[21]

While a vocal backlash emerged from many in the scientific community who publicly condemned any suggestion that labs had played any role in the public health crisis, other conversations were going on in private.

Le Duc was just one of the many knowledgeable scientists around the world who were taking seriously the possibility of a lab accident. Le Duc had an impressive background in research and public health. Before joining the Galveston National Laboratory, he had been the director of the Centers for Disease Control and Prevention's division of viral and rickettsial diseases.

For several years, Le Duc had been working with the U.S. National Academies of Sciences, Engineering, and Medicine to increase communication among U.S. and Chinese scientists on issues of emerging infectious diseases, laboratory safety, and global health security. These joint China–U.S. workshops had included presentations by the Wuhan Institute of Virology's top coronavirus researcher, Shi Zhengli.[22]

Shi had been warning for years about the risks of one of these viruses making the jump from bats to humans and causing the next pandemic.

"I have the utmost respect and admiration for Dr Shi and I am in no way casting doubt on her or her colleagues. I just think that we need to aggressively address these rumors and presumably false accusations quickly and provide definitive, honest information to counter misinformation. If there are weaknesses in your program, now is the time to admit them and get them corrected," Le Duc wrote in his email to Yuan.

Attached to the email was a list of dozens of questions that Le Duc suggested the Wuhan Institute of Virology should be asking[23] about its labs' research activities, physical security, virus stocks, and personnel during the period from October 1, 2019, to the present. The document called for an "investigation into the possibility that the nCoV was the result of a release from the Wuhan Institute of Virology (main campus or new BSL3/BSL4 facilities)," referring to the WIV's older main campus and the institute's new high-containment biosafety level 3 and level 4 lab facility that was located a few miles away.

Among Le Duc's questions:

Where is coronavirus research conducted? What level of biocontainment? Is there any evidence to suggest a mechanical failure in biocontainment during the period in question? Were biological safety cabinets used and appropriately certified? Were exhaust air filtration systems working correctly? Were disinfection systems for lab waste working properly?

When was nCoV first handled in your laboratory? What was the source of that virus? What are the coronaviruses in your possession that are most closely related to nCoV based on genetic sequences? Is anyone on your team conducting gain-of-function studies, recombination studies, or any other studies that may have resulted in the creation of the nCoV?

How many people have access to the coronavirus stocks and laboratory? Senior investigators? Junior investigators? Technical support staff? Students? Animal handlers? Janitors and other cleaning staff? Building support personnel? Others?

Is there any evidence to suggest that a disgruntled employee may have had access to the coronavirus stocks?

Does the institute have an occupational health clinic where employees and students can go to seek medical care? If so, was there any indication of unusual illness similar to that seen for nCoV among institute staff? Do any staff members of the Institute reside in the districts serviced by the hospitals/clinics that treated the first identified Wuhan cases?

Do staff members of the Wuhan Institute of Virology frequent the seafood/live market first associated with the nCoV outbreak? Did any staff member visit the market in the weeks prior to it being closed?

It was a difficult email on an incredibly sensitive topic.

"I trust that you will take my suggestions in the spirit of one friend trying to help another during a very difficult time," Le Duc said as he ended the email.

Months passed.

The email was met with silence.

"Unfortunately, I never received a response," Le Duc said in an April 2020 email[24] to David Franz,[25] a former commander of the U.S. Army Medical Research Institute of Infectious Diseases at Fort Detrick, Maryland, and an international expert on biosecurity who worked closely with Le Duc on projects in China and other countries.

✳

A LAB ACCIDENT, AT least initially, was a very real fear for the Wuhan Institute of Virology's top coronavirus researcher, Shi.[26]

Shi had been attending a conference in Shanghai on December 30, 2019, when she was told that a new kind of coronavirus had been identified in pneumonia patients hospitalized in Wuhan.

"I had never expected this kind of thing to happen in Wuhan, in central China," Shi told science writer Jane Qiu in an interview published in *Scientific American*[27] in March 2020 during the early weeks of the pandemic.

Shi had dedicated much of her career to preventing a pandemic. Since 2004 she had been collecting bat coronaviruses in remote parts of China and studying the specimens in her lab in Wuhan. Shi knew from her research that the types of coronaviruses that posed the greatest risk of jumping to humans were found far away from the huge city where people were now falling ill.

It made her wonder: Could the virus have come from her own lab?[28]

Shi described to Qiu how she frantically reviewed her lab's records to see whether there had been any incidents. Shi indicated she was especially concerned about the disposal of materials that had been used in experiments.

It was a relief, Shi said, when her lab found that the genetic sequence of the virus spreading in Wuhan didn't match any of the viruses in her lab's collections.

"That really took a load off my mind," Shi told *Scientific American*. "I had not slept a wink for days."

There were reasons to be concerned about biosafety.

In the fall of 2019, about two months before the outbreak emerged, Yuan—the director of the WIV's new biosafety level 4 lab—had published an article in a scientific journal[29] noting some concerning issues with biosafety in high-containment labs in China.

Yuan described how biosafety level (BSL) 3 and 4 labs, whose names and locations were not disclosed in the article, faced challenges getting adequate funding for operations and maintenance, as well as ensuring that their workers had sufficient training in biosafety and operational skills.

"Currently, most laboratories lack specialized biosafety managers and engineers," Yuan wrote.

Yuan said that "several high-level BSLs have insufficient operational funds for routine yet vital processes. Due to the limited resources, some BSL-3 laboratories run on extremely minimal operational costs or in some cases none at all." While China had a comprehensive set of regulations governing the construction, management, and operation of high-containment labs, Yuan said "their enforcement still needs to be strengthened."

Yuan's paper seemed to echo the types of concerns that U.S. embassy officials wrote about in their January 2018 cable after visiting the Wuhan Institute of Virology's new BSL-4 lab.

In that diplomatic cable to the U.S. State Department,[30] the embassy team noted that the WIV was working with the University of Texas Medical Branch's Galveston National Lab to help train its workers, "which may help alleviate this talent gap over time."

Despite this collaboration, the cable said WIV "would welcome more help from U.S. and international organizations as they establish 'gold standard' operating procedures and training courses for the first time in China."

AFTER THE PANDEMIC BEGAN, Yuan and Shi would say repeatedly that the new coronavirus didn't come from the Wuhan Institute of Virology. The first time the virus was ever in the WIV, Shi has said, was December 30, 2019: That's when clinical samples from pneumonia patients sickened in the outbreak were sent to her lab for testing. By the next day, they had identified the pathogen as a novel SARS-related coronavirus.

"Before that, we had never been in contact with or studied this virus, nor did we know of its existence," Shi told *Science* magazine in July 2020.[31,32]

Shi said tests performed on all of the institute's staff and students showed nobody had been infected with either a SARS-like bat coronavirus or the new SARS-CoV2 that causes Covid-19. In response to questions from *Science* about how the institute was certain that none of their specimen collection contained the pandemic virus or a close relative, Shi said the institute had tested everything and found no connection.

"We tested all bat samples that we collected, including bat anal swabs, oral swabs and fecal samples," Shi said.[33] While Shi said that 2,007 samples were positive for the presence of coronavirus, none of them had a gene sequence that was close enough to have given rise to the virus that causes Covid-19.

Yuan, in an interview with the global Chinese state television outlet CGTN,[34] said it was "understandable" that people would make associations because the WIV was located in Wuhan. But he decried rumors, political accusations, and conspiracy theories that the Wuhan Institute of Virology could be the source of the pandemic or that the facility wasn't as well run as any in Europe or the United States.

"As we said early on, there's no way this virus came from us," Yuan said in the April 2020 interview, which was dubbed in English. "We have a strict regulatory regime. We have a code of conduct for research, so we are confident of that."

He dismissed the possibility of the virus being man-made, saying he didn't think humans had the capability to make such a virus.

Meanwhile, the Chinese government has gone further, not only saying that Covid-19 didn't come from the WIV—but also asserting that the virus originated somewhere outside of China.

China's propaganda apparatus has pushed claims that members of the U.S. military brought the virus to Wuhan[35] in October 2019 when they attended the Military World Games. (U.S. officials said no illnesses were tied to the nearly 300 athletes sent to the games.)

One of the most enduring story lines promoted by Chinese state media, going back to the earliest months of the pandemic[36] and continuing to this day, was that a high-containment military laboratory at the U.S. Army's Fort Detrick in Maryland was the source of the virus. China also has pushed the idea that the virus had spread on imported frozen foods,[37] a risk that many experts considered marginal.

IN FEBRUARY 2021, WHEN a joint World Health Organization–China team completed a much-anticipated trip to Wuhan to study the origin of the Covid-19 pandemic, the group summarily dismissed the lab-leak hypothesis as "extremely unlikely."

In fact, the group considered a lab accident so unlikely that it was the only hypothesis the group deemed unworthy of further study.[38]

Despite the initial big headlines that fed into the narrative that the lab hypothesis was the stuff of tinfoil hats, it would later be disclosed that the WHO team had done no meaningful investigation of the possibility of a research accident, yet still drew its conclusions.

While the WHO group was taken on highly organized tours of lab facilities in Wuhan, the members never reviewed the laboratory notebooks, incident reports, or volumes of other records that might have shed light on whether a lab origin should legitimately be ruled out.[39]

Instead, they were comfortable making this important finding based on conversations where assurances were made—scientist to scientist—by those who were operating the labs at the center of the controversy.[40]

"Extremely important meeting today with staff at WIV including Dr Shi Zhengli. Frank, open discussion. Key questions asked & answered," tweeted zoologist Peter Daszak,[41] a member of the WHO team and president of the New York–based nonprofit research organization EcoHealth Alliance.

It was no secret in some parts of the scientific community that Daszak had deep personal and professional relationships with the Wuhan Institute of Virology going back years. Daszak and Shi had published several scientific papers together, and EcoHealth had provided funding for some of WIV's coronavirus studies, including some of the very research that should have been under scrutiny.[42]

Yet respected scientific institutions like the WHO and also a Covid-19 commission convened by the prestigious medical journal the *Lancet*—at least in the beginning,[43] before the public backlash[44] over potential conflicts of interest[45]—saw no problem with Daszak playing a key role.

At the joint WHO–China team's press conference on February 9, 2021,[46] the international members of the team were represented on the stage by Peter Ben Embarek, the WHO scientist leading the mission,[47] and team member Marion Koopmans, a virologist who heads the department of viroscience at Erasmus MC in the Netherlands.

The mission, Ben Embarek said, identified four main hypotheses for how the virus could have emerged. The "most likely pathway," he said, involved the virus jumping to humans through some kind of intermediary animal host—such as a wild or farmed animal brought into the Huanan seafood market. It was also possible that the virus spilled over directly from its initial animal host, likely bats, to humans. Both of these deserved further studies, he said.

The team also thought further studies should be done to examine the potential role of frozen animal products in spreading the virus.

"However, the findings suggest that the laboratory incident hypothesis is extremely unlikely to explain introduction of the virus into the human population," he said, and it was not a hypothesis the team would pursue any further.

Ben Embarek spoke about the team's visit to the Wuhan Institute of Virology, where they had met with scientists and lab leadership and discussed a wide range of questions.

"It was very unlikely that anything could escape from such a place," Ben Embarek said. "If you look at the history of lab accidents, these are extremely rare events."

But lab accidents aren't rare.

As an investigative reporter, I had spent nearly fifteen years revealing shocking safety breaches at prestigious U.S. laboratories.

At the *Atlanta Journal-Constitution*, where I was the full-time beat reporter covering the Centers for Disease Control and Prevention during the mid-2000s, I had exposed serious safety and engineering problems inside one of the world's newest and most advanced laboratories. Later, as a member of *USA TODAY*'s national investigative team, I had reported on several serious, high-profile CDC lab accidents involving anthrax, a deadly strain of avian influenza, and Ebola virus that had resulted in potential exposures of dozens of lab workers.

In 2015, I led a *USA TODAY* Network team investigating more than 200 labs[48] operated by universities, federal agencies, the military, and private firms across the United States. Their internal records showed widespread and troubling lapses.[49]

Bacteria had escaped a high-security lab by hitching a ride on workers' dirty lab coats. Respirators and space suit–like protective gear used to deliver safe oxygen to scientists had developed holes while scientists were working in them or had fallen apart with troubling frequency. There were numerous needlesticks, animal bites, spills, and splashes of infectious specimens. Vials of dangerous pathogens had gone missing. Cattle used in experiments with a highly regulated bacteria had even been sent to a slaughterhouse and their meat sold for people to eat.

Over the years, I have spoken with dozens of lab workers who risked their careers to share with me documents and details about the accidents and shoddy safety practices inside the lab buildings where they worked. And I had also reported on the deaths of other lab workers who had become infected during their research but didn't realize it until it was too late.

What I had come to learn through more than a decade of reporting on these failures was that the only thing rare about lab accidents was the public finding out about them.

I also learned that when accidents happen, powerful people and institutions often work hard to keep the information secret.

IN THE WAKE OF the initial joint World Health Organization–China team's report declaring a lab accident "extremely unlikely," there was an international backlash and calls for greater transparency from China.

WHO director-general Tedros Adhanom Ghebreyesus and some members of the international team had raised concerns[50] starting in February 2021 about Chinese officials not sharing raw data during the initial study trip[51] to Wuhan. Tedros also had been troubled by what he said was "a premature push" to eliminate the lab-leak hypothesis.[52]

"I was a lab technician myself, an immunologist," Tedros said.[53] "I have worked in the lab and lab accidents happen. It's common; I have seen it happening and I have myself had errors so it can happen."

Even world leaders attending the Group of Seven summit[54] in the summer of 2021 were calling for a new study of the origins of Covid-19.

But after the WHO announced that its new plan to look for the source of the pandemic would include audits of labs in the area where the virus first emerged,[55] Chinese officials said the country wasn't going to participate.

Zeng Yixin, China's deputy health minister, slammed the new WHO plan as showing "disrespect for common sense and arrogance toward science."[56]

As much as the lab-leak hypothesis had been portrayed as ludicrous in some news coverage, it wasn't viewed that way by key U.S. government officials.

President Joe Biden, in May 2021, called on the U.S. intelligence community to redouble its efforts[57] during the following ninety days to determine the origin of the virus, noting that the intelligence agencies at that time considered the "two likely scenarios" to be the natural and lab theories. And that assessment remained the case when the intelligence community released its declassified report[58] a few months later with the top-line finding that "all agencies assess that two hypotheses are plausible: natural exposure to an infected animal and a laboratory-associated incident."

In Congress, investigations of the lab-leak theory have been largely the purview of Republican members[59,60] whose efforts have helped to extract important information[61] about U.S.-funded research in Wuhan[62]—but have also devolved into political theater[63] partially rooted in the Covid-19 culture wars[64] over masks and a general disdain for Anthony Fauci, the president's chief medical adviser.

A bipartisan oversight investigation into the origins of Covid-19 by the U.S. Senate Committee on Health, Education, Labor and Pensions began in June 2021. In October 2022, the committee's ranking Republican member, Richard Burr of North Carolina, released a thirty-five-page "interim" report from the committee's minority staff that concluded the pandemic was "more likely than not, the result of a research-related incident."[65] The report was based on an analysis of publicly available data.

U.S. Senator Patty Murray, D-Washington, and the committee's chair, said at the time that a bipartisan report was still in the works and that it is "absolutely critical" to learn lessons from the pandemic "and that, of course, includes undertaking a full examination of how Covid-19 first emerged."[66]

Throughout 2022, more groups of experts from around the world—including a new WHO Scientific Advisory Group for the Origins of Novel Pathogens[67,68] and the Covid-19 Commission[69] created by prestigious medical journal the *Lancet*—continued to call the lab-accident hypothesis credible and in need of investigation.

"The proximal origins of SARS-CoV-2 are still not known," the *Lancet* commission report said[70] in September 2022. "Independent experts consulted by the *Lancet* COVID-19 Commission shared the view that hypotheses about both natural and laboratory spillovers are in play and need further investigation."

For three years, while the lab-leak hypothesis has been dismissed, scientists from around the world have searched for evidence of the natural origin of the virus—testing more than 80,000[71] animal samples in China[72] and beyond,[73] and analyzing the limited data the Chinese government has released about the earliest known human cases of Covid-19 in Wuhan.

A prominent and vocal[74] group of U.S. and international scientists made big headlines in 2022 when they published a pair of studies that analyzed a range of publicly available data that indicates the Huanan seafood market was "the early epicenter of the COVID-19 pandemic."[75]

Their work suggests that animals sold at the market—which included species susceptible to the virus—launched the initial outbreak.

However, as of late 2022, no tests had found any animal anywhere that was infected with the virus that gave rise to SARS-CoV-2.

Was the market where the virus made its first jump from animals into humans? Or was it the location of a super-spreader event, with the first infection occurring somewhere else?

That remains unclear.

Thanks to stonewalling by Chinese authorities, the hamstrung World Health Organization inquiry, and the passage of years, we may never know the source of the virus and whether it was unleashed through a laboratory mistake.

One thing is certain. If the pandemic began with a lab accident in Wuhan—or even if the public and world leaders believed it was the likely source—it would be the biological equivalent of the nuclear industry's Three Mile Island or Chernobyl. It would put biological research facilities at risk of being subjected to international safety standards and regulations, limits on dangerous experiments, and mandates for public transparency.

And that's something this sector of the sciences has largely avoided in the more than 300 years since a self-taught Dutch scientist fashioned an early microscope and observed the microorganisms he referred to as "animalcules," or little animals.

Much of what science does is truly miraculous. The stunning speed at which lifesaving Covid-19 vaccines were created is a testament to the critical importance of biomedical research.

But behind these miracles is a disturbing reality, one that gets far too little scrutiny and that scientists, labs, and government agencies actively try to hide.

History shows there are a stunning number of ways that "lab leaks" can happen.

This book will reveal the shockingly lax safety practices inside some of the world's most prestigious labs and show how the current lack of rigorous national and international oversight should make all of us concerned.

Most of the time, laboratories get lucky, despite the inevitable human mistakes and sometimes brazen acts of carelessness.

But when will that luck run out? And has it already?

The current battle lines over whether the lab-leak hypothesis is worthy of investigation started forming decades before the Covid-19 pandemic. How we got to the current stalemate is a tale that begins during World War II in the U.S. biowarfare labs at what is today known as Fort Detrick in Maryland.

It was a time when rigorous scrutiny of potential safety lapses was seen as improving science, not harming it.

PART 1

"SKELETONS" AT THE BIRTHPLACE OF BIOSAFETY

CHAPTER 1

Martyrs to Science

U.S. Army Biological Laboratories
Camp Detrick, Frederick, Maryland
November 1950

A T FIRST, SHERWOOD Davis[1] tried to ignore the headaches. He could not afford to be sick, especially not with a baby on the way.

Each morning, well before dawn, he would quietly climb out of bed to get ready for work, trying not to wake his wife, Geraldine, who was seven months pregnant. She would need to be up soon enough to get to her own job.

The couple lived in a two-story frame house in Bartonsville, Maryland, a historically Black community where Davis grew up. He was the son of a sharecropper and from a young age had learned the importance of hard work.

Their neighborhood was just three miles southeast of downtown Frederick, Maryland. It still had a rural feel, even though the community was only about an hour from the nation's capital. The Monocacy River flowed just a few blocks away from their house.

Landing a job as a dishwasher a few years earlier at the U.S. Army's Camp Detrick on Frederick's northwest side had been a huge opportunity for Davis. The hours were early and long, starting at 5:30 a.m., but the pay was better than he could hope to get anywhere else.[2]

Of course, that was because of the risk.

Davis wasn't washing dishes in the base's cafeteria. He was cleaning and disinfecting specimen plates, beakers, tubes, and other glassware inside Camp Detrick's high-security biological research laboratories. In addition to studying germs, the scientists there were leading the U.S. government's

3

efforts in an international biological arms race that escalated during World War II.

By 1950, most everyone in the Frederick area had some idea of what went on at Camp Detrick, even if the residents didn't know the specifics of the secret work. Detrick was home to the U.S. Army Biological Laboratories, and at the end of World War II the U.S. government had disclosed publicly that the army had been developing biological weapons, a revelation that generated significant news coverage.[3]

In 1943 the military had converted a small airport[4] on the outskirts of Frederick into a sprawling base for scientific research. The base brought an influx of workers—not just military officers and troops, but also numerous civilian scientists who arrived with their families.

Until 1969, when President Richard M. Nixon ordered the end of the United States' offensive biological weapons program and only allowed research considered to be defensive, Camp Detrick's civilian and military workforce was creating batches of toxins, anthrax, and other bacteria and figuring out ways to turn them into bombs and other weapons. The goal was to counter what the U.S. saw as threats posed by enemy states[5] like Germany, Japan, and later the Soviet Union.

But it took a lot more people than just the scientists in their white coats to operate these laboratories.

The high-tech equipment and buildings required ongoing maintenance and repair. Reports on experiments had to be typed. Floors needed to be mopped. Lab animals had to be fed, their cages cleaned, and their spent carcasses disposed.

So the labs also employed scores of support staff like Davis. And their jobs were far riskier than most knew.

Until now, Davis had avoided becoming infected with any of the dreaded diseases that were the focus of the base's work. But recently he wasn't feeling well.

Maybe he just had a cold or the flu? It was November, after all.

The headaches had started about a week earlier, a few days after Davis celebrated his forty-fifth birthday.

It didn't seem like a big deal at first.

As the days went by, though, he started having chills and muscle aches. Then the fevers began.

By the time he felt sick enough to go to the station hospital at Camp Detrick, an infection had been taking hold inside his body for what had probably been weeks. As teams of doctors drew blood and tried to determine whether he had been sickened by one of the base's deadly microbes, his fever spiked to 104°F.[6]

THE REPORT OF SHERWOOD Davis's hospital admission on November 20, 1950, recorded under his full given name of William S. Davis, joined a growing pile of similar reports being investigated by the Safety Division of the U.S. Army Biological Laboratories.

He would soon become one of more than 145 Detrick lab workers[7] with confirmed lab-acquired infections during 1943–1950. In these first several years, there were no recorded deaths.

While some of the lab-acquired infections were minor, many caused serious illnesses that resulted in workers being hospitalized for days or weeks at a time. The fortunate ones eventually recovered completely. Others, however, ended up with chronic infections or on permanent disability.

The mounting human toll weighed heavily on Dr. Arnold Wedum, the safety division's director, who would later be hailed as the father of modern biological safety.[8,9]

Wedum arrived at Camp Detrick in 1946.[10] He and his safety team had methodically documented and studied the extraordinary number of ways that bacteria and viruses could get out of their laboratories and spread infection among those who never knew they were at risk. Wedum's team also pioneered many of the cornerstone biosafety practices still used today to contain microbes in laboratories throughout the world.

Wedum had a PhD in bacteriology and also a medical degree from Northwestern University, a background that allowed him to understand both how biological research was conducted in the lab and the serious health impacts of laboratory-acquired infections.

In the four and a half years since he left a career in academia as an assistant professor of bacteriology, Wedum had been on a crusade at Camp Detrick to eliminate lab accidents and infections.

He knew from personal experience the life-changing impact of occupational illnesses.

His wife, Bernice, a physician and medical researcher, had contracted tuberculosis from a patient during her medical training while the couple lived in Cincinnati. It had been a crushing setback after she had become one of only two women[11] to receive medical degrees in her class of seventy-seven graduates from the University of Cincinnati College of Medicine in June 1941.

Nearly a decade later, she was still battling the disease and eventually needed surgery to remove part of one lung.[12] It was one more hurdle for her as a woman in science trying to pursue her own research into rheumatic heart disease while helping raise the couple's two young children.

In his new job at Camp Detrick, Arnold Wedum made it his mission to search for clues about how each person had become infected in the hope of finding ways to prevent other lab workers from being exposed in the future.

Much of what is known today about how biological research laboratories should safely work with dangerous microbes can be traced to the work of Wedum and his colleagues. They did groundbreaking studies to determine who at Camp Detrick—and at labs across the United States and abroad—was getting sick and why.

Their work revealed the kinds of activities that were most likely to allow deadly microbes to escape the laboratories where they were being studied, infecting people who had no idea they were being placed at risk. And by the 1950s, they had helped create futuristic devices and safety concepts that are still considered best practices today.

Along the way, Wedum also learned that keeping workers safe in biological research laboratories was far more difficult than protecting the safety of workers in chemistry, radiological, or engineering labs.

"Medical personnel as a rule tend to be more reluctant than, for instance, engineers or chemists to enter into a professionally planned safety program that involves critical scrutiny of the entire research process," Wedum would later tell a group[13] of occupational safety experts in 1964.

Part of the challenge was the invisible threat from bacteria and viruses.

The microbes couldn't be seen with the naked eye and signs of their attack might not appear for days or weeks. Even then, infections were often difficult to prove as having been occupationally acquired, especially if symptoms were flu-like and mild.

But there was another, even bigger challenge, he found. It was the pervasive culture of self-sacrifice and resistance to safety measures among many of the researchers drawn to work with dangerous microbes.

They didn't want safety getting in the way of their science.

ARNOLD WEDUM INHERITED SAFETY oversight of a research program that had been quickly launched in 1943, during World War II, amid the growing threat of biological warfare by Germany and Japan.

It was a concern fueled in part by the use of biological agents[14]—including cholera, dysentery, and anthrax—by the Japanese military. (At the end of World War II, an investigation revealed that Japan's biowarfare program had also conducted deadly experiments[15] on prisoners of war, many of them Chinese nationals, including exposures to aerosolized anthrax.)

The possibility of a biological attack on the U.S. seemed urgent and real for those working at Detrick's secret, high-security labs.

In 1942 a committee of experts, convened by the National Academy of Sciences at the request of Secretary of War Henry L. Stimson, said their review found[16] that the use of bacterial weapons was "entirely possible, even probable," and that the country must take actions to develop both offensive and defensive measures.

The United States had already faced some biowarfare plots during World War I, including an effort[17] by German agents in 1915 to infect horses and cattle with deadly bacteria, including anthrax, as the animals were about to be shipped from U.S. ports to battlefields in Europe.

With recent advances in microbiology, the experts warned about the potential for larger scale attacks on U.S. civilians that could range from contaminating water and food supplies to spreading organisms from airplanes, bombs, or missiles.

Dozens of organisms showed potential to be used by enemies, the experts warned. They included the bacteria that cause typhoid, dysentery, brucellosis, plague, and cholera, and viruses that cause various types of encephalitis, smallpox, yellow fever, and psittacosis.

These lists of pathogens contributed to the research agenda for Camp Detrick's secret labs.

Fortunately, the deadly organisms studied during the base's early history generally only caused infection via direct contact with the microbes—such as by inhaling bacteria-laden dust or drinking contaminated water. They weren't capable of easily spreading from person to person and causing a chain-reaction pandemic.

From the beginning, Detrick's labs had a safety program. It was established by Order No. 1[18] on May 17, 1943. But initially much of the research that focused on growing and testing dangerous microbes was done on open benchtops.[19] In those days, microbiology labs looked a lot like chemistry labs—even though the hazards were different.

As a result, Detrick's lab workers during World War II fell ill at alarming rates.

Depending on the organism being studied, 13 percent to 48 percent of the lab workers ended up becoming infected, Major Harold V. Ellingson, the post surgeon[20] at Camp Detrick's hospital, estimated in one internal army report.[21]

What he didn't point out is that many of them were women.

The labor shortage during World War II had created job opportunities for millions of women, including in Camp Detrick's laboratories, where they worked in both civilian and military roles, such as through the Women's Army Corps and the Navy's WAVES program.

One of the first Detrick workers to be stricken with a documented lab infection was Dr. Elizabeth M. Smadel, who became ill in April 1944, the safety division's case records show.[22,23,24]

Smadel, a pathologist, was hospitalized for six days with what the records say was a mild case of a disease called tularemia, one of several being explored as a biological weapon.

She was among seventy workers infected during 1944 and 1945[25] with a wide range of organisms, including those causing anthrax, glanders, valley fever, brucellosis, and psittacosis. These were microbes that in nature primarily sickened livestock and other animals but that also could cause disabling or deadly disease in people.

The tularemia labs had the highest number of workers with documented infections during the war years: twenty-five. And at least twelve were women.[26]

Tularemia, with a long connection to warfare, was an obvious pathogen for Camp Detrick to study. The bacterium *Francisella tularensis* causes disease in many kinds of animals, especially rabbits, muskrats, prairie dogs, and other rodents.

Sometimes an accident in the tularemia lab preceded an infection, such as when Eleanor G. Chapman in 1945 accidentally spilled a specimen of the bacterium two weeks before she developed a fever and other symptoms. Chapman had to be hospitalized twice and needed five months to recover.

Most of the time, however, there was no obvious cause of the infections, which left workers battling extreme fatigue, fevers, and other symptoms, often for weeks or months.

Ruth Doiron, a young army recruit working as a lab tech, was hospitalized with tularemia for ten days in 1944. Years later, Doiron, under her married name Ruth D. Herring, would be credited[27] with assisting Henry T. Eigelsbach with critical research at Camp Detrick that led to the development of a live tularemia vaccine.

Lab tech Ruth A. Penfield, who had enlisted[28] in the Women's Army Corps in 1942, needed to be hospitalized for about three weeks because of her tularemia infection, as did lab techs Alice H. Klauber and Alice L. Devine.

Mary P. Clapp, a 35-year-old scientist, suffered a severe tularemia infection that invaded her lungs, making it impossible for her to work for three months. Jeanne R. Smith,[29] a 24-year-old bacteriologist, had such a severe case, possibly from exposure to aerosolized bacteria, that it took nine months for her to recover.

The work in Detrick's labs was "as dangerous and important as actual combat,"[30] said Cornelia "Cora" M. Downs, who took a leave from her position as a professor of bacteriology at the University of Kansas to help lead Detrick's tularemia research.

Downs had been studying tularemia since 1929, an expertise that started when a Kansas doctor sought her help identifying the source of an infection in a man who developed lesions after killing rabbits for food.[31]

She went to Camp Detrick in the summer of 1943 and was there during many of the war years.[32] "We worked on all diseases we thought might be used against us," Downs said.

The research resulted in significant scientific advances, but it came at a cost.

"In spite of preventive measures a high percentage of the workers became infected but none of them died," Downs said in a 1946 news article.[33]

Infections didn't have to be fatal to be devastating for Detrick's lab workers.

That was especially true for those infected with *Brucella* bacteria, which in nature tended to sicken people who drank contaminated raw milk[34] from infected cattle or goats.

Of seventeen Detrick lab workers infected with *Brucella* during the war, at least nine became permanently disabled or required medical discharge,[35] the safety division's records show.

In one dramatic case, the navy had to send an emergency flight to Mexico City to evacuate[36] a lab tech who had gone there to visit her father in September 1945. Lupe M. Zarraga, a navy WAVE stationed at Camp Detrick's labs, began feeling ill during the visit. In the weeks before her trip, a mishap with a syringe had resulted in her face being sprayed with infectious fluid[37] containing *Brucella* bacteria.

Zarraga ultimately required months of hospitalization.

By 1950, ARNOLD WEDUM was making progress changing the safety culture at Camp Detrick, but it wasn't happening fast enough.

Intensely analytical, Wedum was a meticulous record keeper. He learned from a young age in the family's mercantile business in Glasgow, Montana, the value of tracking and analyzing data.

Wedum required that every illness of every worker in Detrick's lab buildings, regardless of their job type, be investigated and studied.

Because people exposed to dangerous pathogens don't always develop symptoms of illness, Camp Detrick regularly monitored its workers with blood and skin tests, detecting infections that would have otherwise gone unnoticed and that potentially could have spread disease beyond the base's secure gates.

Wedum thought it was critical to maximize the detection of worker infections—and not just wait until there was an obvious accident or serious illness. Otherwise, the safety division would be blind to the true frequency of infections and the risks throughout Detrick's labs.

It was dangerous to assume workers who appeared healthy weren't carrying infections.

The safety division's data showed, for example, that ten of the sixty-two[38] Detrick workers who contracted tularemia between 1944 and 1956—despite being vaccinated—showed no signs of illness. Six of them were working with the bacterium but had no memory of any incident that could have caused their exposure. The other four didn't work with the organism, but had on occasion visited the tularemia lab.

Their cases were only identified through regular worker testing. Such hidden infections posed a risk of sparking outbreaks if they involved a pathogen that was capable of spreading easily from person to person. Luckily, tularemia and the other organisms used at Camp Detrick at the time didn't spread that way.

One of the biggest issues in assessing the safety of biological research labs in the U.S. and abroad—and one that remains to this day—is the lack of any uniform and universal collection of data on laboratory incidents, exposures, infections, and asymptomatic infections detected through medical testing.

Even within individual research institutions, the type of data that is privately collected and tracked can vary significantly, and that was something that Wedum was concerned about.

"A major obstacle to critical comparison of figures from different laboratories is that there are no uniform standards for collection of data," Wedum said.[39]

The kind of broad medical monitoring and scrutiny put in place at Detrick ran counter to a long-standing tradition of courage and personal sacrifice among microbiologists throughout the world, who were accustomed back then to routinely becoming infected by the organisms they studied.

"These dedicated people, particularly in the field of infectious diseases, seem to take pride in the number of diseases they have acquired," Wedum noted.[40]

Lab workers had a tendency to dismiss their illnesses as unimportant or attribute them to sources unrelated to their work, Wedum found. Scientists and their supervisors also resisted reporting laboratory incidents and accidents.

To counter this, it became Camp Detrick policy that every illness suffered by a lab employee would be considered an occupational illness[41] unless the base's medical and safety officials determined otherwise.

Wedum also wanted to remove any financial disincentives that might keep employees from reporting accidents and illnesses. So it became Detrick policy that employees hospitalized because of suspected or known work-related illnesses wouldn't have to pay for their medical care. They also wouldn't be forced to use up any sick leave or vacation days.

The safety division's data showed worker infections had dropped from a high of forty-eight infections in 1945 to twenty-six in 1949.

During the first half of 1950, it appeared cases were continuing to drop. Through July, there had been just five infections.

But by fall of 1950, the numbers were rising.

During just September and October 1950,[42] eight of Camp Detrick's lab employees were stricken with serious infections that required hospitalization—often for weeks.

The types of infections reported at Detrick varied, coming in waves, depending on what pathogens were the focus of current research projects and the volume and type of work being done.

In the early 1950s the Detrick labs were pushing hard on projects involving various species of *Brucella* bacteria, the biological component that the military would use in its M114 antipersonnel bomb.[43]

The M114 looked like a pipe bomb. It was a four-pound tube, twenty-one inches long and about two inches around, that was filled with a species of the bacterium called *Brucella suis*. More than 100 of the tubes would then be assembled inside a larger 500-pound biological cluster bomb.

Brucella was chosen for the weapon because it spread easily[44] through aerosols and could disable troops with debilitating fevers, muscle pains, and other symptoms.

That fall the station hospital at Camp Detrick had been treating a steady stream of infected lab techs who were sickened with brucellosis. Lab tech

Richard Delauter was hospitalized for nineteen days; Albert Maxian for thirty-five days.

Another lab tech, Mary Kraft, was infected with *Brucella melitensis* and spent thirty-five days in the station hospital.[45] Kraft had moved across the country to accept a research position at Detrick after earning a bachelor's degree in home economics in 1946 and a master's degree in bacteriology in 1948 from the University of Wisconsin at Madison.[46]

Brucellosis was rarely fatal, but even with treatment it could cause chronic illness. Kraft, who had just turned 26, was among those who had to battle the infection for years to come. Her case was described in the safety division's records as "chronic, repeated relapses."

Tests at Detrick's hospital confirmed that *Brucella* bacteria were the culprit causing dishwasher Sherwood Davis's raging fever.

It took four days for antibiotics to get Davis's fever under control, and another two weeks[47] of hospital care before he recovered enough to go home.

It was suspected he became exposed while handling and washing contaminated laboratory glassware, but no specific accident was identified.[48]

After Davis was discharged from the hospital, he initially felt okay except for occasional fatigue and a backache that would come and go. But by January 3, 1951, as he and his wife prepared their home for the arrival of their new baby, he was dragging with fatigue.

Over the next week, the headaches came back along with a dry cough that wouldn't stop. Cultures again showed he had a *Brucella* infection in his body.

With his wife due to give birth any day, Davis had to be readmitted to the hospital.

For the next twenty days, Davis again suffered from fevers up to 103°F as doctors treated him with a second course of two types of antibiotics.[49]

He was still hospitalized when his wife, Geraldine, went into labor. Neighbors drove her to the hospital[50] to give birth to their son, Bruce.

Sherwood Davis continued to battle chronic brucellosis for years, dealing with bouts of significant fatigue and back pain that doctors later chronicled in a medical journal. But he continued to work in the labs through it all.

In 1954, Davis was struck again with another lab infection. This time he contracted tularemia pneumonia, the safety division's records show,[51] despite being vaccinated against it.[52] He was hospitalized again, and X-rays showed the infection in his lungs lasted thirty-six days.[53]

When he was well enough, he was back at work in Detrick's labs so he could provide for his family. He remained employed at the base until he retired.

DAVIS WAS ONE OF at least thirteen dishwashers[54] infected by Detrick's laboratories from 1943 to 1964.

The worst case among the dishwashers was that of June Hope Ellis, who suffered a devastating *Brucella suis* infection in March 1945 that kept her hospitalized for 194 days[55] and left her permanently disabled, safety division records show.

Before enlisting in the Navy WAVES in 1943 and becoming a pharmacist's mate third class,[56] Ellis had worked as a toll operator for Illinois Bell Telephone. But her passion was music. She had been an aspiring opera singer,[57] landing roles such as the courtesan Violetta in *La Traviata* in her hometown of Chicago.

After going through boot camp, Ellis initially worked in a medical office at a recruiting station in Chicago. She was transferred to Fort Detrick's laboratories in September 1944.

Within six months of starting work cleaning test tubes, petri dishes, and other laboratory glassware, she had become infected.

"I knew what I was working with," she later said[58] in a 1946 newspaper story. "But I don't know how I caught it. I guess no one will ever know."

Ellis spent months in Fort Detrick's hospital battling a cascading series of complications from her brucellosis infection. She developed an inflammatory condition, enlarged spleen, blood clotting, and blockages of the flow of blood and oxygen to her lungs. The severe course of her illness ended up being described in a medical journal article, without using her name.[59]

After the end of World War II, Ellis—who was just 22 years old—was transferred to Bethesda Naval Hospital. Her doctors said her disease was incurable. Perhaps with time, the disabling attacks would become less frequent, they said.

She was sent briefly to a Veterans Administration hospital in suburban Chicago, and after her discharge, she was given a disability rating of "zero." As her fever attacks continued, she spent years battling the VA[60] for her disability benefits.

Eventually, her disability rating was changed from 0 percent to 50 percent, entitling her to compensation of $69 a month.[61]

In addition to dishwashers, the safety division's records show at least forty other support staff performing a wide range of non-science jobs contracted lab-acquired infections through 1964.

The work that had put them in harm's way included handling laundry or trash that wasn't fully sterilized, performing building maintenance, conducting equipment inventories, and simply opening mail containing samples of bacteria.

IN 1958 ELECTRICIAN JOEL Willard became one of three Detrick workers to die from documented lab-acquired infections.

He started feeling ill around 1:00 p.m. on Sunday, June 29,[62] but didn't mention anything to his wife until 6:00 p.m. A few hours later she called his private physician, who prescribed aspirin under the assumption it was a common virus. On Monday, Willard was admitted to Detrick's hospital; by Wednesday, tests showed a serious anthrax infection; and by 1:00 a.m. Saturday he was dead.

Willard's death was front-page news in Frederick, but mostly because he had been a well-known local fireman before going to work at the army base. There was no mention of anthrax in his obituary.[63]

The army successfully covered up the cause of Willard's death for years.

At 10:00 a.m. on the morning Willard died, army officials summoned the Frederick County public health officer, Dr. Forbes Burgess, to a meeting at the base.

"After discussion of the security aspects, it was decided the death certificate would specify anthrax as the cause of death, and the newspaper release would specify 'occupational death from respiratory disease,'" according to a copy of a 1969 memo[64] that details the deaths of Willard and two other Detrick employees. It is signed on the last page by Wedum and Dr. Paul

Kadull, chief of medical services and research at the base, which had been renamed a few years earlier as Fort Detrick.

The army cultivated a close relationship with Burgess. The military gave him "secret" clearance.[65] During his rare visits to the base, they impressed him with their elaborate safety equipment and protocols.

"They know what they're working with and how to handle it," he would later say.

Unlike the hundreds of serious illnesses that Detrick's lab workers managed to survive, the cover-ups of Willard's death and the deaths of two other civilian employees—William Boyles and Albert Nickel—generated national headlines in 1975 after an unsigned version of what appears to have been the Wedum-Kadull memo was released in Washington[66] by a member of the House Armed Services Committee. The memo included the three men's names.

Boyles, a microbiologist, died in November 1951 of pulmonary anthrax. When he first started feeling ill, neither Boyles, his private physician, nor the post surgeon at Detrick thought that he had an occupational illness, the memo said. He was initially admitted to Frederick Memorial Hospital around 7:30 p.m. on November 22, but a few hours later he was transferred to the Detrick hospital. Three days later he was dead.

Frederick County's health officer, Burgess, attended a series of meetings at the base. He also was present at Boyles's autopsy, where the examiners and observers all suited up in extensive protective gear, face masks, and boots. Burgess, however, considered himself to be present out of personal curiosity, not in his official capacity as a representative of the health department, he would later explain.[67]

Once again, the health department's press release about Boyles's death made no mention of anthrax, instead saying that Boyles died of "acute bronchial pneumonia." The death certificate said: "Bronchopneumonia, with gastric ulceration and hemorrhage."[68]

In actuality, Detrick's scientists were never able to culture anthrax bacteria from Boyles's blood, tissues, or fluids.[69] But by January 1952, the final autopsy report established a diagnosis of anthrax after the scientific team, using a microscope, observed a few bacteria in his brain tissue that looked like *Bacillus anthracis*, the type that cause anthrax disease.

Wedum telephoned Burgess and asked about adding "anthrax" to the death certificate. "Dr. Wedum was told by Dr. Burgess that it was not customary for a physician to come in a month later to add further details to a death certificate," the Wedum-Kadull memo said.

The last of the lab workers to die of an infection from Fort Detrick was Albert Nickel, an animal caretaker stricken in January 1964 with the Machupo virus, which causes Bolivian hemorrhagic fever.

But when Nickel came down with watery diarrhea, vomiting, and a headache, neither he nor his private physician initially recognized the gravity of his symptoms. He fell ill on Sunday, January 26, 1964, and finally on Tuesday went to his private doctor, who sent him home with only an anti-diarrhea pill, similar to Pepto-Bismol. It made him feel a little better.

It wasn't until Thursday that Nickel was admitted to the Fort Detrick hospital. But even then, the memo says, the disease wasn't believed to be an occupational illness. By the following week, however, Nickel's condition was so serious that Fort Detrick officials contacted Burgess at the Frederick County health department to let him know of a "possible serious illness from an unknown probable virus."

Nickel's wife, Gladys, watched him dying through a small window into the quarantine room at the Detrick hospital, unable to hold or comfort him because of the danger.

Nickel died at 1:25 a.m. on February 10, 1964. The base notified Burgess eleven hours later.

It took months of tests by Detrick's scientists on Nickel's tissues and fluids to determine what killed him. The Wedum-Kadull memo says: "Finally, after hundreds of tests in hundreds of animals, a virus was identified as the virus of Bolivian hemorrhagic fever." The work-related diagnosis in July 1964 let Nickel's family receive survivor benefits.

Still his wife never learned what killed him until after his death became public.[70] "They promised to tell me what he died from," she told the *Frederick Post* in 1975, "but they never did."

The Machupo virus had been brought to Detrick's labs at the request of the U.S. Public Health Service, which was helping fight an outbreak of a new kind of hemorrhagic fever disease that had emerged in Bolivia and was killing as many as 30 percent of those who became infected.

There is no indication in the Wedum-Kadull memo that anyone contracted the Machupo virus from Nickel. It also doesn't say how Nickel became exposed.

Investigation of his death was left up to those at Fort Detrick.

During his sixteen years as Frederick County's health officer, Burgess never made any written reports about Fort Detrick's deaths,[71] though he later said he verbally reported them to Maryland's state health department.

Burgess said he purposely kept the information secret from local Frederick officials to avoid "causing a panic."[72]

It was fortunate that the pathogens that Camp Detrick—later renamed Fort Detrick[73]—was studying in those days didn't cause highly contagious illnesses, like exotic strains of influenza or coronavirus that had the potential to cause a pandemic.

Yet even though the microbes studied in Detrick's labs couldn't easily spread from person to person, they sometimes still did.

A Detrick secretary ended up in the hospital for twenty-five days after contracting Q fever from a friend who had worked in the lab. And the wife of a lab worker got Q fever from her husband, who the safety office determined was a carrier of the disease. She spent a week in the hospital even though he never showed signs of illness, the safety division records show.

Another secretary at Camp Detrick, who was the wife of a lab technician, was hospitalized for ten days after developing lung issues from psittacosis, the parrot fever disease caused by another kind of bacterium, *Chlamydia psittaci.*

And in 1946, Alice M. Watson, described in the safety division's records as a housewife who was not employed at the base, contracted anthrax. Her husband worked in Detrick's anthrax lab.

The small anthrax lesion was growing on her face for nearly three days before the couple realized it wasn't an ordinary pimple and might be an infection from bacteria that had somehow escaped Detrick's labs.

Alice Watson spent more than a week in Camp Detrick's hospital. She was given penicillin as the small lesion continued to grow[74] before it began to dry up and formed the black crust over the wound that is typical of anthrax skin infections.

These kinds of incidents, where people in the surrounding community were occasionally becoming infected by escaped research organisms, were occurring at other non-military labs as well and were sometimes written up in scientific journals.

A group of scientists from the U.S. Public Health Service's Rocky Mountain Laboratory in Hamilton, Montana, published an article[75] in 1949 in the *American Journal of Hygiene* documenting how six employees of a local laundry facility became infected with Q fever by handling the lab's soiled coveralls, towels, and other items that needed washing. Three of them were seriously sickened with symptoms that included coughing blood and battling fevers and pneumonia.

In another small community outbreak, a couple living in the Washington, D.C., suburbs contracted Q fever from a lab worker who was a tenant renting a room[76] in their basement.

The tenant, who was a researcher studying Q fever at the National Institutes of Health in Bethesda, Maryland, somehow unknowingly tracked the bacteria into the couple's home.

The researcher, who was vaccinated against Q fever as part of his job, never showed any signs of illness. But the people the researcher was living with were completely vulnerable to the disease.

The first member of the household to fall ill was the 39-year-old wife, who did housework in the tenant's room, cleaning it weekly and washing the sheets and pillowcases. She became severely ill and was hospitalized at Walter Reed General Hospital for nearly a month.

While she was in the hospital, her husband helped with cleaning the researcher's room, and then he fell ill with Q fever, too. Even though his symptoms were milder, he still was hospitalized for nearly three weeks.

It turned out that around the same time as the couple started falling ill, the NIH was experiencing a small outbreak of Q fever that had sickened seven laboratory and maintenance workers.

Imagine what might have happened if the researcher had carried something more contagious.

CHAPTER 2

Invisible Mist

A s Wedum and his team examined each case of infection among Detrick's workers, they observed an unsettling trend. Most became infected without ever knowing they had been exposed.

There rarely was any kind of recognized accident—like a spill or a needlestick or an animal bite. By the time workers started to develop symptoms, they had usually been going about their jobs and lives for days or weeks unaware the infection was growing inside them.

This wasn't just an issue at Detrick.

Research by two professors at the University of Texas Southwestern Medical School, S. Edward Sulkin and Robert Pike, found that infection without obvious lab accidents was the norm. The research they did would become some of the most authoritative on the subject, with their papers still being cited decades later.

One of the biggest challenges in evaluating the safety of biological research labs then—and now—is the lack of any universal system for collecting data on worker infections and lab accidents.

Wedum had been contributing information about Camp Detrick's cases to Sulkin and Pike, and with support from the American Public Health Association and the National Institutes of Health, the researchers sent surveys[1] in 1950 to about 5,000 U.S. laboratories working with biological specimens. They included labs run by medical and veterinary schools, local and state health departments, hospitals, undergraduate teaching institutions, biologic manufacturers, and government agencies.

About half of the labs wouldn't share information. Among the other half, many acknowledged they weren't tracking lab infections and that the information they shared came from memory.

Still, Sulkin and Pike were able to initially identify 1,342 lab-acquired infections through the survey results plus other worker infections that had been written up in scientific journals. It was clearly a significant underestimate of the true toll, but far more than the 467 cases they had been able to identify through journal articles alone.[2]

Perhaps their most concerning finding, one that Arnold Wedum would cite repeatedly in his own scientific journal articles: Recognized accidents accounted for just 16 percent of the infections.[3,4,5] At Camp Detrick during the Wedum era, even with exhaustive and immediate investigations by a safety team that at times had forty full-time employees,[6] they only could determine the cause of worker infections about 35 percent[7] of the time.

In the years that followed, Sulkin and Pike and other researchers continued to find the same issue: When lab workers become infected, they often have no idea that anything has happened.

A KEY REASON FOR this, researchers at Camp Detrick and elsewhere found, was that even the most mundane lab tasks launched an invisible plume of microbes into the air[8]—helping spread them around rooms and even entire buildings.[9]

Without knowing it, unsuspecting workers were coming into contact with or breathing in the infectious fallout.

Using air samplers, Detrick scientists showed how aerosolized particles were created by the removal of stoppers from bottles or the mere act of using a hypodermic syringe to withdraw infectious liquid.

Using high-speed photography,[10] Detrick's scientists captured images of otherwise invisible bacteria-laden particulates spewing into the air as researchers carefully measured and transferred liquid specimens by pouring or using a tube-like pipette.

High-speed blenders,[11] used to cut up infectious tissues, sometimes had leaking gaskets or lids.

Although much of the work at Camp Detrick was secret, Wedum and his team were regularly allowed to share their growing expertise in lab safety measures through dozens of scientific papers and presentations.

The first meeting of what would eventually become the American Biological Safety Association was held at Camp Detrick in 1955 as a small gathering[12] of military lab officials who wanted to share best practices.

The Detrick safety team warned that centrifuges were among the riskiest pieces of lab equipment, prone to invisible leaks. These important scientific devices, which evolved from early efforts to mechanically separate cream from milk, spin test tubes to concentrate bacterial cells and purify virus.

The spinning machinery ran the risk of breaking tubes and leaking fluids. Studies also found that some tubes that looked sealed actually sprayed an invisible microbial mist because of the way their caps were designed. The result was an infectious fallout zone in a seven-foot radius that infected Detrick workers like Agnes Baldwin, a Detrick lab tech, who was sickened with tularemia in December 1948 following a centrifuging accident. She was hospitalized for eleven days, though her symptoms continued for forty-six days.

Animals used in experiments, especially those exposed to aerosolized pathogens, didn't just pose a risk of infections from bites or scratches. They also could potentially spread contagion through the air by shaking their contaminated fur or through human contact with cage litter that had been soiled with infectious urine[13] and feces.

The aerosol exposure experiments, even when conducted in enclosed chambers, posed a significant risk. Leaking or defective aerosol chambers at Detrick were cited in worker infections in 1949, 1952, and 1953.[14]

But in many cases, when bacteriologists and lab techs fell ill after conducting aerosol studies, there was no obvious mishap, the safety division's records show.

The more Wedum's safety team looked, the more they found that the routine activities in a microbiology lab had the potential to create varying amounts of infectious mist. The larger droplets would settle on nearby surfaces, risking contamination of anything nearby, from workers' clothing, desks, and equipment to specimens and animals being used in other experiments.

Other liquid or solid particles were so small they became airborne, spreading on invisible air currents, pushed along by heating and cooling systems, the opening and closing of doors, and the movement of people between rooms and down hallways. The result was contamination in areas where workers or visitors might never think they were in danger.

This eventually led to the use of negative air pressure inside modern high-containment labs. But before that sophisticated engineering was put in place, there were shocking outbreaks.

In 1945–46 at the federal government's National Institute of Health[15] in Bethesda, Maryland, forty-seven workers and visitors on multiple floors of a laboratory building were sickened with Q fever during a six-month period.

The outbreak began[16] soon after scientists started studying Q fever in a single lab located in the south wing of the first floor of Building 5—and ultimately resulted in workers becoming infected throughout the building. Aerosols spread by centrifuge work during Q fever experiments were suspected.[17]

At what was then called Michigan State College in East Lansing, an outbreak[18] of brucellosis in a campus bacteriology building sickened forty-one students plus a lab stockroom attendant, a plumber, a stenographer, and a salesman. One student died.[19] But those who had symptoms were not the only ones infected. Blood tests revealed an additional forty-nine people had been infected, even though they didn't show signs of illness.

A definitive cause of the outbreak wasn't found by state and college investigators, but a member of the Camp Detrick safety team who later studied the incident wrote in an internal army report[20] that use of a centrifuge in the basement lab likely resulted in airborne spread of the bacteria throughout the building.

THE SINGLE MOST IMPORTANT way to contain bacteria and viruses, Wedum and his team found, was for scientists to handle the organisms inside a high-tech ventilated biological safety cabinet.

In chemistry labs, where fumes could be hazardous, fume hoods had started being adopted in the 1860s.[21] Biological safety cabinets, which applied some of the same safety principles, were slow to be embraced by microbiologists when they started becoming commercially available in the United States in the 1950s.

"Bacteriologists have been comparatively slow to accept this idea, partly because of absence of proof that conventional technics are hazardous and partly because of a tradition of personal sacrifice," Wedum wrote in a public health journal article[22] in 1953.

German microbiologist Robert Koch is credited with using a primitive type of safety cabinet around 1905,[23] but it was the safety division[24] at Camp Detrick that used modern engineering to help create far more effective devices.

In most cases these modern biosafety cabinets were essentially stainless steel cabinets with glass viewing panels, an exhaust blower, and an opening at the front where users could insert their hands and do their scientific work.

A key feature was that the cabinets used directional airflow, sucking air into the cabinet. This inward airflow helped to keep any infectious mists inside the cabinet and away from workers as they opened test tubes, created specimens, and performed various other tasks and experiments.

For work that was especially hazardous, the Detrick labs had even more protective gas-tight safety cabinets. Scientists inserted their arms into these completely sealed units through attached glove boxes, allowing them to manipulate specimens inside the cabinets without any direct contact.

Depending on the cabinet, the contaminated air could be vented outside the lab through an air incinerator or high-efficiency HEPA filters. Scientists at Camp Detrick and the U.S. Army Chemical Corps contributed research[25] to the early development of the HEPA filter.

"Dr. Wedum would come into the shop with an idea he had the night before and we would build it for him," longtime Detrick employee Hubert Kaempf recalled in an interview[26] with a Frederick newspaper decades later. Kaempf, who was drafted in 1942, came to Camp Detrick as a military policeman. He was eventually assigned to the sheet metal shop, learning on the job while installing ductwork and fabricating equipment for the base's laboratories. "There was little formal engineering in those days," he said.

During the 1950s and 1960s, Wedum and his team increasingly became the source of authoritative guidance[27] on biosafety for labs across the United States and around the world—everything from use of safety cabinets to the design and construction of laboratories, to safety procedures for housing animals, and a wide range of procedures and protocols.

To this day, many of the practices remain cornerstones of modern biosafety.

The Detrick safety team advised separating lab buildings into "clean" and "contaminated" areas, and routing entry into contaminated areas through a clothes-changing locker room and shower area.

They discussed the value of maintaining positive air pressures in rooms that were in "clean" areas and having negative air pressures in "contaminated" areas. Just as in a biosafety cabinet, this created an airflow in lab rooms and buildings that drew potentially infectious air inward and away from people not directly working with the pathogens.

They encouraged installing electronic communication systems and glass viewing windows to allow scientists to communicate without unnecessary entry to contaminated areas. They called for restricting visitors and support staff from entering infectious areas unless they were familiar with safety procedures.

They warned of the risk of pathogens contaminating lab workers' clothing and urged the use of gowns and shoes that were reserved for lab use only.

Wedum mocked the failure of scientists to recognize how some of their traditional practices and beliefs fueled the spread of pathogens.

"There seems to be some magic protection connected with the wearing of white," he wrote in one journal article.[28] "Otherwise how can one excuse the entry of 30 persons into a surgical operating room or laboratory personnel in the lunch room or wards, wearing white gowns and white shoes seeded with assorted microorganisms?"

The safety team called for an end to eating and smoking in labs and cautioned about the risks of microbes contaminating the beards[29] of men working in labs.

And they advocated that labs be designed in ways that encouraged safe practices: reducing or eliminating open benches to force the use of biosafety cabinets; providing an adequate number of devices called *autoclaves* that are used to sterilize materials; and only providing tools, such as pipetting devices and hypodermic syringes, that were designed to reduce exposure accidents.

But having the finest high-tech equipment wasn't enough to stop workers from becoming infected. Human factors—from mistakes and accidents, to willful breaking of safety rules, to ignorance about risks—all played a role in lab worker infections.

"The major problem is one of communication and conviction," Wedum wrote in one journal article.[30]

By 1953, there were sixty-two bacteriological safety cabinets in use at Camp Detrick, and these, combined with rigorous protocols, were resulting in dramatic drops in worker infections—but only in the buildings and labs where the safety measures were being used.

In a secret internal report that year, Wedum told army officials that safety equipment and protocols showed it was possible to handle the most dangerous agents without employees becoming infected. Yet infections were continuing where safety equipment—and lab supervisor cooperation with safety protocols—was lacking.

"This situation puts a grave burden on the Safety Director, Biological Laboratories, who is given the hard choice of permitting additional illnesses among employees, with an accompanying risk to health and life, when means to reduce or eliminate such illnesses and risks are known, or of ordering the stopping of these operations," the report said,[31] referring to Wedum.

It had been a difficult few years, and Wedum felt the weight of his work in the safety division—and at home as well.

Wedum's job had exacerbated wider tensions in his marriage. His wife Bernice disapproved[32] of the biological warfare program and her husband's involvement in it. Bernice Wedum was concerned that he was using his medical training to enable the development of weapons,[33] and that bothered her deeply. Her view was that doctors were supposed to save lives, not help kill people.

As Bernice Wedum faced her own career challenges and a desire for greater independence, their marriage was strained to the breaking point. They separated after a bitter argument and ultimately divorced a few years later in 1955.[34]

THE BIGGEST IMPEDIMENT TO making labs safer was often the scientists themselves.

"We take a well justified pride in our martyrs to public health research—those who have sacrificed their lives to save others from disease—but the time has come for us to take an equal pride in efforts to prevent such martyrdom," Wedum said in one journal article.[35]

Wedum saw what he called the "martyr-to-science complex" as a deterrent[36] to lab safety. He frequently lamented in journal articles, interviews, and at conferences that efforts to make labs safer often collided with an ingrained culture of scientific independence that resisted oversight of the safety of biological research.

The culture in microbiology labs contributed to a downplaying of risks. And as a result, Wedum found,[37] safety is not practiced fully "because of lack of agreement on the danger by the administrators and lack of awareness by the workers."

Those leading the research in labs tended to be chosen for their scientific ability, he said, not their rigorous respect for safety. Meanwhile, scientists in positions of authority were reluctant[38] to impose rules and regulations on other scientists or to criticize their work.

An effective safety program, Wedum believed, required not only education and engineering, but also rules, standards, and operating procedures. And those had to be backed up with inspections, investigations, analysis of data, and corrections.

"Oftentimes these directly oppose the philosophy of scientific freedom which comes with academic training," Wedum later wrote.[39]

Even at the Detrick labs, which were considered the gold standard for safety, some holdouts thought many precautions were unnecessary, protocols too burdensome, and that the use of biosafety cabinets and other safety equipment made conducting experiments too awkward and slow.

The disregard for safety policies and procedures among some Detrick scientists was an ongoing frustration for Wedum. The safety division files on infected workers included frequent notations about scientists who failed to follow safety rules or use important safety equipment:

"failed to decontaminate materials"
"working on benchtop counting plates"
"careless handling of dry spores"

"animal inoculation on table top—no respiratory protection"

"unsafe technique with mortar and pestle"

"inadequate safety test on aerating equipment"

"grinding in mortar in open"

"inadequate safety test"

"aspiration—mouth pipetting"

"violation of safety rules"

"took off respirator"

The culture of downplaying safety risks and avoiding looking for infections ran deep and wide in the field. That's what Wedum's colleague G. Briggs Phillips found in a review of U.S. and international labs during 1959–1960.

Phillips, who rose through the ranks of the safety division to eventually become its assistant director,[40] traveled more than 80,000 miles by plane, car, train, and boat to visit 111 labs in sixty cities in eighteen countries, including the U.S., Canada, England, Germany, France, Sweden, Switzerland, the Netherlands, Australia, and Japan.

Only twenty-nine of these institutions kept any records on laboratory-acquired illnesses, Phillips learned during his meetings with the directors and staff at each facility. At nearly 90 percent of the labs, accidents were neither investigated nor logged in any records. He detailed his findings in a 289-page technical study[41] submitted to the army in 1961 from Fort Detrick's safety division.

At lab after lab, Phillips observed a pervasive culture of ignoring and downplaying accidents and infections.

"Too much emphasis on laboratory safety will scare people," was a sentiment Phillips heard repeatedly as he tried to understand the lack of awareness of hazards by lab techs and support staff.

At one institute, when Phillips asked the director whether there had been any laboratory-related illnesses, the director initially recalled only two long-ago infections that had happened decades earlier, between 1920 and 1930. One was a finger infection from a needlestick with the organism that causes syphilis; the other was a case of diphtheria after a worker accidentally breathed in some of the culture while using their mouth to draw samples into a pipette.

As Phillips and the lab director chatted about the two old cases, an assistant spoke up after several minutes and reminded the director that there also had been two cases of brucellosis in just the past two years.

This spurred the director to add that he had also forgotten about an epidemic of Q fever cases that had sickened more than a dozen of his workers in 1947. Among those infected was the director himself—who after the initial illness had battled lung problems for the next three years. The outbreak was never investigated, and the facility's leadership had simply chalked it up to being caused by the centrifuging or grinding of tissues by one sloppy worker who left the facility a short time later.

When Phillips asked the director whether there had ever been any tuberculosis infections at the lab, the director initially said no, providing his assessment that most of the work with that type of bacteria had been relatively safe.

But that wasn't accurate, either.

Later in the afternoon, while Phillips and the director were discussing animal exposure experiments, the director remembered there actually had been five tuberculosis infections among his staff—and that two of those workers had died. One of the TB cases even involved the director's own wife, who suffered an eye infection that had permanently damaged her vision. The infections weren't ever investigated but appeared to have been caused by the use of a crude device to expose guinea pigs to aerosols.

"To sum up, at first I was told there had been only two laboratory infections, but before the day was over I had noted 24 infections in my notebook," Phillips wrote in his report.

"Many laboratory directors do not enjoy thinking or talking about their occupational illnesses," he wrote. "Laboratory infections are sometimes skeletons in the closet which are not to be taken out."

IN NOVEMBER 1969, PRESIDENT Richard M. Nixon renounced the use of biological weapons, which he said have "massive, unpredictable and

potentially uncontrollable consequences," including the potential for causing global epidemics.

"Mankind already carries in its own hands too many of the seeds of
its own destruction," Nixon said[42] in announcing the United States would
dispose of its stockpile of biological weapons and restrict future biological
research to defensive measures, such as the development of vaccines, treatments, tests, and safety measures.

As a result, Fort Detrick's role shifted to biodefense. The old Army
Chemical Corps laboratories were replaced by a new unit at the base, one
that had been established in 1969 under the Office of the Surgeon General
of the army.

The new unit was called the U.S. Army Medical Research Institute of
Infectious Diseases, or USAMRIID, which today remains the military's
flagship infectious disease research facility.

Wedum retired as safety director at Fort Detrick in 1972, ultimately
helping document 423 lab-acquired infections and three worker deaths.[43]

As the years went on, documented lab infections dropped dramatically.
Since 2010, there has been no incident at USAMRIID's biosafety level 3
and 4 labs that has involved reports of "symptoms" or "signs of illness,"
according to the limited data the facility disclosed on its website through
most of 2022.[44]

Until Wedum's own death from a heart attack[45] in 1976 at the age of
73,[46] he continued to work as a laboratory safety consultant for national
scientific organizations, the National Cancer Institute, and other firms.

"All who knew Dr. Wedum revered him as the person most responsible
for creating our profession," wrote W. Emmett Barkley, when the *Journal of
the American Biological Safety Association* published its first edition in 1996.[47]

In his final years, in response to scientific advances, Wedum was helping
create a national framework for scientists to safely work with genetically
engineered organisms, what was then an emerging new field of study.

Wedum had no doubt that lab workers faced potential risks from these
engineered pathogens. But he appeared somewhat skeptical about how
much risk there was of engineered diseases being transmitted to the general
public by an infected lab worker or as a result of the microbes riding out of
the lab on clothing, in the trash, through sewage, or in the air.

There was an absence of proof that labs could pose a wider public health hazard, Wedum said in one of the last papers he wrote.[48] "It has not been possible to find reports of laboratory-attributed infection in persons who never were in the laboratory building or who were not associated in some way with the laboratory," he said.[49]

Because most of the microbes studied in labs weren't capable of causing human-spread epidemics, the chances of a community outbreak were low.

Still, Wedum saw a potential risk when research occurred with highly contagious pathogens—citing those like measles or smallpox—that were capable of quickly and easily spreading from person to person.

Wedum's experience at Fort Detrick had shown it was possible for a well-trained and well-disciplined scientific workforce using the world's best safety equipment to experiment with even the most dangerous pathogens without workers becoming infected.

But the safety division also learned that under less stringent conditions and with lesser equipment, even minor lapses would result in microbes infecting at least some of those working around them.

For twenty-six years, Wedum chronicled the many ways things could go wrong in laboratories. They include risks that continue to exist decades later across the United States and around the world, but that many in the biological research community are reluctant to discuss with the general public or even share among themselves.

History shows this devotion to science—and avoidance of acknowledging, quantifying, and addressing laboratory safety risks—has been a challenge within the culture of microbiology going back hundreds of years.

Today's labs, in most cases, aren't brewing up the large batches of pathogens that the Detrick labs were using decades ago, and advances in technology and vaccines have continued to make research safer.

Yet even with all of the advances since Wedum's time, one thing hasn't changed: Laboratories are still filled with devices that can break and human beings who will inevitably make mistakes and have lapses in judgment and moments of hubris.

And these days, laboratories are increasingly working with far more dangerous pathogens than during Wedum's time.

CHAPTER 3

The Leak

T HE LINE OF severe thunderstorms spreading south toward Frederick, Maryland, on the evening of May 15, 2018, stretched from the Pennsylvania border into New England.

As it approached, a brutal series of storm cells erupted just north and east of the city, fueled by an unusually hot and humid spring day that had neared ninety degrees, plus another squall line approaching from the south. On weather radar the cells glowed like menacing dark red-hot explosions, dumping torrential rainfall and large hail.

In less than three hours that Tuesday evening, parts of Frederick were deluged with seven inches of rain. The situation was so severe that the National Weather Service issued a flash flood emergency alert.

It was among the kinds of severe storms that batter elite biological research labs around the world every year.

In the United States during 2018, there were at least nine severe weather events and natural disasters—from hurricanes and tropical storms to nor'easters and an earthquake—that prompted federal lab regulators to check on 144 facilities.[1] These regulators would later assure the public and policy makers, at least those reading their annual statistical report, that none of these unidentified labs had required any assistance and that none of the events resulted in any organisms being released.

Not included in the report's "Emergency Management" disclosures:[2] the lab at the army's Fort Detrick that *did* have a catastrophic event because of a natural disaster.

The storm that stalled out over Frederick that May dropped huge amounts of water and was followed by another one the next day. The storms turned Carroll Creek, which normally meanders gently through historic downtown

Frederick, into a roiling river. Across the region, numerous roads became impassable, cars and even a commuter train became stranded, and homes and businesses were flooded. Frederick's mayor declared a local state of emergency.

The back-to-back storms set off a chain of events at Fort Detrick, ultimately resulting in the kind of laboratory safety crisis that Arnold Wedum had sought to prevent sixty-five years earlier.

The weeks and months that followed would reveal how dangerously lax the revered birthplace of biosafety had become in its handling of deadly microbes.

Most concerning of all: What happened at Fort Detrick that spring illustrated how ill-equipped, or perhaps disinclined, local, state, and federal agencies can be in aggressively investigating and responding when a lab leak occurs.

IT WAS THURSDAY MORNING, May 17, 2018, when Fort Detrick workers made a shocking discovery in the basement of Building 375. It was the location of the steam sterilization plant responsible for treating the potentially infectious liquid waste coming out of labs working with Ebola, anthrax, and other lethal pathogens.

The basement was filling with water[3] that eventually became four to five feet[4] deep. Some of it was rainwater seeping in from outdoors. But a lot was fluid leaking[5] out of the basement's long-deteriorating tanks that held thousands of gallons of unsterilized laboratory wastewater.

As basement sump pumps[6] forced huge volumes of flood water into these tanks, the influx disgorged lab waste through cracks along the tops of the tanks, sending it streaming back toward the floor.

The steam sterilization plant, referred to as "the SSP," was constructed and tested under Arnold Wedum's supervision in 1953.[7,8]

It was designed to use steam to essentially cook the large volumes of wastewater produced by Fort Detrick's biological laboratories. The goal was to ensure the destruction of any research organisms that weren't killed before being washed down lab drains and that might otherwise survive a trip through a typical sewage treatment plant.

Going back decades, officials at Fort Detrick had worried about the potentially serious consequences of unsterilized wastewater being released into the surrounding community.

Records from Wedum's safety division show that at least two waste-water treatment plant operators[9] at Fort Detrick suffered anthrax infections, J. P. Cafferty and a person referred to as J. Kennedy. Each was hospitalized for two weeks in the late 1940s because of serious anthrax skin lesions.

In 1952, before the SSP was operational, several gallons[10] of viable anthrax cultures were discharged into the base's other sewage steriliza-tion plants, resulting in contamination that persisted for months, despite repeated washings with disinfectant solutions.

In 1978, when the SSP storage tanks were drained, tests found that the sludge accumulated inside[11] contained anthrax. This was despite large quantities of disinfectant that in 1972 had been pumped through the tanks and the dedicated laboratory sewer system that leads to them, after the shutdown of the biological weapons program.

When tank sludge was again tested in 1988, no anthrax was detected. The army wouldn't tell me what more recent testing has found.

To get from Fort Detrick's labs to the SSP, the liquid waste traveled through a dedicated laboratory sewer system built from 1949 to 1969.[12] This aging network, made up of 12,500 linear feet of buried pipes,[13] was designed to keep dangerous laboratory fluids separate from Fort Detrick's sanitary sewer system that handled routine wastewater from the base's offices and housing.

In the 1990s, various investigations identified leaks from laboratory sewer system (LSS) pipes. A 1997 army investigation "detected a range of viable microbes[14] both within the LSS and within the soil surrounding the system" and raised concern about the potential for "LSS hazards" to contaminate ground-water. But there was "no confident indication at the time of the report that the groundwater had been impacted."

After years of studies, in 2001 a particularly problematic section was abandoned in place[15] and a new line installed next to it.

While several types of pathogens can survive in wastewater for hours, days, or longer, anthrax spores were a top concern because they were so difficult to kill—and because they can be deadly.

When the organism is inhaled, the resulting anthrax disease is gener-ally fatal without treatment, and even with aggressive treatment about 45 percent of patients will still die. When it enters through a cut in the skin, anthrax usually causes lesions, but the death rate still can reach 20 percent without antibiotics, and it can be more than 50 percent when swallowed.[16]

The bacterium is good at protecting itself. *Bacillus anthracis*, when stressed, encases itself in the equivalent of an armor-plated chamber. This kind of spore can withstand a wide range of assaults—from air drying to temperature extremes to sunlight to ionizing radiation—that would kill other kinds of bacteria.

The ability of anthrax to enter this hardy, dormant state—which allows it to be effectively weaponized without killing the bacteria—is a key reason it has long been a target of bioweapons development and defensive research to counter that threat.

Over the decades, scientists found[17] that certain chemicals, like bleach, could break inside the spore's structure when given enough time. So could wet heat, which forces steam inside the spores to kill the organism.

That's why heat sterilization by the SSP remained a critical safety measure at Fort Detrick even in 2018.

Over the course of a three-hour cycle, the SSP gradually heated each batch of wastewater[18] first to 190°F, holding it at that temperature for sixty minutes. Then the heat was increased to 270°F for another twenty minutes. Finally, there was a cool-down period before the sterilized lab wastewater was discharged into Fort Detrick's regular sanitary sewer system, where it flowed through the army's municipal wastewater treatment plant. In an eight-hour shift, the sterilization plant would process 50,000 gallons of fluid.

Fort Detrick's laboratory and other wastewater is ultimately discharged into the Monocacy River, a favorite for bass fishing and kayaking amid scenic stretches that flow through farmland and forests of maple, sycamore, and oak trees. The Monocacy merges fifteen miles downstream into the Potomac River, then travels through Washington, D.C., before emptying into the Chesapeake Bay.

DESPITE THE STERILIZATION PLANT'S importance to protecting public health, by May 2018 it had become a rusting, leaking, temperamental hulk.

It was sixty-five years old and was supposed to have been torn down already. But a replacement plant completed at a cost to taxpayers of more than $30 million[19] had suffered a "catastrophic failure" in 2016[20] and couldn't be repaired. Fort Detrick, USAMRIID, and Army Corps of Engineers officials refused to explain what happened[21] when I asked.

Whatever happened, it required the Wedum-era SSP to keep sterilizing lab waste.

Tucked away on the western edge of Fort Detrick's 1,200-acre campus,[22] the SSP had two main components. The high-pressure steam heating of lab wastewater occurred in the mostly one-story redbrick building, known on the base as Building 375. In its basement were five 50,000-gallon storage tanks that received and stored the incoming lab wastewater before it was cooked.

Fort Detrick officials had been aware[23] for some time that the tops of these aging storage tanks had multiple leaks caused over the years by chlorine gases accumulating on the surface of the wastewater. It was so much of an issue that the army garrison's Directorate of Public Works employees, who operated the plant, had to make sure the tanks didn't ever fill up completely or the potentially infectious water would spill out.

Their workaround was to try to limit the amount of waste[24] in each of the basement tanks to about half capacity—storing just 23,000–28,000 gallons in the 50,000-gallon tanks.

The second component of the SSP was outdoors. Next to Building 375 were another nine interconnected 50,000-gallon storage tanks, which held more of the wastewater awaiting sterilization. One of those tanks, however, was in such bad condition it had been out of service[25] for a while. The huge tanks were surrounded by a short concrete containment wall less than one-third of their height.

Even though the SSP system was in significant disrepair, two research facilities at Fort Detrick still relied on it to sterilize their liquid waste. On a typical day in 2018, they sent about 30,000 gallons[26] of laboratory wastewater into the plant.

Some of the water was coming from a research and greenhouse facility run by the U.S. Department of Agriculture that experimented with exotic and potentially invasive agricultural weeds and diseases.

Most of the wastewater sent to the steam sterilization plant came from USAMRIID, the U.S. Army Medical Research Institute of Infectious Diseases.

USAMRIID—pronounced *you-SAM-rid*, or simply called RIID for short—was the medical and biodefense research organization that in 1969 replaced Fort Detrick's former biowarfare labs.

USAMRIID's labs had become one of the world's largest centers of bio-defense research, studying the medical aspects of pathogens that might be used in warfare or by terrorists. They focused on creating medical treatments, detection systems, protective equipment, and vaccines for use by military personnel and civilians.

USAMRIID was an elite institution, one of only eight research facilities[27] in the United States to operate suites of BSL-4 laboratories, the highest level.

Only about fifty-nine of these "maximum containment" BSL-4 labs operate worldwide.[28] They are sealed, pressurized, and have numerous safety systems, and are used to study dangerous and exotic pathogens—such as the Ebola virus—that pose a high risk of life-threatening infections that are frequently fatal.

Airtight BSL-4 labs are the type often portrayed in movies where researchers wear full-body pressurized protective gear that looks like an inflated space suit. To leave these labs after doing their work, scientists first enter a chamber where a chemical shower decontaminates the outside of their suits. Then, after changing out of the suits and medical scrubs, they must take an additional personal shower before putting on their street clothes.

The goal is to prevent organisms from hitching a ride out of the facility.

Labs operating at lower biosafety levels have progressively fewer safeguards in how they are engineered, the types of personal protective equipment used, and the procedures that govern the work.

Workers in all labs, regardless of the biosafety level, are supposed to follow standard microbiological practices such as no eating or drinking within lab spaces; washing hands after work with pathogens and also before leaving the lab space; and regularly decontaminating surfaces.

In a BSL-1 lab, where microbes are not known to routinely cause disease in healthy adults, the space often looks like the kind of open bench labs found in school classrooms.

Additional safeguards[29,30] start being added at BSL-2, where pathogens that can pose a moderate risk are studied. In these labs, workers wear laboratory coats and gloves, and may add other gear as needed. Work that generates aerosols or splashes is done in biosafety cabinets, and these labs have procedures or devices, such as an autoclave, to decontaminate materials.

BSL-3 labs are used for microbes that cause serious or deadly diseases, especially by inhalation. Scientists work inside biosafety cabinets and, depending on the nature of the microbes being studied, may be required to wear a respirator. To help contain any aerosolized pathogens, these labs operate under negative air pressure, drawing air inward from clean areas toward the contaminated lab space.

The higher the biosafety level, the more expensive the lab is to operate and maintain and the more cumbersome it is to work in.

The laboratories at USAMRIID, especially the BSL-3 and BSL-4 labs, produced a significant amount of wastewater.

About half[31] of the water sent for sterilization came from lab workers showering after being in infectious areas.

Another big water source came from workers washing down animal holding rooms, where hundreds of creatures from mice to monkeys were being infected with bacteria and viruses in a wide range of experiments.

As was documented by Wedum's safety team decades earlier, the soiled bedding from cages and other waste products could pose a significant hazard because lab animals can shed infectious organisms in urine and feces and via contaminated fur and dander.

Another 5 percent of USAMRIID's liquid waste came directly from experimental fluids and the washing of plates, tubes, and other experimental materials.[32]

To prevent organisms from escaping, USAMRIID's safety protocols called for a two-step kill process for wastewater.

Before the wastewater was sent down drains into the laboratory sewer system for heat treatment at the SSP, workers were supposed to pretreat it with bleach or other chemicals.

But chemical disinfection can be tricky.

To be effective, it requires workers to use the right kind of disinfectant at the right concentration and, importantly, to ensure that the disinfectant remains in contact with the microbes long enough to kill them.

As living organisms, any that are left behind have the potential to multiply.

Animal rooms posed a special challenge, especially those housing larger animals such as monkeys and other non-human primates that generate a lot of waste. If a lot of excrement was present, it could be more difficult to quickly inactivate infectious organisms.

To visualize the wastewater coming out of these animal rooms, one biosafety expert told me[33] to think about when you take your car to be washed. It might have a splat of bird poop on the windshield, mud caking the wheel wells, and, depending on the time of year, it could be covered with a white film of road salt. To clean the car, there is usually an initial rinse cycle to knock off the visible grime. Then comes a foamy soap mixture and maybe some scrubbing, and finally another rinse cycle.

In general, that's the kind of process used to clean up the animal holding rooms in a high-containment lab. But in labs, the foam step could be a straight chemical or a foaming chemical mix. And it has to stay in place for a specific amount of time, then be rinsed away, because the fumes can be hazardous to animals, the expert explained.

As the room is hosed down, all of the excrement, hair, dander, and anything else present on the ground, walls, and in cages is flushed down into the facility's plumbing system.

Human error is a constant risk. Nobody is perfect, and there is always the potential for busy workers to not wait the full kill time before rinsing everything down the drain.

While many microbes are too fragile to survive outside of a laboratory, some have the potential to escape in sewage.

Among those that Fort Detrick's environmental assessments have said have the potential to survive[34] in water and soil for extended periods of time if they aren't completely killed before leaving the base: the bacteria that cause anthrax and Q fever, and some species of *Mycobacterium*, which include the bacteria that cause tuberculosis, as well as some hepatitis viruses.

That's why USAMRIID's laboratory wastewater was sent to the SSP for heat sterilization.

The SSP was the final line of defense against human error.

THE FLOODING INSIDE THE steam sterilization plant on May 17, 2018, was a serious problem that was about to get worse.

As the basement filled with water, it put the plant's struggling equipment at risk of further damage. It also jeopardized the important research underway at USAMRIID—which needed the SSP to stay operational to keep doing much of its work.

Unlike when your home basement floods, the standing water in the SSP basement couldn't just be pumped outdoors because of the risk that it contained deadly microbes.

So workers pumped the water into the SSP's auxiliary tanks in the outdoor tank farm, where it could be stored until it could be heat sterilized. This additional floodwater strained the already compromised SSP.

Dozens of Fort Detrick personnel, including top base commanders, were going in and out of the SSP as they tried to assess the situation, identify where leaks were coming from, make repairs—while also keeping the plant operational.

Many of the workers who responded during those first few days apparently were not wearing the kind of respiratory and full-body protection that would be called for later in the response, according to records and statements from base officials.

The repair efforts and splashing had created risks of them breathing invisible droplets and aerosolized wastewater—and not just in the basement flood area. Officials worried about the spread of these particles throughout the building, noting in a meeting with workers the importance of keeping doors to high-risk areas closed at all times.

A total of fifty-five people[35] worked in or visited the SSP at some point during the flooding. At least two men had some sort of "incidental contact" exposure that was of particular concern.

All fifty-five were sent for medical evaluations. Blood sampling and other testing were done on some, depending on what duties they had performed in the plant, the duration of their exposure, and their vaccination status. Fort Detrick told me "there were no instances of health issues reported."[36]

It is unknown whether any of these workers were quarantined or told to take precautions with their families and friends. Fort Detrick and USAMRIID wouldn't address this when I asked.[37]

There was no independent worker safety investigation by the U.S. Occupational Safety and Health Administration (OSHA) because nobody reported the incident, an OSHA spokesperson told me.[38]

To address concerns from the dozens of workers who had been exposed to potentially infectious wastewater, leadership from the army garrison, USAMRIID, and the base's safety office met with those involved in the SSP response.

Their first talking point was to assure the workers that their safety was the base's top priority and that it was believed that their risk of exposure was "extremely low,"[39] based on the chemical treatments that USAMRIID's wastewater was supposed to undergo before it was sent to the SSP for sterilization.

But their assurances belied their actions.

They told the workers that entry to the SSP would be restricted and that anyone going into certain areas would be required—at a minimum—to wear protective Tyvek suits, nitrile gloves, boots, and powered air-purifying respirators. These kinds of respirators, used in some biosafety level 3 laboratories, delivered a constant supply of HEPA-filtered air through a hood or helmet device to prevent workers from inhaling infectious aerosols and droplets.[40,41]

ON THE DAY THE steam sterilization plant flooded, USAMRIID notified lab regulators in the Division of Select Agents and Toxins at the Centers for Disease Control and Prevention (CDC) in Atlanta.

Federal law required the lab to tell them about the incident.

But state and local health departments, and Maryland's environmental regulatory agency, were left in the dark about the growing lab-leak problem at Fort Detrick. The base didn't begin to start notifying any of them about the safety concerns for another week.[42]

And there was no requirement to inform the public. Doing so would only draw unwanted attention to a messy situation that still wasn't under control.

USAMRIID didn't have to worry about the CDC select agent division publicizing the safety breach. Its regulators could be trusted to keep the accident a secret. This was in part because of how Congress wrote the legislation[43,44] governing the division, but also because that's how the division had a tradition of operating.[45]

In the United States, the vast majority of biological laboratories are not subject to federal biosafety inspections and most accidents with microbial pathogens don't have to be reported to any federal or state lab oversight authority.

Notifying the CDC of the SSP flooding was required only because USAMRIID's labs were among a small subset of government, academic, and private biological research facilities—at that time about 250 nationwide[46]—that study certain types of pathogens that are regulated by the Federal Select Agent Program.[47]

Labs are subject to this federal biosafety inspection and regulation if they possess any specimens of about seventy types of viruses, bacteria, or toxins that have been designated by the federal government as "select agents." These are pathogens considered to pose a severe threat to public health and safety, or to agriculture, animals, or plants. Their potential for use by bioterrorists is also a factor.

The select agent list[48] includes many pathogens widely known to the general public, such as *Bacillus anthracis* (which causes anthrax), Ebola virus, botulinum neurotoxins (which cause botulism), *Yersinia pestis* (which causes plague), and SARS-associated coronavirus (the family of viruses involved in the Covid-19 pandemic). It also includes the organisms that have long held the potential to be used as bioweapons, such as those that cause Q fever, tularemia, and brucellosis.

Many of the other pathogens on the list have names most people have never heard of, some because they primarily pose a risk to agriculture, others because they are so rare and exotic.

Not all dangerous microbes are subject to this federal oversight.

Tuberculosis bacteria, including multi-drug-resistant strains, and the deadly MERS (Middle East respiratory syndrome) coronavirus are among those not on the federal select agent list.

The Federal Select Agent Program is jointly run by the CDC, which takes the lead inspecting labs working primarily on human pathogens, and the U.S. Department of Agriculture, which focuses on oversight of a smaller group of labs predominantly working with microbes that harm animals and plants.

The regulatory program in its current form was created in 2003,[49] largely out of concerns about bioterrorists getting their hands on specimens of dangerous pathogens. It was born in the wake of the 9/11 terrorist attacks of 2001, which were soon followed by anthrax-filled letters sent anonymously through the U.S. postal system to members of Congress and the news media. Five people were killed and another seventeen were infected.[50]

In a way, USAMRIID played a role in shaping the regulatory approach.

The FBI concluded[51] that the 2001 anthrax attacks were planned and executed by Bruce Ivins, a microbiologist at USAMRIID, who died from an overdose of painkillers before he was charged. Although questions remain[52] about whether the FBI got the right man,[53] Ivins became an enduring symbol of the insider risk posed by lab employees intent on doing harm.

It's a key reason for the select agent program's focus on security.

Critics have long felt that ensuring labs were rigorously following safety practices—like those pioneered during the Wedum era—has taken a back seat to the program's inspection focus on security. Too much emphasis, they say, seemed to be on paperwork reviews of procedure manuals—which may or may not be followed in real life.

And there was what some considered an absurd focus on policing labs' inventory counts of vials[54] containing select agent pathogens. It was a time-eating task that ignored the fact that a bad actor didn't need to steal the whole vial, just a few drops of the organisms that could be grown elsewhere.

The program's terrorism-fighting ethos contributed to its zeal for keeping secret the accidents, safety lapses, and regulatory violations occurring at the laboratories it regulated.

So did its close relationship with the laboratory community.

The divisions of the CDC and USDA that regulate these select agent labs belong to agencies in the federal government that also operate their own biological research labs in addition to funding or collaborating on research at regulated facilities across the country.

It's a potentially incestuous system.

When the USAMRIID crisis happened, Samuel Edwin, who was in charge of the CDC's select agent regulatory program, was very familiar with the Fort Detrick facility.

Two years earlier, in 2016, the CDC had hired Edwin from USAMRIID[55]—where he had spent eight years as the biological surety officer and responsible official in charge of making sure USAMRIID's laboratory work complied with federal regulations.

I wanted to know: What awareness did he have of the state of disrepair at the steam sterilization plant when he was still working at USAMRIID? Had he been aware of the serious corrosion, leaking tanks, and other issues at the SSP that predated the plant's failure in 2018?

Edwin said he wasn't aware of any corrosion or leak issues at the SSP during his time as USAMRIID's responsible official.

"I visited the SSP multiple times with FSAP [Federal Select Agent

Program] inspectors during my tenure at USAMRIID," Edwin said in a statement[56] sent to me by a CDC spokesperson. The SSP was inspected annually by the CDC select agent program, he said, adding: "FSAP did not observe, and I did not report any issues with the SSP during this time."

Despite his name being on the CDC's regulatory correspondence with USAMRIID during 2018 and 2019, Edwin said others in the select agent program and at the CDC led the oversight of his former employer "to ensure there were no issues related to conflict of interest."

It is unclear how CDC inspectors failed to recognize the SSP was in such disrepair prior to the crisis in May 2018. The CDC offered no explanation and could produce no record of any report[57] showing the agency went back and examined the effectiveness of the select agent program's oversight of biosafety at USAMRIID's labs before the SSP failed.

FOUR DAYS AFTER THE SSP flooded, CDC select agent inspectors arrived at Fort Detrick and spent May 21 and 22, 2018, inspecting the facility.

By then, the problems at the steam sterilization plant were impossible to miss.

A few weeks later, the CDC select agent program issued a policy statement[58] making clear that inspectors had a right to regulate such facilities even when located in buildings outside of the registered lab spaces where waste originates. The CDC also created a team "specifically dedicated to conduct more focused inspections around effluent decontamination systems," the agency told me. "We believe that this will reduce EDS-related issues in the future."

As the CDC inspectors left Fort Detrick on May 22, they allowed USAMRIID to resume some select agent research activities.[59]

The long Memorial Day weekend was coming up, and the weather forecast showed more rain headed toward Frederick. It had been one of the area's wettest Mays on record.[60]

To protect the SSP against more flooding, a decision was made to pump the water inside the basement's waste storage tanks into the auxiliary tanks outdoors. The hope was to free up an additional 80,000 gallons of storage capacity.

But things didn't go as planned.

Somewhere along the way, an automatic shut-off feature designed to keep the outdoor tanks from overfilling was deactivated.[61]

CHAPTER 4

Nothing to See Here

Wastewater spewed out the top of one of the SSP's 50,000-gallon outdoor tanks, the pressure catapulting it over the short concrete wall[1] that was supposed to contain hazardous spills.

It was the Friday morning before the holiday weekend, and the tank had become over-pressurized, forcing the unsterilized lab waste out a vent pipe.

It sprayed for as long as three hours.[2]

An estimated 2,000–3,000 gallons[3] streamed into a grassy area a few feet from an open storm drain inlet that dumps into Carroll Creek—a centerpiece of downtown Frederick's residential and entertainment district.

But none of Fort Detrick's workers assigned to the SSP apparently noticed the tank had burst a pipe.

Instead, an employee of the National Cancer Institute, which has a research building located near the SSP, reported the leak that Friday morning, May 25, 2018. The person called it in to the "trouble desk" of Fort Detrick's Directorate of Public Works.

But nobody from public works went to check on the tank until noon.[4]

The dispatched workers reported back that they didn't see any leaking fluid. They checked the SSP tanks again at 2:00 p.m.[5] and still saw nothing. So nothing was done.

If not for the persistence of the unidentified National Cancer Institute employee, the leak would have been completely ignored.

On the Wednesday after the holiday, the same institute employee contacted the Fort Detrick safety manager. They wanted to follow up on their previous report—and this time they provided photos[6] proving the tank had been spraying wastewater nearly a week earlier.

The photos got the base's attention.

The Fort Detrick Command was immediately notified. So was USAMRIID's leadership.

But another day passed before they alerted state and local authorities.

THE WORKER AT THE Maryland Department of the Environment who took the call from Fort Detrick at 11:00 a.m. May 31, 2018, jotted down just a few handwritten words on the intake form[7] used to take telephone reports of a sewage overflow.

"Ft. Detrick"
"storage tank overflow"
"Carroll Creek"
"2,000 gal"
"lab ww tank overflowed"
"stopped flow to tank"

The seriousness of the event isn't obvious from the information collected on the form. And it also may not have been obvious to the worker, either, because the form and information about the release didn't reach any of the department's water compliance regulators[8] until another day had passed.

Meanwhile, Fort Detrick officials did manage to meet with local Frederick health officials that Thursday.

USAMRIID issued a six-paragraph press release making public for the first time that there had been an incident involving their laboratories.

The press release's headline: Flooding to Fort Detrick Steam Sterilization Plant.

Here's how the press release,[9] dated May 31, 2018, described the event:

Fort Detrick officials today announced that its Steam Sterilization Plant (SSP) is undergoing repairs following recent flooding in the Frederick area.

The SSP provides steam sterilization of liquid waste from research laboratories at Fort Detrick. Workers initially discovered flooding rain water in the plant May 17. On May 25, a leaking storage tank was also discovered.

Initial reports indicate that storage tanks were filled beyond capacity as a result of unprecedented rain in the region, causing a backup that eventually resulted in a leak outside the plant's concrete containment wall.

The press release explained that the wastewater was chemically disinfected before being routed to the SSP. And it assured: *"Fort Detrick is taking the necessary precautions to ensure the safety of its employees and the surrounding community."*

At the end, it added that USAMRIID, which uses the SSP, was temporarily halting all of its BSL-3 and BSL-4 operations until heat sterilization was restored.

No public mention was made about what my public records requests would reveal: that dozens of workers had been potentially exposed to the liquid waste or that the "leaking storage tank" had actually sprayed what base officials later estimated was 3,000 gallons[10] of the wastewater into the grass next to an open storm drain that led to Frederick's Carroll Creek.

A SIGNIFICANT QUESTION REMAINED unanswered: What exactly was in the lab wastewater that went down the storm drain and into Carroll Creek on May 25, 2018?

If viable organisms like anthrax bacteria had been sent into a creek running through downtown Frederick, the consequences could be disastrous for USAMRIID, Fort Detrick—and also the CDC regulators who allowed them to keep operating despite the jury-rigged SSP.

The risk that people or animals would become infected was probably low, with any organisms likely reduced below infectious levels as the waste became diluted by the floodwaters still surging through the area's streams and rivers.

But public backlash and international headlines were certainties.

So what was in the wastewater?

Nobody seemed to be looking very hard to find out.

USAMRIID and Fort Detrick offered only generalized assurances that their tests hadn't detected any pathogens.

Rather than serve as watchdogs in the public interest, all levels of government seemed to largely defer to USAMRIID and its expertise—despite the organization's egregious safety breach and potential self-interest in damage control.

The head of the Frederick County Department of Health, Dr. Barbara Brookmyer, remembers her department asking a slew of questions[11] after USAMRIID and Fort Detrick officials first notified them of the wastewater release on May 31, 2018. And she also reached out to officials at the Maryland Department of Health to discuss her concerns.

"I was told that Fort Detrick notified [the Maryland Department of the Environment] that there was a Sanitary Sewer Overflow event. I advised that this is not a typical SSO event and that they should make it clear,"[12] Brookmyer said in an email she sent at 9:04 p.m. that Thursday evening to two senior officials at the state health department, plus an official at the state's environmental agency.

"People were planting lily pads in Carroll Creek this past weekend," Brookmyer noted.

Brookmyer wanted to see the actual testing reports from the army's sampling around the SSP. In addition to the potential risks to human health from USAMRIID's wastewater, she also was concerned about the potential environmental impact from any plant pathogens that may have been in wastewater from the USDA lab.[13]

Brookmyer said she requested that additional sampling be performed along Carroll Creek—since that's where the unsterilized wastewater went.

Her requests went nowhere.

"Follow-up responses indicated that they were not planning to conduct testing along Carroll Creek," Brookmyer told me.[14] And neither USAMRIID nor Fort Detrick ever provided Brookmyer any of their testing reports.

The county health department didn't have the expertise to do the sampling itself, she said; the agencies with the expertise and authority were at the state and federal levels.

The Maryland Department of Health, unlike other state and local agencies, got an early heads-up from USAMRIID[15] on May 24, 2018, through a phoned-in report alerting them to the initial SSP flooding. This was the day before the wastewater tank overflowed into Carroll Creek—and possibly at a time when additional oversight might have prevented it from happening.

But officials at Maryland's state health department appear to have kept secret whatever they were told during their call with three of USAMRIID's top biosecurity and emergency management officials. And the department may have been required to under an unusual law passed by the Maryland legislature in 2002.[16] The law mandates that labs working with "select agent" pathogens register with the state health department's lab division and notify it about incidents—but the law also requires the information be kept confidential.

The Maryland Department of Health wouldn't answer my questions[17] about the Fort Detrick incidents or the actions the department took to investigate what was in the wastewater. A spokesman told me to file an open records request,[18] which after a four-month wait yielded only a handful of records.

Because the incident involved sewage, regulators from the Maryland Department of the Environment went to Fort Detrick on June 6, 2018, to investigate the wastewater overflow.

Inspector Charlie Hatfield documented the lax maintenance and failed safety procedures[19] at the SSP that led to the release. He didn't go inside the SSP, but he took photos of the outdoor tanks and of the open storm drain a short distance below them.

Hatfield's report cited Fort Detrick for multiple violations of state environmental regulations, including unauthorized discharge of partially treated wastewater and failure to operate facilities to minimize discharges.

Joseph Gortva, chief of Fort Detrick's Environmental Management Division, had assured the state regulators that the incident didn't pose a public health threat. He told them that USAMRIID had tested wastewater from the leak to see whether it contained any *Bacillus anthracis*, and because anthrax wasn't found, "no other pathogens are present."[20]

The reasoning was that anthrax bacteria were the hardiest pathogen being studied, and the type most likely to be environmentally stable[21] outdoors.

"As a further precaution, USAMRIID conducted additional environmental sampling of the area on May 31–June 1. No growth of any organism handled at USAMRIID was detected," Gortva told them.[22]

In the weeks before the tank started spewing wastewater, USAMRIID had been experimenting with sixteen organisms, and lab officials said they had tested the concrete pad and the ground adjacent to the tanks[23] for all of them.

The organisms that were possibly in the wastewater were *Bacillus anthracis*, Ebola virus, Lassa fever virus, Junin virus, Marburg virus, Venezuelan equine encephalitis virus, eastern equine encephalitis virus, Crimean-Congo hemorrhagic fever virus, Nipah virus, *Burkholderia pseudomallei*, *Burkholderia mallei*, *Francisella tularensis*, western equine encephalitis virus, Dobrava-Belgrade virus, Seoul virus, and Chikungunya virus.

As further evidence that no deadly microbes had escaped, Gortva and army officials noted to state and local officials—without providing reports or details—that they had also done some additional validation testing inside USAMRIID's laboratories that showed lab drains contained sufficient disinfectant to kill anything poured down them. The implication was that there was no risk from the SSP's unsterilized wastewater and that the heat-treating process was nice, but not necessary.

Officials at the Maryland Department of the Environment declined to be interviewed. In a short emailed statement,[24] the department said that because sampling for these kinds of pathogens is highly specialized, it relies on the expertise of those—like the army and CDC—who regularly work with the organisms.

WHEN IT COMES TO environmental sampling, the locations and number of samples and methods used to collect them often determine whether anything is found. This is especially true when samples are collected on outdoor surfaces—where rain can wash contaminants away.

USAMRIID and Fort Detrick officials didn't even do any environmental tests until May 31 and June 1—about a week after the SSP tank overflowed. By then, it had already rained[25] at Fort Detrick between the overflow and the testing.

How meaningful was USAMRIID's testing?

Did USAMRIID test two samples or twenty samples or two hundred samples? What were the detection limits of the testing methods that they used? How might the rain—or wind or sunlight—have impacted the ability of their tests to detect organisms a week after the release incident?

You would think if they had performed tests that supported their position, USAMRIID would *want* to publicly release reports showing what they did.

Yet USAMRIID and Fort Detrick officials refused to release copies of the testing reports involving the SSP or the surrounding area. For months they wouldn't even say how many samples were tested.

"The test plan was reviewed and approved by the CDC," USAMRIID told me in a written statement.

CDC select agent officials were equally unhelpful, saying USAMRIID developed and conducted its own testing.

"USAMRIID test results indicated the public health risk associated with any potential release was negligible; however, you would need to contact USAMRIID for full information about the testing methods and results," the CDC said.[26]

The U.S. Environmental Protection Agency has experts who develop protocols on how to test for bioterror pathogens in the environment. But they were never alerted or consulted about what happened at USAMRIID, the EPA said in response to my questions.[27]

Lab leaks of wastewater potentially containing dangerous pathogens—a circumstance that might benefit from an EPA emergency response—fall into a loophole in federal environmental regulations that were designed to protect against traditional pollutants like chemicals, petroleum products, or heavy metals.

But bacteria and viruses are not regulated as hazardous substances or hazardous wastes.

"Since this seems to be a release involving pathogenic organisms, it would not fall under the EPCRA program, which means there appears to be no requirement for Fort Detrick to contact the National Response Center," the EPA told me.

EPCRA[28] stands for the Emergency Planning and Community Right-to-Know Act, which was passed in 1986 in the wake of the disastrous accidental chemical release in Bhopal, India, that killed or severely injured more than 2,000 people. The law requires U.S. facilities to immediately report accidental releases of certain "hazardous substances" and provides increased public access to information about chemical storage and incidents.

It appears USAMRIID and Fort Detrick, with a somewhat detached CDC looking over their shoulder, were entrusted with investigating the extent of their own contamination and managing any potential risks to the public.

It was a lot of trust to put in an organization that was failing to take appropriate safety precautions in its own lab operations.

Eventually, after months of requests, USAMRIID told me their testing to determine whether pathogens had escaped involved just five swab samples collected from "various locations" at the SSP. But lab officials still didn't answer how many water samples were taken.[29]

By June 28, 2018, CDC regulators formally put USAMRIID's authorization to work with select agent pathogens on a "limited suspension," noting that the facility had already voluntarily suspended work in its BSL-3 and BSL-4 labs.[30]

In the months that followed, USAMRIID stopped sending its liquid waste to the SSP because the repairs[31] it needed were too extensive. As a stopgap, USAMRIID's wastewater was redirected in February to a temporary chemical effluent disinfection system set up outside the lab building.

Within five months that system overflowed, too.

Once again, it was a combination of equipment failures and human error.

The result was 100 gallons of wastewater[32] that sloshed out of a storage tank that was part of the chemical disinfection system on July 1, 2019. The waste had received only 26 minutes of the 120-minute contact time with a bleach solution that was required to fully inactivate any organisms in it.

This time the spill remained on Fort Detrick's property. But it was yet another sloppy mistake.

The situation at USAMRIID had become so alarming to CDC lab regulators that a top official sent a letter directly to the army commander at USAMRIID, rather than corresponding with the lab facility's designated regulatory compliance official.

"The [Federal Select Agent Program] is bringing what it believes to be a serious situation to your attention based on the FSAP concern that a systemic and sustained unsafe biosafety culture has developed at USAMRIID that requires immediate command attention," the July 9, 2019, letter said.[33]

In the previous eighteen months, there had been thirty-six incidents at USAMRIID that required the labs to notify the CDC of the potential release of select agent pathogens. "Sixteen of the thirty-six reports documented departures from USAMRIID's SOPs," the letter said, referring to the standard operating procedures that are a cornerstone of biosafety.

This was a deeply troubling finding. The entire regulatory and safety structure for USAMRIID and labs like it around the world is based on facilities having written safety procedures and their assurances that they are consistently following them in their day-to-day work when nobody is watching.

But that clearly wasn't happening at USAMRIID.

"USAMRIID is displaying an ongoing pattern of unsafe biosafety practices that can best be described as deviations from nationally recognized biosafety standards," the letter said.

During inspections in March and June 2019, CDC inspectors had observed USAMRIID workers not wearing appropriate protective gear inside infectious disease labs. In one biosafety level 3 animal room, they watched a worker repeatedly going partway into the lab "multiple times" without wearing any respiratory protection despite procedures that were underway with an infected primate.

The worker did this even knowing inspectors were in the facility.

Other lab workers told inspectors they weren't following USAMRIID's specified animal cage cleaning procedures because they believed the exact protocol "did not really matter."

Two days after the CDC official's letter, USAMRIID had yet another spill of potentially infectious material.[34] This incident, on July 11, 2019, resulted in a worker being put on a twenty-one-day fever watch.[35]

The CDC ordered USAMRIID to immediately cease all work with select agent pathogens, suspending the facility's participation in the select agent program effective July 12, 2019.[36] The formal letter cited significant violations in the areas of training, security, and oversight by the facility's designated regulatory compliance official.

It was a stunning blow to the crown-jewel lab at the revered birthplace of biosafety.

But the CDC select agent program kept this information secret and made no public announcement, as is its standard practice when it shuts down labs for severe safety problems.

People living in Frederick didn't learn about the shutdown until a few weeks later, and only then because a reporter at the local Frederick newspaper[37] started asking questions forcing the lab's spokesperson to issue a short public statement.

DRESSED IN ARMY CAMOUFLAGE uniforms, Brigadier General Mike Talley and other top officials from Fort Detrick strode into Frederick City Hall on a mission to quell mounting concerns about laboratory safety at USAMRIID.

"I will apologize right up front," Talley said. "If one of our laboratories is under, you know, this type of scrutiny for practices, or were shut down by regulatory organizations, you shouldn't be hearing about this in the news before we talk about it."

Talley had come to answer questions at the October 8, 2019, meeting of the city's Containment Lab Community Advisory Committee (CLCAC),[38] a group established in 2010 with the hope of increasing information sharing between Fort Detrick's labs and concerned citizens who live nearby.

But as a committee of volunteers with no direct authority,[39] they could only do so much.

Nearly 280,000 people call Frederick County their home.[40] And for decades, the area's relationship with Fort Detrick has been a complicated one as a growing number of biological research facilities have been constructed inside the base's secure perimeter.

In addition to USAMRIID and the USDA lab, they include labs operated by the U.S. Department of Homeland Security, the National Institutes of Health's National Institute of Allergy and Infectious Diseases, and the National Cancer Institute.

The base is the area's largest employer,[41] with about 9,500 military, federal employees, and contractors[42] assigned to work there. It drives an estimated $7 billion[43] in economic impact to the state of Maryland.

Fort Detrick has fueled the growth of high-paying jobs by also attracting other life sciences employers to the region.

For all of Fort Detrick's positive impacts, a climate of distrust had developed over the years within segments of the community.

The base and its labs had a long history of downplaying risks and withholding information from area residents. This was on display when USAMRIID began the process of building its massive new $700 million[44] laboratory facility at Fort Detrick in 2006—a facility that as of late 2022 was still not operational.

In 2010, after USAMRIID faced vocal opposition to the new lab facility from area residents, a panel of experts from National Academies of Sciences, Engineering, and Medicine found that the army had failed to adequately assess the risks of deadly pathogens being released into the community.

"The calculations of risk from the release scenarios appear to be incomplete and potentially incorrect," said the National Academies group, which chastised USAMRIID in its eighty-six-page report[45] for not providing enough data in its risk assessments to allow for transparent and independent review of their conclusions.

"No attempts were made to systematically account for the biological characteristics of the organisms, and the analyses did not assess the potential for a local epidemic within the community or the efficacy of mitigation plans for minimizing the effects of such an epidemic."

While USAMRIID's environmental impact assessment for the new facility found no substantial risks, the expert panel said the lab "did not exhaustively consider the various possible routes through which members of the general public may be exposed to pathogens studied at USAMRIID."

For example, the report said, there had been no in-depth evaluation of a reasonable and credible scenario of a lab worker becoming infected through an unrecognized exposure while working at a biosafety cabinet yet ignoring proper specimen handling practices.

The experts criticized USAMRIID for not exploring the potential "low-level/long-term risks" posed by an escaped research pathogen to become established within a local population of animals or insects, such as fleas, ticks, and mosquitoes, which can spread disease.

And they also said USAMRIID had failed to address "the performance, reliability, and security concerning the operations and maintenance of USAMRIID's wastewater treatment and conveyance systems."

Despite all of USAMRIID's failures in its risk assessment, the members of the scientific review group ultimately said they had a "high degree of confidence that policies and procedures are in place to provide appropriate protections to workers and the public."

But they did call for USAMRIID to be more transparent with the community in order to develop and sustain public trust.

"Safety and security failures, along with their countermeasures, should be reported promptly to the public," their 2010 report said. "The tendency to minimize such rare accidents has created mistrust among the local population."

Just because events are rare doesn't mean concerns are unimportant, the committee wrote, noting that the U.S. government spends an enormous amount of money to protect the country against the potential for a biological attack.

"The entire U.S. biodefense program is predicated on low-probability, high-consequence risk of an attack, so it is easy to see why many Frederick area residents view the risk of an accidental release or intentional diversion from USAMRIID laboratories in the same manner, that is, low probability, but high consequence," the report said.

The expert panel recommended that USAMRIID create a community advisory group to facilitate two-way communications—a true dialog and not just press releases and public relations.

USAMRIID never created a community group.

So the city of Frederick created one itself. USAMRIID usually sent only a public relations representative to the meetings.

Except when there was a crisis.

"WE'RE HONORED TO BE here to talk to the Containment Laboratory Community Advisory Committee," Talley said as he began his opening remarks[46] at the October 2019 meeting.

Joining Talley were Colonel E. Darrin Cox, commander of USAMRIID, and Colonel Dexter Nunnally, commander of the Fort Detrick garrison, which oversees the base infrastructure and operations.

They were the latest in the ever-changing string of leaders at USAMRIID and the base, where military commanders routinely rotate in and out every few years. And Talley made clear that he, Cox, and Nunnally had arrived after the July incident that led to the USAMRIID shutdown.

In Talley's few short months overseeing Fort Detrick, he had concluded that the ongoing series of safety violations at the base had their roots in an undisciplined culture.

The issues he identified sounded a lot like those Arnold Wedum had confronted decades earlier.

Those working in USAMRIID's labs, Talley said, had become accustomed over time to doing things the way they wanted to and ignoring safety recommendations from outside inspectors.

"I think it really came down to being held accountable to a standard of performance," Talley told the committee.

One challenge, he said, was that the majority of workers in USAMRIID's labs were employed by private contractors, not directly by the federal government. The arrangement made it easier to swap workers in and out depending on changing research needs, but contracts should have "teeth" added to ensure the workers were accountable for following procedures.

"Frankly, culturally, we've had to make adjustments. We can't keep doing things the way we've always done it," Talley said.

Committee members seemed reassured by what they heard from Talley and the others.

The committee members[47] were a serious and respectful group of appointed Frederick residents who, in many cases, had deep knowledge of biological research. Some had worked as bench scientists or biosafety experts, including at USAMRIID; others had experience in health care or at federal agencies.

The committee's chairman, Matt Sharkey, was a federal health policy analyst who held a PhD in biochemistry and molecular biology and had completed postdoctoral research that included work done at USAMRIID.

Sharkey's main question for Talley, Cox, and Nunnally involved the testing by USAMRIID and Fort Detrick in the wake of the May 2018 SSP flooding incidents. It was the testing that could answer questions about what was in the laboratory wastewater that spewed out of the plant.

A little over a year earlier, in July 2018, the previous group of army commanders had met with the committee and said the testing found nothing, but they hadn't provided any data.

"I was just wondering if you could arrange to share your data from that environmental sampling," Sharkey said,[48] "what the procedure was, where the samples were taken, what type of samples were taken, and what type of tests were done."

By sharing that data, he continued, it would allow the committee to verify that an appropriate sampling method was used and provide reassurance to the public. "Also, did you have that procedure verified or validated by any external partner?"

Nunnally, the garrison commander, told Sharkey: "I'll get you that information."[49]

But no testing records were ever provided. Three years later, the committee was still asking for the data.

Back in July 2020, I filed a federal Freedom of Information Act request with the army seeking the SSP wastewater testing records. More than two years later as I write this book, the army says it is still processing my FOIA request.

I have repeatedly asked spokespeople for USAMRIID and Fort Detrick to voluntarily share the testing reports. "The report itself is not releasable," said the statement I got back from USAMRIID's spokesperson Caree Vander Linden.

At this point, it will likely take a congressional oversight investigation or a Freedom of Information Act lawsuit to find out.[50]

One of my other FOIA requests eventually dislodged from the army the report of the tests done on disinfectant levels inside USAMRIID lab drains—tests that USAMRIID had represented as providing reassuring evidence that all the microbes in the liquid flowing into the SSP would have already been killed before they got there.

However, the five-page report[51] from USAMRIID's drain testing exercise indicates the samples weren't collected under real-life operating conditions. Eventually the army admitted to me that the tests were done in empty labs where no work had been occurring and no animals were present.[52]

Of perhaps greater concern: These validation tests checking the adequacy of disinfecting chemicals in USAMRIID's lab drains were performed solely in response to the regulatory and public relations crisis from the lab leak in May 2018.

It was the only time—from January 2015 through at least March 2022—that USAMRIID had ever checked the adequacy of the disinfectant in their drains, the army's FOIA response said.[53]

As EVIDENCE OF ITS safe operations, USAMRIID's website for many years[54] displayed data indicating there hasn't been a single laboratory-acquired infection since at least 2010. The web page also provided some aggregate tallies of laboratory incidents by year.

"It is important to note that in every incident from 2010 to present, no symptoms were reported and there were no signs of illness," the website stated in its "Safety Report Information" section.

But the data that USAMRIID shared publicly throughout much of 2022 was incomplete, out of date, and potentially misleading. And in the wake of my questions, USAMRIID removed all of its lab safety data from its website.[55]

Until that happened, the data posted on USAMRIID's website in 2022 was only for the period of 2017–2019[56]—and it only covered incidents occurring in the facility's BSL-3 and BSL-4 labs. This excludes the disclosure of laboratory incidents and exposures occurring in biosafety level 2 labs[57] or spaces outside of labs, such as the steam sterilization plant.

As a result, there appears to have been no accounting in USAMRIID's online safety report of the serious 2018 SSP incident where fifty-five people were exposed to potentially infectious wastewater. USAMRIID's online safety data showed zero incidents during 2018 involving equipment malfunctions, illustrating how serious incidents can be kept out of publicly reported numbers based on how labs choose to slice and dice their data.

There have been 486 disclosed incidents in USAMRIID's BSL-3 and BSL-4 labs during 2010–2019, archived images of the lab's safety page show.[58] In sixty-two of these incidents, workers were placed on medical surveillance because USAMRIID assessed the circumstances to have involved a "potential biological exposure."

USAMRIID's online data showed zero "occupational illness" incidents from 2010 through 2019.

The few USAMRIID worker infections that have become publicly known illustrate the potential for more to occur undetected if workers don't report them.

In November 2009, a researcher studying the bacterium *Francisella tularensis* inside one of USAMRIID's BSL-3 labs somehow became infected from her work despite the lab's safety equipment and policies.

When she fell ill, she didn't notify the lab. She simply assumed that her fever, chills, and headache were just something she'd caught from her children,[59] who were also ill at the time.

It was only after her symptoms wouldn't go away that she went to USAMRIID's clinic, which confirmed she had tularemia pneumonia and treated her with appropriate antibiotics. It was fortunately a disease that doesn't spread from person to person. No other tularemia cases occurred.

An even worse example of a USAMRIID microbiologist failing to report their illness occurred in 2000.

This 33-year-old man had been studying a bacterium called *Burkholderia mallei*,[60] which causes a deadly disease called *glanders* and is considered a potential biowarfare agent. Any infection with this bacterium is serious. Without proper treatment with specific antibiotics, as many as 90 percent of people infected will die.[61] And even if treated, about half still will die.

This particular scientist, who had insulin-requiring diabetes, was at even greater risk from an infection because of his health status. Yet during his two years working with these bacteria, he did not routinely wear gloves.[62] And *B. mallei* often enters the body through tiny, unrecognized abrasions in the skin.

The man's symptoms started in March 2000[63] with an increasingly painful mass in his left armpit and a fever of 101.5°F. He went to his primary care doctor, who gave him antibiotics. But he had increasing episodes of fever, felt overwhelming fatigue, and started having night sweats and losing weight. He received more medical tests and a different antibiotic—but multiple blood cultures were negative for bacteria.

He continued to get worse. Eventually in May he was admitted to Frederick Memorial Hospital[64] after a CT scan revealed multiple lesions[65] on his liver and spleen. It was only then that the man's work history at USAMRIID was considered a possible cause of his illness—but he was now in critical condition, having developed respiratory distress and needing a ventilator.

He was transferred to a hospital in Baltimore, where blood cultures eventually identified the bacteria that was killing him and finally enabled doctors to prescribe effective antibiotics that saved his life.

The microbiologist couldn't recall any accident or break in his skin[66] that might have caused his exposure.

Experts from the National Academies, who examined the infection incidents of these two workers as part of their 2010 review of the new USAMRIID facility, noted they highlight how "human actions are probably the weakest link in biosafety."[67]

THE LACK OF TRANSPARENCY by USAMRIID and Fort Detrick about laboratory incidents has made the army base a favorite target for propaganda efforts by China's government and Chinese state media in the wake of the Covid-19 pandemic.

As part of an ongoing campaign to shift attention away from the Wuhan Institute of Virology, Chinese officials have attempted to implicate Fort Detrick in somehow causing the pandemic. This is despite Fort Detrick being more than 7,000 miles from Wuhan, which was the epicenter of where the pandemic emerged in late 2019.

"The Fort Detrick horror: a closer look at the US' largest biochemical weapons research center"[68] was the headline of one article in a state-affiliated Chinese media outlet, which said: "Experts slammed the US for its evasive, ostrich-like attitude towards the rising voices calling for a USAMRIID investigation, while slandering a laboratory in China's Wuhan city for 'originating' the coronavirus."

Since the spring of 2020, Chinese government diplomatic and state-run social media accounts have pushed a similar narrative: "It might be US army who brought the epidemic to Wuhan," tweeted Zhao Lijian,[69] spokesman for China's Foreign Ministry Information Department in March 2020.

In a 2021 tweet, the spokesperson for China's Ministry of Foreign Affairs asked:[70] "On #COVID19 origin-tracing, when will the #US show the same openness & transparency as #China? When will it invite #WHO experts in to investigate? When will it open up #FortDetrick to international experts for probe or research?"

China's state-controlled Xinhua News Agency has even used the Frederick Containment Lab Community Advisory Committee's ongoing efforts[71] to force transparency from USAMRIID to help fuel propaganda.

It's been infuriating for the committee members to see their work twisted in this way.

"This highlights how important it is for high containment laboratory research to be absolutely transparent and accountable to their communities," Sharkey, the committee's chairman, told me. "The Army has done itself and the American people no favors, either at home or on the world stage by refusing to engage with our community about safety and security issues."

There's been a lot of tough talk by the administrations of Presidents Biden and Trump about the lack of China's transparency about any role played by Wuhan's labs in the start of the Covid-19 pandemic. But neither administration—nor any of the Republican or Democratic administrations before them—have done anything to ensure transparency about lab safety failings here in the United States.

Beyond that, they have continued to entrust the oversight of U.S. biolabs working with the most dangerous pathogens to federal agencies like the CDC that are deeply engaged in biological research and whose own labs have a troubled safety record.

PART 2

WARNING SIGNS

CHAPTER 5

Lightning Strike

T HE DUCT TAPE seemed shockingly out of place.

Yet there it was, stripped around a containment door inside a $214 million lab building.

Teams of engineers, architects, and biosafety experts had spent years designing, constructing, and testing the new Emerging Infectious Diseases Laboratory at the Centers for Disease Control and Prevention's headquarters in Atlanta.

The gleaming concrete-and-glass structure, informally known as Building 18, was touted when it opened as the most advanced facility of its type in the world, an impenetrable fortress where about 500 scientists and staff engaged in the study of lethal viruses and bacteria.

This was not where you would expect to find a biosafety level 3 lab with a containment door sealed with duct tape. And especially not a lab used for experimenting with highly infectious Q fever bacteria.

Yet there I was in the summer of 2008, reporter's notebook in hand, staring at this duct-taped door while five CDC officials tried to convince me that it was all perfectly normal.

During my years of reporting on laboratory safety lapses at the CDC and hundreds of other U.S. facilities, I came to learn that the bizarre scene that played out in front of the duct-taped door was emblematic of how labs and regulators approach safety.

At the time I was the beat reporter covering the CDC for the *Atlanta Journal-Constitution*—the hometown newspaper read by many of the agency's 9,000 employees and 5,000 contractors who mostly lived in the Atlanta metro area.

The CDC has long been considered one of the world's premier public health agencies, home to legions of disease detectives revered worldwide for their ability to track down and help extinguish outbreaks and epidemics ranging from *E. coli* in ground beef to global plagues like malaria, polio, tuberculosis, and SARS.

Yet in early 2020, when the CDC's labs produced contaminated and flawed test kits[1] that delayed the country's ability to diagnose Covid-19 infections at the start of the pandemic, the agency already had a history of sloppy practices in its laboratories.

Despite this history, the CDC remains the primary U.S. lab regulatory agency overseeing biosafety at facilities possessing select agent pathogens.

Like most people, I had never given much thought to the safety of biological research labs. I had assumed they were highly regulated and operated with the strictest attention to safety.

Yet during my first three years covering the CDC, the duct-taped door was one of several disturbing situations that my reporting uncovered inside the agency's labs.

My first CDC lab story involved horrifying animal welfare issues. Following up on a tip, I reported that the CDC's labs had secretly been put on probation by an international accreditation organization because of multiple serious animal care failures that included two monkeys dying of dehydration because nobody noticed their water devices weren't working. The problems left CDC director Julie Gerberding "simply appalled," she told me at the time.[2]

When the CDC did an internal review in 2006 examining how its lab animal program had failed so badly, it found several root causes: fragmented lab oversight, lack of centralized accountability, and inadequate training.

In hindsight, the report had diagnosed the causes of a much wider, more invasive safety problem spreading unchecked throughout the agency's labs.

Another tipster contacted me in 2008 about the duct tape.

The tape had been put around the edges of the door a year earlier after a malfunction of the lab's air-handling systems. The incident, in May 2007, had pulled potentially contaminated air out of a biosafety level 3 Q fever lab and into a "clean" hallway where workers aren't expected to wear protective safety gear because no microbes are supposed to be present.

The bacterium that causes Q fever is especially risky. It takes a very small exposure—as few as ten organisms[3]—for a person to become infected. Because of this, the organism has a long history of causing infections among researchers around the world. It's also among the reasons that Q fever bacteria, which cause debilitating flu-like symptoms, are considered a potential biowarfare agent and are regulated by the Federal Select Agent Program.

BSL-3 labs, like the one used for Q fever at the CDC, are supposed to maintain negative—or inward—airflow. It's an important safety layer, on top of scientists using a biosafety cabinet to manipulate specimens, that helps keep any aerosolized microbes inside the lab and not wafting invisibly into other parts of the building.

The air circulation in these kinds of high-containment labs is an ongoing cycle of drawing air from clean areas into labs; then this potentially contaminated air is vented outdoors after passing through HEPA filters that remove any microbes.

But when a Q fever researcher arrived at the problematic CDC lab at 6:20 a.m. on May 25, 2007, they discovered the air blowing outward from the lab—an alarming situation of the lab going "positive" that continued for another forty-five minutes,[4] until the system was fixed at 7:05 a.m.

The air imbalance in the Q fever lab was so significant that in addition to air blowing into the clean corridor, the "Q-lab went so positive it blew open the door to the vivarium,"[5] a CDC scientist said in an email that morning, referring to a door that led to where research animals were kept.

The good news was that no scientists were actively working with specimens at the time. But members of the Q fever team had concerns that bacteria might have been present on contaminated equipment[6] and surfaces inside the lab.

Nine CDC workers potentially exposed that day received blood tests and had to monitor their temperature twice daily for ten days. The CDC said none developed infections and the public was never at risk.

A year later, as my CDC escorts and I stood in the corridor outside the Q fever lab, the agency officials emphasized that the lab's air handling systems had worked properly since the incident.

"Then why is the door still sealed with duct tape?" I asked.

"It's an enhancement,"[7] Patrick Stockton, who was the CDC's safety and occupational health manager at the time, told me. "We could take it off."

But they weren't taking it off.

It made no sense.

"I do not believe the CDC would approve this arrangement in a laboratory other than their own,"[8] Richard Ebright, a molecular biologist at Rutgers University in New Jersey, told me for my article in the *Atlanta Journal-Constitution*.

Lab inspectors from the CDC arm of the Federal Select Agent Program at that time were still allowed to inspect the agency's own labs, a practice that the agency defended as not posing any conflict of interest.

These CDC inspectors were fine with the duct tape, the agency told me.

What apparently worried the agency more was the unwanted public attention that my article would bring to the situation.

Behind the scenes, while I was peppering the agency with questions, the CDC engineering office was completing designs for a new self-sealing door for the Q fever lab, which it purchased on an expedited basis.[9] It was installed after the article was published—though the agency kept saying it wasn't really necessary.

It was a reminder of the old adage: Sunlight is the best disinfectant.

THE DUCT-TAPED LAB ARTICLE prompted concern from Congress.

"This is yet another incident that calls into question the CDC's self-inspection policy," U.S. Representative John Dingell (D-Mich.), chairman of the House Committee on Energy and Commerce, told me at the time. "If the going rate for a leaky door and a roll of duct tape is $200 million, then I think I'm in the wrong line of business."[10]

Dingell and his committee, along with the U.S. Government Accountability Office (GAO), had been investigating the potential safety risks posed by the post-9/11 building boom of high-containment laboratories.

Back then and in the decade that followed, examining the threats posed by laboratory accidents was a bipartisan issue, with both Democrats and Republicans actively engaged in asking uncomfortable questions, compelling agencies to release documents, and holding hearings that sought to uncover problems and look for solutions.

When the duct tape story broke, congressional investigators and the GAO were already investigating another problem with CDC Building 18 that my reporting had revealed the previous summer.[11]

During a thunderstorm in June 2007, Building 18 lost power for an hour after its emergency backup generators failed to come online following a lightning strike and power surge.

It was 6:30 p.m. on a Friday when the outage happened. A battery system provided[12] enough power to sound alarms and keep doors and lights working for about fifteen to twenty minutes while workers in the 368,000-square-foot building evacuated.

The CDC wouldn't say what experiments were underway at the time.

Building 18 housed BSL-3 labs that had been operational since at least January 2006.[13] It was in these types of labs that CDC scientists had a history of working with a reconstructed strain of the 1918 pandemic influenza virus, as well as avian influenza and anthrax.

Neither workers nor the public were ever in any danger, the agency told me.

The building's new BSL-4 labs—where scientists would work with smallpox and Ebola virus—were still undergoing testing and were not yet operational when the power outage occurred. While the CDC downplayed the significance of the outage, George Chandler, who was in charge of the CDC's buildings and facilities, told me that the agency was considering adding a special backup power supply[14] for the BSL-4 labs as a result of the incident.

The CDC quickly determined that construction on an adjacent building had caused unrecognized damage to Building 18's grounding system,[15] cutting a cable that protected it from lightning strikes.

But there was an unsettling backstory about the design of Building 18 that the CDC wasn't sharing with the public.

AS A REPORTER, YOU can't just rely on what people and agencies want to tell you.

In addition to contacting the CDC media office and doing other interviews, I also filed a federal Freedom of Information Act (FOIA) request seeking the agency's internal emails and documents about the lightning strike and any other safety concerns about Building 18.

The FOIA, enacted in 1967, gives any member of the public the right to access government records. We, the people, are the ones actually paying for all of those documents generated by government workers. And the ability for the public to know what its government is doing—or not doing—is critical to a functioning democracy.

Yet the federal government routinely breaks this transparency law. It's not a partisan issue. It's really more of a power issue. Whatever party is in power, it doesn't want its dirty laundry hanging out for the public to see.

The FOIA generally requires federal agencies to respond to a request for records within twenty business days. Early in my journalism career, that actually happened with many of my requests. But that's not been the norm for many years, as the government allowed the backlogs of records requests to balloon and learned that delay is a tactic that can effectively kill stories when media organizations can't afford to file lawsuits over every FOIA request.

(By the way, journalists file only a small fraction of FOIA requests.[16] Most are filed by businesses, law firms, advocacy groups, and other non-profit organizations.)

The CDC had no plans to quickly release documents about Building 18's power outage and other problems, denying my request for expedited processing, saying, "There is no urgency to inform the public."[17]

The agency ultimately took more than three years to release the records—far longer than the thirty-eight-day median processing time for complex records requests that it had touted in FOIA compliance reports back then.

During that extended wait, the agency attempted to throw out my FOIA request administratively—without releasing any records—simply because I had taken a new job with USA TODAY. It took multiple appeals to the CDC's parent agency, the U.S. Department of Health and Human Services, to get the FOIA request restored so that I didn't have to file a new request and start the wait all over again.

When the Building 18 documents were eventually released to me in September 2010,[18] the CDC completely withheld nearly half of the 555 pages discussing the building's safety and engineering problems; the other 268 pages were heavily redacted.

Information can be withheld only for certain specific reasons outlined in the FOIA, such as information that would harm national security, personal privacy, law enforcement, or certain pre-decisional discussions.

The desire to avoid negative publicity is not a recognized exemption under the FOIA.

Yet at the CDC and other federal agencies, regardless of the political party in office, public relations interests too often seem to play a role in how FOIA requests are processed and what information is and is not released.

I later learned, through sources and internal records, that the CDC was performing public relations risk assessments on the documents[19] that I was seeking.

The result was that the public documents the agency had gathered would frequently take a time-consuming detour through the CDC Office of Enterprise Communications before anything was released to me. In this office, staff would review the records and write up memos on how to counteract the threats the information posed to the agency's image.

Among the official purposes of this office was "conducting environmental scanning to determine emerging threats to the agency's reputation"[20] and implementing strategies "to promote and protect the agency's brand."

Your taxpayer dollars at work.

There was significant concern at that time about the direction of the agency under then CDC director Julie Gerberding.

Gerberding, the first woman to lead the CDC, was named director in July 2002 following her high-profile role in the agency's response to the previous year's anthrax attacks. As CDC director, she quickly launched a reorganization of the agency with the stated goal of making the CDC more nimble in responding to modern public health threats like bioterrorism and pandemics.

But many longtime CDC scientists felt the initiative, which dragged on for years, was adding layers of bureaucracy—and bureaucrats—that were threatening the agency's scientific focus and ability to respond in a crisis.

Dozens of high-profile CDC leaders and scientists left the agency[21] between 2004 and 2006—including all but two of the directors of the CDC's eight primary scientific centers. It was a shocking exodus from an institution that had long been seen as a career destination.

The situation became so dire that five of the six former CDC directors—who had led the agency during Republican and Democratic administrations over the previous forty years—even privately sent Gerberding a rare joint letter about their concerns for the organization.[22]

It was against this backdrop of turmoil inside the CDC that the power outage occurred in Building 18 in June 2007.

THE CDC HAD LONG been one of the most trusted agencies in the federal government. The agency was full of smart, idealistic public health professionals, people who could have made a lot more money working in private industry, but who chose the CDC because they believed in its mission. They wanted to save lives and make the world a safer, healthier place.

The crass efforts by the agency's leadership to use PR spin—both internally with employees and externally with the public—to cover up issues that needed fixing rubbed many CDC employees the wrong way.

It resulted in a stunning range and number of people finding ways to leak information to me, especially when they knew the agency's leadership was trying to hide it.

Envelopes of records were left for me under park benches and sent through the mail. There were anonymous phone calls and meetings in cars, bars, homes, parks, and empty stadium bleachers.

When the CDC denied expedited processing of my FOIA request for records about Building 18's power outage, I made sure to include that fact in one of my articles.

Within days, people who knew what the agency wanted to hide were in contact with me.

It turned out that multiple government construction officials had been warning since 2001 that the complicated design of Building 18's backup power system—at a remote, centralized power farm rather than a simple unit at the building—put its labs at risk of power failures.

While the CDC told me that the system's design had nothing to do with the outage, the trove of emails,[23] leaked to me by sources, included blunt assessments like this one from CDC mechanical engineer Johnnie West in 2003: "I've been saying this for over three years now, but having the generators in this configuration gives us no protection whatsoever from many types of failures."

Others expressing concerns in various emails included a CDC architect and the head of the CDC's facilities office, plus the lead engineer for the private contractor designing the building.

Even back in the days of Arnold Wedum, a reliable source of power was among the cornerstone criteria for safe lab operations. Among the questions that should be asked when designing infectious disease labs, Wedum in 1964 wrote:[24] "How reliable is the source of power for the building? The major danger to employees is an air flow stoppage in a protective ventilated cabinet during a hazardous experiment with aerosolized microorganisms."

To say the CDC was unhappy about my coverage of the power outage would be an understatement. In the hours after the article was published, CDC officials crafted a letter to the editor[25] to share "reassuring facts" about the agency's "excellent track record" in biosafety.

"CDC has operated laboratories in Atlanta for over 60 years," the letter said. "Throughout this entire time, there has never been an environmental release from a CDC lab that would have endangered a member of the community. Not a single one. This track record reflects both exceptional technical design of our laboratories and well-trained laboratory and safety people dedicated to careful control of the risks related to our work."

JUST THIRTEEN MONTHS AFTER the lightning strike that hit Building 18, there was another major power outage on the CDC's Atlanta campus.

This time Building 17—which housed infectious disease labs working with the deadly H5N1 avian influenza virus and multi-drug-resistant strains of tuberculosis—lost power for one hour and fifteen minutes on July 11, 2008.

The cause? A bird shorted out a power transformer[26] on the edge of the CDC's property.

Once again, negative airflow was lost after the complicated, centralized backup generator system failed—coming on briefly, but then shutting back down because two of its units had been offline since April[27] for upgrades.

The outages in 2007 and 2008 pointed out the agency's failures to monitor the integrity of systems[28] that support critical operations for its highest-containment labs, according to a 2009 review by the U.S. Government Accountability Office, the nonpartisan investigative arm of Congress.

The GAO's review of the CDC's incidents was part of the watchdog's larger examination of the risks posed by the U.S. biodefense laboratory building boom that followed the 9/11 and anthrax attacks in 2001. It was being fueled by $1 billion a year in funding for new research to address biothreats as part of the National Institutes of Health–led research agenda.[29]

Members of Congress, both Democrats and Republicans, were concerned about the increased potential for deadly pathogens being accidentally or intentionally released from the growing number of labs receiving federal funding. The GAO review had been requested by a bipartisan group of more than a dozen members[30] of the Senate and House, including both the chairs and ranking members from four committees.

"The public is concerned about these laboratories because the deliberate or accidental release of biological agents can have disastrous consequences," the GAO wrote.

Yet the GAO found the oversight and funding of these labs was fragmented across multiple federal agencies. The lab expansion lacked a coordinated strategy, the report said. And since "no single agency is in charge of the expansion, no one is determining the aggregate risks associated with this expansion."

The incidents at the CDC showed how highly sophisticated research facilities that are expensive to build and maintain are at risk of engineering and design flaws and operational failures.

The GAO noted that while there are voluntary guidelines for how to safely construct and operate high-containment laboratory buildings, the guidance isn't universally followed. A "clear and unambiguous" set of national standards is needed, the report said, and these standards should address the potential for one or more critical systems to fail.

The GAO pushed back on how the CDC had downplayed the significance of its outages and airflow issues, saying the CDC needed "to create understanding throughout the organization that effective biosafety involves layers of containment and, furthermore, that the loss of any one layer is serious even though the remaining layers, as intended, do maintain containment."

❋

IN THE YEARS THAT followed, my reporting continued to uncover numerous other failures of building engineering, safety systems, and equipment in the CDC's lab facilities.

Yet another lightning strike occurred in July 2013, this time hitting another CDC lab tower called Building 23. The power surge caused air flow changes that "made it nearly impossible to open the lab hallway doors over approximately 1 hour."[31] The phone service also went down within this $365 million building, which it turned out had no plan for backup communications.

Several CDC buildings have had incidents where negative air pressure systems have temporarily failed, sometimes reversing the airflow so that potentially contaminated air is blown outward from individual lab rooms into adjoining clean areas. While airflow is just one layer of safety in high-containment labs, such failures increase the risks of workers unknowingly becoming infected.

At a CDC lab facility in Fort Collins, Colorado, the air pressure in lab Building 401 became reversed in November 2016, blowing outward from eleven laboratory suites, some of them for five to eight hours.[32]

The problem was caused by an overnight maintenance crew replacing a fan motor around 4:00 a.m., but it was compounded by the facility's failure to effectively notify all workers of the safety risk in impacted labs. In addition, an airflow alarm system didn't sound in at least one lab, resulting in a lab worker—unaware of any problem—performing animal autopsies, called necropsies, on mice as the lab blew air outward.

Fortunately, the pathogen being studied in that lab was *Borrelia burgdorferi*, which causes Lyme disease through the bite of infected ticks. The CDC considered it a low-risk exposure event.

DURING MY MANY YEARS reading CDC lab accident reports, one building stands out for its pervasive problems with physical containment and safety systems: Building 18—the one in Atlanta with the duct-taped door and where the backup generators failed.

A particularly dramatic incident involved a chemical decontamination shower that failed[33] inside one of Building 18's biosafety level 4 labs, where scientists study deadly pathogens like Ebola and smallpox for which we lack reliable treatments.

Four scientists clad in space suit–like gear had just finished inventorying a freezer of specimens. Before they could leave the BSL-4 suite and enter the safety of the adjacent changing room, they first needed to douse their suits with a shower of virus-killing chemicals.

Once inside the lab's sealed decontamination chamber, the shower wouldn't start; then warning lights started flashing as the gasket seal around the exit door kept deflating. They could even see light coming through from the changing room.

As they tried to hold the door shut and start an emergency spray of chemicals, the back door into the infectious side of the lab burst open so "forcefully" they couldn't keep it shut. It kept happening over and over.

Records about the incident and internal agency emails—which took more than three and a half years to pry out of the CDC with a Freedom of Information Act request—showed several agency officials sought to avoid reporting the 2009 incident to lab regulators[34] at the Federal Select Agent Program. Their justification was that no work with pathogens was under-way at the time.

Numerous other incidents in Building 18 have involved repeated failures of negative airflow systems inside its laboratories. While CDC leadership sought to publicly minimize potential safety issues, in 2012 I uncovered internal agency meeting minutes showing that scientists working with pox-viruses, such as monkeypox, "don't want to go into that facility because they don't feel comfortable with the way it is currently designed."[35] A top CDC safety manager was quoted in the minutes as saying: "Bottom line is we can't continue to operate the building the way it is...if [the Federal Select Agent Program] finds out air is moving this direction they will shut this place down."

As CDC engineers tried to address Building 18's airflow problems, at one point the tinkering caused extreme negative air pressures that made it difficult to open doors. To escape in an emergency, workers would need to use more than three times the force that the fire code allowed,[36] internal records showed. A contractor's report noted that the CDC assumed respon-sibility for reopening the lab with the "known code violation."

These kinds of problems persisted.

"We've had a number of air flow problem induced evacuations[37] in our basement and first floor labs in bldg. 18," wrote one worker in a long 2016 complaint to agency safety officials. The CDC lab worker was troubled that the maintenance contractor responsible for addressing problems "didn't seem to understand the air flow system" and lacked awareness of the bio-safety implications of warning alarms sounding, acting "as if the air flow in the labs is no big deal."

While CDC officials maintain that there have never been any significant problems with the design or operation of Building 18, the agency announced in 2018[38] that it would be building a new infectious disease lab facility at their Atlanta headquarters.

The new multi-story CDC High-Containment Continuity Laboratory (aka Building 28) will cost $480 million.[39] It will house BSL-3 and BSL-4 laboratories and provide 95,000 square feet of space for research on emerging infectious diseases.

Construction is scheduled to be completed in 2025, and the building is expected to be fully operational by 2027,[40] after its systems undergo testing and commissioning.

The CDC says Building 18, which opened in 2005, has computerized systems that are obsolete and cannot be upgraded without taking the agency's BSL-4 labs out of service for an extended period of time.

Whether that's the full story is unclear.

When I filed a FOIA request in 2021 seeking documents about the CDC's assessments of Building 18's useful life span and the agency's decision to construct the new lab building, I received two documents totaling twenty-seven pages. Much of the information was redacted.

The documents said the CDC facilities team expected that Building 18's high-containment labs would start having increasing potential for "unplanned outages"[41] starting in 2019, with frequent system outages "likely" to occur starting around 2025.

CHAPTER 6

"Losing Credibility"

Q UESTIONS ABOUT WHETHER the Covid-19 pandemic could have started with a lab accident in Wuhan may have brought laboratory safety concerns into wider public view. But the problems have been known for decades.

It's just that little has been done to address them.

The summer of 2014 should have been a wake-up call to the world.

Over the course of just twenty-three days, news of lab safety breaches at prestigious U.S. labs—presumably among the safest in the world—kept emerging. And in the months that followed, even more shocking lab accidents became public.

First, the CDC announced on June 19 that seventy-five of its lab workers in Atlanta[1] had been potentially exposed to anthrax bacteria after a serious safety breach. The number of at-risk workers undergoing antibiotic treatment or medical monitoring was soon increased to eighty-four.[2]

The CDC's Bioterrorism Rapid Response and Advanced Technology Laboratory had used an unapproved method to inactivate anthrax spores[3] before sending the supposedly killed specimens to lower-level CDC labs that didn't use the kinds of safety gear and protocols needed to protect against infections from live anthrax.

Tests later showed that some of the spores were still alive and could grow. While nobody became infected, the head of the lab resigned after being reassigned.[4]

Then, on July 8, federal officials announced the shocking discovery of forgotten vials[5] of variola virus, which causes smallpox, in an unlocked cold storage room on the National Institutes of Health campus in Bethesda, Maryland.

This highly contagious smallpox virus was one of the deadliest the world has ever known. Before it was declared eradicated from the planet in 1980, the virus killed as many as three out of every ten people who became infected and marked many survivors with scars from the disease's hallmark skin pustules. Others were left blind.

It was so dangerous that under international agreement only two labs in the world—one at the CDC in Atlanta and the other at a facility in the Russian Federation—were allowed to hold the last known specimens of live variola virus. There had been debate for decades about whether even those specimens should be destroyed because of concerns about the devastating consequences should a lab accident occur.

Nobody had been routinely vaccinated against smallpox in decades. If a lab worker accidentally became infected, it could launch a devastating pandemic.

The fragile vials of smallpox virus discovered in 2014 on the NIH campus were in some old cardboard boxes containing an assortment of pathogen specimens from the 1940s and 1950s that had somehow been overlooked for decades.

There were 327 of the small glass vials filled with powdery freeze-dried specimens.[6] Most had a typewritten label that indicated contents ranging from Q fever and Rocky Mountain spotted fever to Russian spring and summer encephalitis virus and eastern equine encephalitis virus. But it was the labels that said "variola" that alarmed the workers who first looked through the boxes on July 1, 2014.

What wasn't shared publicly at the time, but came out later in government records,[7] was the cavalier handling of the vials after their discovery.

Wearing just lab coats and gloves, two lab workers put the smaller boxes containing the vials into a larger cardboard box. Then a solitary lab worker hoisted the box into their arms and carried it through the hallways of one building, then walked with it outside to another NIH building about two blocks away.

With each step, the worker could hear the glass vials rattling and clinking together. One vial was found shattered when the box was later unpacked.

Fortunately, it was a tissue specimen, and nobody became infected.

"Had any of the six glass vials containing the Variola virus been breached, there would have been nothing to contain the agent and prevent its release to the surrounding environment," according to the joint investigation by the FBI and CDC[8] select agent lab regulators.

The anthrax exposures and smallpox discovery were shocking events and drew news coverage around the world.

THE DAY AFTER THE smallpox discovery became public, CDC director Tom Frieden was working in the agency's Washington, D.C., office when he got a disturbing call about yet another serious lab safety breach.

It had occurred yet again in Atlanta at his own agency, this time involving specimens of deadly H5N1 avian influenza—a virus capable of jumping species to infect humans and a feared candidate for causing a future pandemic.

Workers and experiments at multiple laboratories at the CDC and the U.S. Department of Agriculture had been jeopardized, and lab animals had died unexpectedly because of the carelessness.

Even worse: Some CDC lab workers had known about the safety breach for six weeks, but key managers and the agency's leadership were just now being informed. Also kept in the dark: regulators at the Federal Select Agent Program—even though the incident involved researchers at both the CDC and USDA, the two agencies that ran the U.S. lab regulation program.

"Nobody had been informed," Frieden recalled[9] as we discussed the event recently. "It was appalling."

The details that emerged of the sloppy safety practices in the avian influenza accident—and how even supervisors within the CDC were left unaware—revealed deep issues with lab safety and oversight at the CDC, especially when viewed alongside the recent anthrax incident and the other lab problems revealed in past years.

"I think there were folks at CDC who didn't like me saying there was a problem with the culture of safety because they felt that was too sweeping of a critique," Frieden told me. "But that is the way it seemed to me."

THESE BACK-TO-BACK LAB INCIDENTS were so alarming that Frieden temporarily closed both the anthrax and the influenza labs[10] and halted the movement of all biological specimens in and out of the agency's BSL-3 and BSL-4 labs until the practices in individual labs were reviewed. Frieden further announced the creation of a new position of laboratory safety director[11] to serve as a single point of accountability within the agency.

Meanwhile, Frieden began recruiting an outside group of experts to help advise the CDC on lab safety and had the agency post on its website its investigation reports into the anthrax and avian influenza accidents.

"Our agency has a tradition of competence, scientific integrity, service, and courage in the face of danger," Frieden wrote in an email[12] sent to everyone at the agency on July 15, 2014. "We are proud of our familiarity with risk, but it is also a potential problem. The overriding culture at CDC must be a culture of safety."

That means reporting incidents and assessing risks, he wrote.

Frieden knew from personal experience the threat posed by occupational infections. Early in his career, as a CDC Epidemic Intelligence Service Officer, he had volunteered in a tuberculosis control clinic where he became infected with TB bacteria.[13] He never became ill but had to take preventive antibiotics. And when he eventually became director of the program that oversaw the clinics, one of his first actions was to implement overdue infection control practices.[14]

"We cannot continue to improve safety in a 'business as usual' mode, and we cannot fix problems one-by-one as they become apparent," he told the CDC's employees and contractors. "We can only succeed in our mission of protecting people from health threats with a culture of safety, and the first step is ensuring the safety of our own staff."

THE DETAILS OF THE avian influenza incident were particularly unnerving.

Once again it illustrated how the culture inside labs too often seeks to downplay safety issues and avoid the reporting of incidents.

The first sign of trouble was when the USDA's chickens started dying unexpectedly on May 23, 2014.

The chickens were part of an experiment at the USDA Southeast Poultry

Research Laboratory in Athens, Georgia, testing the effectiveness of a poultry vaccine. Months earlier, USDA scientists had asked the influenza lab at the CDC for a specimen of a relatively mild H9N2 strain of bird flu that was circulating at the time in China.

The CDC shipped them the specimen by overnight courier.

But after the chickens died, the USDA lab team tested the original CDC specimen and found that it wasn't pure. It also contained a deadly second strain of avian influenza called H5N1. This H5N1 strain not only was dangerous to poultry, but it also had the ability to cause severe and fatal illness in humans.

Fortunately, the USDA researchers had been using the same safety equipment and precautions that they would have used if they had been knowingly working with the deadly virus.

"We were very lucky,"[15] said Anne Schuchat, who at the time was director of the CDC's National Center for Immunization and Respiratory Diseases.

The CDC's investigation determined the flu specimens became cross-contaminated inside one of its labs back on January 17, a few days after they arrived at the agency. The specimen of the mild strain of H9N2 influenza virus had been shipped to the CDC from Hong Kong, and the two dangerous H5N1 influenza virus specimens had arrived from Vietnam.

An experienced CDC scientist apparently cut significant corners during their work growing the newly arrived viruses in cell cultures in one of the agency's biosafety level 3 labs.

The unnamed scientist initially insisted to agency officials that proper procedures had been followed[16] to ensure that the viruses weren't cross-contaminated.

Yet the lab's security card reader logs told another story. They showed it was impossible for the scientist to have performed all of the steps as they claimed.

It would have taken a minimum of one and a half hours to gather the specimens and necessary supplies, then do the cell culture work with the two different strains separately, while also adhering to required wait times for chemicals to decontaminate the biosafety cabinet. Yet the scientist had been in and out of the lab in just fifty-one minutes.

The scientist later acknowledged being rushed that day to complete the tasks before having to attend a lab meeting at noon.

While it remained unclear how the specimen of the mild strain became contaminated with one of the deadly strains, the CDC's investigation concluded there were two likely explanations, and both involved very bad lab practices.

Either the scientist had handled both the mild and deadly virus strains in the biosafety cabinet at the same time, or they had started their work with the deadly strain and didn't thoroughly decontaminate the biosafety cabinet before handling the mild strain.

"We just don't think shortcuts are permissible when working with these kinds of dangerous pathogens," Schuchat told me[17] after the agency completed its investigation, releasing a detailed report to the public.

The dangers posed by the sloppy lab practices were further compounded by the failures to immediately report the contamination issues once they were recognized.

When researchers at the USDA lab first discovered the H5N1 cross-contamination problem, they alerted the team leader of the CDC influenza division that had provided the specimen. But this team leader—yet another experienced CDC scientist—did not report the problem to any of the key supervisors overseeing the division and its labs.

Because it is such a risky virus, the H5N1 flu virus was regulated as a select agent pathogen. But neither the CDC influenza lab's team leader nor anybody at the USDA lab reported the incident to regulators at the Federal Select Agent Program. The team leader later said they didn't think it was necessary—when in fact it was required.

The scientists in the CDC influenza lab also failed to track down and notify the other labs that had received dangerously contaminated specimens. As a result, another CDC biosafety level 3 lab had been using the contaminated virus in a mouse experiment that was also producing unexpected results.

It was only after this other CDC lab reported on June 23 that their research had been compromised that the CDC influenza team leader finally told the lab's branch chief about the continuing fallout from the safety breach.

When the CDC finally started rounding up and destroying the contaminated specimens, it had been about to ship a sample from the contaminated virus specimen to influenza researchers at St. Jude Children's Research Hospital.

But there were still more delays alerting Frieden and others in the CDC's leadership. That didn't happen until July 9, as the lab finally reported the incident to select agent regulators.

To help Frieden get a better idea of the scope of incidents occurring across the agency's labs, CDC staff cobbled together a spreadsheet, pulling information from the agency's occupational health clinic and individual labs across the organization's many divisions.

For an agency so adept at using data to spot public health trends and stop outbreaks, the CDC had done little over the years to actively gather and analyze data about incidents occurring across its own laboratories.

The spreadsheet, which looked like it had been slapped together in a hurry, included about 170 line items with short summaries[18] of mishaps and certain clinic visits from 2013 through August 2014. Some appeared to be duplicate reports, and others indicated the description was one of several similar events. (And in the version that I obtained under the Freedom of Information Act, the CDC had blacked out the names of the pathogens involved in the incidents when the bacteria or viruses were classified as select agents.)

The listed incidents included workers suffering a wide range of accidental needlesticks, cuts, spills, animal bites and scratches that potentially had exposed them to various types of undisclosed select agent pathogens and other disease-causing agents.

In one incident, workers had potentially been exposed to select agent pathogens in an incident with infected prairie dogs and another with infected fleas. Several reports involved workers potentially exposed to tuberculosis bacteria, including a researcher who wasn't wearing any respiratory protection.

Another worker had a possible aerosol exposure to Chikungunya virus after they took a broken specimen tube out of a biosafety cabinet without wearing any respiratory protection.

Lack of proper personal protective equipment (PPE) was noted in several other incidents, including workers in a BSL-2 influenza lab growing a weakened strain of H7N9 flu virus without using N95 respirators.

Multiple incidents involved equipment, ranging from defective "space suit" full-body protective gear used in BSL-4 labs, to biosafety cabinets that failed certifications because of leaks or other defects, to malfunctions of freezers used for storing specimens and autoclaves used to disinfect materials.

The list, the CDC acknowledged, was likely not comprehensive. Part of the problem, it would later come out, is that workers inside the agency had a culture of avoiding reporting lab incidents.

As FRIEDEN'S INTERNAL AND external lab safety teams worked to identify problems across the CDC's labs, yet another serious incident occurred.

On Christmas Eve 2014, I was cooking a holiday dinner for my family when my cell phone rang. One of the agency's laboratory technicians in Atlanta had potentially been exposed to deadly Ebola virus and would be undergoing twenty-one days of monitoring.

The incident involved potentially live Ebola virus samples that, because of a color-coding mix-up, had been accidentally sent to a CDC biosafety level 2 lab where workers typically only wear gowns and gloves—not the full-body pressurized moon suits used by scientists working with live Ebola virus in a BSL-4 lab.

The mistake occurred in CDC's Viral Special Pathogens Branch, which was helping respond to a devastating Ebola outbreak that was occurring in West Africa.

Some color-coded tubes were prepared for live-virus studies that would be done in BSL-4 labs; other tubes were prepared containing killed virus specimens that could be safely sent to a BSL-2 lab.

Because the tubes were similar and a worker was inattentive, the wrong set of tubes was sent to the BSL-2 lab where the laboratory technician processed the material without adequate personal protective gear.

The mistake was discovered a day later, on December 23, and reported immediately. The worker never became ill, and CDC said additional testing later found that the vials didn't actually contain any live virus.[19] But none of this was known on Christmas Eve as the news was covered by many national media outlets.

"We've made sweeping changes to our lab safety protocols over the last couple of months," CDC spokesman Tom Skinner said as I began typing up sections of a story for *USA TODAY*[20] while others took over in the kitchen. "But these incidents that involve human error simply cannot happen and we'll get to the bottom of what happened here."

THE ELEVEN-MEMBER TEAM OF outside experts that Frieden appointed to review the CDC's safety practices was made up of prestigious and respected figures in microbiology and lab safety.[21]

Their report,[22] delivered privately to Frieden in January 2015, was scathing.

"We are very concerned that the CDC is on the way to losing credibility," said the report, which the CDC waited two months to quietly post onto a page within its vast website.[23] "The CDC must not see itself as 'special.' The internal controls and rules that the rest of the world works under also apply to CDC."

The agency's leadership commitment toward lab safety has been "inconsistent and insufficient at multiple levels," the experts said.

Their report identified many of the same systemic issues at the CDC that Arnold Wedum had warned about decades earlier while battling against what he described as microbiology's martyr-to-science culture.

Many scientists working in the CDC's labs viewed safety as something that was separate from their primary public health mission, the outside experts warned.

Risk assessments of proposed research—a cornerstone practice of biosafety that allows appropriate precautions to be determined in advance— "are either not being done in a standardized manner or are not being done at all," the group found.

Lab safety training was inadequate, fragmented, and inconsistent. There was a reluctance to report lab incidents and potential exposures because of fears about experiencing negative repercussions.

While select agent regulatory requirements seemed to get worker attention, "there were no mentions of people being similarly concerned with biosafety."

It was critical that the CDC establish a culture of responsible science and safety, the report said.

"My marching orders to this external group was don't pull any punches, tell us all of the problems so that we can fix them," Frieden told me. "It was a very blunt review."

It was a rough time at the agency, which has more than 1,700 scientists working in more than 200 laboratories[24] located not only at the agency's large Atlanta headquarters campus, but also at a major zoonotic disease facility in Fort Collins, Colorado, that studies pathogens that can spread between animals and people, and at additional lab buildings in several cities across the country.

"I think there were some people who were doing a good job and felt that they were being unduly attacked," Frieden said.

But change needed to happen, and the report provided the road map.

"We went through every single laboratory and we identified challenges and best practices," Frieden said.

It was a wake-up call that strengthened the safety inside the agency, he said.

But as happens in labs all across the United States and around the world, accidents continue to occur. Some are minor, some more significant.

In a recent batch of CDC lab incident reports for 2019 that I obtained with a FOIA request, there were reports of researchers being cut, scratched, and splashed during their work with pathogens. There were malfunctions of biosafety cabinets and autoclaves and repeated issues with holes in the positive-pressure full-body suits worn in BSL-4 labs.

Laboratory workers, maintenance contractors, and visitors were spotted not wearing adequate PPE.

CDC Building 23 suffered a power failure[25] on August 21, 2019. Labs on floors throughout the building lost their negative air flow "resulting in a near miss for anyone working in the lab," the incident report said. Because the agency's procedure for notifying labs was "not immediately performed... some lab work may have occurred in labs that should have been closed."

As is usually the case, most of these incidents posed a health risk to a small number of workers who were inside the room where the issue happened. A few of them were put on fever watches or were prescribed antiviral or other medications to prevent infections, the records show.

Yet seemingly small biosafety lapses that go unrecognized can have enormous consequences, as became apparent in early February 2020 when the CDC's flawed Covid-19 test kits[26] delayed the country's ability to track and respond to the early spread of the pandemic.

Within days of sending the test kits to public health labs nationwide, the kits were suspected of producing unreliable results. Investigations flagged contamination issues[27] in the manufacturing of the kits inside the CDC's labs as well as a design flaw[28] in the tests.

The failure of these test kits illustrated how compromised science from lax biosafety can also pose a significant threat to the wider public.

"It's not unrelated," Frieden said. "Laboratory safety isn't just about releases. It's about working in a way that avoids cross-contamination. It's about having the right trainings and protocols."

CHAPTER 7

Cloaked in Secrecy

W HEN BIOLOGICAL RESEARCH labs are operating in unsafe ways, the public and policymakers almost never hear about it.

That's because the system is designed in ways that largely conceal the failures of lab operators—and regulators—from scrutiny and accountability.

Every year, scores of incidents are happening at labs across the country and around the world. But it's impossible to know the full extent of biosafety problems because oversight of biological research is fragmented and relies largely on individual facilities and scientists to police themselves.[1]

In the United States, there is no comprehensive federal regulation and inspection of biosafety at laboratories experimenting with dangerous infectious organisms to ensure their safe operation. There is no government entity that even knows where they all are,[2] the GAO has warned since 2007.

The oversight system has been cobbled together over time, often in reaction to individual safety and security incidents. It's a hodgepodge of biosafety guidance documents, policies within individual research organizations, conditions that are placed on research funding, sometimes regulations, and occasionally community ordinances.

As a result, the safety net protecting lab workers and the public against serious accidents varies greatly depending on the type of organism being studied, the institution operating the lab, and the funding source for the study.

"Although technology and improved scientific practice guidance have reduced the risk in high-containment laboratories, the risk is not zero," the GAO's Nancy Kingsbury testified at a congressional hearing in 2014.[3]

"Many experts agree that as the number of high-containment laboratories has increased, so the overall risk of an accidental or deliberate release of a dangerous pathogen will also increase," she said.

FROM 2015 THROUGH 2021, federal regulators have taken about forty-five enforcement actions against U.S. labs with serious biosafety or biosecurity problems, according to the Federal Select Agent Program's vaguely written annual reports.

What are the names of these labs? And what were their violations and what kinds of pathogens were involved?

The CDC and USDA, which jointly run the Federal Select Agent Program, won't say.

They cite provisions in the Public Health Security and Bioterrorism Preparedness and Response Act of 2002 as justification for the secrecy, though in a few instances they have made an exception and released the identities of sanctioned labs after information had already become public, as they eventually did after USAMRIID was suspended.

This refusal to name names, the CDC and USDA have said, is mandated by law and is also justified as a safety measure to protect the labs from terrorists and others from gaining illegal access to dangerous pathogens.

It's a dubious claim and a policy approach that arguably makes these labs less safe when problems are allowed to fester under ineffective oversight.

White House science and security advisers[4] called for greater transparency and public accountability about lab accidents in a government-wide memo in 2015. "In most cases, withholding this information has negligible security value, since the research, researchers, institutions, and agents involved with [select agent] research are often published in scientific journals or can readily be inferred from public materials,"[5] concluded the panel of federal experts cited in the memo.

Even a federal appeals court in 2019 told the CDC[6] that it was violating the Freedom of Information Act by withholding many details about lab safety violations under an overly broad interpretation of the 2002 bioterrorism law's secrecy provisions.

But it has made little difference.

Unless Congress changes how the law's secrecy provisions are written, the CDC and USDA will continue to largely keep secret the identities of laboratories with troubling safety records.

It's an arrangement that for years has benefited the CDC and USDA, my reporting has found.

It turned out that before the CDC's high-profile string of accidents in 2014 with anthrax and avian flu, the agency's labs had one of the worst regulatory histories in the country.

In the preceding years, the CDC's labs had already faced secret federal enforcement actions seven times.[7] But it was all kept secret—allowing the agency to avoid embarrassment and public accountability.

One research group at the CDC's lab facilities in Fort Collins, Colorado, was even suspended from the Federal Select Agent Program for three years after serious violations during its work with Japanese encephalitis virus,[8] which can cause fatal brain inflammation.

But this was all hidden within the Federal Select Agent Program's anonymous statistics that protect the identities of failing labs.

Neither the public nor members of Congress knew about the CDC labs' regulatory problems until nearly two years after the agency's 2014 safety meltdown.

And it only came to light because I had managed to win a Freedom of Information Act appeal that forced the agency to finally admit[9] that its own labs had a shocking track record of failing to comply with regulations.

Until that time, the CDC—as both regulator and lab operator—had simply insisted on keeping secret the names of sanctioned labs, while also refusing to answer my questions about its own labs' enforcement histories.

What if the CDC labs' inspection failings had been known years earlier? Would public accountability have given the CDC greater incentive to recognize and address its safety culture sooner?

Would lab accidents have been prevented?

The USDA—the CDC's partner in regulating select agent labs—has also benefited from the secrecy.

In July 2020, select agent program inspectors privately threatened the USDA

National Animal Disease Center in Ames, Iowa, with suspension or revocation[10] of its permit to work with dangerous pathogens because of "repetitive failures of and releases from" its wastewater system, my reporting has found.

In a batch of enforcement records I recently obtained with a FOIA request, the CDC had tried to conceal the USDA lab's name along with the names of other previously unidentified labs that had faced recent enforcement actions. Two versions of the same letter to the USDA lab were included in the stack of documents released to me; in most of the two letters the lab's name was redacted, but it was left behind in one spot.

According to the enforcement letter, the USDA National Animal Disease Center had three releases of wastewater that was potentially contaminated with select agent pathogens. The incidents occurred on June 5, 2019; April 16, 2020; and May 3, 2020.

"The continued, compounding failures," CDC regulators told the USDA lab, "represent risk to the safety of agriculture and public health."

The USDA lab was facing sanctions because it knew it had a serious problem as far back as June 2019, when there were three leak detection alarms in the double-walled drain lines feeding into the treatment plant for laboratory wastewater. But the facility didn't begin repairs on the faulty lines until ten months later, in April 2020.

Many of the details about the incidents were redacted from the letter I obtained with my FOIA request.

Neither the CDC nor the USDA would talk with me about the leak incidents, which were not reported to the Iowa Department of Natural Resources[11] even though federal regulators deemed them to pose a risk to agriculture and public health.

The Iowa lab's waste pipe issues occurred about a year after the wastewater release at USAMRIID in Maryland.

"There was never a leak of waste effluent into the environment," the USDA said in an emailed statement,[12] adding that the lab had "fully satisfied" the terms of a regulatory corrective action plan.

"Through root cause analysis and testing, all three leaks were determined to be ground water intrusion through the external wall of the pipe and not leakage from the effluent carrying inner wall of the pipe," the USDA said.

When I asked for more details about how the USDA made this determination and whether they would share a copy of any report or test results, the agency stopped responding to my questions.

I will need to file yet another FOIA request.

VIEWED ON THE WIDER global stage, the United States is considered to have one of the world's strongest systems of regulatory oversight[13] of biological laboratories.

Yet from his front-row seat as director of the CDC, Tom Frieden saw a system that caused him to be concerned.

"I felt that the inspections were not as rigorous as they needed to be," Frieden told me.[14]

He was particularly concerned that the select agent program didn't do any unannounced inspections to see how labs operated when they thought nobody was looking. All inspections were scheduled in advance.

Before Frieden was appointed CDC director in 2009, he served as New York City's health commissioner, overseeing an agency that he said did about 100,000 inspections a year—everything from restaurants to child care facilities. He had seen the tragic consequences of ineffective oversight when two city inspectors failed to fully inspect an overcrowded apartment day care center[15] in the hour before an infant was found unconscious and later died.

When Frieden pressed regulators in the CDC's select agent division to do unannounced lab inspections, the division resisted.

"The answer came back: 'We find so many problems with announced inspections, we don't think it's necessary,'" Frieden told me. "Which was hardly reassuring."

Following an internal review of the select agent program, the CDC replaced the division's longtime director in late 2015.[16]

During 2013 and 2014, just 9 percent of inspections had been unannounced.[17] In recent years the agency has set a goal of 30 percent unannounced inspections and in some years has exceeded that percentage.

But any progress that was made was lost when Covid-19 emerged.

Since April 2020, citing the pandemic, most of the lab inspections conducted by the Federal Select Agent Program have been done remotely,[18] focusing on reviewing labs' documentation and conducting employee interviews. While some on-site and hybrid inspections were done in 2021, as of July 2022 the program told labs it plans to use a hybrid inspection approach for most future inspections.

The CDC says its remote, hybrid, and on-site inspections are effective at ensuring labs comply with regulations.[19]

The select agent program relies largely on the premise that labs are responsible for overseeing their own compliance with safety and security regulations. The regulations require that labs have written policies and procedures for safety and security, but they largely leave it up to each facility to determine their own best approach.

Since 2015, between three and seven facilities each year faced enforcement actions.[20]

During 2021, two unnamed lab facilities were suspended for multiple regulatory failures, according to the program's most recent annual report. Three other unnamed labs were allowed to continue doing research despite systemic compliance problems dating back to 2020; they remained on corrective action plans into 2022.

From what Frieden observed during his time at the CDC, he told me he thought the select agent program had been made more effective, "but I think it still had a long way to go."

One way to improve the safety and oversight of labs, Frieden said, is to have fewer labs.

"Partly I think it comes down to reducing the number of places that do these experiments because you know, any person who has access might on purpose or by mistake, result in a release," he said.

Frieden's conclusion won't sit well with many in the life sciences: "There should be fewer labs working with fewer dangerous pathogens with fewer staff having access to those laboratories, and fewer experiments being done, because there is always going to be a non-zero risk of a problem. You can minimize it, lots of things you can do to minimize it, but you can't make it zero."

THE SECRECY THAT SURROUNDS lab accidents and a desire to dismiss and downplay warning signs can allow facilities and regulators to become complacent.

Consider what happened at labs at the U.S. Army's Dugway Proving Ground in Utah. Labs at the facility were responsible for preparing killed specimens of anthrax bacteria for use in research that doesn't require live spores, such as the development of tests and detection technologies.

Between 2004 and 2015, Dugway's Life Science Test Facility mistakenly shipped live anthrax specimens—certified as dead—that ended up putting researchers' lives at risk in nearly 200 private, academic, and government laboratories[21] located in every U.S. state and at least nine foreign countries.[22]

Dozens of lab workers received antibiotic treatment as a precaution against potentially deadly infections. Fortunately, anthrax is not contagious; infections are caused through inhalation and direct contact with the organism.

Despite warning signs going back more than a decade, neither the scientists at Dugway nor the lab regulators at the CDC were the ones that caught the problem.

Dugway's serious safety issues were only revealed because a private biotech company in Maryland didn't just blindly trust the death certificate that accompanied the supposedly inactivated spores. The company's tests showed some of the spores were still dangerously alive.

It was only then that Dugway and CDC regulators went back and retested reserved specimens from thirty-three lots of *Bacillus anthracis* that had been issued death certificates following irradiation at the army facility. More than half of the batches were still alive.[23]

The tests showed that Dugway "had a long-standing, widespread problem that they failed to reasonably recognize or correct," the military's accountability investigation later found.[24]

It shouldn't have come as a surprise. There had been plenty of warning signs, but each time they were ignored, dismissed as unimportant, or treated as isolated incidents rather than an indicator of a systemic problem.

In 2007—three years into the period where Dugway was mistakenly shipping live anthrax to unsuspecting labs—CDC inspectors cited the facility for this very problem. But they failed to uncover the wider issue despite the egregious nature of the specific incident.

One of Dugway's labs had used a chemical method to kill anthrax specimens, dosing them with chlorine dioxide[25] rather than using its typical gamma irradiation method.

Before shipping the spores to another facility, the Dugway lab conducted a critical safety test to ensure they were dead.

Nothing was supposed to be growing in the five test tubes filled with samples from a recent batch of chemically treated anthrax spores.

Yet when anthrax bacteria started growing in one of the tubes—a warning sign about the safety of the entire batch—the army scientist simply destroyed the bad tube and certified the rest of the specimens as dead.

But they weren't.

The scientist had simply ignored the results of the sterility test. The fact that the tube had bacteria growing in it showed the kill method had been ineffective.

In April 2007, testing by scientists at the federal government's Lawrence Livermore National Laboratory in California found a live anthrax spore in the specimen they received from Dugway. Lawrence Livermore officials reported the issue to select agent regulators at the CDC, who eventually cited Dugway for shipping the live anthrax and referred the army lab for potential fines or other enforcement actions.

But Dugway was never fined because of its status as a federal entity. And the CDC didn't disclose the incident in the vaguely written annual reports of the Federal Select Agent Program[26] that are sent to Congress.

Rather than address its own problems, Dugway disputed the CDC's findings and claimed the spore wasn't theirs, blaming the Lawrence Livermore lab[27] for contaminating the specimen after arrival. Officials at Dugway didn't do anything to dig deeper.

That a scientist at a major biodefense lab would use such a faulty approach to sterility testing should have set off alarm bells for regulators. The incident begged an obvious question: If the Dugway lab was so nonchalant in its approach to anthrax inactivation in this one incident, had other batches failed sterility tests before?

But nobody would go looking for another eight years—and by that time hundreds of labs around the world had received live anthrax that they thought was dead.

As the anthrax crisis grew in 2015, the CDC tried to downplay the significance of the 2007 violation as a warning sign. In a hair-splitting statement, the agency told me: "It should be noted that this incident is not similar to the current investigation where Dugway was using an established irradiation protocol and no growth was observed following the gamma irradiation."[28]

Yet the core issue was the same: mistakenly certifying live anthrax as dead.

What if the incident had been required to be publicly reported soon after the lab was cited by federal regulators? Would the prospect of public scrutiny have encouraged greater curiosity and accountability for both the lab and regulators?

The military's accountability review in 2015 was blistering in its assessment of the warning signs that were missed on its end.

The report detailed repeated issues with specimen shipments in the preceding years and a culture where management and leadership's response to incidents "was to blame external entities or to downplay the seriousness" of issues.[29]

Dugway supervisors and leadership had failed to investigate "multiple accusations of unsafe laboratory practices"—even when they came from "prominent" biosafety level 3 workers,[30] the military investigation found. When investigators reviewed video surveillance footage from inside the labs, they identified three separate incidents of sloppy and unsafe practices involving two individuals—and this was just in the most recent ninety days and when workers knew an investigation was underway.

The facility had an unqualified biosafety officer overseeing lab work, and for many years had failed to follow its own policies to routinely test surfaces like countertops, floors, and door handles for anthrax contamination—which the investigation found was on floors and other surfaces in the room.

"This complacent atmosphere resulted in an organization plagued by mistakes and unable to identify systemic issues in the high-risk, zero-defects world of biological select agents and toxins,"[31] the military found.

EXPERTS SAY ONE WAY to address the current patchwork of lab oversight in the United States is to create a new federal agency that is focused on reducing biorisks in a holistic manner.

It's a concept that's been advocated for many years but has gone nowhere amid resistance from researchers and scientific agencies, as well as a lack of action by Congress.

In the broadest sense, the idea is to create for biological laboratories a single regulatory authority like the Nuclear Regulatory Commission (NRC), which was created by Congress in 1974 as an independent agency to ensure the safe use of radioactive materials.

The Nuclear Regulatory Commission not only regulates nuclear power plants, but it also licenses, inspects, and enforces safety compliance at organizations using radioactive materials in medical, industrial, and academic facilities, as well as providing oversight of the transportation, storage, and disposal of radioactive materials.

Like biological pathogens, information about radioactive materials also comes with security sensitivities. Yet the NRC says it considers public transparency integral to good regulation. While the NRC has faced criticism over the years for being too close to industry, details of enforcement actions[32] are posted on the NRC website soon after they happen and the names of the institutions and individuals violating rules are publicly disclosed, too, as are copies of regulatory documents. Inspection reports[33] and findings also are posted.

The Covid-19 pandemic and the questions over the virus's origin have renewed calls for an overhaul of current research regulation, which some say is too narrowly focused on select agent pathogens and ignores many other dangerous organisms.

Too much work with highly transmissible and harmful organisms lacks appropriate oversight, said Rocco Casagrande, chair of the board of Gryphon Scientific, a Maryland-based biosafety and biosecurity consulting firm.

The current system, for example, would allow a privately funded U.S. lab to work with a variety of highly transmissible and harmful organisms— even engineer them in ways that make them more dangerous—without any federal entity overseeing the safety of the work, Casagrande and colleagues noted in a recent journal article.[34]

"They could do basically anything they want to it," Casagrande told me. "And no one could tell them not to."

But the leadership of the major professional organizations for microbiologists and virologists have a different worldview.

"The system of oversight that we have in the U.S., we think it works and we think this is evidenced by the track record of accomplishment that we have on safety in our BSL-3 and BSL-4 labs in the country," Stefano Bertuzzi,[35,36] chief executive officer of the American Society for Microbiology, said at an NIH meeting in 2022 on the oversight of research involving enhanced potential pandemic pathogens.

Felicia Goodrum,[37] who at the time was president of the American Society for Virology, spoke at the same meeting and also cited the "exemplary record" of U.S. labs. She cautioned about the negative impacts additional restrictions might have on growing the future science workforce and on international collaboration.

Rather than "placing additional burden on an already highly regulated system," Bertuzzi said the NIH should be looking for ways to provide more resources to bolster lab facilities and workforce training.

There is a belief by many in the research community that the current system of biosafety oversight works. This appears to be based in part on perceptions that the diligent safety practices that individual scientists observe in their own labs are being applied universally. The lack of publicly available data about lab incidents, worker infections, and safety inspection findings seems to reinforce that view.

It's not surprising that the politicization of questions surrounding the origins of Covid-19 and the growing engagement of stakeholders who aren't scientists is fueling worries that important, lifesaving research will be unnecessarily threatened.

Unlike the high-profile lab accidents at the CDC in 2014, the Covid-19 lab-leak hypothesis has captured far more attention from the general public, not just in the United States but around the world.

"My greatest concern is just even the fact that this is being considered is going to erode trust in the scientific community," Michael Imperiale, a professor of microbiology and immunology at the University of Michigan who is active on biosecurity issues, told me.[38]

"Even if it's proven definitively that this was not a lab leak, and I think we're pretty close to that, just the fact that it gained as much traction as it did means that there's going to be more scrutiny of laboratories," Imperiale said, referring to studies in 2022 pointing to Wuhan's Huanan market as where the pandemic began. "And we've got to be wary of that as the research community, right, and again kind of double down if you will to make sure that we're really working safely. We owe it to the public. They fund our research. We owe it to ourselves."

Others see now as the time to talk about setting baseline standards for labs around the world.

"There is no such thing as zero risk in research. Something going wrong in a lab may be rare, but it is a reality; one we all need to talk about and face," said David Gillum, assistant vice president of environmental health and safety at Arizona State University and a past president of ABSA International, which until 2015 was called the American Biological Safety Association.[39]

Gillum told me there is a need for minimum standards for biosafety—covering such areas as facility design, personnel training, and the use of protective equipment—that would be followed by labs around the world. "It's challenging to do anything like that, but I think we're at a moment where we should encourage it, we should be pushing for it," he said.

But as a result of past U.S. lab accidents and concerns about a Wuhan lab leak, the idea of a new U.S. regulatory agency is of growing interest among even some who would have been unlikely supporters a few years ago.

"I am kind of warming up to the idea of a separate kind of biorisk management authority," said Gerald Parker, a former commander of USAMRIID who has held an array of government leadership positions overseeing biodefense and global health security issues.[40] Parker was chairperson of the National Science Advisory Board for Biosecurity at the NIH and an associate dean at Texas A&M University at the time we spoke.

While emphasizing the importance of life sciences research and worrying about potential unintended consequences from a new bureaucratic entity, Parker said a broader approach is needed to overseeing biosafety and biosecurity. "It would help, I think, if Congress would take this on as a bipartisan dialogue and discussion," he said.

There are grave risks if the U.S. and other countries don't take action, he warned.

"If we don't harmonize and do something to enhance laboratory biosafety, biosecurity," Parker said, "we just increase our probability of a catastrophic lab accident."

CHAPTER 8

The Biolab Next Door

IT WAS FRIDAY evening, and Richard Din had finished what seemed like a typical week as a researcher at San Francisco's VA Medical Center, where he was working with bacteria specimens in a biosafety level 2 lab as part of a vaccine project.[1]

Din, 25, had earned his bachelor's degree in microbiology just eight months earlier, and this job as a researcher was an important first step toward his goal of finding cures for diseases like the cancer that killed his mother.

But after meeting up with friends for dinner that Friday evening in April 2012, Din wasn't feeling well.

As he sat in a car in the restaurant's parking lot, his head was throbbing, his neck was aching and stiff. As his girlfriend drove him home, his waves of dizziness were getting worse. So was his fever.

By morning, Din's body was covered in an alarming, deep purple rash. Lawrence Tsai, who carried Din down two flights of stairs and raced his friend to the medical center, was horrified by what he saw.

"His body was very hard, very straight," Tsai told me.[2] "Only his eyes were open. He could not say anything."

Within hours, Din was dead, his body torn apart by the bacteria he had been studying. And about seventy people who had come in close contact[3] with him—friends, family, and medical workers—were in danger, too. They all received antibiotics to protect against infection.

Richard Din didn't have to die.

There were a range of safety protocols, equipment, and recommended practices that could have protected him from infection. But they weren't followed.

101

Just as it was in the 1950s when Arnold Wedum was pioneering the bedrock concepts of biosafety, the health of thousands of lab workers today depends largely on the attitude and sense of responsibility that their supervisors and research organizations have toward creating a culture of safety.

By far, the people most at risk of exposure to dangerous microbes are those working directly in the labs. Unlike the viruses that cause flu and Covid-19, many pathogens studied in labs don't spread easily from person to person. Often, to become infected, a person must come into direct contact with the virus or bacteria.

That's why lab workers are most at risk.

What happened to Richard Din shows how badly things can go wrong in labs even when research is done at biosafety level 2 with a pathogen that is not classified as a select agent and therefore isn't subject to inspection and regulation by the Federal Select Agent Program. The case also illustrates the potential for one lab worker to unknowingly become infected and expose dozens of others to a dangerous, contagious pathogen.

It takes just one unrecognized lab infection from the right kind of invisible virus or bacterium to launch an outbreak.

Just one.

WHEN STATE OCCUPATIONAL HEALTH and safety inspectors from Cal/OSHA visited the VA-operated lab and interviewed Richard Din's co-workers, they identified a stunning number of safety breaches that contributed to the young researcher's death from infection with *Neisseria meningitidis* bacteria.[4]

This bacterium already had a long history of occasionally infecting and killing microbiologists. While lab-acquired infections with this organism were rare, when they occurred, the fatality rate was 50 percent.[5]

In 1991, following the deaths of two lab workers in separate incidents, the CDC recommended[6] that lab workers handling specimens of *N. meningitidis* should take extra precautions beyond usual biosafety level 2 practices.

The CDC specifically advised researchers use a biosafety cabinet when engaging in activities that have a high potential to generate invisible aerosolized particles. Work with high concentrations or large quantities of bacteria should be performed in a biosafety level 3 lab, the agency advised.

But it was just advice.

In the United States the biosafety precautions taken by labs working with dangerous pathogens are largely determined by the professional judgments made by individual researchers and institutions as they assess the risk of the work they plan to perform.

The cornerstone manual governing biosafety in this country since 1984 is a document called *Biosafety in Microbiological and Biomedical Laboratories*,[7] or *BMBL* for short, which is published by the CDC and NIH. Currently in its sixth edition, the *BMBL* is 604 pages long and is considered the bible of biosafety. It describes what are considered the gold-standard practices and best biosafety levels for working safely with various pathogens in microbiological labs.

The document, however, also seeks to give wide discretion to labs and scientists, while acknowledging that it is sometimes used in regulatory activities.

"We wish to emphasize that the sixth edition of BMBL remains an advisory document recommending best practices for the safe conduct of work," the foreword of the tome says. "The BMBL is not intended to be a regulatory document although we recognize that some may use it in that way."

When Richard Din died on April 28, 2012, the *BMBL* was in its fifth edition,[8] and it specifically warned that the most likely risk of infection from *Neisseria meningitidis* came from working with isolates out on an open laboratory bench. It recommended manipulating specimens inside a biosafety cabinet to help contain infectious droplets and aerosols.

YET DIN AND HIS colleagues often worked with the deadly bacterium out in the open.

Over and over, researchers in the lab scraped and heated specimens in ways that had the potential to create invisible plumes of infectious particles, according to the Cal/OSHA inspection report.[9]

When he became infected, Din appears to have simply been following the same poor lab safety practices already used by his far more experienced colleagues.

The lab's researchers routinely worked out on open bench tops, while an enclosed biosafety cabinet sat nearby. The microbiologist who worked most often with Din told of how the two of them would harvest bacteria from the plates out on an open bench top, scraping as many as twenty to fifty plates at a time that contained *Neisseria meningitidis*—a "serious" safety risk, the inspectors wrote in the 135-page report.

The disinfectant solution they used to sanitize their workspaces and equipment was inadequate. Lab coats were infrequently laundered, eye protection wasn't adequate, and double-gloves were never used. Lab staff did not routinely wear respiratory protection, except when cleaning up spills.

The lab's workers lacked training on airborne transmissible diseases, the report said, adding that the "proficiency and competency program in this laboratory were non-existent."

It was a scathing report.

"The microbiologists in this laboratory did not seem to have an awareness of the highest risk procedures, which were conducted on the open bench," the Cal/OSHA report said. In observing how the lab's microbiologists manipulated specimens, the inspectors noted techniques that were "not ideal in many instances creating dangerous aerosols."

The report warned that if current practices continued in this laboratory, the workers would be at "EXTREMELY HIGH" risk of infection.

"We will never be able to identify a single microbiologist responsible for Mr. Din's exposure," the report said. "All of the microbiologists working in this laboratory share responsibility with regard to the creation of infectious aerosols. High hazard procedures were conducted outside primary containment without the use of respirators by three different microbiologists. These manipulations took place at the deceased's work station."

The San Francisco Veterans Affairs Medical Center was ultimately cited by the federal Occupational Safety and Health Administration[10] for three serious violations involving the lab's failure to require use of a biosafety cabinet, failure to provide workers with vaccines, and a failure to train staff on the signs and symptoms of illness from agents studied in the lab.

"Richard Din died because the VA failed to supervise and protect these workers adequately," OSHA regional administrator Ken Atha said at the time.[11]

In the wake of his death, the San Francisco VA Medical Center enacted a wide range of safety reforms,[12] including improved training, reviews of worker vaccines, and a requirement that all work with viable organisms, not just those that generate aerosols, occur inside biosafety cabinets.

How OFTEN DO ACCIDENTS happen with dangerous pathogens?

Nobody knows.

There is no universal, mandatory system for reporting laboratory accidents and lab-associated infections, nor is there any system to analyze mishaps and share lessons learned.

Nobody even knows how many labs are working with dangerous pathogens.[13] And labs and lab workers have long resisted voluntarily sharing details about safety breaches.

"Our ability to accurately quantify laboratory-associated infections (LAIs) is hampered by an indifference to and, frequently, an unwillingness to report these incidents," a reference book on microbiological safety bluntly noted in 2006.[14]

In the United States, the Federal Select Agent Program—which regulates only a small subset of labs working with a few dozen types of pathogens—requires labs to report incidents.

From 2015 through 2021, labs registered with the program reported nearly 600 incidents with select agent pathogens where there was either an occupational exposure or the pathogen was considered to have been released outside of its primary containment inside the lab.

As a result of these incidents, more than 780 lab workers received medical assessments, diagnostic testing, or treatments to help prevent infections, according to the select agent program's annual reports to Congress.[15]

More than 100 of these incidents involved pathogens being manipulated outside of biosafety cabinets or other equipment designed to protect workers from infectious aerosols. At least 140 incidents involved failures or problems with personal protective equipment, and more than 100 incidents were caused by other kinds of mechanical or equipment failures.

In at least thirty-two incidents, lab workers failed to properly follow procedures, such as not wearing appropriate protective equipment before entering the laboratory. There were at least eighty incidents involving needlesticks or cuts, ninety-seven spills, and twenty-one animal bites or scratches.

Since 2013, labs reported a handful of workers who unknowingly became infected with select agent pathogens in recent years, the reports show. Their exposures were detected only because their employers had programs to periodically test their blood for antibodies to the pathogens they work with, something that isn't required. Fortunately, these workers did not have any symptoms and what they had been exposed to were the types of bacteria that cause Q fever and brucellosis, which don't spread easily from person to person.

How representative these incidents are of what is happening at all labs is unclear.

FOR MANY YEARS, KAREN Byers, a biosafety manager at the Dana-Farber Cancer Institute in Boston, has been scouring the scientific literature and limited publicly reported data to keep a running tally of reported incidents of lab-associated infections in the U.S. and abroad.

From 1979 through 2015, about 3,230 lab-associated infections with forty-one deaths[16] had been publicly described in various scientific journal articles and other publications, her research has found. Of these known infections, most occurred in either clinical or research labs.

That tally, without using their names, includes those whose deaths have received news coverage, like Richard Din from his 2012 infection with *Neisseria meningitidis* and Malcolm Casadaban, a scientist with underlying health conditions at the University of Chicago who was killed in 2009 by a weakened strain of *Yersinia pestis*, the bacteria that causes plague.[17,18]

Also included are scores of infections with strains of *Salmonella* typhimurium bacteria that the CDC over the years has linked to microbiology laboratories in clinical, college, and university settings. Those who were sickened often told CDC investigators that they didn't wear gloves or lab coats and even failed to wash their hands. In one outbreak, several children of the exposed lab workers also became ill.[19]

But the cases in Byers's tallies are just a fraction of the infections that are actually occurring among lab workers.

Underreporting is a widely acknowledged problem, with lab personnel fearing stigma and reprisal when incidents occur. For many years, biosafety professionals have sought the creation of a nonpunitive and potentially anonymous reporting and surveillance system for lab incidents and infections. But it hasn't happened.

Having good data helps improve safety, Byers said.

"As a former person who worked at the bench, you need to know why not to take a shortcut to get the work done," Byers told me.[20] "These people are very committed. It's not a nine-to-five job in any sense. And they're very committed to getting results."

Laboratory work could be made safer, some experts say, if the federal government invested in applied biosafety research in the way it did back in Arnold Wedum's day.

When it comes to studying lab accidents and assessing the evidence for various safety practices and equipment, "There isn't any funding for it," said biosafety consultant Rocco Casagrande.[21] "Basically, almost all of the data on performance of these equipment, accident source terms, accident frequency... especially the things that are truly empirical where someone has set up the test to actually determine what the evidence is from 1980 and before."

There also is a need for more biosafety training, and not just among lab employees, the current leadership of ABSA International, which was previously called the American Biological Safety Association, said in a statement sent to me. The fundamentals of biosafety and biosecurity are not currently widely integrated into graduate and undergraduate science programs in the United States, ABSA officials said.

"We believe that instilling biosafety awareness and sound risk assessment in future scientists is critical to identifying safety issues and preventing accidents or exposures," they said.

MOST OF THE TIME, experts told me, there is little risk to the general public when accidents happen inside biological laboratories.

Even when accidents occur, organisms usually remain contained inside the facilities and workers don't become infected. And even when workers do become infected, the organisms may not be deadly or capable of spreading from person to person.

While rare, however, labs have been the source of deadly outbreaks.

It just takes the right set of circumstances.

PART 3

WHEN GERMS ESCAPE

CHAPTER 9

The Many Lab Leaks of SARS-CoV-1

M ORE THAN A decade before Covid-19 emerged, there was another, even more lethal,[1] SARS coronavirus. It surfaced in China's Guang-dong Province in late 2002, then spread among families and health care workers who treated them, jumping to Vietnam, Canada, and Hong Kong[2] and ultimately twenty-nine countries and territories around the world, including the United States.

Several months of intensive, international public health measures brought the epidemic to a halt in July 2003.[3]

After the international outbreak ended, this first SARS virus escaped from labs at least four times.

Four times.

In just eight months.

From labs in Singapore, Taipei, and Beijing.

Over and over, lax safety practices in these labs threatened to reignite the epidemic of severe acute respiratory syndrome, which had infected about 8,000 people and killed nearly 800 of them.[4] In the United States, eight people were sickened; none died.[5]

Early in this first SARS epidemic, officials at the World Health Organization worried about lab infections spreading the virus and issued safety recommendations[6] for research and diagnostic specimens.

Accidents still happened.

They happened with such frequency that the WHO eventually determined that laboratories potentially posed a greater risk of launching a new SARS epidemic than did the virus making a second jump from nature.[7]

While rare, outbreaks that spread from labs to people and animals in

111

the surrounding environment have happened around the world with deadly consequences. The names, dates, and places may change—but human error is a constant.

The dismissal of the possibility that labs in Wuhan could have sparked the Covid-19 pandemic illustrates how many in the scientific community have failed to learn the lessons of past mistakes.

THE FIRST SARS LAB escape occurred in Singapore in the fall of 2003—three months after the epidemic had been extinguished in that country.

It was an alarming development that prompted the country to quickly ask the WHO for expert advice, and resulted in two scientists from the U.S. Centers for Disease Control and Prevention being dispatched to help determine what had happened.

As epidemiologist Sonja Olsen was en route to Singapore from a CDC field office near Bangkok, Thailand, she read up on the lessons learned from other cases of lab-acquired infections and started thinking through the kinds of questions that had to be asked.

"Each outbreak is a puzzle you're trying to solve, and to solve it quickly," she told me.[8] "You don't really know enough until you get on the ground and start talking to people."

The WHO had removed Singapore from its list of countries with active SARS outbreaks in late May 2003. Yet scientists across the 275-square-mile island nation were continuing to work with specimens of the SARS virus. The 27-year-old graduate student who eventually fell ill with SARS wasn't one of them—or at least he didn't know he was.

The man, in his third year of a doctoral program in microbiology at the National University of Singapore,[9] had been studying West Nile virus at the university and also in lab facilities at Singapore's Environmental Health Institute.

He began feeling achy and feverish on the evening of August 26, 2003. Over the next week, he repeatedly sought medical care for his symptoms, including at a hospital emergency room. But nobody tested him for SARS, and he kept being sent home. Only after his fever continued was he admitted to a hospital and finally tested. The results on September 8 showed he was positive for SARS.

The man's illness, and the risk it posed of reigniting the epidemic, prompted officials in Singapore and at the WHO to quickly assemble an eleven-member team of local and international experts to determine how the student was sickened and whether he had spread the virus to others.

The CDC experts on the team were Olsen and Dr. Pierre Rollin. Olsen had joined the CDC a few years earlier, after completing her PhD. She initially honed her skills as a disease detective in the CDC's storied Epidemic Intelligence Service. In 2001 she had moved to Thailand as part of the agency's International Emerging Infections Program, and she had been working on the front lines of the SARS epidemic since it emerged in Asia.[10]

Rollin, who was based at the CDC's Atlanta headquarters, was perhaps best known for his expertise combating Ebola virus in villages in Africa. Rollin had spearheaded the CDC's response[11] to each Ebola outbreak since 1995. But he also was a skilled and respected laboratory scientist with expertise in biosafety.

Since the SARS epidemic began in 2002–2003, officials in Singapore had worked closely with lab scientists at the CDC, sharing specimens and data that helped provide early clues that it was a new kind of coronavirus that was causing the outbreak.

The collaborative relationship prompted Singapore to ask for the CDC's help[12] to investigate how the graduate student studying West Nile virus became infected with SARS—and also to review the biosafety practices at Singapore's BSL-3 labs.

Olsen, Rollin, and the other members of the expert team interviewed the student, his family, plus the man's work colleagues, twenty-five of whom had been quarantined. They toured the labs and examined their equipment, as well as the building systems and the kinds of pathogens being studied. They reviewed the written safety procedures and compared those with how lab work was actually being performed.

The facts that emerged showed a doctoral student who had never worked with the SARS virus—but who was working in a lab where that virus was handled by others. The student also was accessing a freezer where many different microbial specimens, including SARS virus, were stored.

"There is always the potential for human error," Rollin told me.[13] Did he open the SARS virus by mistake? Did he share the biosafety hood at the same time with someone working with SARS? Did he come into contact with someone who was ill?

"You have all the scenarios possible," Rollin said, "and then you try to go through everything and try to figure out: How would I screw up something and get infected?"

The student's research had initially begun at the National University of Singapore. It was there he gained experience working in a biosafety level 2 lab with a weakened strain of West Nile virus. Because he had an interest in comparing this strain to a more dangerous New York strain, an agreement was made for him to go to the Environmental Health Institute's biosafety level 3 lab[14] to do this work during July and August 2003.

The student, however, had no prior training in how to work safely in a biosafety level 3 lab.

Before the SARS epidemic, the Environmental Health Institute had traditionally focused on vector-borne diseases,[15] which are spread by mosquitoes, ticks, and fleas. But in April 2003, as the SARS epidemic grew, the institute's biosafety level 3 lab had also begun working with one specific strain of SARS coronavirus,[16] growing virus in flasks and twenty-four- and ninety-six-well plates.

While there were some design problems with the Environmental Health Institute's lab space, what concerned Rollin the most was how the lab was being used. "You have different viruses, at different times, with people with different training and really no supervision inside the lab," he recalled.

When the student entered the institute's BSL-3 lab for the first time in July 2003, he received only twenty minutes of instruction on how to work safely in the lab and then was allowed to start inoculating cells with West Nile virus.

But something went wrong with how his specimens were prepared. The flasks that should have only contained West Nile virus appeared to also have bacteria growing in them, so they were destroyed. To help out the student, who was only occasionally coming to the lab, one of the institute's lab techs prepared a new set of West Nile specimens, then tended to the cells for a few weeks.

That lab tech's job also included working with SARS coronavirus.

When the student returned to the institute on August 23, 2003—three days before he started getting sick—he initially entered the BSL-3 lab just wearing his street clothes.

After being given some instructions by the lab tech, the student put on a gown and two sets of gloves, then spent twenty minutes unsupervised transferring the specimens into vials. When he was done, they put the vials into the lab's freezer.

About three days later, the student developed a fever and started feeling sick.

As the expert team tried to figure out what had happened, Olsen remembers chatting with some of them outside the building one day. As they talked, she was thinking back over what they had been shown during one of the lab tours. Then she remembered the freezer where the student's West Nile specimens had been stored.

"Wait a minute," Olsen said.[17] "You know what, why don't we test the samples? What if it's cross-contaminated and he thinks he's working on West Nile, but he's also working on SARS?"

All of the clues were pointing toward some kind of microbial contamination having occurred in the BSL-3 lab or within its inventory of specimens.

The case reminded Rollin of the time health officials in India[18] had contacted the CDC with concerns that a mutant strain of measles had infected a patient who had a puzzling set of symptoms that were yielding odd test results.

After the CDC's lab examined the patient's specimen, it turned out that the patient was actually infected with Nipah virus, which can cause deadly swelling of the brain. Measles virus was present, too—but because of cross-contamination.

"They had a cell line that was chronically infected with measles by mistake," Rollin said.

When the Singapore student's specimens were examined, tests showed that the vial he had handled on August 23 contained both West Nile virus and also high levels of the strain of SARS coronavirus studied in the institute's lab.[19] The amount of SARS virus that had grown in the vial indicated that the contamination occurred sometime before the student's last visit.

In addition, other tests showed that the SARS virus that sickened the student was a near match with the strain used in the BSL-3 lab.[20]

The international expert team's conclusion, in a thirty-one-page report produced quickly and shared publicly on September 24, 2003,[21] was that "inappropriate laboratory standards and a cross-contamination of West Nile virus samples with SARS coronavirus in the laboratory led to the infection of the doctoral student."

Exactly how the SARS virus got into the West Nile specimen could not be determined.

Fortunately, none of the student's family, friends, co-workers, or medical caregivers ended up contracting SARS.

Nonetheless, the incident revealed significant issues with biosafety at multiple institutions at the time. Singapore lacked legislated standards for biological safety, the report said, and the microbiology department at the National University of Singapore (NUS) needed to improve its culture around safety.

"What is clear is that not all students are being adequately trained to understand and act safely," the report said, faulting the university for assuming the labs where students went to work would make sure they stayed safe.

"This was not a good assumption for the student who worked at EHI," the report said, referring to the Environmental Health Institute.

Given the large number of BSL-3 labs that were planned to open in the near future, the expert panel said, it was critical that those who would be staffing them were properly trained.

"If the safety culture of many of the students coming out of NUS does not improve, then [there] will be more microbiological incidents, some of which could have serious consequences," they warned.

DESPITE WORLDWIDE ALERTS ABOUT the Singapore SARS lab escape, increasingly dangerous accidents continued to happen at other labs.

About three months after the Singapore microbiology student fell ill, a far more experienced military scientist, a lieutenant colonel, became infected with SARS at his lab in Taiwan. He then traveled to a medical conference[22] before realizing he was ill.

In this second SARS lab infection, the 44-year-old man was a senior scientist at the Institute of Preventive Medicine[23] at the National Defense University in Taipei. He had been working on a study using the SARS virus since June 2003 inside Taiwan's only biosafety level 4 laboratory.

When he fell ill in December 2003,[24] his lab work was suspected as the likely source, according to the initial case description published by health authorities in Taiwan.[25]

The details that emerged in the weeks that followed were even more troubling than what had played out at the lab in Singapore with an untrained graduate student.

This high-ranking military scientist, in hindsight, had a good idea of exactly when, where, and how he had become infected. He had done something stunningly unwise on December 3, a few days before he flew to the conference in Singapore.

The scientist had been doing research testing antiviral drugs[26] against the SARS virus in his facility's biosafety level 4 lab, where protections should have made it nearly impossible for him to be exposed to the virus.

While the military scientist was doing a final cleaning of the lab to prepare for being away at the conference, he noticed some spilled material in a crevice inside a sealed biosafety cabinet with attached chamber gloves.[27] This special type of cabinet was designed to keep microbes and infectious air contained inside the device—and safely away from scientists. But as he used some alcohol spray to disinfect that area, it became clear that the spill was beyond what he could reach using the cabinet's attached gloves.

In the minutes that followed, his actions put him at greater and greater risk of infection.

While wearing just a "normal mask and surgical gloves," he opened the chamber door to try to clean up the spilled substance, but it was still out of reach.

"As a result, he physically poked his head into the negative-pressure transporting chamber to clean up the leakage," according to a report of the incident by the Taiwan Centers for Disease Control.[28]

When investigators later tested surfaces inside the lab, they detected SARS virus on a light switch for the safety cabinet and on the handle of the alcohol spray bottle kept on top of the chamber.

It's unclear why a senior scientist would put himself—and others—at so much risk to clean up a spill without using appropriate procedures and safety gear.

He then flew to Singapore on December 7, attended a medical conference sponsored by the Defence Medical and Environmental Research Institute, then flew back on December 10. When he landed in Taipei around 1:00 p.m., he had no fever and passed through the airport's still-ongoing temperature screening of passengers.

However, at home later that night, he developed a fever of 101.3°F. He initially thought it was just the flu. Then he developed diarrhea, a symptom that 10–20 percent of SARS patients experienced. The next day, his wife drove him to a clinic, and after that he stayed at home.

As the scientist grappled with the recognition that he may have contracted SARS from his own lab, he refused to get medical help—even as his symptoms worsened—until his father gave him an ultimatum.

"My son had refused to go to the hospital and said he wanted to die at home because he feared his illness would bring shame to his lab and the country," the scientist's father said in a TV report broadcast at the time.[29] "He finally agreed to go to the hospital after I threatened to kill myself."

On the evening of December 16, the scientist was taken by ambulance to Tri-Service General Hospital. A chest X-ray showed he had pneumonia in his right lung. Within a few hours, tests showed he had SARS.

More than 100 people who came into contact with the scientist were monitored for potential infections. They included seventy-five people in Singapore and thirty-five in Taiwan, the five colleagues who accompanied him on the trip[30] to the conference, as well as members of his family.

Of the fourteen at-risk people who sat in the three rows around the scientist during his flight from Singapore back to Taipei, five were international travelers to other countries. Two of these passengers ultimately landed in the United States,[31] one in San Francisco and the other in Los Angeles.

Nobody contracted SARS from the scientist, who also recovered from his illness. It was fortunate that this first SARS virus didn't tend to spread until after patients started experiencing symptoms.

But this second laboratory escape of SARS further alarmed the World Health Organization, which called on governments around the world to assess the safety of labs possessing specimens of the virus.

While national and international safety guidelines were available to scientists in Taiwan at the time of the incident, as was the case in Singapore, Taiwan lacked national laboratory biosafety regulations governing work with the most dangerous types of pathogens.[32]

"There should be no more cutting corners and procedures should be followed to the letter," WHO spokesman Peter Cordingley told Reuters.[33] He acknowledged that the WHO had no idea how many labs were experimenting with the SARS virus.

"We are not the lab Interpol," Cordingley said. "We can't go out busting laboratories and inspecting them."

The WHO issued more safety guidelines[34] that bluntly warned of the significant risk to public health from laboratories mishandling SARS specimens: "These laboratories currently represent the greatest threat for renewed SARS-CoV transmission through accidental exposure associated with breaches in laboratory biosafety."

Countries seemed to take the warnings seriously.

In Beijing, the Chinese Health Ministry called for SARS specimens to be consolidated into a small number of designated labs. The ministry enacted regulations[35] for the use of SARS specimens and called for labs to intensify safety practices to prevent accidents.

But the SARS virus was about to be on the loose yet again—this time with deadly consequences.

THE NATIONAL INSTITUTE OF Virology in Beijing, operated by the Chinese Center for Disease Control and Prevention, was among the labs China had designated in December 2003 to be entrusted with securing the nation's specimens of SARS virus.

But by late April 2004, the virology institute had accidentally released the SARS virus, and the WHO and Chinese health authorities were scrambling to contain a growing outbreak of cases linked to the lab's researchers, their family members, and the health care workers who had treated them.

The WHO said in an emergency update at the time that investigators "have serious concerns about biosafety procedures at the Institute—including how and where procedures using SARS coronavirus were carried out, and how and where SARS coronavirus samples were stored."[36]

Two researchers at the institute had become infected in what appeared to be two separate events and without any obvious laboratory accident.

One was a 26-year-old medical student, identified in official Chinese state media as Ms. Song,[37] who became ill on March 25. The other was a 31-year-old researcher, identified as Mr. Yang, who became ill on April 17 and was hospitalized on April 22.

While Mr. Yang apparently didn't transmit the virus to anyone else,[38] Ms. Song did.

Ms. Song was a medical student from Anhui Medical University who had spent two weeks in Beijing conducting research at the virology institute, where live SARS virus studies were being conducted. After she completed her lab work, she returned to Anhui, where she began feeling ill on March 25.

Even though she wasn't well, Ms. Song took two train trips[39]—risking further spread of the virus. She traveled from Anhui back to Beijing, where she became so ill that on March 29 she was admitted to a hospital for pneumonia.

But nobody knew she had SARS, and she wasn't tested.

While in the hospital, Ms. Song was cared for by a nurse, identified as Ms. Li. In addition, Ms. Song's mother, who was identified as Mrs. Wei, spent significant time at the young woman's bedside.[40] Soon, both fell ill.

Ms. Song, after being discharged from the hospital, traveled by train from Beijing to Anhui on April 2. Once there, Ms. Song was hospitalized again. And within a week, her 53-year-old mother developed a fever and pneumonia and was admitted to the same hospital;[41] she eventually became critically ill and died on April 19.[42]

Meanwhile, Ms. Li, the 20-year-old nurse who cared for Ms. Song at the Beijing hospital, also fell ill with SARS—spreading it to several of her family members.[43]

By April 22, China had identified eight people clinically diagnosed or under investigation for SARS infections. Six of them were in Beijing, and two were in Anhui Province. Within days, the country had put nearly 1,000 people[44] under medical observation because of potential exposures. Authorities closed the virology institute and also put more than 200 of its employees under medical observation.

By summer the outbreak that began at the National Institute of Virology had been contained—but only after three generations of transmission, with nine confirmed cases of SARS and one death.[45]

It was lucky that the toll wasn't much higher.

An investigation by the WHO[46] uncovered evidence that SARS viruses from inside the lab likely had been infecting the institute's workers months before the illnesses of Ms. Song and Mr. Yang caught the attention of health authorities in April 2004.

The WHO team identified two additional lab workers who suffered SARS-like illnesses in February 2004. Although they weren't diagnosed with SARS at the time they were ill, tests showed they were positive for SARS antibodies.

All of these researchers had worked in the same general laboratory at the virology institute. While work with live SARS virus wasn't done in this lab, some research had been done there in early 2004 with inactivated SARS specimens that weren't supposed to be dangerous.

Investigators concluded that these specimens hadn't been fully killed, putting those who worked with them—and who worked with other pathogens in the shared lab space—at risk of infection.

Compounding these mistakes was a lack of any health monitoring[47] of the institute's staff to identify lab-acquired infections. Despite the exposure risks of their jobs, none of the lab workers who fell ill received tests for SARS infections until weeks after they started getting sick.

When the World Health Organization published a comprehensive report of how the SARS epidemic was stopped[48] a few years after the epidemic ended, it discussed the ongoing concerns about the lack of consistency in biosafety standards and oversight across countries and within individual labs.

There were two ways the SARS virus had the potential to cause a future outbreak, the WHO experts wrote. It could emerge from an animal reservoir, or it could be released by a lab doing research with live cultures or handling stored clinical specimens.

The report concluded: "The risk of re-emergence from a laboratory source is thought to be potentially greater."

CHAPTER 10

Frozen in Time

W HILE IT MAY seem incredible to think that a research-related accident could cause a worldwide pandemic, such an event is believed
to have already occurred.

During 1977, a decades-old strain of H1N1 influenza virus suddenly
emerged and swept the globe, sickening younger people with what was generally a mild form of the disease.[1]

The first reported cases were in what was then the Soviet Union. There
was a 22-year-old man in Moscow[2] who started feeling ill on November 1,
1977. Nine days later, there was an outbreak among 152 trainees at a mari-
time school[3] in the village of Nakhodka in a far eastern area of the USSR.
Those sickened were between 15 and 20 years old. And by early December,
large numbers of flu cases were reported across the Soviet Union's fifty
largest cities.[4]

By January 1978, this H1N1 flu virus was spreading around the world,
with cases starting to be identified in the Philippines and United Kingdom.

It was only then—six months after the virus started sweeping across
the Soviet Union—that health officials in China notified the World Health
Organization[5] that they, too, had been dealing with an H1N1 influenza
epidemic since May 1977. The first cases to draw attention in China had
been among children, and the epidemic there also had primarily sickened
people between the ages of 8 and 20.

Early on, the flu strain was recognized as unusual. Curiously, most of
those who were sickened were young people and children. Yet the virus
largely bypassed people who were older than 30,[6] perhaps because they had
already been sickened by it decades earlier.

The newly emerged flu appeared to be nearly identical to the H1N1 flu that had circulated in 1950. Its genetic information seemed "preserved over the last 25–27 years by some unusual mechanism," wrote one team of researchers in a July 1978 journal article.[7]

They stopped short of directly raising the specter of a lab accident but said one possibility was that a 1950 flu virus "was truly frozen in nature or elsewhere and that such a strain was only recently reintroduced into man."

Over the years, other prominent flu experts have been far more blunt, saying "this virus from 1950 almost certainly escaped back into nature from frozen storage"—or, more specifically, that it "probably escaped from a laboratory."[8]

Although the source of the 1977–1978 H1N1 flu epidemic remains unknown, it is widely believed to have been caused by some kind of a lab or research-related mishap.

Did a lab worker unknowingly become infected while working with a frozen specimen or through a cross-contamination accident, then spread the virus to family and friends and beyond? Or was the virus perhaps set loose during some kind of vaccine trial[9] using a live, weakened influenza virus that didn't go as planned?

In 1978, a team of researchers from the Chinese Academy of Medical Sciences dismissed a lab accident as a possible source of the virus in a paper published that year in the *Bulletin of the World Health Organization* detailing the epidemic's spread across China.

"Laboratory contamination can be excluded because the laboratories concerned either had never kept the H1N1 virus or had not worked with it for a long time,"[10] wrote the team, led by the pioneering Chinese molecular virologist Chi-Ming Chu.

At some point in the decades that followed, Chu told a prominent U.S. influenza researcher that the 1977 virus had come from a mishap involving vaccine research.

Peter Palese, a virologist at the Mount Sinai School of Medicine in New York City, included this revelation, almost as an aside, in a 2004 journal article discussing the flu pandemics that occurred in 1918, 1957, and 1968.

"Strictly speaking, there was a fourth pandemic strain in the last century, an H1N1 strain which appeared in 1977," Palese wrote.[11] "Although there is no hard evidence available, the introduction of this 1977 H1N1 virus is now thought to be the result of vaccine trials in the Far East involving the challenge of several thousand military recruits with live H1N1 virus...Unfortunately, this H1N1 strain (and its descendants) has been circulating ever since."

Palese cited personal communication with Chu as the source of the vaccine trial information. Chu died in 1998.[12] Palese did not grant me an interview.

In recent years, some researchers have downplayed the relevance[13] of the 1977 influenza epidemic as a real-world example of a global epidemic caused by biological research.

They don't dispute that the origin of the virus almost certainly was not natural. But they say the event didn't occur in the context of modern biosafety practices. And they essentially argue that if the type of research that led to the escape involved a "vaccine trial or vaccine development gone awry," it is somehow not as relevant to debates over biosafety risks as other kinds of microbiological research.

WE MAY NEVER KNOW exactly how the 1977 H1N1 strain emerged. But it showed how a safety breach, especially with a respiratory virus that spreads easily from person to person, can launch a global pandemic.

More than any other type of pathogen studied in labs, respiratory pathogens pose the greatest risks of causing pandemics, experts told me.

"Respiratory pathogens are spread through coughing, laughing, sneezing, breathing, and that's not something that's easy for public health interventions to disrupt," said Dr. Amesh Adalja, a senior scholar at the Johns Hopkins Center for Health Security.[14]

Viruses pose a greater risk of pandemics than bacteria, he said, because fewer broad-spectrum treatments are available for viruses. And those pathogens, like SARS-CoV-2, that are capable of spreading before any symptoms appear are of particular concern.

Adalja led a study published in 2018 examining the characteristics of pathogens that pose the greatest risks of causing widespread disaster through natural emergence, deliberate creation and release, or laboratory escape.[15] The report said that although most classes of microbe "could evolve or be manipulated in ways that would cause a catastrophic risk to humans, viruses—especially RNA viruses—are the most likely class of microorganism to have this capacity."

Among the families of viruses the report said pose the most likely threat: influenza viruses and coronaviruses, which are well known to most people. Also on their list are virus families that the public may be less familiar with, including paramyxoviruses, pneumoviruses, and picornaviruses.

"Respiratory spread, being a virus, and being contagious during the incubation period are the three key factors," Adalja told me.

Biosafety has always been important when it comes to protecting lab workers against infections, Adalja said. "I also think that it is important, especially when you're working with pandemic pathogens, to think about how biosafety has to be in place so the work you're trying to do to prevent the next pandemic doesn't end up contributing to it."

CHAPTER 11

The Last Smallpox Death

T HE YEAR 1977 was notable not just for the likely flu virus escape. That's also when the last known natural case of smallpox occurred— an infection in a hospital cook[1] sickened in Somalia[2]—before the deadly virus was finally eradicated through vaccination and public health efforts. It is the only infectious disease that science, so far, has been able to stamp out.

The following year, that monumental achievement—ridding the world of a disease that for at least 3,000 years had killed millions—was jeopardized by a laboratory at Birmingham University Medical School in England that sparked a deadly smallpox outbreak.[3]

This outbreak was tiny in comparison to the worldwide H1N1 influenza epidemic, but it showed how some of the world's leading scientists can badly misjudge safety risks with high-stakes pathogens while oversight authorities defer to their expertise even in the face of obvious warning signs.

What happened in Birmingham further illustrated the flawed logic behind the pervasive belief across the biological research sector that the absence of catastrophic lab-caused pandemics is somehow evidence of current and future laboratory safety.

In August 1978, Janet Parker, who worked as a medical photographer in the school's anatomy department—one floor above a smallpox lab—fell ill with headache and muscle pains, then eventually developed a rash. Parker was ill for two weeks—and continuing to come into contact with various family members, medical personnel, and other people—before she was finally hospitalized and diagnosed with smallpox.

Even though Parker, 40, had been vaccinated against smallpox in 1966, she still died from the infection and became the last person in the world to die of smallpox.

Her 70-year-old mother also contracted smallpox, but recovered. Her father, who was 71, died[4,5] after being admitted to an isolation hospital, but officials said his cause of death was a heart attack. More than 300 people[6] were quarantined, though nobody else was infected.

As the investigation into the source of Parker's exposure got underway, the head of Birmingham University's pox virus lab, Professor Henry Bedson, died from self-inflicted throat wounds.[7]

Bedson, an international expert credited with playing an important role in the worldwide smallpox eradication campaign, left behind a note[8] saying: "I am sorry to have misplaced the trust which so many of my friends and colleagues placed in my work..."

Three months before Parker's infection, in May 1978, inspectors from the World Health Organization—which was funding some of Bedson's research—had expressed concerns to Bedson[9] about safety measures that needed improvement in his lab. Yet they allowed his work with variola, the virus that causes smallpox, to continue since it was being phased out by the year's end. (Investigators later learned that university officials had not been told about the WHO's concerns.)

To protect the world against smallpox reemerging from a lab accident, the WHO had embarked on a program to dramatically limit the number of labs holding specimens of variola virus. The Birmingham lab was not among those chosen, which is why it was scheduled to cease its smallpox research by the end of 1978.

(Today, just two labs in the world—one at the U.S. CDC in Atlanta and the other at the VECTOR Institute in Russia—are the only places authorized under international agreement to possess variola virus.[10])

While acknowledging that the Birmingham lab didn't meet the physical standards of facilities that were to be among some of the final repositories of smallpox virus, Bedson downplayed the risks posed by his lab in a June 2, 1978, letter to WHO officials.

"Although all work with pathogens involves some risk and no one concerned can afford to be complacent, I see no reason to depart from my previous statement that the risks must be minimal," Bedson wrote to the chief of the WHO Smallpox Eradication Unit in Geneva, citing his lab's long history of conducting research on smallpox viruses without disastrous consequences.[11]

At least one member of the WHO inspection team agreed that the risks posed by the Birmingham lab were "probably minimal," but expressed concerns that it still should discontinue its smallpox research "at the earliest possible date."

As the back-and-forth correspondence continued between Bedson and the WHO, Janet Parker became infected with smallpox.

While investigators were certain that the Birmingham lab was responsible for Parker's infection, they ultimately were not able to determine how she was exposed.

Of the two scenarios they considered likely,[12] one involved the virus traveling through a service duct to a room regularly used by Parker that was located one floor above the lab. The other involved the possibility that a visitor from the medical microbiology department had somehow unknowingly carried the virus to Parker in her darkroom.

But those theories, especially the air duct theory, have been the subject of controversy. In 1979 a court dismissed a workplace safety prosecution[13] brought by the Health and Safety Executive, clearing the university of blame in Parker's death after it couldn't be proven how she became infected.

The bottom line: Although nobody knows for certain how Parker became infected, it never should have happened.

A government-commissioned investigation found that while the university and the medical microbiology department had biosafety policies, "no effective system" was in place to determine whether they were followed.[14] The university and the WHO appear to have largely relied on assurances that Bedson—a leading smallpox expert—was properly overseeing the lab's safety.

Yet because of an increased focus on administrative and teaching responsibilities, Bedson had spent very little time inside the lab[15] in the three years before Parker was infected.

As investigators scrutinized the operations of the pox virus lab, they found far more safety problems than had been identified by the WHO.

They ranged from critical pieces of lab equipment that were poorly maintained or potentially unsafe to an alarming lack of training and supervision.

A PhD student in the lab told investigators that from when she first started working with smallpox in 1975 she had never received supervision from Bedson.[16]

Investigators questioned the smallpox lab's ability to maintain negative air pressure[17] and tests of the lab's airflow[18] "demonstrated without a doubt that airborne particles can and do escape from the smallpox laboratory and could reach sensitive unrestricted areas." And while exhaust air from the room was supposed to be exhausted through two HEPA filters, the smallpox lab had no air filtration system.

Containers of smallpox virus specimens were stored in a freezer alongside specimens of other organisms, such as herpes virus, that were being used by labs elsewhere in the department. Investigators learned the outsides of the smallpox containers, which were potentially contaminated, were not disinfected before they were put in the shared freezer.

"This presented a risk to anyone subsequently retrieving stocks of virus from the freezer," their report said.[19]

Those working in the smallpox lab also didn't always wear gloves to protect against contaminating their hands with the virus, an issue flagged by WHO inspectors a few months before Parker's infection. Yet Bedson questioned whether gloves were really necessary,[20] saying that "one could argue about the extent to which they affect the safety of the work."

Investigators in their final report expressed their "deep concern"[21] about the lab's failure to follow safety procedures—and the failure of the WHO, university, and other health agencies to recognize the extent of the risk posed by the lab. Too much trust had been placed in the lab to police itself, and too many were blinded for too long by Bedson's expertise as a scientist.

They added, "if the situation like that found at Birmingham exists elsewhere, the need for identification and remedy is urgent."

CHAPTER 12

Anthrax Cloud

A FEW YEARS after smallpox was briefly set loose in the U.K., an anthrax lab in the former Soviet Union was linked to the deaths of more than sixty people who were in a fallout zone downwind of the facility.

The 1979 anthrax outbreak in Sverdlovsk involved labs that were part of a suspected biological weapons facility. But the disaster demonstrated how countries that are determined to cover up a major lab accident can use secrecy, misdirection, and the sharing of carefully curated information to bolster a false narrative.

The official Soviet story, which over time had slight variations, was that the outbreak was a result of people in Sverdlovsk eating black-market meat from anthrax-infected animals. Soviet officials insisted that the people who died had suffered from intestinal anthrax, proof that they had ingested the spores and didn't inhale them. Other victims had developed skin lesions from touching sick animals, they said. Any airborne release was denied.

But U.S. intelligence believed[1] that the facility in Sverdlovsk had been manufacturing dry anthrax spores in bulk quantities and that in early April 1979 some kind of pressurized system exploded, releasing as much as twenty-two pounds of this lethal dust into the air. Those in the fallout zone, the U.S. Defense Intelligence Agency said in a 1986 report, inhaled the spores and contracted pulmonary anthrax. Some may have had skin infections and, later, consumed contaminated meat.

In the wake of the accident, the initial efforts to decontaminate the area were "largely ineffective," the U.S. intelligence report said, adding that "the extraordinary efforts to 'clean-up' are inconsistent with the Soviet explanation." Fortunately, however, the outbreak involved anthrax—which does not spread from person to person and requires people or animals to directly touch, eat, or inhale it in doses large enough to cause an infection.

For years, the Sverdlovsk incident led to heated speculation about whether the anthrax deaths were evidence that the Soviets had violated the Biological Weapons Convention of 1972.

In 1986—seven years after the outbreak—an official from the Soviet Ministry of Health for the first time offered up a new layer of details to the official story. In response to continued U.S. allegations that the Sverdlovsk facility was working on biological warfare agents, the Soviet official said that the anthrax outbreak originated with contaminated cattle feed[2] that had been distributed by the government.

But the Soviets weren't forthcoming with any documentation.

In 1988, nearly a decade after the outbreak, three top Soviet health officials traveled to Washington, D.C., and made an elaborate presentation to their American scientific peers, U.S. officials, and journalists assembled for a three-hour seminar at the prestigious National Academy of Sciences.[3]

The Soviet delegation shared personal stories of racing to Sverdlovsk in the Ural Mountains to help contain what they said was suspected from the start as a foodborne illness outbreak.

They presented data and showed autopsy photographs that they represented as evidence of victims' intestines that had been ravaged by anthrax after consuming tainted meat. They explained away U.S. intelligence reports of victims having difficulty breathing, saying that was a consequence of the toxin produced by the ingested anthrax bacteria causing lung tissue to swell and fill with fluid.

They detailed efforts to contain the outbreak[4] that included searching homes for suspect meat, burning contaminated buildings, and killing 300 street dogs. And they explained how Soviet investigators determined that a twenty-nine-ton lot of anthrax-tainted bone meal, which was used as a livestock feed supplement without being properly heat treated, was the source of the meat's contamination.

Dr. Pyotr Burgasov, former deputy Soviet health minister, said: "The whole idea of some sort of aerosol is impossible."[5]

The Soviet display of apparent scientific openness and the prospect of reducing mistrust between the nations swayed the opinions of several high-profile scientists who had long been skeptical of the tainted meat story. The event drew coverage from major news organizations, including the *New York Times*, the *Washington Post*, and scientific publications.

A report of the event in *Science*,[6] which is published by the American Association for the Advancement of Science, proclaimed: "Sverdlovsk's 'mystery epidemic' of 1979 lost much of its mystery this month when a group of Soviet doctors came to the United States and met with scientists and reporters to give a firsthand account of what happened . . . They gave the same explanation as in 1980, but provided many more details, convincing some long-time doubters that the account was true."

Dr. Alexander Langmuir, a former director of epidemiology at the CDC, said he found the scientists' explanation credible[7] and that "the current position of the U.S. military needs thorough re-examination; that is clear."[8]

Dr. Philip Brachman, an anthrax expert at Emory University, said the presentation was a "landmark report"[9] and that it gave "a pretty good indication that this incident was an outbreak of gastrointestinal anthrax."[10]

Harvard molecular biologist Matthew Meselson, who organized the visit by the Soviet officials, called their explanation "completely plausible and consistent with what we know from the literature and other recorded experiences with animal and human anthrax."[11]

It was a weighty statement coming from Meselson, who had played a key role in the creation of the 1972 Biological Weapons Convention that prohibited weapons research and stockpiling.[12]

But not everyone was swayed.

Gary Crocker, an intelligence analyst from the U.S. State Department, told reporters that many questions remained unanswered and the controversy surrounding the source of the outbreak might never be resolved.

An important lesson to be learned, Crocker told *Science*,[13] was that when catastrophes of international significance occur in the future, treaties must allow investigators to immediately be given access to evidence to assess what happened.

The favorable headlines from the event helped change the narrative from a bioweapon accident toward a foodborne illness outbreak.

Yet as the years went by, new information kept trickling out.

In 1992, Russian president Boris Yeltsin surprised the world by making a public statement in a Russian newspaper, *Komsomolskaya Pravda*, acknowledging that the Sverdlovsk anthrax outbreak had been caused by military bioweapons research.[14] When the accident occurred in 1979, Yeltsin had been the head of the Communist Party in Sverdlovsk, and he said the KGB had privately told him that "our military development was the cause."

The same Russian newspaper, a few months earlier, had reported accounts of people living near the facility remembering "a discharge in the form of a pink cloud that rose behind a high fence."[15]

Meanwhile, Matthew Meselson, the Harvard molecular biologist who had organized the 1988 presentation in Washington by Soviet scientists, continued to look for answers to what had happened in Sverdlovsk and organize scientific fact-finding missions to Russia.

As the years passed, more data became available in Russia, and political changes allowed Russian scientists in Sverdlovsk to speak more freely. Eventually, multiple studies of the anthrax outbreak were published in scientific journals. They documented how the deaths and illnesses were most likely the result of an explosion at a laboratory facility—and concluded the story of tainted meat was part of the cover-up.

Faina Abramova and Lev M. Grinberg, Russian pathologists, had managed to hide their handwritten autopsy notes, specimen slides, and even some patients' preserved organs, keeping them for years after Soviet authorities destroyed the official autopsy reports and hospital records. They ended up co-authoring a study, published in 1993 in the *Proceedings of the National Academy of Sciences* with Meselson's involvement, detailing their review of the original autopsy findings on forty-two patients who died during the anthrax outbreak.[16]

The team determined that "these patients died because of inhalation of aerosols containing *B. anthracis*."

The following year, in 1994, a collaboration between U.S. and Russian scientists produced a study that painstakingly examined a wide range of records[17] that hadn't been confiscated by the KGB at the time of the 1979 accident.

Among the documents was an administrative list, compiled from KGB records, that had been created to compensate victims' families. It contained the names and home addresses of sixty-eight people who died.

The researchers interviewed the relatives and friends of people on the list. They gleaned information from grave markers, tapped into the newly disclosed autopsy information, and obtained veterinary records of animal deaths. They mapped victims' locations, reviewed meteorological data, and created detailed timelines.

Their research showed that most victims lived or worked in a narrow, straight-line fallout zone between the military facility and the city's south side, and that it followed the path of a northerly wind that had prevailed before the outbreak.

In their journal article, Meselson and several of the co-authors acknowledged that in 1988 they had felt the Soviets had made a "plausible case" for the tainted meat story during their U.S. visit. But they also believed more information was still needed. As a result of further requests by Meselson, he and other U.S. scientists were invited to conduct on-site research in Sverdlovsk in June 1992 and August 1993.

These scientists' shoe-leather epidemiology found that the Sverdlovsk outbreak was caused by aerosolized anthrax spores from a military compound in the city. Although it remained unclear whether the spores were released as a result of a catastrophic accident during an aerosol experiment or a weapon that exploded by accident, the tainted meat story was refuted by some of the same scientists who had once given it credence.

"This should end the argument about where the outbreak came from," Meselson told the *New York Times* in 1994.[18]

The process of gaining access to data and candid witness accounts took more than fifteen years.

That's something worth remembering during the current search for the origin of Covid-19.

CHAPTER 13

The Plague from Pirbright

LABORATORIES INVOLVED IN vaccine research and production can pose significant safety risks because of the large volumes of pathogens they are working with, incidents in China and the U.K. have shown.

More than 10,000 people in Lanzhou, a provincial capital in northwest China, tested positive for exposure to *Brucella* bacteria during 2019 and 2020 after a disastrous safety failure at a vaccine production facility.[1]

While rarely fatal, these bacteria can cause debilitating fevers, weakness, joint pain, and other symptoms that in some people can last for months or years.[2]

City health officials traced the outbreak to the Zhongmu Lanzhou biological pharmaceutical factory, which manufactures a veterinary vaccine against brucellosis, the disease caused by *Brucella* bacteria. These bacteria mainly cause disease in livestock, but they also can sicken people, usually through consuming unpasteurized dairy products or having contact with infected animals.

The investigation by Lanzhou health officials found that the vaccine factory had been spewing live, infectious bacteria into the outdoor air through emissions from a fermentation tank. The emissions weren't fully sterilized because the factory was using an expired disinfectant during July and August 2019. As a result, live bacteria were carried downwind, where people became exposed.[3]

The outbreak was first identified because of infections diagnosed among students and faculty members at the nearby Lanzhou Veterinary Research Institute of the Chinese Academy of Agricultural Sciences, which is downwind from the vaccine factory. There were 181 initial reports of infections at the institute, according to a report from Xinhua, a Chinese state-run news agency.[4]

Widespread testing in the wake of the accident identified more than 10,500 people in Lanzhou with exposures to the bacteria. The factory's vaccine production license was withdrawn, and several company officials were warned or fired as a result of the bacteria release.[5,6]

IN THE U.K., ANOTHER vaccine research and production complex was the site of a devastating escape of foot-and-mouth disease virus in 2007 that showed how lax biosafety can cause outbreaks among animals and significant economic damages to individuals and entire industries.

To bring the Pirbright foot-and-mouth disease outbreak under control required the slaughter and incineration of the carcasses of 982 cattle, 1,128 pigs, 43 sheep, and 7 goats over the course of two months.[7] The initial economic cost of the outbreak to the government and livestock industry was estimated at more than £147 million,[8] but may have been far higher.

As is often the case, despite warning signs, there wasn't an obvious lab accident. Nobody knew that a highly contagious virus had been leaking out of the facility in Pirbright, England, until after cattle started falling ill on a nearby farm.

The Pirbright facility was home to multiple laboratories spread across several buildings in a secure compound. The two main organizations on the site were the government-run Institute for Animal Health (IAH) and a commercial vaccine manufacturing facility operated by Merial Animal Health, one of the world's largest animal health companies. Both organizations did research on foot-and-mouth disease virus.

To keep intruders out, the Pirbright site was surrounded by a perimeter fence topped with razor wire. It even had a trembler wire and microwave beams to detect movement inside the fence line. The property also was monitored by video surveillance as part of its many security systems.[9]

Yet the biosafety systems critical to keeping pathogens inside the facility had been neglected for years.[10]

The IAH labs at Pirbright, some dating to the 1950s, did research on exotic animal diseases and developed diagnostic tests. Five years earlier, an expert review had warned parts of the facility were "shabby" and that "some of the laboratories...are not of a standard that would be expected in a modern bio-medical research facility."[11]

Just a few months before the outbreak began, the director of IAH Pirbright had sent a letter[12] raising similar concerns to the U.K. Department for Environment, Food and Rural Affairs (Defra)—a government agency that both regulated the facility and funded some of its research.[13] The IAH director's letter said "the laboratories at Pirbright are old and in urgent need of replacement...the overall infrastructure does not allow IAH to maintain a risk profile as low as other sister laboratories in Europe."

Still, the facility had passed its most recent inspection,[14] in December 2006, without any significant issues being flagged.

Plans had been in the works for years to build new facilities at Pirbright, but construction and commissioning weren't expected to be completed for five more years.

The facility operated by Merial was originally developed in the 1960s[15] for foot-and-mouth disease (FMD) vaccine production by the Wellcome Foundation Laboratories. It had been modernized in the 1990s and its facilities were considered to be "state-of-the-art."[16]

While the IAH labs worked with only small amounts of virus inside biosafety cabinets, the Merial facility had to grow large quantities of virus in 6,000-liter vessels[17] containing tissue culture cells as part of the process to make its FMD vaccine. The contents of the vessels were centrifuged to remove cell debris. Then the concentrated virus was inactivated and stored until it was turned into batches of vaccine.

The scientific research and vaccine production done at Pirbright was critical to protecting animals and agriculture from one of the most dreaded livestock diseases on the planet.

The consequences of foot-and-mouth disease may be unfamiliar to many in the United States who aren't involved in agriculture. The disease was eradicated in the U.S. in 1929, and the U.S. Department of Agriculture has spent decades working to prevent it from being re-imported.[18]

But in other parts of the world, this highly contagious disease still ravages livestock, including cows, pigs, and sheep. Once infected, animals develop fevers and painful blisters that swell and burst in and around their mouths, on their mammary glands, and in their hooves. Because they pop so quickly, the blisters are not always easy to see, and the first signs of trouble often involve drooling and limping animals.

While the FMD virus isn't usually deadly, it weakens infected animals and harms milk and meat production. When outbreaks occur, entire herds of animals are killed in an effort to stop further spread of the virus.

As few as ten infectious virus particles[19] are enough to infect a cow, and it spreads easily and quickly from their drool and excretions. This happens not only from direct contact, but particles can also be tracked from place to place on shoes, clothing, and vehicles, and it even can be carried by the wind under the right conditions.

It's such a scourge for agriculture that if it is detected even in just one animal, it can shut down international livestock trade for an entire country until the threat of further spread ends.

So it was alarming when some cattle at the small, family-run[20] beef finishing operation at Woolford Farm[21] in Surrey developed what appeared to be symptoms of foot-and-mouth disease in August 2007.

AROUND 6:00 A.M. ON August 3, a Friday morning,[22] a veterinarian collected blood samples from the sick animals and notified the Veterinary Exotic Notifiable Diseases Unit at Defra. The samples were taken to the nearby Institute of Animal Health, which had the expertise and containment to perform the tests.

By late afternoon, U.K. chief veterinary officer Debby Reynolds had confirmed the first tests were positive for foot-and-mouth disease virus. And by the following day, additional tests had linked the strain of virus to the research and vaccine production being done at the Pirbright facility.

The virus was a laboratory strain isolated from Great Britain's 1967 foot-and-mouth disease epidemic. Since that time, it had been used worldwide for research and vaccine production. It was not naturally found in the environment.

"This strain is present at the IAH and was used in a batch manufactured in July 2007 by the Merial facility. On a precautionary basis Merial has agreed to voluntarily halt vaccine production," Defra said in a statement on August 4.[23]

As often happens when labs have serious safety breaches, the facilities at Pirbright insisted their operations were safe.

IAH director Martin Shirley told news organizations there had been no safety breach at his facility. "The IAH operates under strict biosecurity procedures," Shirley said.[24]

Meanwhile, Merial told reporters[25] that its facility "operates to the very highest international standards" and insists on "stringent adherence to processes and procedures." Merial managing director David Biland added: "We have been operating from this site for 15 years and during that time have produced hundreds of millions of vaccine doses. In all that time we have never had a breach in our biosecurity."

But it only takes one breach.

Government agriculture officials locked down the areas around the Pirbright facility and oversaw the culling of livestock at what became a growing number of farms. It was a disaster for families that had worked the land for generations.

"It has just wiped us out. It is our only income," John Gunner, one of the farmers hit by the outbreak, told a reporter.[26]

Gunner had hoped his cattle would be spared. Then they started drooling and limping. "By this time, my old bull Ned, he was not very well. He was like having a pet dog... He had a great pedigree, he was so gentle."

Multiple investigations—not only by government agencies, but also by an outside panel of experts—began an urgent search for the source of the virus, focusing on three possible routes of escape[27] from the Pirbright facility.

Investigators looked at the possibility of wind-borne spread. Laboratory wastewater, possibly carried by recent local flooding, was another suspect. Lastly, they searched for evidence that someone had deliberately or accidentally infected the livestock by carrying the virus, perhaps on a contaminated object, car, or clothing.

In addition to the investigations being done by Defra, the U.K. agriculture agency that had been funding and overseeing research at the Pirbright facility, the government also launched two additional probes.

The U.K. Health and Safety Executive (HSE), which is Britain's national regulator of workplace health and safety, began a forensic investigation within days of the first cattle testing positive for FMD virus. These investigators checked equipment and records at Pirbright's several labs, examined research and safety protocols, inspected waste-handling systems, and performed environmental sampling.

A separate team of outside scientific experts, led by Professor Brian Spratt, a molecular microbiologist at Imperial College London, was charged with scrutinizing the underlying science and advising the government on the plausibility of the various escape scenarios.

Liquid waste, or effluent, from the laboratories soon became the prime suspect.

The wastewater from IAH and Merial was supposed to undergo a two-step chemical disinfection process. The first step involved treating the wastewater inside each of the lab facilities, before it was sent into dedicated pipes that took it to the Pirbright facility's treatment plant. This plant provided a second round of chemical treatment to ensure all pathogens were killed.

At the time of the outbreak, the plant was more than fifty years old.[28]

"There had been concern for several years that the effluent pipes were old and needed replacing but, after much discussion between IAH, Merial, and Defra, money had not been made available," the Spratt report found.[29]

THE PIRBRIGHT FACILITY HAD had two previous accidents[30] in 2006 during which it had releases into the public sewer system of a "small amount" of wastewater that had only been partially sterilized. The release events, in February and September 2006, involved valve failures that allowed wastewater overflows. IAH officials determined neither posed a risk of infection.

During the week of July 20, 2007—shortly before the foot-and-mouth disease outbreak began and around the time the cattle likely became infected—storm systems dropped heavy rain that flooded some parts of the Pirbright site.

IAH employees found rainwater was seeping into the wastewater system's pipes,[31] and it was adding to the water in its holding tanks. The effluent treatment plant didn't flood, but the labs had to temporarily stop discharging into the system because so much excess rainwater was seeping into it.

As investigators took a closer look at the Pirbright facility's wastewater system, they found "long-term damage and leakage, including cracked pipes, unsealed manholes and tree root ingress." The wastewater system was owned by the Institute for Animal Health,[32] but the responsibility for maintaining a key stretch of pipe was a matter of dispute between IAH and Merial.

Adding to investigators' suspicions: Construction work was being done inside the Pirbright compound in the period before the outbreak. That work included soil excavation around one of the wastewater discharge pipes from the Merial facility.

Investigators concluded this soil likely was contaminated with live virus and the heavy rains may have further spread the virus, allowing it to be picked up on the muddy tires and underbodies of vehicles. The investigation found that some trucks had traveled along Westwood Lane,[33] alongside the first affected farm.

While there was "very little doubt"[34] that the outbreak was caused by biosafety and biosecurity failures by one or more of the labs at Pirbright, investigators couldn't say for sure how the virus got out of the facility.

"This was unsatisfactory and frustrating but identifying the source of an outbreak of this kind with any certainty is always likely to be inconclusive, unless some gross and obvious breakdown in a safety critical feature occurred," the Spratt report said.[35]

THE PIRBRIGHT OUTBREAK WAS hardly an isolated incident with this dangerous agricultural virus.

A government-commissioned review of the accident[36] identified that from 1960 to 2008 there had been at least thirteen additional reported incidents of foot-and-mouth disease virus accidentally being released from labs around the world, with many involved in vaccine production.

These other FMD lab accidents had occurred in the U.K. (1960), Denmark (1968), Czechoslovakia (1969 and 1975), Hungary (1972), Germany (1974, 1976, 1977, 1987, and 1988), Spain (1979), and Russia (1993).[37]

Missing from that list was yet another FMD virus release incident that occurred in the United States in 1978[38] at the Plum Island Animal Disease

Center, which fortunately was located off the tip of Long Island, New York, and not near farms.

Clean animals being held on Plum Island—outside of the laboratory buildings—became infected with the virus. The exact source of their infections was never determined, but prime suspects were contaminated air from poorly maintained lab vents and filters, or a leak of contaminated water through a construction barrier.

What happened in Pirbright and in these other FMD virus escapes is why controversy and concern has dogged the U.S. government's decision to relocate the country's research on the disease from the isolation of Plum Island—two miles off the coast—to a new lab facility in the heart of Kansas cattle country.

Construction was nearing completion in 2022 on the new $1.25 billion National Bio and Agro-Defense Facility (NBAF) in Manhattan, Kansas, which will then undergo months of tests to ensure its systems function properly.

The NBAF facility is being built by the U.S. Department of Homeland Security and will be operated by the U.S. Department of Agriculture. It is located adjacent to Kansas State University and will work on a wide range of foreign animal diseases in addition to FMD virus, including some that can spread from animals to humans.

The NBAF will be the first facility in the United States, and one of only a handful around the world, to have biosafety level 4 labs that can house cattle and other types of large livestock. And, once operational, it will for the first time since 1937[39] bring FMD virus research onto the U.S. mainland.

Officials from the U.S. Department of Homeland Security, which has led the facility's construction, for years have provided assurances that the many high-tech and redundant safety features of the NBAF's labs will keep foot-and-mouth disease virus from escaping.

But scientific experts assembled by the U.S. National Academies of Sciences, Engineering, and Medicine have repeatedly warned that the government's risk assessments have been "overly optimistic" and have failed to take into account the real-world experiences of lab accidents—including what happened at Pirbright.

In an official risk assessment for the facility, Homeland Security officials even claimed that the chance of a wastewater treatment failure was essentially nonexistent—something their official risk analysis estimated would occur only once every 2.1 million years.[40]

It was a credulous claim that in 2010 was challenged[41] by the National Academies' National Research Council panel that had been asked by Congress to evaluate the government's risk assessment. The experts took DHS to task for its apparently failing to consider the FMD virus escapes that occurred from Pirbright, Plum Island, and in more than a dozen other international lab incidents.

But even with the limited risks identified by the department's assessment, the National Academies' panel found they showed a nearly 70 percent chance over the facility's fifty-year lifetime[42] that there would be some kind of FMD virus release causing an infection outside the laboratory.

The economic cost of an FMD outbreak in the United States was estimated at $9 billion to $50 billion.

In response to the criticisms, the Department of Homeland Security revised its risk assessment in 2012, saying that changes to the design of the lab facility had dramatically reduced the risk of an accidental release from 70 percent to just one-tenth of 1 percent.[43]

But once again, a panel from the National Academies found the assessment was based on "questionable and inappropriate assumptions,"[44] used "overly optimistic and unsupported estimates of human error rates," and placed too much emphasis on using reinforced construction to control risks posed by natural hazards, like tornadoes and earthquakes.

In the coming months, as the NBAF starts working with live pathogens, we'll see how these varying assessments of risk ultimately play out in real life.

History continues to show that biosafety technology is only as good as the people maintaining and using it.

CHAPTER 14

"Time Bomb" in Louisiana

T HE MONKEYS IN the Tulane National Primate Research Center's huge outdoor compound of open-air cages, about forty miles north of New Orleans, should never have come into contact with the lethal bacteria that were killing them in 2014 and 2015.

It was a type of soil-dwelling bacteria that most people in the United States have never heard of: *Burkholderia pseudomallei*.

It's pronounced *Ber-kol-dairy-uh su-do-mal-ee-eye*, but it's often referred to by its abbreviation: Bp. And the strain that was infecting the monkeys isn't found in nature in Louisiana or anywhere else in the continental United States.

In tropical and semi-tropical areas of northern Australia and southeast Asia, where Bp long ago colonized the soil and water, the bacteria cause a disease called *melioidosis* that can kill a person within forty-eight hours.[1] Yet in some people, for reasons science still can't fully explain, these hardy bacteria can lurk inside their bodies for months, years, or even decades before unleashing a cascade of flu-like symptoms that doctors may not recognize as deadly until it is too late.[2]

One of the nicknames for this bacterium is the "Vietnamese Time Bomb," earned from the infections it caused among veterans of the Vietnam War after they returned home to the United States.[3,4]

It's also called the Great Mimicker[5] because it causes a wide range of symptoms that can make it appear to be many diseases.[6] It can turn into a blood infection or it might create abscesses or instead cause lung or kidney or heart problems.

In parts of the world where this bacterium has had decades to take root, it is believed to kill about 90,000 people a year[7] who had the misfortune of coming into contact with contaminated soil or water and getting infected through cuts in their skin or by breathing bacteria-laced dust or mist kicked up during storms.[8]

The only place in the United States that this strain of *Burkholderia pseudomallei* was supposed to be found was inside a high-containment laboratory—like the biosafety level 3 labs that were experimenting with it at the Tulane National Primate Research Center in Covington, Louisiana.

The U.S. government has spent millions of dollars funding Bp research at Tulane and other institutions in an effort to create vaccines, more accurate tests, and better treatments—all of which are desperately needed. As a result, *Burkholderia pseudomallei* is among the most frequently held specimens[9] of select agent pathogens in U.S. labs.

But this research comes with risks.

Burkholderia pseudomallei poses such a severe threat to public health and safety that lab regulators at the Federal Select Agent Program have designated it a Tier 1 select agent—taking its place alongside about a dozen other better-known pathogens like those that cause anthrax, plague, Ebola, and smallpox.[10] Labs working with Bp are supposed to take additional precautions to ensure these bacteria don't escape.[11]

That's why it was alarming when tests revealed in late 2014 that two sick monkeys kept outdoors at the Tulane National Primate Research Center—monkeys that had never been used in any experiments—were infected with *Burkholderia pseudomallei*.

These animals were part of the center's monkey breeding operation. It was a massive endeavor involving about 4,000 animals kept in dozens of huge outdoor cages that stretched across much of the center's 500-acre property.

Since the 1960s, Tulane has operated one of the original U.S. primate centers that were created by the National Institutes of Health to help scientists conduct specialized biomedical research using monkeys and apes as stand-ins for humans. The centers also help supply specific disease-free primates for use in research facilities across the country.

The magnitude of Tulane's breeding operation can only be fully appreciated from the air. It is set on 300 acres in the compound's South Campus, carved out of the densely wooded forests lining the nearby Abita and Bogue Falaya rivers, which ultimately flow into Lake Pontchartrain.

The area is covered in a grid pattern of open-air, chain-link cages. Many of these field cages were more than half the size of a football field. Inside each of them, monkeys forage throughout the dirt-and-grass-covered enclosures. Some sit on perches suspended from the chain-link roofs, while others watch the coming and going of keepers distributing food and making twice-daily checks on them.[12]

In addition to breeding monkeys, the Tulane primate center also conducted its own biological research, including with *Burkholderia pseudomallei*. But those experiments were done in labs located on the far north side of the sprawling property, a five-minute drive from the breeding colony.

It should have been impossible for *Burkholderia pseudomallei* to escape from the center's labs and infect the monkeys—at least according to Tulane's written safety protocols.

The center had multiple layers of high-tech safety equipment plus detailed policies and procedures. On top of that was the sheer physical distance between the labs and the breeding colony, plus a series of locked doors, gates, and barrier fences that required badges for entry.

Yet this deadly pathogen still escaped from one or more of the center's biosafety level 3 labs in 2014, infecting multiple monkeys as it spread undetected for weeks.

The center's sloppy biosafety practices, as would later be documented by federal investigators, have raised the specter that *Burkholderia pseudomallei* may be growing undetected in soil or water near the compound or that it has entered the nearby rivers and traveled much farther downstream.

Louisiana's soil and climate, federal scientists later determined, would make a great home for the bacteria.

WHEN THE MONKEYS STARTED falling ill in early November 2014, nobody initially realized the gravity of the situation.[13]

Monkeys, like people, sometimes get sick. And the first two monkeys, macaques known by identification numbers IL38 and ID22,[14] didn't seem to have anything in common.

They lived in separate cages located far from each other. And their symptoms, which developed a few days apart, didn't point toward any obvious diagnosis. They were just lethargic and appeared dehydrated.[15]

The monkeys were loaded into a transport van and driven out of the breeding colony, across Three Rivers Road, and onto the center's separate North Campus. That's where the veterinary clinic, administrative offices, and laboratories were located across several buildings.

Despite batteries of diagnostic tests and even exploratory surgeries, the center's veterinarians couldn't figure out what was wrong with these two monkeys.

Initial tests indicated they might be infected with some kind of *Pseudomonas* species of bacteria. These bacteria are frequently found in soil, water, and plants, but they don't usually cause deadly infections.

While one of the monkeys seemed to be getting better, the other one, called IL38, had become so ill and unresponsive that it had to be euthanized on November 26. (Monkey ID22's recovery didn't last long, and it also was euthanized less than three months later.)

As the veterinary staff tried to figure out a diagnosis, further testing provided a troubling clue. It indicated the monkeys were actually infected with some type of *Burkholderia* bacteria.

Tulane sent specimens to the CDC's labs in Atlanta, where tests confirmed the infections were caused by *Burkholderia pseudomallei*.

The diagnosis had serious implications, not just for the monkeys but also for the health of people working at the center, as well as those outside its gates.

For weeks, the primate center's staff had been repeatedly put at risk of infection as they cared for these monkeys—providing medical treatments, feeding them, changing their water, and cleaning their cages—all the time unaware of the danger posed by the organism causing their infections.

Yet Tulane did not notify the center's occupational health providers[16] about the potential worker exposures until December 16—nearly a month after *Burkholderia* was first suspected and ten days after it was confirmed.

There seemed to be some hope among center officials that the bacteria infecting the monkeys had come from somewhere other than Tulane's labs. Maybe *Burkholderia pseudomallei* was naturally occurring in Louisiana and just hadn't before been identified?

It wasn't until December 22—a time when many were focused on the holidays—that the center held a meeting to inform staff about their possible health risks. And even then, not all of the workers at high risk were notified.

Some workers later told regulators they had to rely on word of mouth, colleagues who attended the meeting, later news coverage, or even a call from a concerned neighbor to learn they may have been infected.

The result was a three-month delay for some workers to get medical attention, surveillance, and counseling.[17]

By mid-January, more tests by the CDC showed the strain killing the monkeys was the same one that the center was using in its experiments. This laboratory strain, called 1026b, had been isolated from an infection suffered by a rice farmer sickened in Thailand[18] in 1993.

Records showed the primate center's scientists had acquired a specimen of this strain in May 2013.[19]

The CDC's strain tests confirmed what everyone feared: *Burkholderia pseudomallei* had escaped one of Tulane's biosafety level 3 labs.

The risks went beyond the potential exposures of Tulane's own workers. The infected monkeys had been kept in dirt-and-grass-covered outdoor cages. Had they spread the deadly soil-burrowing bacteria into the environment through their urine and feces?

The wider public still hadn't been alerted.[20]

IN THE MONTHS BEFORE the monkeys became ill, experiments with *Burkholderia pseudomallei* had been conducted in at least two separate research buildings on the primate center's North Campus.

Tulane's primate center had been among the big winners in 2003 of what *Science* magazine at the time called a "biodefense bonanza"[21] that gave hundreds of millions of dollars in federal funds for construction and operation of what would ultimately be a dozen Regional Biocontainment Laboratories[22] across the country.

The National Institutes of Health and a panel of outside experts had determined that a lack of BSL-3 and BSL-4 research space was a barrier to scientific progress.[23]

Tulane, which was the largest of eight national primate centers at that time, was the only primate center to be chosen to construct one of the

state-of-the-art labs, receiving $21 million from the NIH's National Insti-
tute of Allergy and Infectious Diseases (NIAID), with the university chip-
ping in about $5 million of its own money.[24]

"With input from the scientific community, we have crafted a biodefense
research agenda emphasizing rapid translation of basic findings into real
products," NIAID director Anthony Fauci said at the time.[25] "Although the
agenda is ambitious, America's scientists have the commitment, creativity
and energy equal to the task. The new laboratories will give these dedicated
scientists space to conduct this critical research, and equally important,
they will be able to conduct it safely."

As part of the deal, Tulane's scientists and NIAID entered into a twenty-
year cooperative agreement[26] to collaborate on research projects involving
biodefense and emerging infectious diseases.

Tulane's Regional Biocontainment Laboratory, a 40,000-square-foot
BSL-3 facility[27] that had its ribbon-cutting ceremony in December 2008,[28]
brought an influx of federal research funding and enabled the primate center's scientists to do more work with increasingly dangerous pathogens. At
the time, the center only had one BSL-3 lab, which was about ten years old.[29]

Before the new facility came along, the center had focused on pathogens[30] that caused HIV/AIDS, malaria, Lyme disease, West Nile virus, and
tuberculosis. With the new facility, the center announced it planned to
conduct research into additional infectious diseases, including SARS, botulism, plague, tularemia, and brucellosis.

TULANE AND THE CDC have long refused to identify by name the
researchers whose lab work was involved in the *Burkholderia pseudomallei*
release incident. They would only say that the research involved work to
develop a vaccine and that it primarily involved rodents, but also involved
some experiments with monkeys.[31]

Grant records,[32] scientific journal articles, and promotional material[33]
on Tulane's website show research matching this description was being conducted at the primate center by microbiologist Lisa Morici and Chad Roy,[34]
director of infectious disease aerobiology at the primate center. Morici and
Roy did not respond to interview requests.

Tulane and other labs routinely justify their refusal to answer questions about lab accidents with blanket claims that disclosing details about their work poses a security threat. Yet those security concerns only seem to apply when it involves safety breaches, not when it comes to promoting scientific accomplishments.

For example, the university's medical school prominently featured Morici and Roy's research on *Burkholderia pseudomallei* at the primate center in an article for the winter 2019 edition of *Tulane Med* magazine.[35]

The article details how their research to create a Bp vaccine candidate for the U.S. military started with Morici getting an initial $25,000 pilot grant that over time grew into a $7.68 million project.

"From the very beginning I wouldn't be where I am right now without the primate center—without a doubt," Morici told the magazine.

Experiments conducted with Roy have showed the vaccine can protect animals against aerosol exposures to *Burkholderia pseduomallei*, the article said, noting that much of the work was done in the primate center's Regional Biocontainment Laboratory.

"It's an amazing feeling to work on something that could save lives or prevent disease," Morici said in the article.

IT WAS A FEW weeks after the holiday season when a team of Federal Select Agent Program investigators descended on the Tulane National Primate Center in a four-day visit from January 20 to January 24, 2015.[36]

Their mission was to try to determine how the monkeys became exposed and the extent of the risk in the surrounding area. Louisiana's homeland security department activated a command center to help coordinate local, state, and federal response.

The Tulane primate center's labs had no history of regulatory problems, and the CDC had said their most recent inspection in December 2013 found no significant problems. (When I later obtained the report, it showed thirty violations.[37])

Although the CDC was responsible for overseeing the Tulane primate center's labs, the USDA arm of the select agent program also sent investigators to Covington, Louisiana, because of concern about the threat Bp posed to animals and agriculture in the surrounding area.

In a strange twist, a day after completing the inspections, one of the USDA's inspectors fell ill and was hospitalized. Results of a blood test that came back on Saturday, February 7, indicated she had either a current or past exposure to *Burkholderia pseudomallei.*

It was likely a coincidence, federal officials thought. The USDA inspector, who wasn't identified and recovered from her illness, also had a history of international travel that possibly explained tests showing she had antibodies to Bp.

Still, it was an unnerving development that pushed the CDC's lab regulators to order the primate center to halt all research[38] with Bp and other select agent pathogens while the investigation continued.

It also helped prompt the decision to let the public know that a lab accident had occurred.

That Saturday afternoon, Pat Brister, the local St. Tammany Parish president, held a news conference. She was joined by the other state and local officials who had been investigating Tulane's lab accident.

The primate center's director, Andrew Lackner, had sent a letter[39] dated January 17, after a local TV reporter began asking questions, disclosing some information about the sick monkeys to a small group of people on the center's community advisory board as federal investigators were headed into Covington. But it was the press conference that made the wider public aware of what was going on.

Dr. Jimmy Guidry, Louisiana's state health officer, told the *Times-Picayune* that the hastily called press conference late on a Saturday during Mardi Gras was no reason for alarm.[40]

"We don't want the public to know we have information that they don't have," Guidry said. "We want people to know we're on top of this. We don't want people to think we're holding something back."

The CDC's secretive select agent program even issued a rare public announcement of a safety breach.[41] "At this time, there is no known public health threat," the CDC emphasized in its press release that day and subsequent interviews with reporters.

IN THE WEEKS THAT followed, more details trickled out as I wrote a series of articles[42] about the episode in *USA TODAY,* helping to extract information about what had happened and contributing to the reporting being done by local journalists in Louisiana.

As the Tulane primate center started testing more of the 4,000 monkeys in their supposedly disease-free breeding colony, they discovered more macaques that had antibodies to *Burkholderia pseudomallei*—signs that they had been exposed even though they showed no signs of illness.

By March 3, tests of 159 monkeys had found a fifth monkey exposed[43] to Bp. By March 6, testing had identified two more monkeys with antibodies, bringing the total to seven that had been exposed[44] or infected. Among them was yet another monkey that had become so seriously ill it became the third to be euthanized.

Amid these troubling developments, state agriculture and wildlife officials were developing a plan to test wildlife and domestic animals on—and off—the primate center's grounds.[45] The realization was sinking in that this escaped pathogen was a threat to the surrounding area.

As the number of documented monkey exposures rose, Tulane officials increasingly seemed to try to downplay the significance of the lab accident.

In interviews with me for my *USA TODAY* articles, Lackner repeatedly questioned whether *Burkholderia pseudomallei* was already naturally present in Louisiana's soil and water. Maybe it just hadn't been detected before now, he said, because nobody had previously been looking for it.

It was a message he also was pushing out to local residents, many of them living in homes that bordered the massive facility, or who had children who attended a nearby school.

In one community update, Lackner wrote: "Data from state records demonstrate that various Burkholderia species have been present in domestic animals in Louisiana since at least 2004, long before any scientific study of the organism began at TNPRC."[46]

When I asked his spokespeople at the time what he was referring to, they declined to answer my questions.

It was a curious spin to put on the situation—given that the CDC's tests showed the strain infecting Tulane's outdoor monkeys was a specific, known lab strain from Thailand that matched the Bp specimens used in the center's research.

At that time back in 2015, Bp had never been found in the continental

United States, although testing had detected it in soil in the U.S. Virgin Islands[47] and Puerto Rico.[48] (In July 2022, the CDC announced that a new strain of *Burkholderia pseudomallei,* unrelated to the strain from Thailand that sickened Tulane's monkeys, was identified in soil and water samples in the Gulf Coast region of southern Mississippi.[49])

As I reported on the growing Bp crisis at the Tulane primate center, Lackner and Tulane's PR team sought to brush off some of the concerning details that my *USA TODAY* articles were making public.

"This coverage in *USA TODAY* and other national outlets is part of the predictable news cycle in which local stories eventually receive the attention from the national media," Lackner told local residents.[50] "This coverage does not contain any additional news or discovery that has come about during the investigation by Tulane, federal, state and parish officials, including CDC, USDA and EPA. As the CDC and parish officials have stated in the past, there continues to be no known threat to public health as a result of this incident."

Tulane was bristling over my front-page and online investigative articles that had started appearing in *USA TODAY* since March 1.

My articles made clear the risks of the pathogen spreading into the surrounding environment, and they exposed how grossly inadequate the investigation's soil testing had been in looking for evidence that any bacteria had been released.

Tulane had been touting to the public that the absence of Bp being detected in any tests of soil, air, and water indicated it was "increasingly unlikely" that the bacterium had ever even been in their outdoor breeding colony.[51]

But rather than take their word for it, I obtained copies of the actual soil sampling plans that detailed the testing that had been done so far. Then I researched scientific journal articles about protocols for testing soil for the bacteria.

What I found was that even in countries where Bp has been living and growing in the soil for hundreds of years, it was still very difficult to detect its presence without testing a large number of samples.

The reason: Bp doesn't become evenly distributed across the soil like powdered sugar dusted across a cake. It forms individual colonies—with large gaps of soil that contain no bacteria.

And in the case of the Tulane primate center, if the bacteria had gotten into the soil, it had only had months to start multiplying—not hundreds of years.

"So unless a shovel is put in the right spot, the test will yield a false-negative result," my March 1 article reported.

Yet the records I obtained from the Environmental Protection Agency's contractor showed that only thirty-nine soil samples had been collected.

Inside field cage G12, where one of the sick monkeys had lived, only four samples were collected. These field cages, Tulane had told me, were 100 feet by 200 feet—an area that according to the scientific literature[52] should have been sampled in more than 100 spots.

As I pressed for the scientific justification of the testing approach, the EPA began trying to distance itself from the sampling plans,[53] referring me to the CDC, Tulane, and state officials. And all of them were pointing to one another.

THE GOVERNMENT'S INVESTIGATION—AT LEAST from what the CDC and Tulane were telling me at the time—seemed to be zeroing in on the center's veterinary clinic as the source of the monkeys' infections. It is only recently, however—by obtaining documents that Tulane fought hard to keep secret—that I have learned they weren't telling the public everything.

Early in the investigation, the one thing the sick and infected monkeys had in common was that they had all been in the center's veterinary hospital.

The first monkeys became obviously sick while still in their outdoor cages. But Lackner told me that they may have been sick with something entirely different while outside in the breeding colony. It was possible, he said, that they caught a secondary infection with *Burkholderia pseudomallei* only after they were inside the veterinary clinic.

He noted that two of the asymptomatic monkeys that tested positive for Bp had also been in the hospital because of injuries.

The theory that Tulane and CDC were increasingly latching on to was that somehow the veterinary clinic's exam tables or equipment or another shared item had become contaminated with Bp—and it was inside the clinic, not outdoors, that all these monkeys had come into contact with the bacterium.

But the hypothesis lacked any tests showing Bp bacteria on surfaces or equipment inside the clinic. Tulane had thoroughly decontaminated the clinic using vaporized hydrogen peroxide on February 2, after the federal investigation was underway but before the clinic became the prime suspect.

I began hearing rumblings about tensions between the CDC and USDA inspectors who were jointly investigating the incident. The CDC increasingly believed the spread of *Burkholderia pseudomallei* may have been limited to the clinic. But the USDA believed it had spread in the outdoor breeding colony.

Making the vet clinic ground zero had the potential of making a bad situation less bad—because it at least meant that *Burkholderia pseudomallei* had only spread indoors where it couldn't start colonizing the state of Louisiana's soil.

It was a potentially reassuring message for the public.

But was it true? Did this theory really mean Bp had never reached the outdoors?

Tulane seemed to have difficulty answering my questions about how many monkeys had passed through the clinic—and then been returned to their outdoor cages—during the period the clinic was suspected of being contaminated.

If the clinic were the source of a super-spreader event, wouldn't the monkeys that had been treated in the clinic during the period it was being portrayed as a Bp hot zone pose a risk of carrying the bacteria back outdoors with them? The narrative that Bp was confined to the clinic didn't make sense if the monkeys were sent back to their field cages.

As I kept pushing for answers, Tulane finally acknowledged that 177 rhesus macaques had been treated in the clinic—and then returned to the outdoor breeding colony[54]—during the several weeks the clinic was suspected of being contaminated.

Even if the vet clinic theory was true, Bp should never have been there. The clinic wasn't designed or operated in ways to safely handle animals infected with that kind of dangerous pathogen.

The only place these bacteria were supposed to be was in one of the designated biosafety level 3 labs that were doing the vaccine development research.

Neither of the labs working with Bp was anywhere near the breeding colony, which was a short drive away.

WHEN THE CDC ANNOUNCED the findings of the federal investigation on March 13, 2015, the agency blamed contaminated worker clothing as the likely way the bacteria escaped Tulane's labs and infected the breeding colony's monkeys.[55]

"Although the specific transmission event has not been identified, plausible mechanisms were uncovered during the investigation," the CDC's media statement said.

Inspectors found that staff at the center frequently entered the Bp lab without wearing appropriate protective clothing, a practice that increased the risk of accidentally bringing the bacteria out of the lab, then tracking it into the breeding colony or to the veterinary clinic.

Tulane issued its own statement apologizing for "any anxiety, discomfort or inconvenience" and emphasizing the primate center's commitment to "rebuild and sustain the trust, goodwill and support we have received from our neighbors as we conduct vital research to combat a range of human diseases."

The safety problems the CDC announced publicly focused on worker clothing and related entry and exit procedures.

"CDC has found no evidence to date to suggest the organism was released into the surrounding environment and therefore it's unlikely there is any threat to the general population," the statement said.

As I covered this breaking news story, I also reached out to the USDA—the CDC's partner in the joint investigation. USDA spokesperson Joelle Hayden told me that her agency had not yet reached any conclusions[56] on whether a threat existed to agriculture in the wider environment.

The public wasn't being told the whole story.

IN THE WEEKS BEFORE the CDC announcement, Tim Clouse, a USDA risk analyst, and Katie Portacci, a USDA veterinary epidemiologist, had traveled to Louisiana to begin their own investigation.[57]

They worked for the USDA's Center for Epidemiology and Animal Health in Fort Collins, Colorado, and their job was to conduct a formal risk assessment of the Tulane lab accident, focusing on the risks to the area's livestock and domestic pets.

When Clouse was tapped for the assignment, he read everything he could about *Burkholderia pseudomallei*, then sat at his desk, looking at Google satellite images of the primate center and worrying about its proximity to the nearby wetlands and rivers.[58]

In warm climates, the bacterium can survive for years in soil and muddy water.

Once in Covington, Portacci and Clouse met with Tulane officials and reviewed the center's records and the findings of the other federal inspectors. They toured the facility, donning protective Tyvek suits, shoe booties, and head coverings as they went out into the breeding colony.

Clouse wanted to get a closer look at the field cages, the locations of swampy areas—and where the primate center discharged its wastewater.

The troubling details of the risks Portacci and Clouse identified are contained in a fifty-eight-page USDA report that Tulane and its lawyers tried to keep me from obtaining after I learned about its existence in the summer of 2020.[59]

The biosafety problems at the primate center went well beyond what the public was told in 2015. The USDA risk assessment identified not one but "several plausible pathways" for Bp to have escaped from the primate center.

USDA investigators were especially concerned about the facility's lax decontamination of potentially infectious wastewater, an issue that their report documented going back years. And their report examined old veterinary records that raised shocking concerns that Bp had been infecting animals in the supposedly disease-free breeding colony earlier than what federal officials had told the public.

"CDC, in our opinion, kind of trivialized the whole thing," Clouse, who retired from the USDA at the start of the Covid-19 pandemic, told me in an interview in 2022.[60]

Without a bunch of people infected or ill, Clouse said, the CDC was inclined to say there wasn't a problem.

There was a difference in cultures between the agencies. The USDA had long been a regulatory agency; the CDC primarily was a public health agency whose scientists subscribed to a no-shame, no-blame philosophy of helping people live healthier lives. Regulation wasn't in the CDC's DNA.

"They're clinicians, physicians, they don't like being second-guessed, which is kind of what a risk assessment can look like," Clouse said. "A lot of the friction had to do with they were relying on informed professional judgment. And due to the nature of our work, we have to document everything."

The tensions also extended to Tulane officials. "And they preferred CDC because we were asking awkward questions," Clouse said. "It felt like it was Tulane and CDC versus us."

IF TULANE HAD ITS way, you wouldn't be reading about any of the USDA investigation's findings.

After I filed a Freedom of Information Act request for the report in July 2020, the USDA's records staff initially saw no reasons to keep any of it secret, internal USDA emails show.[61] It didn't contain any security sensitive information, and it wasn't disclosing facts about the types of select agent pathogens held at the primate center that weren't already widely known.

But then the USDA alerted Tulane about my FOIA request and sought their input on the agency's plan to make the report public.

Tulane sent the agency a letter[62] detailing numerous reasons why the university believed the report should be kept secret.

"Because the Risk Assessment directly relates to the release of a listed agent or toxin, its public disclosure is prohibited," the letter said, citing a 2002 bioterrorism law[63] that exempts only certain types of regulatory records from the FOIA.

In addition, Tulane argued that the risk assessment contained proprietary business information, such as the "novel techniques" Tulane used to respond to the bacteria release.

The letter went on to say that making the report public would cause an unwarranted invasion of privacy, arguing: "Documented violence by animal rights extremists against faculty members and others performing animal research places Tulane/TNPRC-affiliated individuals at risk if the information is released."

Tulane's letter doesn't mention any of the many ways the center and its researchers routinely publicize the primate center's research when it is of promotional benefit.

The USDA did much of what Tulane asked, blacking out most of the report's detailed findings about the primate center's safety failures from the copy released to me in February 2021.[64] I filed an administrative appeal, but the USDA still wouldn't budge.

Ultimately, I obtained unredacted copies of the full report that had been shared with Louisiana's state agriculture[65] and wildlife departments.

It's no wonder Tulane didn't want the public to see it.

ACCORDING TO THE USDA's risk assessment,[66] the lax approach Tulane's workers took to wearing protective lab clothing when working around *Burkholderia pseudomallei* may have tracked deadly bacteria beyond the compound's breeding colony and the veterinary clinic.

"It remains possible that *B. pseudomallei* was carried home on contaminated clothing," the report says.

But it was unknown how frequently this might have occurred or whether any of the workers' pets had become infected because only fifteen of the fifty-six Tulane primate center employees who had worked with the exposed monkeys would answer the USDA's questions.

Contaminated clothing, however, wasn't the USDA team's biggest worry.

The USDA risk assessment concluded that contaminated laboratory wastewater was the most likely way the bacteria escaped the facility and infected the monkeys outdoors.

Their report detailed evidence of lax laboratory wastewater treatment practices going back to 2013, when Tulane was doing an earlier round of research with *Burkholderia pseudomallei*.

The USDA investigation found that during experiments on monkeys in July and August 2013, bodily fluids from the Bp-infected animals were flushed down the drain without adequate disinfection.

The serious safety breaches occurred during animal autopsies—called necropsies—that were conducted on the Bp-infected monkeys following the 2013 experiments. Written safety procedures required the use of absorbent pads to capture all of the blood, fluids, and tissues from the infected animals. These pads were then supposed to be disposed of as solid waste—sterilized at high heat in an autoclave before being thrown out.

Meanwhile, the necropsy sink was supposed to have been plugged with a stopper and filled with a 10 percent bleach solution, with any water held for a minimum five-minute contact time to ensure it was sterilized.

But those procedures weren't followed, the USDA investigation found.

The report says the Bp-infected monkeys were "exsanguinated"—essentially drained of blood—"directly into the sink during the course of euthanasia and that fluids were not retained for any contact period with disinfectant before entering the drain."

The USDA report does not say how many Bp-infected monkeys were killed this way. These necropsies occurred in a BSL-3 necropsy suite in Building 20.

This contaminated liquid waste and water containing the blood and other fluids from infected monkeys was discharged into the primate center's on-site wastewater settling ponds, which the report said were located near the outdoor breeding colony on the center's South Campus.

"These necropsies provide an alternate hypothesis for the date of initial release of *B. pseudomallei* from the BSL-3 laboratory directly into the breeding colony," the USDA report said.

Although the CDC said nothing in its public press release about wastewater contamination, records show its inspectors also were concerned that the center had been sending blood and tissue waste from infected monkeys down the drain without giving the bleach enough time to disinfect the fluids.

"This observation raises serious concerns regarding environmental contamination due to improper decontamination of infectious fluids," they wrote in an inspection report[67] sent to the primate center in March 2015. The redacted document released to me by the CDC in 2022 under the Freedom of Information Act is stamped: "Sensitive But Unclassified."

USDA investigators expressed concern about the lack of chlorination in the center's wastewater treatment system when the first breeding colony

monkey was necropsied at the center's veterinary hospital after being euthanized for its Bp infection on November 26, 2014.

"The possibility of B. pseudomallei in the environment around the field
cages cannot be ruled out," the USDA report says.

While Bp had not been found in tests of water or soil, the report said too
few samples had been collected to detect a small amount of the organism.

There were many opportunities for Bp to remain viable in the water
around the primate center and beyond. "Chlorine concentrations in the
wetland treatment area [for wastewater] are not sufficient to kill the organism," the report said.

The USDA investigators were concerned that the center's wastewater
wasn't always thoroughly decontaminated before it was discharged into the
nearby Bogue Falaya River. The river, they noted, "is within the optimal
temperature range for *B. pseudomallei* April through October."

The Louisiana Department of Environmental Quality's records, the
USDA team noted, showed the center's wastewater discharges "frequently
exceed allowable levels" of fecal coliform—a type of bacteria that is used as
an indicator of ineffective treatment.

"Fecal coliform counts more than 100 times the monthly permitted
amount demonstrate the ability for organisms to survive TNPRC's water
treatment," the report said.

And the risks of the primate center ineffectively treating its wastewater
went up during severe rainfall events.

"When rainfall is greater than 1 inch, water bypasses the treatment processing," the USDA report said. When such a surge occurs, "this water is
untreated and drains into the local waterways."

THE USDA INVESTIGATORS WERE clearly skeptical that the monkeys that
showed signs of illness while still in their outdoor field cages had somehow
only become infected with Bp once they went inside the veterinary clinic.

While the vet clinic may well have helped further spread Bp infections,
the USDA report noted the first two monkeys were never given any other
diagnoses to indicate they were simultaneously suffering from additional
infections.

The USDA inspectors dug deep into Tulane's veterinary records to raise concerns that the pathogen may have been spreading within the breeding colony long before the first two monkeys fell ill in November 2014.

Remember how the first test results on those monkeys initially misdiagnosed them as being infected with *Pseudomonas* bacteria?

The center's veterinary records showed several other monkeys with *Pseudomonas* infections as far back as May 2014 and others with medical symptoms similar to those experienced by the first two monkeys.

Pseudomonas and *Burkholderia* bacteria have so many similarities that tests can't always tell them apart. In fact, until it was reclassified in the 1990s, *Burkholderia pseudomallei* was called *Pseudomonas pseudomallei*.[68]

The USDA's detailed analysis of the soil in Louisiana—including the soil pH, moisture, and temperature, as well as the overall climate—found it was an environment where Bp bacteria could establish a foothold and start slowly multiplying over time.

"If *B. pseudomallei* did escape, the environmental conditions around St. Tammany Parish are similar to those of endemic areas, making environmental establishment a possibility," the USDA team wrote. "The long-term consequences could be intermittent cases of melioidosis in livestock and pets."

Humans, too, would likely suffer infections, but they were beyond the scope of the USDA review.

In other countries, water and storms are often associated with outbreaks of Bp infections, and the investigators noted that Louisiana's frequent tropical storms and hurricanes had the potential to spread the bacteria far beyond the local area.

The lack of soil or water tests detecting Bp didn't mean the bacteria wasn't in the soil and waterways around the primate center, the report said.

"Because *B. pseudomallei* proliferates in soil, a small amount of *B. pseudomallei* in the environment may not be detectible immediately," they wrote, "but over time more cases would be expected in animals, particularly following significant wind/rain events."

Tulane officials declined to answer my questions about the USDA risk assessment's findings.

"The questions that you ask are based on an assessment of an incident that occurred nearly eight years ago and offer conjectures, using incomplete and self-selected information, about possible risks to the environment and public health following that incident," Michael Strecker, Tulane's assistant vice president for communications, said in an emailed response in 2022.[69]

"From the time of the incident you reference to the present day, comprehensive testing by numerous federal and state agencies, as well as independent laboratories, has shown no evidence of human or environmental exposure to BP as a result of activities at the TNPRC," Strecker said. "In response to the 2015 incident, we have improved our biosafety program which is widely regarded as a model program for other institutions throughout the country."

IN OCTOBER 2017, THE USDA offered the Tulane National Primate Research Center a deal to settle multiple biosafety, security, and incident response violations of the Agricultural Bioterrorism Protection Act of 2002 stemming from its Bp release incident.

The USDA's settlement letter[70] noted that the primate center could face fines of up to $600,000. But if Tulane waived its right to a hearing and agreed to pay a reduced fine, they could do so for $39,062.50.

Tulane took the deal and paid the fine.[71]

Today, all these years after the Bp outbreak began with the first monkeys falling ill in their outdoor field cages, Tulane says that hundreds of tests have failed to detect the bacteria: not in soil or water or monkeys or wildlife or its employees.

"All tests for B. pseudomallei among TNPRC employees in 2015 were negative, and the bacteria have never been found in wildlife tested on the center's grounds or in the surrounding community," the center said in an emailed statement to me in 2021.

"The TNPRC breeding colony of nonhuman primates has been regularly tested for B. pseudomallei beginning in 2015 and since that time, all have tested negative. Since 2015, year over year testing of thousands of animals in the breeding colony has never produced evidence of the bacteria in the breeding colony's nonhuman primates.

"If the bacteria were in the center's outdoor facilities, it would first appear in this population. Similarly, testing of environmental samples has never found evidence of the bacteria in the center's soil, wastewater or run-off," Tulane said in the statement.[72]

The statement wasn't entirely accurate. Some wildlife on and around the primate center property actually did test positive for Bp in 2015, according to the USDA risk assessment that Tulane wanted kept secret. Yet further testing had not been able to grow the bacteria out of specimens taken from these animals.

"These findings indicate either cross reaction with another organism in the environment or infection that cannot be cultured," the USDA risk assessment said.

Tulane said experts, including at the CDC, had deemed the wildlife tests to be "false positives."

Did Louisiana get lucky and no Bp took root outdoors despite Tulane's practices? Or is the bacteria still out there slowly growing somewhere, but in colonies too small and dispersed to be detected?

There is no way to know.

Jim LaCour, Louisiana's state wildlife veterinarian, told me in 2022 that he continues to watch for signs of Bp infections among animals in the area around the primate center.

"I still have worries to this day that it's possible it may pop back up sometime. It is a very tenacious organism. And if it can get hold in the environment, it can set up shop and live for quite some time," LaCour said. "It's always on my radar."[73]

You MIGHT THINK THAT after all of this that the Tulane primate center would be extra careful about the safety of its wastewater.

But that's not what happened.

Around the same time as the USDA was offering Tulane the settlement agreement, workers at the primate center made a new round of mistakes that yet again potentially released *Burkholderia pseudomallei*—and this time also anthrax bacteria—into the environment.

It happened in November 2017 when workers—apparently without consulting with safety officials—mucked out years of sewage sludge from the center's wastewater treatment plant that served the compound's laboratories and offices.

They removed about forty cubic yards of the sludge[74]—an amount that would be enough to fill about three dump trucks—then spread it onto the ground in a remote area of the center's property that was used for decomposing manure and cage waste from monkeys kept in the disease-free breeding colony.

It was the first time this housekeeping task had been performed since the plant became operational in January 2014. But nobody apparently checked first with the primate center's Environmental Health and Safety Office[75] to understand the safety and regulatory implications of their actions.

While the primate center's laboratory wastewater is supposed to be sterilized before getting dumped down the drain, the facility—as the USDA found—has a history of not always following proper procedures.

It's difficult to know how much risk spreading sewage sludge like this from a lab facility posed to the environment.

Charles Haas, a wastewater treatment expert and professor of environmental engineering at Drexel University in Philadelphia, told me that regulations usually require sludge to undergo testing and treatment before being spread on land.

"Whether it's a microorganism or any other pollutant in a facility, the pollutants can absorb to the solids," Haas told me.[76] "Without really testing those solids before they land apply it, who knows what the impact might be."

When Tulane's safety officials learned about the sludge spreading in December 2017, they held off notifying state environmental regulators for another ten months. The reporting delay, the center later told the regulators, was because Tulane felt it needed to first investigate for itself whether a permit violation had occurred,[77] and if so, the extent of the violation.

During that time, the primate center terminated its facilities director and accepted the resignation of its wastewater consultant.[78] The primate center also hired a scientist from Northern Arizona University, who had worked for them during the previous Bp monkey infection crisis, to test the soil in the sludge-spreading areas for the presence of both *Burkholderia pseudomallei* and the bacteria that cause anthrax.

Both were hardy pathogens that had been used in the center's labs and had the potential to survive in the sludge.

In the muggy, oppressive heat of Louisiana in July 2018, Dave Wagner and his Northern Arizona University team dug 210 holes and took 416 samples across the two areas where Tulane's workers had dumped the sludge more than seven months earlier.[79] These same areas were also used for dumping what Tulane called the "spoils" from monkey cages.

None of the tests detected the pathogens.

Wagner told me he thinks enough samples were collected to find the bacteria if it were in the dump sites.

"Absence of proof is not proof of absence, right? But we found no evidence for it there," said Wagner, who has been involved in research establishing the natural presence of Bp in soil in Puerto Rico[80] and the U.S. Virgin Islands.[81]

Tulane finally notified state environmental regulators about the sludge spreading incident on October 20, 2018. In their letter, the primate center's chief operations officer, Mark Alise, conceded the facility likely violated its wastewater permit.

"However, we believe that the land application of the sludge did not have an adverse effect on the environment, did not pose a threat to public health and did not cause an emergency condition," Alise wrote, noting that Wagner's tests hadn't detected any pathogens.

It doesn't appear that the Louisiana Department of Environmental Quality (DEQ) investigated the sludge incident, until the summer of 2021—after I started asking questions.

After coming across Alise's letter while reviewing the primate center's wastewater records, I reached out to the Louisiana DEQ press office to see whether the department had done its own investigation of the sludge incident or reviewed Wagner's test results.

While I was waiting for answers to my questions, on July 28, 2021, DEQ press secretary Greg Langley called Alise,[82] the primate center's chief operations officer, to ask for a copy of Wagner's testing report. A top official in the DEQ's compliance division followed up with a letter later the same day, again asking for the report to be emailed to the department.

Nearly a year later, DEQ officials told me the sludge spreading incident "continues to be under review"[83] and that they couldn't answer questions.

In 2021, Tulane officials asked the National Institutes of Health for millions of taxpayer dollars to improve several safety systems at the primate center's Regional Biocontainment Laboratory—including installing an effluent decontamination system to sterilize their biohazardous liquid laboratory waste.

"Effluent decontamination capabilities are desperately needed and will be realized through installation of the proposed effluent decontamination system," Tulane wrote in its application that resulted in $3.27 million from the NIH.[84] Strecker said the request involved equipment needed for future growth into new research areas and not the center's current programs, which he said comply with select agent program waste treatment requirements.[85]

Lab regulators at the CDC wouldn't answer my questions about whether Tulane reported the sludge incident to them and what, if any, investigation they did to determine any risk to the environment. They instead sent me a statement noting generally that the select agent program requires labs to decontaminate waste before disposal.

"If the [effluent decontamination system] is operating as designed and the entity is following proper methods of decontamination using the system, there should be no risk of select agent release," the CDC said.[86]

The key word in their statement: *if.*

In the United States we may want to believe that if a plausible lab-leak event occurred in this country, that our laboratories and regulatory institutions would scientifically, aggressively, and transparently pursue the truth and tell the public what happened.

But the current oversight structure too often demonstrates a lack of sufficient will or expertise to shine a light deeply into the dark corners of our own laboratories' failings. There also seems to be a reluctance to hold researchers and facilities accountable for lax safety practices that put the public at risk.

And because Congress has empowered the secrecy of the Federal Select Agent Program, this approach to oversight is emboldened because it operates outside of public view, shielding the performance of both labs and regulators from the kind of accountability that can help reduce how often germs escape.

PART 4

PANDORA'S GAMBLE

CHAPTER 15

Engineered Microbes and Viral Ghosts

Inside the high-security Influenza Research Institute at the University of Wisconsin–Madison, two experienced scientists were pulling ferrets out of their HEPA-filtered cages on a Monday in December 2019. Another researcher, still in training, was also in the room to watch and learn.[1]

One by one, the animals were put into a biosafety cabinet, where a solution was washed into their nostrils. It's a procedure used to collect evidence of infection, and this particular experiment involved exposing the animals to a highly controversial lab-engineered strain of H5N1 avian influenza virus.

The task was routine and a bit cumbersome for the scientists, who were clad in layers of protective gear inside a sealed BSL-3 lab with extra safety enhancements.

But the virus they were working with was far from ordinary, and there should have been no room for the safety breach that was about to happen and the oversight failures that followed.

The experiment underway that day involved one of two infamous lab-made bird flu viruses that had alarmed scientists around the world when their creation became widely known in November 2011.[2] In each case, scientists had taken an avian influenza virus that is mostly dangerous to birds and manipulated it in ways that potentially increased its threat to humans.

The ultimate goal of this work was to help protect the world from future pandemics.

Yet these groundbreaking scientific feats by the team in Wisconsin, led by virologist Yoshihiro Kawaoka, and another team in the Netherlands, led by virologist Ron Fouchier, set off a heated international debate over the ethics and safety of "gain of function" research. The controversy continues to this day.

The story of how these viruses came to be created—and then how the University of Wisconsin and the Kawaoka lab would later respond to the 2019 safety breach during the ferret experiment—raises uncomfortable questions about the tremendous trust the world is placing in these kinds of labs.

We are trusting that every hour of every day their layers of laboratory containment equipment are working properly, that all of their employees are sufficiently trained, qualified, and attentive, and that their written safety and incident response protocols are followed in real-life practice.

When something goes wrong, we are trusting that these labs will immediately notify local public health officials who are responsible for preventing outbreaks and the federal authorities who oversee the safety of experiments with genetically engineered organisms.

And given that so much about this work is shrouded in secrecy, what happened in Wisconsin raises the question: Should the public be giving this trust blindly?

THE CONTROVERSIES INVOLVING KAWAOKA, Fouchier, and their engineered H5N1 viruses began eight years before the accident that would happen in Wisconsin in December 2019—a safety breach that was not an isolated event.

These two virologists in labs thousands of miles apart were seeking to address what seemed to be an urgent global health threat.

The H5N1 strain of avian influenza virus, which was first identified in 1996 in waterfowl in southern China,[3] primarily attacked birds and poultry. But on rare occasions, the virus had found a way to infect some people.

It's a worrying sign that this virus might someday evolve naturally to become a significant threat to humans.

When people have been sickened by H5N1, they have usually been in close contact with infected birds. From 1996 through early 2022, fewer than 900 human cases[4] had been reported in twenty countries.

But for these unlucky people, the H5N1 virus was unusually lethal. More than half died.[5]

So it is fortunate that the H5N1 virus isn't capable of spreading easily[6] from person to person. If the virus were ever to evolve in ways that gave it that ability, it could cause a devastating pandemic.

And yet in late 2011 the world learned that Kawaoka and Fouchier had potentially pushed the virus in that direction.

The two scientific teams had used genetic engineering and other manipulations to create H5N1 viruses that easily spread through the air between ferrets, the animal model used to study how flu viruses might behave in humans.[7]

The implications were enormous. As Fouchier once described it, the virus his lab had created was "probably one of the most dangerous viruses you can make."[8]

Fouchier's team in Rotterdam had added mutations to a strain of H5N1 virus,[9] then helped it to further evolve[10] by putting the virus into the noses of a series of ferrets. After ten rounds of passing the evolving virus through ferrets, the virus had gained the ability to spread through the air, infecting ferrets kept in separate cages.

The virus created by Kawaoka's team in Wisconsin used a different method. Their virus was made with genes from both the H5N1 virus and the H1N1 influenza strain that caused the 2009 flu pandemic that sickened humans around the world.[11] Such gene swapping can occur in nature, if an animal or person is infected with multiple flu strains.

This virus created by Kawaoka's team could spread from ferret to ferret through respiratory droplets, the kind that can be created by coughing or sneezing. While the Wisconsin virus made ferrets used in the experiment sick and caused lung lesions and weight loss, it didn't kill them.[12]

In response to the backlash over these viruses, in January 2012 Fouchier and Kawaoka, along with more than thirty other scientists around the world, published an open letter agreeing to a temporary pause on research[13] involving the creation of H5N1 viruses that were more transmissible in mammals to allow for discussion and debate about the "opportunities and challenges" posed by the work.

THE WORK DONE ON those H5N1 viruses is generally considered to be "gain of function" research, in which scientists help microbes gain new abilities such as making them easier to transmit, expanding what species can become infected, or increasing the severity of diseases they cause.

If you have heard the term "gain of function" recently, it's probably because of the heated exchanges during the Covid-19 pandemic between U.S. Senator Rand Paul (R-Kentucky) and NIH's Dr. Anthony Fauci over whether certain bat coronavirus research at the Wuhan Institute of Virology that was supported with funds from the NIH involved gain-of-function experiments.

Part of the Paul–Fauci dispute involves how the term "gain of function" is defined differently by various organizations and scientists. And it goes to how the safety concerns over making microbes more dangerous—no matter what you call the work—was never adequately addressed and comprehensively regulated when Kawaoka and Fouchier were tinkering with their H5N1 avian influenza viruses more than ten years earlier.

Supporters say that even the riskiest experiments that engineer pathogens capable of causing pandemics—sometimes called "gain of function research of concern"—provide critical information that will help lay the groundwork for defenses against disease. Too much oversight, they say, will stifle scientific advances that could lead to lifesaving vaccines, tests, and treatments.

Critics argue that the benefits of the research are speculative and not worth the risks of creating pathogens that are more dangerous than those found in nature and that the research could unleash a pandemic through an act of bioterrorism or a lab accident.

Kawaoka was steadfast that the groundbreaking research he and Fouchier were doing was urgently needed.

"Some people have argued that the risks of such studies—misuse and accidental release, for example—outweigh the benefits. I counter that H5N1 viruses circulating in nature already pose a threat," Kawaoka wrote at the time. "Because H5N1 mutations that confer transmissibility in mammals may emerge in nature, I believe that it would be irresponsible not to study the underlying mechanisms."[14]

The research by Kawaoka and Fouchier was supported—with words and funding—by some of the most prominent scientists in the United States: Dr. Francis S. Collins, director of the National Institutes of Health, and Dr. Anthony Fauci, director of the NIH's National Institute of Allergy and Infectious Diseases.

"Understanding the biology of influenza virus transmission has implications for outbreak prediction, prevention and treatment," they said in a column published in the *Washington Post* soon after the controversial research became public.[15]

Still, other scientists were alarmed by what Kawaoka and Fouchier had done.

"If accidentally released, mammalian-transmissible influenza A/H5N1 viruses could pose a greater threat to public health than possibly any other infectious agent currently under study in laboratories, because of such viruses' likely combination of transmissibility and virulence to humans," wrote the Harvard School of Public Health's Marc Lipsitch and Barry Bloom.[16]

In addition to the risks of a lab accident, there were also larger biosecurity concerns that information about how the teams had made the viruses could be used by bioterrorists with life sciences skills to create their own versions—or worse.

The potential danger posed by these two lab-created viruses was so significant that the U.S. National Science Advisory Board for Biosecurity (NSABB) asked Kawaoka, Fouchier, and the editors of the scientific journals *Science* and *Nature*, which were planning to publish their research, to withhold details from the papers that might allow others to replicate the work.[17]

The NSABB's request sparked further controversy over what some scientists saw as efforts to restrict academic freedom, impose censorship, and withhold important information from legitimate influenza researchers around the world.

"Censorship is considered the ultimate sin of original research," Michael Osterholm, director of the Center for Infectious Disease Research and Policy at the University of Minnesota and a member of NSABB at that time, told the *Washington Post*.[18] "However, we also have an imperative to keep certain research out of the hands of individuals who could use it for nefarious purposes."

Others in the virology community didn't see it that way. Columbia University microbiology professor Vincent Racaniello called the NSABB's decision a "bad day for virology," saying it "sets a precedent for censoring future experimental results whose wide dissemination would benefit, not harm, humanity."[19]

Added prominent influenza virologist Peter Palese at the Mount Sinai

School of Medicine in New York: "I think this is really hyped up, and certainly I think not to publish it is ridiculous."[20]

PALESE HAD BEEN A part of another scientific team that had stirred up controversy a few years earlier when their own genetic tinkering resurrected the 1918 influenza virus that had killed an estimated 50 million people during the world's worst influenza pandemic.[21]

In 2005, that team—which included CDC microbiologist Terrence Tumpey and scientists at several other government and academic labs—used reverse genetics to reconstruct this viral ghost based on a gene sequence pieced together in part from lung tissue samples from victims.[22]

The live virus was constructed by Tumpey inside an enhanced biosafety level 3 lab at the CDC in Atlanta.[23] To further reduce risks to other CDC staff, Tumpey worked alone in the lab and at off-hours.[24]

"Although these experiments seem dangerously foolhardy, they are exactly the opposite," Palese wrote in 2012, defending Kawaoka's and Fouchier's research against censorship by sharing the 1918 flu team's experience being allowed to publish their work.[25] "They gave us the opportunity to make the world safer, allowing us to learn what makes the virus dangerous and how it can be disabled."

While Palese and Tumpey said they thought that the world's population had at least some level of immunity to the re-created 1918 virus, others questioned the safety and merit of the experiment.

"I believe that this was research that should not have been performed," Richard Ebright, a molecular biologist at Rutgers University in New Jersey, said at the time.[26] "If this virus was to be accidentally or intentionally released, it is virtually certain that there would be greater lethality than from seasonal influenza, and quite possible that the threat of pandemic that is in the news daily would become a reality."

Over the years there have been proposals to create an international oversight structure with enforceable rules that would bring independent scrutiny to especially risky biological research.[27] But such proposals have gained little traction, with scientific societies embracing voluntary systems that rely largely on the research community policing itself.

Some argued then—and now—that stakes to humanity are enormous. In 2007 a think tank at the University of Maryland warned that the extraordinary advances in biology are "arguably becoming one of the most consequential problems of public policy ever encountered."[28]

"Unfortunately," they said, "the capacity to alter basic life processes is not remotely matched by the capacity to understand the extended implications."

By the spring of 2012, the National Science Advisory Board for Biosecurity voted in support of the publication of Kawaoka's and Fouchier's revised manuscripts.[29] And their two labs went on with their work studying various infectious diseases.

However, it wasn't long before officials at the NIH—which was funding Kawaoka's continued work with engineered H5N1 viruses—were quietly grappling with "significant concerns" about the biosafety practices at his Wisconsin laboratories.

In November 2013, Kawaoka's research team had two accidents with engineered influenza viruses, just a few days apart.

IT TOOK LESS THAN a second. The needle with an engineered H5N1 virus on it accidentally pierced through the glove and into the finger of a researcher working on a Saturday evening inside one of the University of Wisconsin–Madison's enhanced biosafety level 3 labs.[30]

The researcher was using a syringe to collect a sample from a tissue culture, a procedure that could have easily been done without a needle.[31] In fact, the lab's safety policies prohibited the use of needles except in specific circumstances—and this wasn't one of them.[32]

It was a moment of poor judgment and human error around 6:30 p.m. on November 16, 2013, that set off a series of emergency calls that would eventually raise concerns in the nation's capital.

In the minutes that followed, the scientist sprayed the puncture site with disinfectant, then ran water over the injured finger for five minutes while squeezing blood out of the wound trying to reduce the chance of infection.

Using a radio inside the lab suite, the scientist called out for help to a colleague working in a different lab in another part of the building.

By 6:34 p.m., this co-worker had reached the lab manager, who instructed the injured scientist to try to squeeze a few more drops of blood out of the finger and to keep water running over it for another ten minutes while lab safety and university infectious disease officials were notified.

Just before 7:00 p.m. the lab manager got back to the injured researcher with instructions to "put on new gloves, clean up the work area and then shower out normally. Do not hurry. Go upstairs, sit in the conference room and do not leave the building."[33]

The lab manager and another lab official made a flurry of calls, consulting with the university's infectious disease physicians and obtaining the antiviral medication Tamiflu from a nearby Walgreens.

By 8:34 p.m., they had alerted local, state, and federal public health officials.[34]

An expert at the CDC told officials at Wisconsin's state health department that while the likelihood the scientist would develop symptoms of H5N1 was "low," the needlestick "should be considered a serious exposure" and treated aggressively.[35]

The chief medical officer of the Wisconsin Department of Health Services told the university that the researcher would need to quarantine for seven days and take a treatment-level dosage of Tamiflu twice a day for ten days.[36]

Six months earlier, while seeking funding and approval for the controversial experiments, Kawaoka had assured officials at the National Institutes of Health that the university had a designated quarantine apartment.

But it turned out that wasn't the case.[37]

When the Wisconsin scientist was potentially exposed by the needlestick on that Saturday evening, lab officials called the researcher's family and told them they needed to pack up their belongings. Then the university sent a car to take them to a hotel.

And at 9:30 p.m., the injured researcher finally left the lab facility wearing an N95 mask and a glove on the wounded hand, and was driven home to wait out the seven-day quarantine while doing fever checks and taking Tamiflu.

OFFICIALS IN THE NIH office responsible for overseeing research with engineered organisms were alarmed to learn that the university didn't have a dedicated quarantine facility for such emergencies.

In a series of teleconferences that began the day after the incident, university officials told the NIH that regardless of whether an incident posed a high or low risk of infection, the Kawaoka lab's quarantine policy involved having exposed lab workers stay at home, with any family members sent elsewhere.

"This policy is not what was communicated to us in Dr. Kawaoka's application to perform research with mammalian transmissible strains of H5N1," wrote Dr. Jacqueline Corrigan-Curay, acting director of the NIH Office of Biotechnology Activities, in a follow-up letter to the university.[38]

"In a May 6, 2013, plan provided to NIH, Dr. Kawaoka indicated that he had access to a 'designated quarantine apartment' in which researchers could be placed for 10-14 days in the event of an accidental exposure," Corrigan-Curay wrote.

Trying to provide an explanation, university officials told NIH there had been a "miscommunication" between Kawaoka and the university's administration.[39,40]

Wisconsin officials justified their decision to home-quarantine the injured researcher by telling NIH that the needlestick was not expected to put the researcher at high risk of infection and that although the engineered virus contained the HA gene from H5N1, it "was determined not to be a mammalian-transmissible strain."[41] The scientist with the needlestick ultimately completed quarantine without showing symptoms or becoming ill.[42]

But even if the university were to have what it considered a high-risk exposure with a more dangerous strain, the lab worker's quarantine location would still be at home, Rebecca Moritz, a key university official responsible for safety at Kawaoka's labs, told the NIH.[43]

It was a stunning change by the university to a critical safeguard that federal officials thought was in place for the Kawaoka lab's potentially high-risk research.

The NIH demanded that Kawaoka halt all research with mammalian-transmissible H5N1 virus strains until an appropriate quarantine arrangement was put in place.[44]

A researcher's home, the NIH told the university, was not an appropriate quarantine site for Kawaoka's high-risk studies because influenza viruses can be transmissible through the air, and many residences are in high-occupancy buildings, like apartments, that share air exchange and other infrastructure.

NIH biotechnology oversight officials had additional concerns about other lax biosafety practices that had surfaced in two back-to-back incidents in Kawaoka's labs during 2013.

Just a week before the needlestick incident, another member of Kawaoka's research team was wearing what NIH later considered to be inadequate personal protective equipment when the researcher accidentally spilled a specimen containing a different strain of H5N1 virus.[45]

A culture plate had dropped to the floor while the scientist moved a stack of plates from a biosafety cabinet to an incubator on November 9, 2013. A few drops splashed onto the leg of the researcher's protective Tyvek suit. But the suit had a two-to-three-inch gap near the ankles, exposing the person's skin. None of the drops landed on the person's skin, however.

While UW officials said inspectors for the Federal Select Agent Program had never flagged the suits' ankle gap as a problem,[46] the NIH said that having bare skin in an enhanced BSL-3 lab was "unacceptable."[47]

"NIH has significant concerns regarding the biosafety practices associated with both of the recent incidents," the NIH Associate Director for Science Policy, Dr. Amy Patterson, and Deputy Director for Extramural Research, Sally Rockey, said in a letter to the university.[48]

NIH demanded the university find a dedicated quarantine facility outside workers' residences, such as a hospital isolation room, or face the suspension or termination of its grant funding.[49]

"For high risk exposures, it is critical to isolate the individual in a structure that does not have shared air exchange and can be quickly and efficiently decontaminated,"[50] the NIH told the university in December 2013.

The university and its medical team didn't want to use the UW Hospital to quarantine Kawaoka's researchers.

They had concerns about the "mental health and physical wellbeing" of researchers "as well as a potential impact on the willingness of researchers to come forward following exposures" if they are sent to restrictive hospital isolation rooms, which "are uncomfortable and confining."[51]

The university officials also worried that quarantining researchers at the hospital would increase the chances the public would learn about its lab accidents with exotic influenza viruses. With all the hospital workers and visitors coming and going, "it would be much harder to control the spread of information and as a result there would be a higher probability of incorrect information being told to [the] general public and potentially members of the media."[52]

Despite these concerns, the university eventually agreed to NIH's demands.[53] And on December 24, 2013, the NIH gave its approval for Kawaoka's lab to resume its research manipulating H5N1 virus strains that were transmissible to mammals.[54]

By 2014 THERE WAS growing discomfort at the highest levels of the U.S. government about the risk of an accident with an engineered virus.

While Wisconsin's needlestick incident in November 2013 wasn't publicly known, it had caused significant concern with officials inside the NIH. And it was soon followed by the series of high-profile accidents at federal labs in 2014—from safety breaches with anthrax and avian influenza at the CDC to the discovery of forgotten vials of smallpox that had been kept for decades in a storage room on the NIH campus.

In October 2014, citing the string of recent federal lab incidents, the White House Office of Science and Technology Policy announced an unusual "pause" on new federal funding for certain gain-of-function research while the U.S. government began an extensive study of the risks and benefits of these kinds of controversial experiments.[55] The pause involved certain experiments involving influenza viruses, but also those with MERS and SARS coronaviruses.

The federal funding pause remained in place for three years until it was finally lifted in December 2017.[56] During that time, there were multiple scientific meetings where the issues were debated, and there were reports examining the risks and benefits.[57,58,59]

Ultimately, the federal review concluded that only a "small subset" of gain-of-function studies were of greatest concern.[60] And when the NIH lifted its funding pause, it announced a new framework for how the agency would oversee future decisions about funding research that potentially increased the danger of pandemic pathogens.[61]

It was only in 2019 that some of the halted federally funded experiments were quietly allowed to begin again[62] under the revised federal oversight process,[63] which was criticized for keeping secret the details of the new experiments[64] and the basis for the government approvals.

✳

THE KAWAOKA LAB WAS one of the first to receive approval and NIH funding under this new oversight process,[65] which required a review by a secretive panel of scientific experts called the P3CO Review Group.

The odd acronym stands for "Potential Pandemic Pathogen Care and Oversight" and this review group at the U.S. Department of Health and Human Services makes recommendations to federal funding officials about whether the benefits of the research justify the risks.

The names of the experts conducting the reviews are secret as are the details of how they make decisions, a policy federal officials justify as necessary "to preserve confidentiality and to allow for candid critique and discussion of individual proposals."[66]

The criteria the P3CO Review Group uses to evaluate proposals includes assessing whether the lead scientist and institution planning the research "have the demonstrated capacity and commitment to conduct it safely and securely, and have the ability to respond rapidly, mitigate potential risks and take corrective actions in response to laboratory accidents, lapses in protocol and procedures, and potential security breaches."[67]

It is unknown whether the P3CO Review Group examined the Kawaoka group's past laboratory accidents, its previous "miscommunication" with NIH over quarantine plans, or the university's regulatory history with the Federal Select Agent Program. HHS officials didn't answer my questions about UW's biosafety history, instead issuing a general statement that the reviews consider "the potential scientific and public health benefits, biosafety and biosecurity risks, and appropriate risk mitigation strategies."[68]

It's also unclear what safety promises the Kawaoka lab was required to give to resume its federally funded research with modified H5N1 influenza viruses.

One of the greatest risks posed by this kind of research involves a scenario where a worker unknowingly becomes infected inside the lab, then unintentionally spreads the virus among friends, family, and their wider community.

As research has shown going back to the days of Arnold Wedum, when laboratory-acquired infections occur, there frequently is not any kind of recognized safety mishap.

This raises some obvious questions: What policies or procedures does the Kawaoka research team use to monitor its lab workers for infections with exotic or engineered viruses? And if an issue arises, what procedures are in place to ensure that local and state public health officials are notified so that they can help prevent an outbreak?

Kawaoka and university officials wouldn't agree to be interviewed and provided little information in response to my questions.[69]

However, UW officials wrote a detailed memo in 2015 that answered a series of questions from federal contractors about the safety practices in Kawaoka's labs.[70] The lengthy memo was created in preparation for a site visit that summer by a team of scientists from Gryphon Scientific who had been hired to conduct the federal government's study of the risks and benefits of gain-of-function research.

The Gryphon Scientific team had asked about any standard monitoring procedures used to detect the potential loss of containment of engineered pathogens prior to a worker becoming ill, such as whether surfaces in the lab were swabbed and tested.

Here's what University of Wisconsin lab officials said in their written answers, which they circulated among themselves and a local public health official the day before the July 6–7, 2015, site visit: "We do not have any standard laboratory monitoring procedures aimed at detecting potential loss of containment prior to a researcher exhibiting influenza-like symptoms or the report of an inadvertent exposure."[71]

Think about that: The way the Wisconsin lab said it monitors for a virus release, beyond an obvious accident, involves waiting for their workers to show signs of infection.

The lab said it didn't swab surfaces to test for contamination with pathogens, noting that influenza viruses aren't viable for long on surfaces.[72] But it said it takes extensive precautions to ensure the viruses they are working with stay contained. Safeguards include having equipment that allows for full air exchanges in the labs to occur more than thirteen times an hour, using comprehensive disinfection procedures at the end of all work sessions, and mopping of floors as needed, "but at least weekly" in the BSL-3+ facilities. All aerosol-generating equipment, including centrifuges, are fitted with HEPA filters or housed in a biosafety cabinet.

The Kawaoka lab said it issues thermometers to its BSL-3 workers and requires them "to self-monitor and report influenza-like symptoms."[73] And other staff are also required to report flu-like symptoms, and everyone receives annual refresher training on how to do this.

When incidents occur or if lab workers experience flu-like symptoms, the document repeatedly says that the Kawaoka lab's response would be closely coordinated in consultation with local and state public health officials.

When asked by the Gryphon team whether workers who were only "potentially exposed" would be treated differently from those who were "certainly exposed," the university gave this answer: "No. People with a known potential exposure would be immediately quarantined as described above. Following any potential exposure, the individual is immediately quarantined until there is consultation with university and local/state public health officials, the PI [principal investigator] and laboratory staff member."

Not only would "local/state public health officials" be consulted in the event of a potential exposure, but also the university further assured that there were standard procedures for contacting local health officials. And they listed a wide range of information they said would be provided to local and state health officials about a researcher involved in a potential exposure event, including the researcher's last known entry into the BSL-3 lab, the virus strains they were working with, and the specific biological features associated with those strains—including whether they had the potential for mammalian transmissibility. UW officials also represented that they would share with local health officials the quarantine or isolation procedures that would be followed.

Yet that's not what happened after the Kawaoka team had its accident during the ferret experiment in December 2019 involving its infamous strain of lab-created H5N1 influenza virus, the one that had helped spark the worldwide debate over gain-of-function research.

And in the days and weeks that followed, efforts were made to downplay the significance of the event, avoid notifying public health and oversight bodies, and keep the public and policymakers in the dark.

There was a lot at stake.

Not only would the handling of the incident draw attention to safety issues at the University of Wisconsin's lab, but it would also raise much larger questions about the rigor and effectiveness of the secretive process the U.S. government is using to oversee the riskiest experiments in which scientists are creating enhanced pathogens with pandemic potential.

WHEN THE ACCIDENT HAPPENED on December 9, 2019, Kawaoka's three scientists were working in a biosafety level 3 agriculture lab suite with enhanced safety features at the University of Wisconsin's Influenza Research Institute.[74]

This $12.5 million facility had been built specifically for Kawaoka's research. It was constructed with ten-inch-thick concrete walls, infrared surveillance beams,[75] negative air pressure, watertight and airtight seals, double HEPA-filtered exhaust air, and redundant air handling systems.

The experiment they were performing involved a virus whose name describes the components of its engineering: VN1203HA(N158D/N224K/Q226L/T318I)/CA04.[76] It was the virus described in Kawaoka's controversial H5N1 gain-of-function experiments that had been published nearly eight years earlier.[77]

It was the virus that had gained the concerning ability to spread between ferrets and had raised fears it could do this among humans.

Kawaoka's renewed studies with this virus in 2019 were one of the first two research projects approved and funded under the U.S. government's opaque new P3CO framework for overseeing research involving engineered pathogens that have the potential to cause a pandemic.[78]

The work the UW team was doing was part of the group's studies[79] seeking to understand the mechanisms[80] that would allow highly pathogenic H5N1 bird flu viruses to infect and spread among humans.

On that December day, two experienced researchers from Kawaoka's team were helping train a colleague as they collected samples from ferrets. The animals were part of a transmission experiment and had been in contact with other ferrets infected with this engineered H5N1 virus or another wild-type flu strain.

The three scientists wore several layers of personal protection equipment.[81] Their lightweight full-body Tyvek suits, made of high-density, spunbonded fibers and worn over hospital scrubs, provided a barrier against infectious droplets and splashes.

Their shoes, covered in Tyvek booties, were dedicated for use only when inside the lab. That, too, helped to guard against organisms hitching a ride to the outside world. They also wore two pairs of gloves with Tyvek sleeve covers for added protection.

One of their most important pieces of PPE was the powered, air-purifying respirator that each wore to ensure they didn't breathe any air inside the laboratory. Even though they were using a biosafety cabinet, there was always the potential for invisible, aerosolized virus to be present in the room's air.

These kinds of high-tech respirators, called PAPRs (powered air purifying respirator), encase workers' heads in a protective hood with a clear faceplate. A blower attached to a belt delivers purified air through what looks like a vacuum cleaner hose that runs up the scientist's back and attaches to the hood behind their head.

Labs are responsible for training workers how to properly assemble and use this kind of equipment.

As one of the senior researchers was preparing to start collecting samples from the next round of ferrets, the trainee realized there was a problem with their respirator.

The PAPR hose had somehow become disconnected from the unit that supplied safe, filtered air. Instead, the detached hose dangled loose in the lab's potentially contaminated air.

The hose was "immediately" reconnected, Wisconsin officials later said, and one of the experienced researchers radioed out to the lab's operations manager as the trainee began the process of exiting the lab.[82]

It was a significant incident, especially because it involved the H5N1 avian influenza virus that had been engineered to be capable of spreading in mammals—and potentially humans.

After consulting with a university lab compliance official, the trainee was told to follow the lab's quarantine procedure to keep them from coming into contact with others and spreading the virus if they were infected. The university would later say this was done "out of an abundance of caution."[83]

But at some point, a lab compliance official released the worker from quarantine.

It is unclear whether this quarantine release happened within minutes, hours, or days of the incident occurring. Nor is it clear whether university officials first consulted with any public health and oversight agencies.

The University of Wisconsin–Madison wouldn't answer most of my questions about what happened.

What I was able to piece together after months of reporting reveals troubling gaps in the oversight of high-risk experiments. And it raises questions about the ability of the current fragmented system to ensure public safety.

IF THERE WERE EVER a virus requiring that everyone follow safety and incident reporting rules, this was it. The system of oversight in place that day had been created in response to the international furor over this very virus.

Yet after the trainee's respirator hose disconnected in December 2019, the university didn't notify local or state public health officials about the incident or consult with them before discontinuing the trainee's quarantine,[84] despite representations going back years indicating this would occur following "any potential exposure."[85]

The university says it didn't need to notify them. That's because UW officials, in consultation with the university's health experts, made their own determination that no potential exposure had occurred.[86]

Officials at Public Health Madison & Dane County, the local health department, told me they have no authority over UW–Madison, which is on state property, and that they defer to the university's judgment and expertise when it comes to lab safety issues.[87]

"Public Health Madison & Dane County is not and does not need to be notified of something that was determined to not be a significant exposure. It is also not incumbent on us to further evaluate whether there was a significant exposure, if UW reports that there was not," the department said.[88]

The university also didn't immediately alert other key oversight entities that the public relies upon to ensure the safety of this kind of particularly risky research.

UW officials waited two months—until February 10, 2020—to file a report that should have been made immediately to the NIH Office of Science Policy, which oversees U.S. research with genetically manipulated organisms like the engineered H5N1 influenza virus involved in the experiment.[89,90,91]

Records show the university's internal biosafety committee, which had approved the Kawaoka lab's research, wasn't "apprised" of the December 9, 2019, incident until February 5, 2020.[92,93]

The university was less slow in reporting the incident to the federal funding officials at NIH's National Institute of Allergy and Infectious Diseases (NIAID), which provided the grant for the controversial experiments. But UW still waited ten days—until December 19, 2019—to report the incident to NIAID program staff, according to information provided to me by NIH officials.[94]

The grant's terms required immediate notification in the event of an "illness or exposure."[95] It was UW's contention, however, that "neither of the two criteria were met" because there was "no reasonable risk of virus exposure," NIH officials told me.[96] When the university eventually notified grant officials, it said it was doing so "in the spirit of transparency and responsible conduct of research," the NIH said.

The university says Kawaoka "informed his program officer at NIH in early December," before following up with an incident summary on December 19.[97]

As I pressed NIH to reconcile the agency's statement with UW's account, a few more details emerged. NIH said that the first time UW contacted anyone at the agency was on December 12, 2019—three days after the incident. That's when UW first requested a phone call from an NIAID program officer. A first discussion about the incident happened on December 13, and on December 16, during a follow-up discussion, NIAID staff asked UW to send in a written description of the incident.

Both NIAID director Anthony Fauci and NIAID principal deputy director Hugh Auchincloss "were briefed about the incident," the NIH said in a written response to my questions. But NIH would not tell me when Fauci and Auchincloss were briefed or whether they provided guidance on how the UW incident should be handled.[98]

On December 19, UW sent in a write-up about what happened and NIAID forwarded the incident information to a contact within the U.S. Department of Health and Human Services' secretive P3CO structure that oversees and approves funding for research with enhanced potential pandemic pathogens.[99]

But the P3CO process is focused on "pre-funding" reviews of "proposed" research and this incident involved experiments already underway, a spokesperson at HHS told me; the agency that had the authority to investigate was the CDC select agent program.[100]

The program's guidance indicates that a PPE failure involving a select agent pathogen, like UW's H5N1 virus, is a potential occupational exposure that is required to be reported immediately to lab regulators at the CDC.

UW officials said Kawaoka's lab immediately reported the incident to the CDC's select agent regulators.[101] But the university didn't answer my questions about why the incident was immediately reported to the CDC—and not NIH—given UW's stated position that there wasn't any potential exposure.

It is unclear whether Kawaoka's team consulted the CDC in advance of the university's decision to release the researcher from quarantine. CDC officials—including Dr. Samuel Edwin, who heads the select agent program—didn't answer my questions about this.

Just three months before the December 2019 ferret incident, CDC select agent inspectors cited the university for a "serious" violation[102] involving failure to ensure the immediate reporting of a release of a select agent pathogen outside of primary biocontainment barriers, according to a heavily redacted copy of the inspection report that I obtained under the federal Freedom of Information Act.

The CDC blacked out from the document all of the details about the incident, including the type of pathogen involved, and wouldn't answer any questions about what happened. The university would say only that this violation did not involve Kawaoka's lab.[103]

WHEN THE UNIVERSITY FINALLY notified the NIH Office of Science Policy about the ferret incident—two months after it happened—UW officials unsuccessfully tried to justify their significant delay by saying the incident was "not reportable."[104]

Wisconsin officials told the NIH Office of Science Policy that even though the trainee's PAPR tube had detached, in their view there was "no potential exposure" that had to be reported to this oversight office.[105]

The university's justifications included that the ferrets had been handled inside a certified and properly working biosafety cabinet and that the contact ferrets had only been exposed to infected ferrets for about twenty-four hours "and were not shedding virus yet."

The university also told NIH officials that "the air the observer would have breathed during the few seconds the hose was disconnected would have come from inside the PAPR hood, which would have been HEPA-filtered before the hose disconnected." The lab's report to the NIH doesn't say how they determined this.

The reason UW finally told the NIH oversight office about the incident was because officials at the Federal Select Agent Program—as well as the NIH office that funded the research—"recommended" it be reported.[106]

The report UW finally submitted to the NIH Office of Science Policy includes the following notation: "*Confidential—do not release this information without written authorization of the University of Wisconsin–Madison."

What were the consequences of UW's delayed reporting of the incident? The NIH Office of Science Policy told me it "reminded the institution about its reporting responsibilities under the *NIH Guidelines for Research Involving Recombinant or Synthetic Nucleic Acid Molecules* and noted that it should have been immediately reported to OSP."[107]

If NIH delivered that message, UW officials say they never heard it.

"Multiple people from UW-Madison took part in conversations with OSP after the incident and none of them recall OSP telling the university the incident should have been immediately reported," a UW spokesperson said by email. "This is certainly the kind of information we would have remembered or recorded in notes taken at the time."[108]

UW repeatedly pointed to a short email from an NIH analyst thanking the university for its February 10, 2020, report and adding that "the actions taken in response to this incident appear appropriate."[109] NIH says this email was only referring to UW's "biosafety actions," not to the university's failure to file an immediate report.

In the end, the trainee apparently didn't become infected. But how the university and the lab oversight system handled the incident should be cause for concern.

When I initially contacted the university, a spokesperson took issue with me asking detailed questions about the incident and the lab's policies, first saying UW officials needed more time to answer them; then, after I asked over multiple days how much time they would need, they told me to file a public records request.

"It is all too easy to sensationalize this research, to misconstrue events, and misrepresent the nature of incidents rightfully reported by institutions to regulatory agencies," said Kelly Tyrrell, UW's director of media relations, in a 1,146-word email that spoke in broad brushstrokes about the importance of research, the humanity of researchers as parents, siblings, and community members, and how sometimes there can be differences in interpretations of incident reporting requirements and about regulations.[110]

Tyrrell said UW takes safety seriously and that the Kawaoka lab has never had an incident where public health or safety have been put at risk.

"There are few people in the world trained to understand the nature of the pathogens involved, the biosafety and biosecurity measures in place and the protocols developed and followed," Tyrrell continued. "Most people are also not equipped to appropriately evaluate the risk. It is unfortunate that some seek to capitalize on this knowledge gap."

In the months that followed, UW didn't answer many of my questions. Still, Tyrrell's email made references to what she said was the lab's track record of transparency and openness with journalists.

THE UNIVERSITY OF WISCONSIN is just one of the places around the world where a small but growing number of scientists are engineering microbes in potentially dangerous ways.

When you ask experts in biosafety, public health, and national security about the kinds of laboratory safety breaches that worry them the most, they point to the subset of research that involves deadly microbes that have been engineered or synthesized in a laboratory and that are capable of spreading easily from person to person.

If such a pathogen were to be released from a lab—either accidentally, such as through a worker unknowingly becoming infected, or intentionally by a bioterrorist—the consequences could be enormous.

"There are some areas of work, which if things go wrong, could initiate major events outside a laboratory,"[111] said Dr. Tom Inglesby, director of the Johns Hopkins Center for Health Security in Baltimore, Maryland.

Inglesby, who served as a senior White House adviser on the nation's Covid-19 response during the Biden administration, supports research on highly pathogenic organisms, but has called for greater transparency and stronger oversight of the riskiest kinds of research that pose biosafety risks not just to the scientists inside the lab, but also to the public.[112]

"I am concerned about the possibility of making pathogens more harmful, more transmissible than they are in nature," he told me when we spoke during the summer of 2022. "Those are the ones that I and others have been particularly focused on the last five or ten years."

Even the safest laboratories with the best engineering and equipment are still at risk of workers making mistakes or deciding not to follow safety protocols, he said.

"We can still and do still have laboratory accidents," Inglesby said, "and should those accidents occur where research is going on to make pathogens more transmissible, more capable of epidemic spread, then there could be lab accidents that generate epidemics or even pandemics."

Advances in the field of synthetic biology have increased the stakes, making it easier and cheaper for more people to create deadly viruses from scratch using the recipes provided by publicly available genetic sequences.

Stanford bioengineering professor Drew Endy, who is seen as an ambassador and evangelist for synthetic biology, likes to tell the story of how SARS-CoV-2, the virus that causes Covid-19, first arrived in Switzerland.

"It came in over the internet," he points out, detailing how technological advances allowed for scientists to use gene sequencing to produce the equivalent of a recipe for the virus and then took a variety of steps to re-create the live virus in their lab. "And they did all that thirteen days before the first infected person showed up."

The result, Endy said, was that the internet plus synthetic biology got the virus to Switzerland two weeks before it arrived through the spreading of the pandemic. "Is that good or bad? It depends. It depends on whether or not we have a coherent set of strategies for biosecurity."

When the pandemic began, this technology was among the scientific advances that allowed scientists around the world to quickly begin working on diagnostic tests and other lifesaving tools to respond to the emergence of Covid-19.[113]

But these same technologies and techniques can be used in ways that could inadvertently or deliberately cause significant harm to public health, agricultural crops, plants, animals, the environment, or national security.

In 2016, for example, a team of Canadian scientists at the University of Alberta revealed they had synthesized horsepox virus, resurrecting this extinct animal pathogen.

They purchased the genetic building blocks for the virus from a commercial DNA synthesis company in Germany[114] and had them delivered through the mail. Their work, which took about six months and cost about $100,000,[115] simply used publicly available information to sequence and generate the virus.

While horsepox isn't a threat to humans, it is related to the deadly variola virus, which causes smallpox and can kill 30 percent of those who become infected. The Canadian team's work demonstrated the potential for similar methods to be used by bioterrorists or rogue regimes to create and unleash this eradicated pathogen.

After the Canadian team published their horsepox research,[116] they noted the biosecurity implications of the technologies they had used, saying their work "shows that no viral pathogen is likely beyond the reach of synthetic biology."[117]

In 2020, Tonix Pharmaceuticals, a U.S. biopharmaceutical company that funded the Canadian horsepox research,[118] announced that it had created a synthesized vaccinia virus[119]—which is also related to smallpox—as part of its research to develop vaccines.

These episodes were more warning flags of the enormous gaps in oversight in this area of science.

While an organization of gene synthesis companies, called the International Gene Synthesis Consortium, is working to screen gene orders to identify dangerous pathogen sequences and vet customers, the group's membership represents only about 80 percent of the world's commercial gene synthesis capacity.[120]

That other 20 percent, notes Gregory Koblentz, director of the Biodefense Graduate Program at George Mason University in Virginia, leaves "an uncomfortably large number of companies operating without any sort of regulation on what they can make and who they can sell it to."[121]

Inside Stanford's bioengineering building, Drew Endy spends a lot of time thinking about what the future might look like ten or twenty years from now.

He's excited about the potential for synthetic biology to be a revolutionary force for good in our lives, but he also sees the need for discussions to be occurring now to help create better systems of governance that will help guide that future.

Perhaps what is needed is a "biology code"—something like the framework of building codes we're all familiar with that govern safety and policy goals in how buildings are constructed. Want to put an addition on your house? You need to get a permit. Are you using a contractor? Are they licensed? And have you lined up the building inspector?

"Codes by themselves are wholly insufficient. Codes combined with licensing and inspection have a chance, right? And yes, everybody's going to complain about it. But we know that the reason they're in place is because we have policy goals we're trying to achieve, including like don't die of carbon monoxide poisoning or other things worse than that," he said. "I've never met somebody going to pull their own building permit who's excited about it. Right? Because it's a pain. But it's there for a reason."

And it frustrates Endy that there is a presumption that in the future all of this kind of work will occur inside laboratories.

"What if anybody, anywhere could make any pathogen?" he asks hypothetically.

It's the kind of question that must be part of the discussion now.

GIVEN THE PUBLIC HEALTH and national security threats posed by the pathogens created by such research, you would think that at least this subset of life sciences research would be universally and strictly regulated.

But it's not.

The governance structures around the world are a hodgepodge of voluntary biosafety and biosecurity guidance, institutional self-policing, and fragmented regulatory oversight systems.

Nobody is tracking how many or which labs around the world maintain collections of the most dangerous pathogens—either natural or lab-made—nor does anyone know how many labs are engaging experiments that are making pathogens more dangerous.

"To the best of our knowledge, there is no internationally maintained database or inventory for high consequence biological agents," Kazunobu Kojima, a World Health Organization biosafety expert, told me.[122] "WHO has no access to such information on who's doing what in terms of gain of function (GOF) or similar research work that comes with an elevated risk."

Kojima said that countries' annual emergency preparedness reports show biosafety approaches around the world are uneven, with resource-limited countries struggling to manage biosafety and biosecurity challenges.

Only a tiny fraction of countries around the world have any kind of oversight structure in place to limit who can possess especially dangerous pathogens, to screen buyers of synthetic DNA products, or to regulate so-called dual use research that carries risks of producing knowledge that can be used to cause significant harm, according to the 2021 Global Health Security Index,[123] which examined biosafety and biosecurity capacities in 195 countries.

"Even the governments that are doing the best still have gaps. The United States has quite a lot of guidance in place, but we still have significant gaps and weaknesses," said Jaime Yassif, vice president for global biological policy and programs at the Nuclear Threat Initiative, a nonprofit global security group that is involved in producing the report.[124]

While it's important to recognize and support the many positive outcomes from scientific research—everything from vaccines to biofuels—Yassif told me that safeguards must be put in place to prevent catastrophic accidents.

"There is no existing international organization that has as their primary responsibility preventing the deliberate or accidental misuse of bioscience and biotechnology or reducing emerging risks associated with these biological advances," she said.

Current international structures focus primarily on either naturally emerging infectious disease outbreaks—or on prohibitions against biological weapons.

"There's a huge, yawning divide in between, and I would say the things that fit in that gap include an accidental release event or something where it's just really unclear," said Yassif. "What do you do if you're not sure?"

The World Health Organization has significant expertise and experience in investigating and mobilizing responses to naturally occurring outbreaks. And the WHO also has worked to promote biosafety, especially in the wake of the lab escapes of the first SARS virus, including publishing a laboratory biosafety manual that has been translated into several languages and serves as a de facto code in some countries.[125]

But it can be challenging for the WHO to investigate an outbreak of ambiguous origin, especially if a country doesn't want to cooperate—as has occurred in the investigations into the origin of Covid-19.

Yassif and her organization are trying to build international support to establish a group within the United Nations Secretary-General's Office[126] that would monitor biological risk data on an ongoing basis and have the ability to quickly deploy a credible multidisciplinary team to investigate events.

To be successful, Yassif said, it will need to become an international norm and expectation that countries will cooperate with these assessments and let the team into their borders.

SINCE THE INTERNATIONAL DEBATE over Fouchier and Kawaoka's research was at its peak in 2012, the risks of lab accidents and generating information that could be used by bioterrorists have only grown.

And there are other, less obvious ways information and accidents could combine to cause a disaster.

It's something that Dr. Anthony Fauci pondered a decade ago amid the controversy over Kawaoka's and Fouchier's research. A key issue, he noted, is "whether knowledge obtained from these experiments could inadvertently affect public health in an adverse way, even in nations multiple time zones away."[127]

"Putting aside the specter of bioterrorism for the moment, consider this hypothetical scenario," Fauci wrote in a 2012 commentary article in a scientific journal, "an important gain-of-function experiment involving a virus with serious pandemic potential is performed in a well-regulated, world-class laboratory by experienced investigators."[128]

Afterward, "the information from the experiment is then used by another scientist who does not have the same training and facilities and is not subject to the same regulations. In an unlikely but conceivable turn of events, what if that scientist becomes infected with the virus, which leads to an outbreak and ultimately triggers a pandemic?"

Even in this kind of scenario, Fauci wrote back then, many scientists would believe that the benefits of the scientific knowledge gained to stay ahead of pandemic threats would outweigh the risks.

The debate today over the so-called lab-leak hypothesis includes questions about whether a scenario like what was described in this hypothetical could have caused the Covid-19 pandemic.

CHAPTER 16

Chimeras

VIROLOGIST RALPH BARIC[1] was away from his laboratory at the University of North Carolina at Chapel Hill when the U.S. government announced its moratorium on gain-of-function research in the fall of 2014. His daughter was getting married,[2] and his focus had been on the celebrations surrounding the wedding, not on his email.

By Monday morning, as he caught up on his backlog of messages, Baric was hit with the shocking realization that much of his federally funded research was being halted.

While the gain-of-function debate over the past few years had focused largely on Yoshihiro Kawaoka's and Ron Fouchier's controversial influenza experiments, the research pause announced by the White House also included certain types of experiments with SARS and MERS coronaviruses.[3]

Baric was one of the world's foremost coronavirus experts, and the restrictions seemed like they were going to have a huge impact on the studies underway in his lab.

"It took me ten seconds to realize that most of them were going to be affected," he told NPR a few weeks after the moratorium was announced.

Baric didn't think the kinds of experiments his lab was doing on coronaviruses posed the same risks as the earlier H5N1 transmission studies done in Wisconsin and the Netherlands.[4] There were important biological differences between influenza viruses and coronaviruses, and also in the ways scientists studied them in labs.

From Baric's perspective, the timing of the government's halt on certain experiments couldn't have been worse.

"Emerging coronaviruses in nature do not observe a mandated pause,"

197

Baric and another scientist said in a letter to federal officials a few weeks after the announcement.[5]

As far back as 1995, Baric had been warning that coronaviruses had the potential to become a significant threat to humans.[6] These viruses had a worryingly high rate of recombination and mutation, helping them to evade the immune protection systems of the animals they infected.

After the severe acute respiratory syndrome (SARS) coronavirus started causing dangerous cases of pneumonia in people as it swept across twenty-nine countries and regions during 2003, Baric's research got a lot more attention.

That deadly epidemic, which sickened about 8,000 and killed nearly 800,[7] showed the pandemic potential of these kinds of viruses. With that recognition came more funding. Baric also was able to upgrade his lab space at the University of North Carolina, convincing officials to convert an unused biosafety level 3 lab into a coronavirus lab.[8]

In pushing back against the 2014 funding pause on gain-of-function research, Baric noted that dangerous coronaviruses were continuing to emerge from nature, including two in 2012. One was the porcine epidemic diarrhea virus, which was a threat to agriculture, killing millions of piglets. The other, called Middle East respiratory syndrome virus, or MERS, had made the troubling leap from dromedary camels to people.

Baric's lab was helping combat the ongoing MERS outbreak, which by that time had caused more than 900 documented human infections—with about 35 percent of those people dying. The virus seemed to be a potential candidate to cause a future pandemic.

"The term 'gain of function (GOF)' has become so broadly over-used and encompassing that it now poses a serious risk to block development of new public health intervention strategies to combat the ongoing MERS-CoV outbreak," Baric said in his letter to federal officials.[9]

ONE OF THE PROJECTS underway in Baric's lab at that time involved a virus called SHC014.

It was a virus that had been discovered by scientists at the Wuhan Institute of Virology during one of their many virus-hunting trips to collect samples in bat caves in southern China.

The WIV team, and especially its lead coronavirus scientist Shi Zhengli, had gained international respect in scientific circles for their field research. Their trips to remote parts of Asia had allowed Shi's team to amass an extensive collection of coronaviruses that they were studying in their labs in Wuhan.

The WIV team had found SHC014[10] while collecting fecal samples from Chinese horseshoe bats in a cave in Kunming, in China's Yunnan Province, during 2011–2012. It was an important discovery: SHC014 turned out to be one of the two closest known relatives to the first SARS virus that caused the 2002–2003 epidemic.

Finding these viruses was part of a project that Shi had helped co-lead with Peter Daszak, president of a U.S.-based nonprofit called EcoHealth Alliance that worked on global health and conservation issues. Daszak's and EcoHealth's collaboration with Shi over the years would involve both financial support and co-authorship on several journal articles.

Nearly a decade later, after the virus that causes Covid-19 emerged to kill millions of people worldwide, the scientific relationships between Shi, Daszak, and Baric would come under intense scrutiny. Their history is integral to understanding why there are legitimate questions about whether a lab accident in Wuhan, or perhaps a biosafety lapse during a bat virus-collection trip, could have been the source of the pandemic.

But back then, Baric was just one coronavirus researcher asking another coronavirus researcher to share some data for an experiment.

He told *MIT Technology Review*[11] that he had heard Shi speak at a conference around 2012 or 2013 about some newly discovered coronaviruses, including SHC014. Baric asked her if she might be willing to share the virus's genetic sequence so that he could re-create it in his lab.

Baric was particularly interested in the sequence for its "spike" protein, a key feature that coronaviruses use to enter cells and cause infections. Shi quickly shared the sequences, even before publishing her 2013 paper.[12]

Despite the U.S. gain-of-function moratorium, the NIH allowed Baric to continue his work with SHC014,[13] eventually deciding that his experiments didn't meet the criteria to be halted.[14]

Inside his North Carolina lab, Baric created a hybrid virus using a reverse genetics system for coronaviruses that he had pioneered[15] several years earlier. He combined the spike from Shi's bat coronavirus SHC014 into the backbone of a SARS coronavirus that had been adapted for study in mice.

This lab-created hybrid virus—made up of parts of different viruses—is what is referred to in virology as a chimera. It's a name with roots in mythology, where it is often described as a creature that was part lion, part goat, and part serpent, which had the ability to breathe fire.

The chimera created in Baric's lab had the ability[16] to infect a dish of human airway cells, an indication it could pose a threat to people.

The team had thought this chimera, with its spike protein coming from a bat virus, would have to first spend time learning to infect cells in another kind of animal before it would be able to infect human cells.

That's the sequence of events that scientists think happened before the first SARS virus emerged in 2002–2003. That SARS virus went from infecting bats, to then becoming able to infect other wild animals like palm civets,[17] which in turn started spreading the virus to people when these wild or farmed creatures were sold for food in live markets.

The results of the team's experiments showed the potential for SHC014 to jump from bats directly to humans. It underscored the danger lurking in what are estimated to be thousands of coronaviruses circulating in wild bat populations, Baric said.[18]

"So this is not a situation of 'if' there will be an outbreak of one of these coronaviruses but rather 'when' and how prepared we'll be to address it," he said.[19]

Baric's creation of the chimera renewed concerns about the risks posed by experiments that made viruses more dangerous.

"If the virus escaped, nobody could predict the trajectory,"[20] Simon Wain-Hobson, a virologist at the Pasteur Institute in Paris, said at the time. Others, like Stanley Perlman, a coronavirus expert at the University of Iowa, said the chimera virus probably wouldn't be able to spread widely[21] in people without more adaptation in humans.

It's important to note, as UNC told me, that the chimera created in this study was "a very different strain" from the coronavirus that would later cause Covid-19.

Baric was prepared for the creation of the SARS-like chimera to cause a backlash. The published research paper[22] included a section detailing the enhanced biosafety and biosecurity precautions taken by his team in UNC's biosafety level 3 lab.

The "potential to prepare for and mitigate future outbreaks must be weighed against the risk of creating more dangerous pathogens,"[23] Baric and his team argued.

THREE MONTHS AFTER THE chimera paper was published, Baric's team had an accident with one of its lab-created coronaviruses.[24]

A researcher was weighing infected mice on February 4, 2016, when one bit her.[25] Its sharp little teeth pierced through her double gloves, then plunged into her right ring finger, delivering a potential injection of the virus.

The incident occurred inside the team's BSL-3 lab, despite all its safety enhancements, special gear, and protocols.

The medical director for the university's occupational health program discussed "options for isolation" with the researcher and lab officials.

Instead, the researcher was allowed to move about in the community for the next ten days while waiting to see whether she was infected. She just was asked to wear a surgical mask and report her temperature twice daily.

The university, NIH, and select agent lab regulators at the CDC refused, when I asked, to explain the potential risks to the public or discuss why the researcher wasn't quarantined until it was known she wasn't infected.

Records show Baric's lab had immediately reported the mouse bite to CDC lab regulators and provided the agency with repeated updates throughout the researcher's medical monitoring period.[26] The researcher ultimately did not get sick.

Neither NIH nor the university would describe the nature of the modifications made to the virus.[27]

Eventually, by using a federal Freedom of Information Act request, I obtained documents showing the 2016 incident involved a "mouse adapted SARS CoV (MA15)."

This lab-made MA15 virus was developed several years earlier to cause in mice the kinds of severe SARS disease symptoms experienced in humans.

When my reporting with Jessica Blake revealed the mouse bite incident[28] in an article for ProPublica in August 2020, it wasn't just news to the general public. It was the first time that grant officers at the NIH's National Institute of Allergy and Infectious Diseases—who were helping fund Baric's research—were hearing about the safety breach.

"Was this February 2016 incident reported to NIAID and, if so, for which grant was this incident report filed?" asked an email from a staffer in NIAID's Office of Extramural Research Policy and Operations, attaching a copy of our ProPublica article that had published two days earlier.[29]

Agency officials were trying "to determine whether UNC followed proper procedures with respect to reporting biosafety incidents," the staffer wrote, kicking off an email string[30] that was obtained by journalists at the Intercept as part of a Freedom of Information Act lawsuit against the NIH.

NIAID staffers found nothing about the mouse-bite incident in their files on Baric's grants.

"That just seems to indicate that they do not have their house in order," Filippa Lentzos, co-director of the Centre for Science and Security Studies at King's College London, told the Intercept.[31] "It underscores that as a funder, NIH is not the independent oversight body that you would want for this kind of research."

While the grant officers were unaware of the incident, the Baric team had properly reported it, as required, to a different branch of NIH that oversees research with genetically engineered organisms. In yet another example of the fragmented oversight of risky research, the two NIH offices apparently didn't have any mechanism or practice for sharing incident reports.

The 2016 mouse bite wasn't the only incident in Baric's lab in recent years.

From 2015 through early 2020, it was one of four incidents with lab-created SARS or MERS coronaviruses that resulted in eight UNC researchers[32] having to undergo medical monitoring as a result of potential exposures.

And in each case, records indicate these eight lab workers were allowed to move about in public while they waited to see whether they would develop symptoms. None ended up getting sick.

It was only after the Covid-19 pandemic emerged in early 2020 that records show UNC restricted one lab worker's movements following a safety breach with a lab-created coronavirus.

That UNC scientist, who was bitten in April 2020 by a mouse infected with a strain of SARS-CoV-2 adapted for growth in mice, was told to quarantine at home for fourteen days,[33] even though it wasn't clear their skin was broken.

UNC told the NIH that "we are treating this as a medium/high risk exposure."

LIKE SO MANY LABS, UNC tried to conceal from the public key details about its safety breaches, deleting references to the involvement of SARS viruses from the incident reports it was required to release to me—not only under North Carolina's public records law, but also as a condition of its NIH funding.

When UNC sent over a 170-page PDF of all incidents that labs across its campus had reported to the NIH from January 2015 to June 2020, university officials didn't disclose that they had withheld any information.[34]

Yet scattered throughout the thousands of sentences in that sometimes-mind-numbing PDF were a few places with odd spots of extra white space between words.

It turned out that UNC officials had redacted the documents in a crafty way—essentially erasing words from the records—providing no obvious markings of what they had deleted. But SARS is a short acronym, and I suspected that was what had been removed.

As a condition of receiving federal funding for its research, UNC is required to make public copies of its institutional biosafety committee's meeting minutes plus any incident reports involving genetically modified organisms. These public transparency requirements are a part of the NIH Guidelines for Research Involving Recombinant or Synthetic Nucleic Acid Molecules.[35]

To further public trust in the safety of scientific research, the principles of public participation and transparency are "integral" to the NIH Guidelines, the NIH said in a 2014 memo to hundreds of labs[36] specifically reminding them that they are required to provide these records to the public on request.

"In keeping with the NIH Guidelines, institutions may redact certain information from these documents if there are privacy or proprietary concerns. However, information that is widely available from numerous other sources (e.g., agent names and names of principal investigators) is not generally considered private or proprietary," the memo said.

But labs like UNC regularly violate these transparency requirements.

At most, if someone files a complaint about the withholding of public records—as I have dozens of times over the years—NIH staffers will simply "remind" the lab of their obligations under the NIH guidelines.

That's usually enough to get the lab to follow the rules. But it wasn't with UNC, forcing the NIH to eventually step in and tell me that the redacted pathogen names involved types of "SARS-associated Coronavirus."

The accidents at UNC came amid Baric's decades-long quest to combat coronaviruses, which the university notes contributed to the development of Moderna's Covid-19 vaccine as well as antiviral medications like remdesivir and molnupiravir.

"Dr. Baric's research has helped us chart a path to safety and recovery during the pandemic,"[37] UNC system president Peter Hans said in 2021, as Baric received an award recognizing faculty who have "made the greatest contribution to the welfare of the human race."

That same year, Baric was elected into the prestigious National Academy of Sciences, a nonprofit society of scholars founded in 1863 through an act of Congress that was signed by President Abraham Lincoln. The academy is charged with providing independent and objective advice to the nation on scientific issues.

"Baric's work has expanded our understanding of RNA virus genetics, pathogenesis, cross-species transmission, and evolution,"[38] said academy president and geophysicist Marcia McNutt, as Baric walked across the stage to sign his name into the academy's registry book during his induction ceremony.

Membership in the academy, through the vote of other academy members, is considered one of the highest honors a U.S. scientist can receive.

WHILE SCIENTISTS FROM THE Wuhan Institute of Virology were listed as co-authors of the controversial 2015 scientific paper about the SARS-like chimera, the potentially risky experiments were done at the University of North Carolina.

The credit given to the Wuhan lab was largely in recognition of the institute's top coronavirus researcher, Shi Zhengli, providing the genetic sequence[39] of the spike from the bat virus SHC014.

But Shi's team at the Wuhan Institute of Virology—with U.S. funding from the National Institutes of Health through WIV's partnership with Peter Daszak and EcoHealth Alliance—was soon working to make their own coronavirus chimeras.[40]

The Wuhan lab focused some of this genetic tinkering on a SARS-like bat virus they called WIV1.[41] The NIH says that the chimeras created with the agency's funding and published in the scientific literature and public databases "were so far distant from an evolutionary standpoint from SARS-CoV-2 . . . that they could not have possibly been the source of SARS-CoV-2 or the COVID-19 pandemic."[42]

The WIV–EcoHealth team had created their own reverse genetics system[43] based in part on work pioneered by Baric.[44] This gave Shi and her team the ability to more easily manipulate the genomes of bat coronaviruses in the ways that Baric's lab was doing in North Carolina.

THERE WAS A TROUBLING difference, however, between the safety precautions taken in Wuhan and those in North Carolina.

Shi's team at the Wuhan Institute of Virology was doing some of its work with bat coronaviruses in biosafety level 2 labs, some of their published research shows.[45]

BSL-2 labs operate with far fewer safety precautions and less high-tech equipment than the enhanced BSL-3 lab at UNC, where Baric's team wore powered air-purifying respirators to protect against inhaling the airborne viruses that they were studying.

Not only would any lab-created viruses pose risks, but so would natural bat viruses, especially those that were newly collected with properties that weren't fully understood. Field work specimens of guano and swabs from bats brought back to the Wuhan lab—and potentially teeming with unrecognized pathogens—also posed biosafety risks.

Even some of Shi's supporters—top scientific experts who leaned strongly toward the belief that the Covid-19 pandemic emerged from nature—were alarmed to learn that the Wuhan Institute of Virology had been working with risky coronaviruses in BSL-2 labs.

"That's screwed up," Columbia University virus hunter Dr. W. Ian Lipkin told former *New York Times* science writer Donald G. McNeil Jr. in 2021,[46] after learning work he considered dangerous was done in lower level labs. "It shouldn't have happened. People should not be looking at bat viruses in BSL-2 labs."

Lipkin, who has worked in China since 2003,[47] was among five co-authors of a highly influential article in a scientific journal early in the pandemic that analyzed the genome of the SARS-CoV-2 virus that caused Covid-19.[48] The article from these scientists said the virus appeared to have a natural origin and "we do not believe that any type of laboratory-based scenario is plausible."

This article that Lipkin co-authored in March 2020, with the headline "The Proximal Origin of SARS-CoV-2," was instrumental in helping fuel worldwide perceptions among scientists, world leaders, journalists, and ultimately the general public that any lab-leak hypothesis was the stuff of anti-science crackpots.

When I reached out to Lipkin in 2022 to talk with him about the impact this paper had on shaping the narrative around the origin of the virus, as well as his perspective on international biosafety practices, he said he was not giving interviews on this topic.

In a brief email exchange, Lipkin told me his view remains unchanged that the SARS-CoV-2 virus emerged in nature.

"The knowledge that would have been required to design this virus did not exist prior to the pandemic,"[49] he said. "How it jumped into the human population was the question that we tried to address. Was it through an individual infected in the field or a laboratory, or a wildlife market? The bulk of the evidence favors a market origin."

Lipkin, however, said that he had wrongly assumed that all the Wuhan Institute of Virology's work with SARS-like bat viruses had been done in the facility's maximum containment biosafety level 4 labs, where scientists work in full-body, pressurized moon suits, and there are a host of other protocols and policies to dramatically reduce the chances a worker will become infected or a microbe will escape.

"I do believe that all work with potential human pathogens should only be pursued in high level biocontainment," he told me.

It's a position Lipkin has advocated for more than a decade, despite his reputation as a driven virus hunter whose work has helped identify hundreds of infectious agents and even inspired one of the characters[50] in the 2011 movie *Contagion*, in which a fictional deadly virus sweeps the planet.

In 2012, Lipkin publicly called for the World Health Organization to develop specific biosafety requirements[51] for research with pathogens that have pandemic potential, especially when research involves experiments that enhance virulence or transmissibility.

In that commentary article in a scientific journal, Lipkin made clear that he didn't think that even biosafety level 3 containment was sufficient when scientists conduct gain-of-function experiments with a dangerous virus, such as the H5N1 avian influenza virus. Scientists can't know whether such experiments will result in a virus that is capable of spreading from person to person, he wrote.

Lipkin noted that the safety precautions used in biosafety level 4 labs involve far more than the iconic moon suits worn by scientists. BSL-4 operation guidelines also call for daily inspection of facilities and equipment, logging all entries and exits from containment, and the extensive training of workers, plus monitoring them for signs of infection.

There is a level of rigor to lab operations at BSL-4 that goes beyond the usual requirements for training, monitoring, and access control that is generally in place in BSL-3 and enhanced BSL-3-Ag labs, he said.

Because of the worldwide proliferation of BSL-3 labs—which may vary in equipment and the experience of their operators—Lipkin said it was imperative that the WHO establish "strict criteria for biocontainment" for pandemic-capable pathogens so that safety practices can be fairly applied in both low-resource and high-resource countries.

Lipkin told me the views he expressed then still apply.

A lot of the publicity surrounding the Wuhan Institute of Virology has focused on its status as the first biosafety level 4 facility in mainland China,[52] but the institute also had many lower level labs. It is unknown how often WIV scientists did bat virus work in BSL-2 labs because research published in scientific journals doesn't always include descriptions of the biosafety precautions used in experiments.

Working with bat coronaviruses at BSL-2 doesn't mean lab accidents occurred at WIV. But it adds fuel to questions about the potential for a research-related accident in Wuhan or an unrecognized infection of a researcher—two theories that are at the heart of the lab-leak hypothesis.

RALPH BARIC ALSO HAD concerns about some of the experiments being done with bat viruses in BSL-2 labs in Wuhan, something he said he wouldn't do in his own labs in North Carolina.

"Historically, the Chinese have done a lot of their bat coronavirus research under BSL-2 conditions," Baric said in a remarkable interview with science journalist Rowan Jacobsen that was published by *MIT Technology Review* in 2021.[53] "Obviously, the safety standards of BSL-2 are different than BSL-3, and lab-acquired infections occur much more frequently at BSL-2."

It is important to point out that the troubling use of BSL-2 labs at the Wuhan Institute of Virology was not flagged by the joint WHO–China study group[54] that in early 2021 reached its highly publicized conclusion that it was "extremely unlikely" that Covid-19 had come from a laboratory accident.

The conclusion was largely based on "a very long, frank, open discussion" with lab officials at the Wuhan Institute of Virology,[55] the WHO official leading the team said, as well as meetings at other labs the team visited in Wuhan. But there was no critical scrutiny or investigation and no forensic review of lab records.

In the WHO team's final report, the discussion with WIV officials about any potential lab involvement in the pandemic was included under a section labeled "Conspiracy Theories."[56]

When the report was released in March 2021, the U.S. and thirteen other countries—including Australia, Canada, Japan, Israel, and the United Kingdom—issued a statement calling for additional investigation[57] of the origin of Covid-19 that was "free from interference and undue influence."

WHO director-general Tedros Adhanom Ghebreyesus even felt the need to quickly clarify that "all hypotheses remain open and require further study," later saying there had been a "premature push"[58] to rule out the lab theory.

Peter Ben Embarek, the WHO official leading the study team of international and Chinese scientists, told Danish documentarians[59] that the Chinese members of the group had tried to stop the report from even mentioning the lab hypothesis. Ben Embarek said the Chinese members only agreed to include the lab-leak scenario "on the condition we didn't recommend any specific studies to further that hypothesis."

The potential for conflicts of interest during the joint WHO–China mission went beyond just those on the China side of the delegation.

One of the ten international scientists on the team was Peter Daszak, the president of EcoHealth Alliance and long-time research partner of Shi Zhengli and the Wuhan Institute of Virology.[60]

WHILE MANY HAVE CRITICIZED the WHO team's findings, the questions raised by Ralph Baric are particularly noteworthy given his past scientific work with the Wuhan Institute of Virology, Shi, and Daszak.

Baric, in his interview with *MIT Technology Review*, questioned what data the joint WHO–China team relied on to reach its conclusion dismissing the possibility of a lab source. The WHO team's report,[61] Baric noted, provided little detail about how research was conducted at the Wuhan Institute of Virology.

"There must be some recognition that a laboratory infection could have occurred under BSL-2 operating conditions," Baric told the *Review*'s Rowan Jacobsen. "Some unknown viruses pooled from guano or oral swabs might replicate or recombine with others, so you could get new strains with unique and unpredictable biological features."

The WIV's work in BSL-2 labs raises numerous questions that Baric said should have been reviewed in the WHO report, including about worker training, biosafety procedures, the history of exposure events, and procedures for addressing sick workers.

This lack of scrutiny is one of the reasons that Baric joined more than a dozen other scientists in May 2021 who signed a letter published in the journal *Science* that called for a "proper investigation" that took seriously both the natural and laboratory hypotheses of the pandemic.[62]

While Baric in the interview said he believed that SARS-CoV-2 is a natural pathogen that emerged from wildlife, he said the possibility of an accidental lab escape could not be excluded.

"This is serious stuff. Global standards need to exist, especially for understudied emerging viruses," Baric said.[63] "If you study hundreds of different bat viruses at BSL-2, your luck may eventually run out."

Shi Zhengli, who has led coronavirus research at the Wuhan Institute of Virology for many years, has defended the safety of her lab, telling *Science* magazine: "the research and experiments in our institute are in strict accordance with the international and national management requirements of biosafety laboratories... To date, no pathogen leaks or personnel infection accidents have occurred."[64]

But questions persist.

China's lack of transparency and refusal to cooperate with an independent investigation—along with some eyebrow-raising bits of information that have surfaced over time—have continued to fuel suspicion.

"How on earth can I offer up evidence for something where there is no evidence?" a clearly frustrated Shi said after a reporter for the *New York Times* reached her on her cell phone in mid-2021.[65] In a text message to the *Times* she wrote: "I don't know how the world has come to this, constantly pouring filth on an innocent scientist."

Those who have worked with Shi for years have praised her integrity and expressed disgust at the way she has been portrayed in the media.

"You're already guilty until you're proven innocent. You're guilty because you're in Wuhan. That's it,"[66] said Linfa Wang, director of the Emerging Infectious Diseases Program at the medical school in Singapore run by Duke University and the National University of Singapore.

Wang, who has served as the chair of WIV's scientific advisory board,[67] has collaborated with Shi on research projects for years. "In terms of moral high ground and the character," Wang said during a Facebook Live event that of all the scientists he has worked with over the years, Shi is "on top."[68]

Shi's supporters, including prominent scientists who are proponents of the natural origin hypothesis, say Shi should be taken at her word. You can't have a lab leak of a virus that the lab didn't possess. There is no evidence the WIV ever had the Covid-19 virus or any virus that could be manipulated into becoming SARS-CoV-2. And Shi says her lab never had it.

"Shi Zhengli has been pretty clear about this virus not being handled in her lab before the outbreak,"[69] said Michael Worobey, an evolutionary biologist at the University of Arizona, who also spoke at the Facebook Live event. Worobey's research has focused on links between early Covid-19 cases and the Huanan seafood market in Wuhan.[70]

"This really does require a conspiracy and a cover-up if Shi Zhengli was really doing this work with a SARS-CoV-2-like virus, then there's a sort of conspiracy to keep that secret,"[71] said Worobey, who has said there is no evidence this occurred.

SHI'S PUBLIC STATEMENTS HAVE been made amid the Chinese government's restrictions on the release of information about the origin of the virus.

In addition to delaying public warnings[72] in January 2020 about the pandemic emerging in Wuhan, China's central government issued a directive imposing a restriction on research into the origin of the new coronavirus,[73] saying "academic papers about tracing the origin of the virus must be strictly and tightly managed."

It outlined a series of required approvals that went up through the Education Ministry's science and technology department, which would then forward research for further review by a task force under the State Council.

"I think it is a coordinated effort from (the) Chinese government to control (the) narrative, and paint it as if the outbreak did not originate in China," a Chinese researcher told CNN in April 2020.[74] "And I don't think they will really tolerate any objective study to investigate the origination of this disease."

A leaked trove of government documents, obtained and published by the Associated Press,[75] included a February 24, 2020, China CDC lab notice of a new approval process for publication of coronavirus studies that was issued under "important instructions" from Chinese president Xi Jinping.

Another notice the following month said all communication about Covid-19 research needed to go through a special task force. Publication would be guided by propaganda and public opinion teams, coordinated like a "game of chess" under instructions from Xi. Anyone publishing without permission "causing serious adverse social impact, shall be held accountable," the AP reported.

Chinese officials initially focused their search for the virus's origin on a cluster of cases associated with the Huanan seafood market, where live animals were sold for food, including some that had the potential to carry SARS-like viruses.

Government officials had said they were tracing the market's suppliers and testing wild and farmed animals.

"We are close to finding the source of the virus," Tan Wenjie, a researcher for the Chinese Center for Disease Control and Prevention, told the *China Daily* for a January 26, 2020, article.[76] "We have found out which stalls on the seafood market in Wuhan had the virus. It is an important discovery, and we will investigate which animal was the source."

Scientists from the China CDC had analyzed 585 samples from the Huanan market. The thirty-three samples that tested positive for the new virus had come from twenty-two stalls and a garbage vehicle, with most of them coming from the western area of the market where wild animals were regularly traded, the *China Daily* reported.

Multiple news reports and scientific journal articles indicated Chinese officials were conducting an extensive search for an animal source, including investigating vendor records from the Huanan market and examining freezers containing animal parts.[77]

Then Chinese officials began to increasingly press a narrative that the virus had originated outside of the country, while simultaneously blocking efforts for an international investigation into the source of the virus.[78]

By May 2020, George Fu Gao, the director of the Chinese Center for Disease Control and Prevention, was being quoted in the state-owned *Global Times* as saying it was unlikely the market was the source of the outbreak.

"At first, we assumed the seafood market might have the virus, but now the market is more like a victim. The novel coronavirus had existed long before,"[79] Gao said.

✳

SOME SCIENTISTS, AS WELL as government and intelligence investigators who consider the lab-leak hypothesis to be plausible, point to China's refusal to cooperate with international investigations and a potential lack of transparency by Chinese authorities and the Wuhan Institute of Virology about the lab's collection and research.

One example is the delayed, incomplete, and sometimes inconsistent information provided by WIV scientists early in the pandemic about a virus that at the time was the closest known relative[80] of the one causing the pandemic. It was a virus that WIV researchers had collected years earlier.

On February 3, 2020, at a time when scientists and public health officials around the world were scrambling for information about the outbreak's source, Shi Zhengli and her WIV team published an important article in the journal *Nature*.[81] They described how the genome of the deadly new coronavirus that had emerged in Wuhan was only 79.6 percent similar to the severe acute respiratory syndrome coronavirus that had caused the 2002–2003 SARS epidemic. And they announced that the closest relative of the outbreak virus was a bat coronavirus called RaTG13 that was 96.2 percent identical, evidence that SARS-CoV-2 may have originated in bats.

It was an important early clue about where Covid-19 came from.

Yet the WIV team provided little information in this journal article about the history of RaTG13, beyond vaguely saying that it "was previously detected in *Rhinolophus affinis* [a type of horseshoe bat] from Yunnan province," in southwest China.

It later would come out that the WIV team's journal article had left out some key details, including that RaTG13 had been collected by WIV researchers in 2013 from a cave where there had been a deadly pneumonia outbreak among a group of miners who had been shoveling bat guano.

The February 2020 paper also didn't mention that RaTG13 was a new name for a virus that Shi and her team had previously called RaBtCoV/4991 when they wrote about it in a 2016 journal article as one of several coronaviruses found during a two-year virus hunting project during 2012–2013 in an abandoned mine shaft in Mojiang County in Yunnan Province.[82] The multiple species of bats using the cave had a high infection rate with a diverse range of coronaviruses, this earlier paper said.

These details and omissions were among many that came to light because of a disparate international confederation of unofficial investigators who called themselves DRASTIC.[83]

These sleuths came from a variety of backgrounds and countries, connecting over the internet as they searched for answers to how the Covid-19 pandemic began. Some were scientists, like Monali Rahalkar[84] at the Agharkar Research Institute in Pune, India, and Rossana Segreto,[85] who was with the microbiology department at the University of Innsbruck in Austria. Others, like an anonymous Twitter user who called himself "The Seeker," used aliases that obscured their identities as they shared their findings on the social media platform.

While some major news organizations declared, with little independent investigation, that a potential lab origin was a "fringe" or "debunked" theory,[86] these non-journalists were doing important legwork. DRASTIC members were pulling on threads of information, spotting and following up on inconsistencies, digging deep into archives of scientific journal articles and websites in China as they unearthed possible clues.

The Seeker, who turned out to be a filmmaker and teacher in India, demonstrated some ingenious reporting skills by digging into China's online database of master's and PhD theses to look for clues. "I think we filled a void that was created by the media as well as the scientific and investigative community," The Seeker, whose real name is Prasenjit Ray, told *MIT Technology Review*'s Antonio Regalado.[87]

In May 2020, The Seeker found a 2013 thesis written by a student at Kunming Medical University and posted a link to it on Twitter.[88] The thesis, which the *Wall Street Journal* would later cite in its reporting, detailed the miners' illnesses and their diagnosis with pneumonia that was likely caused by a virus. Another doctoral thesis from 2016, supervised by George Gao, who was the director of the China CDC when the Covid-19 pandemic emerged, gave a similar account and said four of the miners tested positive for SARS virus antibodies.[89]

Media organizations that later tried to send reporters to the mine were blocked by authorities. A *Wall Street Journal* reporter who managed to reach the mine by mountain bike was detained and questioned for five hours.[90]

As information kept dribbling out, Shi and her team eventually published an addendum[91] in November 2020 to their February journal article about RaTG13, acknowledging the virus's name change[92] and that it had been collected in connection with the deadly outbreak among the Mojiang miners in 2012. The addendum, however, said the miners' samples were negative for the presence of SARS-like bat viruses, and that more recent tests on the old specimens showed they were not infected with SARS-CoV-2.

At other times, Shi[93] and WIV officials[94] have said the miners were likely sickened by a fungal infection, a cause that was not mentioned in the addendum to the journal article.

Shi has disputed statements in the archived thesis that said the miners had tested positive for SARS antibodies. While early tests on the miners' samples produced some false positives, Shi told science writer Jane Qiu that no antibodies were found in the final, validated results. Qiu also reported that WIV scientists told her that the cause of the miners' illnesses remained a "mystery" and that Gao says the statement in the doctoral thesis is erroneous and possibly based on the false-positive results.[95] The WIV scientists' failure to give a clear and complete picture of the provenance of RaTG13 when they announced it was the closest known relative of the virus causing Covid-19 has contributed to questions about what else the WIV hasn't fully disclosed about its specimen holdings.

U.S. intelligence officials, in a 2021 declassified report on the pandemic's origins, noted: "Although the WIV described the sampling trip to the mineshaft in Mojiang in Yunnan Province where it collected RaTG13 in 2016, it did not explicitly state that RaTG13 was collected from the mine until 2020. Similarly, the WIV collected eight other coronaviruses from the same mine in 2015 that it did not fully disclose until 2021."[96]

In some instances, the intelligence report said, the WIV has described unpublished work in webinars and interviews prior to publication. But analysts expressed concern that "at least some relevant data on coronaviruses of interest has either been unavailable or has not been published."

Shi has said that the WIV's collections include more than 2,000 samples from bats—such as oral and anal swabs and fecal specimens—that have tested positive for the presence of various types of coronaviruses. But from those positive samples, Shi said that over fifteen years of work the

WIV team had only been able to isolate three bat coronaviruses—all of them SARS-related—that could be grown in cell cultures in their lab. RaTG13 wasn't one of them, and as a result the WIV only had this virus's genomic sequence, Shi has said.[97]

More recently the WIV team has successfully synthesized from genomic sequences three bat coronaviruses[98] that are close relatives of the first SARS virus, but all are reportedly too different from SARS-CoV-2 to have been the source of the Covid-19 pandemic.

Further fueling suspicion about the Wuhan Institute of Virology's collection was the removal of a database of viruses from the institute's website.[99] The WIV has said it was taken down because of plans to make it interactive and also because of cyberattacks.[100] As of late 2022, it was not back online.

In addition, in November 2019, around the time Covid-19 may have started spreading in Wuhan, three WIV researchers reportedly became so ill they sought hospital care, according to information from a U.S. intelligence report revealed by the *Wall Street Journal* in May 2021.[101] But the report lacked detail, and the workers could have had a seasonal illness unrelated to Covid-19. Shi has said there were no suspected or confirmed cases of Covid-19 among lab staff and antibody tests of workers were also negative.[102]

The U.S. State Department, in the final days of the Trump administration, had made a similar assertion about sick WIV researchers in a fact sheet it posted on the web,[103] and also alleged that the WIV "has engaged in classified research, including laboratory animal experiments, on behalf of the Chinese military since at least 2017."

As of late 2022, China was still refusing to cooperate with independent investigations and no sick lab workers had been publicly identified and no proof had come to light that the WIV or any other lab in China possessed the Covid-19 virus before the pandemic began.

MANY HAVE BEEN QUICK to dismiss the lab-accident hypothesis as a product of former president Donald Trump's offensive rhetoric, which included calling Covid-19 the "China virus" and use of the slur "kung flu." But concerns about a lab origin and China's resistance to any investigation have persisted during the administration of President Joe Biden.

"The failure to get our inspectors on the ground in those early months will always hamper any investigation into the origin of COVID-19," Biden said in May 2021[104] as he ordered a ninety-day push by the U.S. intelligence community to analyze data around both a natural animal origin and a lab accident, which were considered the "two likely scenarios."

Despite the additional review by the nation's intelligence agencies, no firm conclusions were reached. "All agencies assess that two hypotheses are plausible: natural exposure to an infected animal and a laboratory-associated incident," the unclassified summary[105] of the review's findings said. But analysts disagree on which is more likely—or whether any assessment can be made because so much data is lacking.

While four of the unnamed intelligence entities and the National Intelligence Council assessed that a natural animal exposure was the "most likely" origin of the initial SARS-CoV-2 infection, they did so only with "low confidence." These analysts gave weight to the fact that this is historically how new viruses emerge, coupled with the wide range of animals susceptible to SARS-CoV-2 infection involved in China's wildlife trade, farming, and sale, a longer declassified version of the full report[106] said.

Most of the intelligence analysts thought the virus causing Covid-19 was not genetically engineered, but again they had "low confidence" in this assessment in part because of standard lab techniques that can leave no trace that a modification has been made.

One unidentified intelligence entity assessed with "moderate confidence" that the virus originated from a lab-associated incident, "probably involving experimentation, animal handling, or sampling by the Wuhan Institute of Virology." Fueling this concern was the WIV's history of conducting research on coronaviruses under "inadequate biosafety conditions," the declassified report said.

It was also plausible that WIV researchers "may have unwittingly exposed themselves to the virus without sequencing it during experiments or sampling activities, possibly resulting in asymptomatic or mild infection," the report said.

Meanwhile, analysts from three other entities were unable to decide whether they leaned toward either hypothesis, with some favoring a natural origin, others a lab origin, and still others seeing both hypotheses as equally likely.

The intelligence agencies said they believe the virus that causes Covid-19 probably started infecting people through an initial small-scale exposure that occurred no later than November 2019, resulting in the first known cluster of cases in Wuhan that December.

Analysts think that officials in China probably did not know the SARS-CoV-2 virus existed until it was isolated from patient samples after the outbreak began. "Accordingly, if the pandemic originated from a laboratory-associated accident, they probably were unaware in the initial months that such an incident had occurred," the report said, adding that WIV personnel appear to have been similarly unaware.

"China's cooperation most likely would be needed to reach a conclusive assessment of the origins of COVID-19," the assessment concluded. "Beijing, however, continues to hinder the global investigation, resist sharing information, and blame other countries, including the United States."

A FEW MONTHS AFTER Baric's interview was published in *MIT Technology Review* expressing concerns about biosafety in Wuhan, a shocking document surfaced about a previously undisclosed research project that included his North Carolina lab, the Wuhan Institute of Virology, and EcoHealth Alliance.

The internet sleuths from DRASTIC had scored[107] a major document leak[108] from a whistleblower. It was a 2018 proposal for U.S. funding for a project that outlined plans to collect and genetically manipulate bat coronaviruses, including some research focused on a specialized feature called a furin cleavage site—the same kind of unusual feature that has drawn scrutiny in the virus that causes Covid-19.

This furin cleavage site is a part of the SARS-CoV-2 spike protein—which is not found in other similar coronaviruses—that plays a critical role in the virus's ability to cause infections and disease.[109] While some other types of coronaviruses also have furin cleavage sites, the site has been described as "peculiar"[110] for SARS-like coronaviruses.

The funding proposal for the $14.2 million project, put together by Daszak and EcoHealth, sought grant money from the U.S. military's Defense

Advanced Research Projects Agency, or DARPA. The project was called "Project DEFUSE: Defusing the Threat of Bat-borne Coronaviruses."[111]

While DARPA declined to fund the proposal,[112] the leaked document outlined a detailed research plan that included doing field work to "intensively" sample bats in cave sites where the team had previously identified SARS-like coronaviruses. The team would then sequence the spike proteins of these bat viruses, reverse engineer them, and then insert them back into bat SARS-like viruses. Then these lab-created viruses would be assessed in mouse experiments for their ability to cause SARS-like disease.

While the unfunded proposal called for much of the engineering work to be done by Baric's team at UNC, the leaked document has raised questions about whether scientists in China moved ahead with some of the proposed experiments using knowledge and technology that came from U.S. researchers.[113, 114]

Until seeing a copy of the DARPA proposal, Jesse Bloom, an evolutionary biologist at the Fred Hutchinson Cancer Center in Seattle, had believed like many scientists that it was very unlikely the virus that causes Covid-19 had been engineered. Now he's more open to the possibility.

"Although that particular proposal wasn't funded, it certainly shows that idea was on the table and under discussion," Bloom told me.[115] "When something like that only comes to light due to a leak—even when one of the members of that proposal was actually on the joint WHO–China team that was supposed to be looking into this and apparently didn't release that information—I think that has to make you circumspect about how confident you can be that you've been told everything else that's going on."

Bloom considers both a natural or a lab origin for the pandemic to be plausible. "I don't think from the scientific evidence it's possible to be confident that it was a lab accident," he said. "I also don't think it's possible to be confident that it was a zoonotic jump."

And Bloom thinks the SARS-CoV-2 furin cleavage site could have arisen by natural evolution, but it also could have been introduced into the virus.

It's an assessment of the unusual feature that has been shared by virologist David Baltimore, who received the Nobel Prize for his research into viral genetics and is president emeritus of Caltech.

"There is an insertion of 12 nucleotides that is entirely foreign to the beta-coronavirus class of virus that SARS-CoV-2 is in," Baltimore said in 2021.[116] "There are many other viruses in this class, including the closest relative of SARS-CoV-2 by sequence, and none of them have this sequence."

Is it natural? Or is it the result of engineering?

"You can't distinguish between the two origins from just looking at the sequence," Baltimore said. "So, naturally, you want to know were there people in the virology laboratory in Wuhan who were manipulating viral genetic sequences. It's really a question of history: What happened?"

Shi did not respond to my interview requests, nor did Daszak, who was listed as the principal investigator in the DARPA proposal.

When the Intercept asked Daszak whether EcoHealth Alliance or the Wuhan Institute of Virology ever inserted a furin cleavage site into bat coronavirus genetic sequence he said: "Of course not!" If such work had been done, Daszak said, it would have been published by now. "The DARPA proposal was not funded. Therefore, the work was not done. Simple."[117]

Other experts, like Michael Worobey,[118] the evolutionary biologist at the University of Arizona, have said they think the furin cleavage site evolved naturally, especially since its amino acid sequence is similar to ones found recently in some wild bat viruses from Laos.

"To me it's just not plausible that this sequence that you find in bats naturally, just a slight tweak on that, was what would have been inserted into this genome. It actually makes no sense," said Worobey.[119]

Worobey was among a large group of scientists who published a "critical review" in 2021 of the evidence surrounding the pandemic's origin that deemed a lab-accident origin "highly unlikely."[120]

The paper said there was "no evidence of prior research at the WIV" involving artificial insertion of furin cleavage sites into coronaviruses, as well as no evidence that the facility possessed a SARS-CoV-2-like virus prior to the pandemic. And the paper noted that if SARS-CoV-2 had been engineered, it wasn't constructed in the way that would be expected, saying there is "no logical reason" why scientists would create a virus with "such a suboptimal furin cleavage site" involving "an unusual and needlessly complex feat of genetic engineering."[121]

Alina Chan, a molecular biologist at the Broad Institute of MIT and Harvard, disagreed.

"If you read the DARPA proposal, they said precisely they were copying parts from nature. They were looking for natural furin cleavage sites and putting these into SARS viruses in the lab with slight tweaks," said Chan.[122] "So what we're seeing is completely consistent with a lab escape of a virus that had a furin cleavage site from nature put into it."

Wherever the furin cleavage site came from, its role in causing Covid-19 infections has been the source of so much of the world's misery since the pandemic began.

The virus's spike protein, Worobey said, serves as a sort of Velcro that sticks the virus to the cell it is seeking to invade, and then the furin cleavage site puts the virus on a "hair-trigger so that once it binds to the cell it can get in and be very infective."

"So that's the magic sauce of this virus,"[123] Worobey said. "Whether it's natural or genetically modified, this is why this virus is circulating in humans."

DESPITE LEGITIMATE CONCERNS ABOUT the biosafety practices at the Wuhan Institute of Virology, a group of prominent scientists—proponents of the theory the virus originated via live animal trade—has become increasingly vocal in deriding as conspiracy theorists, or worse, those who persist in calling for the lab-accident scenario to be investigated.

"The acrid stench of xenophobia lingers over much of this discussion. Fervent dismissals by the Chinese scientists of anything untoward are blithely cast as lies," Australian virologist Edward Holmes of the University of Sydney wrote in a column published by the Conversation in August 2022.[124]

Kristian Andersen, a virologist at the Scripps Research Institute in La Jolla, California, has regularly used Twitter to dismiss the lab-leak hypothesis as illegitimate, casting those who consider a lab origin plausible as being ignorant of science[125] or lacking sufficient credentials[126] to assess evidence, and labeling "non-science journalists" investigating the potential lab origin as being "deep in conspiracy theories."[127]

"We're dealing with conspiracy theories so no amount of evidence will put this to ▬," Andersen tweeted in August 2022.[128]

Andersen and Holmes didn't always see the lab-leak hypothesis this way.

CHAPTER 17

Secret Meetings

I N THE EARLY days of the pandemic, just as Covid-19 was starting to explode across the globe, two of the most powerful and influential scientists in the world—Anthony Fauci and Jeremy Farrar—convened a secret meeting of international experts to discuss an unnerving possibility: that the virus looked as if it had been engineered in a lab.[1]

For Fauci and Farrar—as well as for the others on the call—the suggestion that the virus might have been released from a laboratory had significant implications, if that turned out to be true. Fauci was the top infectious disease expert at the U.S. National Institutes of Health; Farrar[2] was the director of the Wellcome Trust, a global scientific charitable foundation based in London.

The organizations that Fauci and Farrar helped lead are among the largest funders of life-sciences and biomedical research in the world. And Fauci's organization at NIH had been funding research on coronaviruses at the Wuhan Institute of Virology through the agency's grant to EcoHealth Alliance.[3]

"The unusual features of the virus make up a really small part of the genome (<0.1 percent) so one has to look really closely at all the sequences to see that some of the features (potentially) look engineered," wrote Kristian Andersen of the Scripps Research Institute[4] in an email to Fauci and Farrar on the evening of January 31, 2020.

Translation: It's possible the virus had been created in a lab.

The meeting was scheduled for the next day, a Saturday, and the small group of invited scientists was asked to treat the discussion in complete confidence.

"We have a good team lined up to look very critically at this, so we should know much more at the end of the weekend," said Andersen,[5] who is an expert in infectious disease genomics. "I should mention that after discussions earlier today, Eddie, Bob, Mike, and myself all find the genome inconsistent with expectations from evolutionary theory." He noted that more analysis needed to be done, "so those opinions could still change."

The alarming possibility that the virus causing Covid-19 didn't look natural was being delivered by some of the world's leading scientists.

Eddie was Edward Holmes,[6] an evolutionary biologist at the University of Sydney in Australia. Bob was Robert Garry, a professor of microbiology and immunology at the Tulane University School of Medicine in New Orleans. And Mike was Michael Farzan, also a researcher at Scripps, who had done groundbreaking research on how the first SARS virus from 2002–2003 entered cells.[7]

Just a few days earlier, Andersen had contacted Holmes to share concerns that the virus had features in part of its genome sequence that seemed to be too perfectly adapted[8] for infecting humans.

It was almost as if the virus's furin cleavage site, which was unusual to see in these types of coronaviruses, had been inserted into the virus.

Even more troubling, Andersen had found a scientific paper[9] that showed this kind of technique had been previously used in an experiment with the original SARS virus, and there also was a major coronavirus lab—the Wuhan Institute of Virology—in the same city where the outbreak had emerged.

"Fuck, this is bad," was Holmes's initial reaction,[10] according to Farrar's account of events in his memoir, *Spike*.

Holmes contacted Farrar, who had been asking a few days earlier[11] about the possibility the virus had gotten out of a lab.

Farrar then alerted Fauci to the concerns. Fauci told me he recalled conferencing Andersen into a three-way call with Farrar to hear more.

"I suggested we bring together a multidisciplinary team," Fauci told me during a short, impromptu telephone interview[12] in June 2021. "We agreed to convene by phone the next day."

What was discussed by the larger group during the February 1, 2020, teleconference became instrumental in shaping the views of influential scientists whose published papers, prominent and prolific quotes in agenda-setting news reports, and use of social media have significantly contributed to shutting down legitimate discussion of the lab-accident hypothesis.

Without news organizations and advocacy groups suing the NIH to enforce the Freedom of Information Act, eventually forcing the public disclosure of government records, the meeting might have remained secret.

CONCERNS THAT THE NEW coronavirus had a lab origin were urgent and troubling enough that the teleconference was quickly scheduled for a Saturday.

The group of scientists invited to the call had agreed in advance that the information discussed would be kept "in total confidence and not to be shared until agreement on next steps,"[13] according to what were initially heavily redacted copies of emails about the meeting. They are among 3,234 pages of Fauci's emails on a wide range of topics that *BuzzFeed News* had to sue to force NIH to release[14] under the Freedom of Information Act.

About a dozen scientists from across the United States and around the world were invited to be on the call that day. They included Ron Fouchier, the controversial H5N1 gain-of-function research proponent from Erasmus MC in the Netherlands, as well as Marion Koopmans, the head of the center's viroscience department. (Koopmans was later named as part of the joint WHO–China mission to investigate the origins of Covid-19.)

Besides the core group of Fauci, Farrar, Andersen, and Holmes, among the others invited were Robert Garry from Tulane; Christian Drosten, director of the Charité Institute of Virology in Berlin; Andrew Rambaut, an expert in molecular evolution at the University of Edinburgh; Patrick Vallance, the U.K. government's chief scientific adviser. NIH director Francis Collins[15] dialed in from his granddaughter's swim meet in Michigan.[16]

The meeting lasted about one hour. According to the agenda, Farrar started the meeting with: "Introduction, focus and desired outcomes." Andersen was next with: "Summary." Then Holmes provided: "Comments." Then there was Q&A from the group.

"It was a very productive back-and-forth conversation where some on the call felt it could possibly be an engineered virus," Fauci said in our 2021 interview.[17] Others on the call thought the evidence was "heavily weighted" toward the virus emerging naturally from an animal.

"I always had an open mind," Fauci told me, "even though I felt then, and still do, the most likely origin was in an animal host."

At the time Fauci called my cell phone one morning, nearly all of the details about what was discussed during and after the February 1 meeting—including extensive notes from Fouchier—had been blacked out by the NIH[18] before the emails and other documents were made public.

New details would trickle out months later after congressional staff for House Republicans were allowed to review and take notes on the unredacted versions of the emails—which they made public in January 2022.[19]

It wouldn't be until November 2022 that an FOIA lawsuit brought by journalist Jimmy Tobias would force the NIH to release the complete text of many key emails.[20]

The emails show that after the meeting, Farrar collected a range of thoughts from those who had been involved in the recent discussions about the virus's origin.

Michael Farzan,[21] Andersen's colleague at Scripps, was "bothered by the furin site and has a hard time explaining that as an event outside the lab (though, there are possible ways in nature, but highly unlikely)," Farrar relayed in a February 2 email to Collins and Fauci.[22] A "likely explanation" for the unusual features of the virus, like the furin cleavage site, "could be something as simple as passaging SARS-like CoVs in tissue culture on human cell lines (under BSL-2) for an extended period [of] time, accidently creating a virus that would be primed for rapid transmission between humans."

Robert Garry from Tulane said, "I really can't think of a plausible natural scenario where you get from the bat virus or one very similar to it to nCoV..." according to Farrar's email.[23]

Andrew Rambaut sent an email to the group[24] after the meeting saying he was "agnostic." His concern: "From a (natural) evolutionary point of view the only thing here that strikes me as unusual is the furin cleavage site," Rambaut wrote. "It strongly suggests to me that we are missing something important in the origin of this virus," such as a missing host species,[25] he said, noting the lack of data and information coming out of Wuhan.

Ron Fouchier's post-meeting email[26] to the group said in part: "It is my opinion that a non-natural origin of 2019-nCoV is highly unlikely at present. Any conspiracy theory can be approached with factual information."

Fouchier then warned about the potential for a wider impact on science.

"An accusation that nCoV-19 might have been engineered and released into the environment by humans (accidental or intentional) would need to be supported by strong data, beyond reasonable doubt," he wrote.[27] "It is good that this possibility was discussed in detail with a team of experts. However, further debate about such accusations would unnecessarily distract top researchers from their active duties and do unnecessary harm to science in general and science in China in particular."

Fouchier, his Erasmus colleague Marion Koopmans, and Christian Drosten were among those who were most firmly in the natural origin camp, according to Farrar's account in his memoir.

These scientists didn't see any signs of lab involvement, essentially because the way they would go about creating a new virus would involve using parts of known viruses—viruses that they assumed would have already been described in scientific journal articles or whose genetic sequences would have been uploaded to massive international databases.

Koopmans described the meeting as the type of discussion that scientists have among themselves. "Of course, the suggestion alone that there might be something 'odd' at the start of a global pandemic is not something to think of lightly," she told me in an email exchange in November 2022.

Koopmans said that the input she provided during the meeting was based on her years working on infectious diseases that had come from animals, especially avian influenza viruses that had a history of picking up mutations that insert cleavage sites like the one that was raising eyebrows in the newly emerged coronavirus.

"Similarly, cleavage sites have been found in some other coronaviruses, just not in the SARS like lineage," Koopmans said. "That is why I (and some others in the meeting) mentioned that finding a cleavage site does not prove that this is a smoking gun. The reverse is also true: it does not prove it can NOT have been inserted in the lab. But proving a negative is virtually impossible."

Koopmans said she viewed China's farming practices and wildlife market system—which were known risk factors for the spillover of emerging viruses—as important evidence supporting a natural emergence of SARS-CoV-2.

If the virus causing the Covid-19 pandemic were a lab-created virus, "there should have been a virus very close to SARS COV 2 in the lab already, because the previously identified viruses that were studied in the lab were far too distant. Given the track record of Dr Shi, if that had happened, I would have expected a publication because she has frequently published," Koopmans said.

"Of course, all that line of reasoning goes out the window if one argues that the information from colleagues in China cannot be trusted, which seems to be a central argument in some discussions. That is not a position that I take. For such accusations, I would expect to see clear evidence," she said.

But coming out of the secret February 1, 2020, teleconference, participants' publicly available emails[28] indicate others in the group still harbored significant concerns the virus may have been created in a lab and the group had not reached any firm conclusion or even a consensus.[29]

"We decided on the call the situation really needed to be looked into carefully," Fauci told me.[30] He said the plan was for Andersen to spend the next two or three weeks taking a closer look at the genetic sequences.

Then a surprising thing happened.

Somehow between Saturday and Tuesday, Andersen went from having significant concerns about genetic engineering to calling suggestions of engineering "fringe" and "crackpot," telling another group of scientists that "the data conclusively show" the virus wasn't engineered.

What data had suddenly been discovered to "conclusively" show anything?

As of Sunday, February 2, according to the available emails between Farrar, Fauci, and Collins, scientists participating in the discussions with Andersen still held a range of opinions.[31] There is no indication in these records that the question of whether the virus had been engineered had been put to rest.

Andersen wouldn't talk with me, despite multiple requests in 2021 and 2022, about how his opinion apparently changed so dramatically in such a short period of time.

His comments dismissing any suggestion of engineering were sent on Tuesday, February 4, 2020, in an email to about ten scientists who were helping craft a letter about the new virus for the National Academies of Sciences, Engineering, and Medicine to send to the White House.

"Reading through the letter I think it's great, but I do wonder if we need to be more firm on the question of engineering," Andersen wrote to the group.[32] "The main crackpot theories going around at the moment relate to this virus being somehow engineered with intent and that is demonstrably not the case. Engineering can mean many things and could be done for either basic research or nefarious reasons, but the data conclusively show that neither was done..."

Andersen closed out the email with this: "If one of the main purposes of this document is to counter those fringe theories, I think it's very important that we do so strongly and in plain language ('consistent with' [natural evolution] is a favorite of mine when talking to scientists, but not when talking to the public—especially conspiracy theorists)."

The National Academies' letter,[33] however, didn't incorporate Andersen's suggestions to stifle questions about engineering. Instead, the February 6, 2020, letter focused on the need for more research and data.

"The closest known relative of 2019-nCoV appears to be a coronavirus identified from bat-derived samples collected in China," the National Academies letter said. The organization's leadership noted that they had consulted with leading experts in the fields of virology, infectious disease genomics, epidemiology, microbiology, coronaviruses, biosecurity, global health, and other fields.

"The experts informed us that additional genomic sequence data from geographically- and temporally-diverse viral samples are needed to determine the origin and evolution of the virus. Samples collected as early as possible in the outbreak in Wuhan and samples from wildlife would be particularly valuable," the letter said.

A FEW WEEKS LATER, on March 17, 2020, Andersen, Holmes, and co-authors Robert Garry, Andrew Rambaut, and W. Ian Lipkin published their analysis of the SARS-CoV-2 virus as a research paper titled "The Proximal Origin of SARS-CoV-2"[34] in the journal *Nature Medicine*.

To scientists around the world, as well as the science writers who cover them, it appeared that the science was settled. These were eminent scientists and the language they used in their paper was firm and definitive.

"Our analyses clearly show that SARS-CoV-2 is not a laboratory construct or a purposefully manipulated virus," their article said. After detailing their observations about the virus, the paper concluded that even the unusual features of the virus are found in nature and "we do not believe that any type of laboratory-based scenario is plausible."

The "proximal origin" paper has been extremely influential.

As of late 2022, it had been cited in more than 3,500 other publications, including scientific journal articles and policy documents; 2,100 news stories from more than 750 news outlets; 100 Wikipedia pages; and more than 74,000 tweets, according to data tracked by Altmetric,[35] which monitors the attention received by scientific research across multiple platforms. The paper ranked number three in the attention it had received among the 22.5 million research articles tracked by Altmetric.

Yet many questions remain unanswered about the backstory of this paper.

What prompted Andersen—in the span of about three days—to go from being concerned the virus wasn't natural to labeling any concerns about engineering "crackpot" and asserting to other scientists that data "conclusively" show it wasn't engineered?

I first started asking Andersen about this in an email on June 8, 2021. After getting no reply, I followed up the next day with Chris Emery, a Scripps spokesperson. Still no reply.

A week later, as I was about to publish an article in *USA TODAY*,[36] Emery emailed and said Andersen was traveling and unavailable to respond to my questions, but suggested I could instead use material in a Q&A with him the *New York Times* had just published.[37]

In it, Andersen said that many of the analyses that led to the "proximal origin" paper were completed in "a matter of days, while we worked around the clock, which allowed us to reject our preliminary hypothesis that SARS-CoV-2 might have been engineered, while other 'lab'-based scenarios were still on the table."

"Yet more extensive analyses, significant additional data and thorough investigations to compare genomic diversity more broadly across coronaviruses led to the peer-reviewed study published in *Nature Medicine*," Andersen said in the Q&A.

But how did Andersen and his co-authors do all that in less than four days? There is no indication in the published Q&A that Andersen was asked detailed questions to reconcile his quote with the timeline in the newly released records.

NIH emails indicate that Andersen and Holmes had already written the first draft of this paper on February 4, 2020—just three days after the secret teleconference and the same day Andersen was pressing for the National Academies' letter to more firmly tamp down theories about engineering.

"Here's our summary so far. Will be edited further," Holmes wrote in a February 4 email to Farrar.[38] "It's fundamental science and completely neutral as written. Did not mention other anomalies as this will make us look like loons. As it stands it is excellent basic science I think, which is a service in itself. Will finish as soon as we can."

Farrar forwarded Holmes's draft to Fauci and Collins at NIH. "Please treat in confidence—a very rough first draft from Eddie and team," wrote Farrar.

"Very thoughtful analysis," replied Collins in a February 4, 2020, email to Farrar and Fauci. "I note that Eddie is now arguing against the idea that this is the product of intentional human engineering. But repeated tissue culture passage is still an option…"

Farrar noted: "Remains very real possibility of accidental lab passage in animals…Eddie would be 60:40 lab side. I remain 50:50…"

Fauci, Farrar, and Collins briefly exchange emails about the possibility that the virus could be a result of experiments using mice that have been genetically engineered to mimic human responses to infections.

"Surely that wouldn't be done in a BSL-2 lab?" asked Collins.

"Wild West…" replied Farrar.[39]

Holmes didn't respond to my requests for an interview or comment about the February 1 meeting, the drafting of the "proximal origin" paper, or these emails. Eventually a university spokesperson said he was unavailable.[40]

Like Andersen, Holmes's view of the SARS-CoV-2 virus changed significantly after the February 1 meeting.

In fall 2022, Holmes told the scientists who host the collegial podcast

This Week in Virology that the change was a result of Fouchier and some others in the February 1 meeting explaining how if someone was going to engineer this virus, they wouldn't have made it this way.[41]

"In that discussion I flipped from being this I think is probably out of a lab, to actually, it really makes no sense," Holmes said. Then, "literally the next day," Holmes said colleagues from the University of Hong Kong sent him some data on coronaviruses found in pangolins that made some of the features of SARS-CoV-2 seem less unusual.

"I'm famously quoted online saying, 'Eddie Holmes thought that, you know, it's 60-40 for a lab leak'...But that phase lasted for like three days. Very quickly, very quickly I changed my mind because of the data. I changed my mind and not because Fauci told me," Holmes said on the podcast, "and then we wrote it up as the proximal origin paper. And that's it."[42]

The account Holmes provided leaves questions unanswered about what available emails indicate was a lack of consensus or certainty among the assembled experts in the aftermath of the February 1 meeting.

"And so I see online, I see these emails and things redacted, people saying, 'Ah ha, this is Fauci ordering people to change their mind because NIH is funding research.' And it's just complete, absolute nonsense. I know what those emails say," Holmes said on the podcast. "It says please go look at the science and tell me what it says." Fauci and Collins, he added, "should be celebrated for what they did, rather than vilified."

A PRE-PRINT VERSION OF the finished "proximal origin" paper was posted online on February 16, 2020,[43] twelve days after the rough draft was shared with Fauci and Collins. It was officially published by *Nature Medicine* a month later.

As the paper was in the process of being published by the journal, Andersen sent an email to Farrar, Fauci, and Collins. "Thank you again for your advice and leadership as we have been working through the SARS-CoV-2 'origins' paper," Andersen wrote.[44] "To keep you in the loop, I just wanted to share the accepted version with you, as well as a draft press release. We're still waiting for proofs, so please let me know if you have any comments, suggestions, or questions about the paper or the press release."

The proximal origin paper generated headlines from news organizations like:

"No, the new coronavirus wasn't created in a lab, scientists say"[45]

"Sorry, conspiracy theorists. Study concludes COVID-19 'is not a laboratory construct' "[46]

"No, the coronavirus wasn't made in a lab. A genetic analysis shows it's from nature"[47]

In his NIH Director's Blog, Collins published a 735-word column highlighting the proximal origin paper, which he said "debunks" claims the virus was engineered in a lab and deliberately released, and that it provides "reassuring findings" that the new coronavirus arose naturally.[48]

The *Nature Medicine* paper, Collins wrote, "leaves little room to refute a natural origin for COVID-19. And that's a good thing because it helps us keep focused on what really matters: observing good hygiene, practicing social distancing, and supporting the efforts of all the dedicated health-care professionals and researchers who are working so hard to address this major public health challenge."

But questions about the lab-leak hypothesis didn't go away.

"Wondering if there is something NIH can do to help put down this very destructive conspiracy, with what seems to be growing momentum," wrote Collins in an April 16, 2020, email exchange with Fauci that the NIH has fought to keep secret despite FOIA lawsuits, but that was revealed through the *in camera* document review by GOP congressional staffers.[49]

Collins shared a link to an article about Fox News anchor Bret Baier talking about "multiple sources" saying "there is increasing confidence" that the virus came from a Wuhan lab—not as a bioweapon, but through a mishap in research activities.[50]

Wrote Collins, referencing the proximal origin paper: "I hoped the Nature Medicine article on the genomic sequence of SARS-CoV-2 would settle this. But probably didn't get much visibility. Anything more we can do? Ask the National Academy to weigh in?"[51]

Fauci replied: "I would not do anything about this right now. It is a shiny object that will go away in times."[52]

Fauci, through a spokesperson, declined to be interviewed or provide comments beyond our short 2021 interview, which occurred before more details about these and other emails became public. Fauci announced in August 2022 that he would be stepping down as director of NIH's National Institute of Allergy and Infectious Diseases at the end of the year "to pursue the next chapter of my career."[53]

Collins, who stepped down as NIH director in December 2021 to go back to his lab and later serve as an acting science adviser to President Biden,[54] also declined to be interviewed or provide comments for this book.

IN THE DAYS IMMEDIATELY following the secret February 1, 2020, meeting organized by Fauci and Farrar, another submission to a scientific journal was being written that would help to further cement early public perceptions of the lab-leak hypothesis as a conspiracy theory.

The letter, which would ultimately be published in the journal the *Lancet*, was organized by Peter Daszak, the president of EcoHealth Alliance and the longtime research partner of the Wuhan Institute of Virology.

A key point of the letter, as circulated among several scientists by Daszak on February 6, 2020, was to deliver the following message from as many well-known scientists as possible: "We stand together to strongly condemn conspiracy theories suggesting that 2019-nCoV does not have a natural origin. Scientific evidence overwhelmingly suggests that this virus originated in wildlife, as have so many other emerging diseases."[55]

As Daszak emailed various scientists and gathered their input on the letter, plus their agreement to put their names on it, he sent an urgent email to Ralph Baric at the University of North Carolina at Chapel Hill.

"No need for you to sign the 'Statement' Ralph!!"[56] was the subject line on the email Daszak sent to Baric on the afternoon of February 6, 2020.

"I spoke with Linfa last night about the statement we sent round," Daszak began, referencing Linfa Wang, professor in the Programme in Emerging Infectious Diseases at Duke–NUS Medical School in Singapore.[57] "He thinks, and I agree with him, that you, me and him should not sign this statement, so it has some distance from us and therefore doesn't work in a counterproductive way."[58]

Daszak, Wang, and Baric had all been collaborators with the Wuhan Institute of Virology on the proposed DARPA research project[59] that involved engineering bat coronaviruses, but information about that unfunded grant proposal hadn't yet leaked out.

Baric agreed it was a good decision to leave his name off the letter. "Otherwise it looks self-serving and we lose impact,"[60] he replied.

Daszak listed the names of several other prominent scientists who had agreed to sign the letter and said he would send it around to some other key people. "We'll then put it out in a way that doesn't link it back to our collaboration so we maximize an independent voice."

The letter was published in the *Lancet*[61] on February 19, 2020, with the headline: "Statement in Support of the Scientists, Public Health Professionals, and Medical Professionals of China Combatting COVID-19."

The twenty-seven signatories included Daszak—who changed his mind and decided to include his own name—as well as Jeremy Farrar and Christian Drosten, who had attended the February 1 meeting.

The letter included the language condemning as conspiracy theories any suggestions that the virus wasn't natural, and even stronger assertions of scientific proof that the virus was natural.

"Scientists from multiple countries have published and analysed genomes of the causative agent, severe acute respiratory syndrome coronavirus 2 (SARS-CoV-2), and they overwhelmingly conclude that this coronavirus originated in wildlife, as have so many other emerging pathogens," the published letter said. "Conspiracy theories do nothing but create fear, rumours, and prejudice that jeopardise our global collaboration in the fight against this virus."

At the end of the letter, the authors encouraged others to add their support for the statement and to sign the letter online. And they pledged: "We declare no competing interests."

It was a statement that some readers of the *Lancet* complained wasn't accurate.

"We take those statements on trust,"[62] Richard Horton, the journal's editor in chief, would later tell a science and technology committee meeting in the U.K. House of Commons.

Horton acknowledged that concerns were quickly raised with the *Lancet* about Daszak's potential conflicts of interest. He said that *Lancet* editors debated with Daszak for months about whether or not he had a competing interest. "His view was, 'look, I'm an expert working in China on bat coronaviruses. That isn't a competing interest. It actually makes me an expert with a view that should be listened to'...It took us over a year to persuade him to declare his full competing interest."[63]

Horton said the journal doesn't have the staff to investigate authors' potential conflicts of interest.

"The whole process of scientific publication depends, rightly or wrongly, justly or unjustly, on an element of trust. We trust authors to be honest with us," Horton said. "Sometimes that system breaks down."[64]

THE LETTER ORCHESTRATED BY Daszak, coupled with the "proximal origin" paper, largely shut down efforts to examine the lab-leak hypothesis and resulted in even legitimate questions being branded as racist or the product of conspiracy theories.

"A false narrative was put in place that science shows SARS-CoV-2 entered humans through natural spillover and that is the consensus of the scientific community...suggestions otherwise are shameful and conspiracy theories," Richard Ebright, Board of Governors professor of chemistry and chemical biology at Rutgers University, told me when we spoke in 2022.

In the weeks that followed these two influential journal papers, President Donald Trump and Secretary of State Mike Pompeo made public statements implying there was evidence of a lab origin of the virus—without offering any proof. That, in Ebright's view, is what cemented perceptions of the lab hypothesis as a fringe conspiracy theory.

On Twitter, Andersen mocks those who see an organized effort to discredit the lab-leak hypothesis.

"The conspiracy theory that there is a conspiracy to label something as a conspiracy theory is a perfect example of a conspiracy theory amplified by self-proclaimed non-conspiracy theory conspiracy theorists," Andersen tweeted in January 2022.[65]

Columbia University's Jeffrey Sachs, a prominent global economist and United Nations adviser who led the *Lancet*'s Covid-19 commission for two years, has provocatively stated that he thinks the failure to investigate a lab origin of the pandemic is rooted in far more than China's failure to be transparent and cooperate.

"I'm pretty convinced it came out of U.S. lab biotechnology, not out of nature,"[66] Sachs said during a speaking appearance in Spain during the summer of 2022. "We don't know for sure. I should be absolutely clear. But there's enough evidence that it should be looked into. And it's not being investigated. Not in the United States, not anywhere. And I think for real reasons that they don't want to look underneath . . . the rug too much."

Even if China won't cooperate with an independent investigation by the WHO, there are numerous other sources of information that could be gathered in the United States and other countries that might provide clues, say those calling for an investigation of the lab-leak hypothesis.[67, 68, 69] These include emails, computer files, and other paper trails involving research partners like EcoHealth Alliance and Ralph Baric's lab in North Carolina, at funding organizations like the NIH, at the publishers of scientific journals, and in international datasets where scientists upload genomic sequences of pathogens.[70]

When the *Lancet* commission issued its final report[71] in September 2022, it warned: "In the absence of an unbiased, independent, and rigorous search for a natural origin by a multidisciplinary team of experts alongside an unbiased, independent, and rigorous investigation of the research-related hypotheses, the public's trust in science will be imperilled, with potentially grave long-term repercussions."

WITHOUT ANY FORENSIC INVESTIGATION of a potential lab origin, the fight to control the narrative surrounding the origin of Covid-19 continued to play out in 2022.

One international group of researchers and co-authors—which includes Andersen, Holmes, plus other participants in the February 1, 2020, secret meeting as well as some scientists who weren't on the call—continue to be among the most vocal proponents of the natural origin hypothesis.

They continue to make bold assertions on Twitter, in op-ed articles, and in media interviews about what they say their science shows, while deriding as conspiracy theorists, or even racists, those who think the lab accident hypothesis still deserves investigation.

Led by Andersen and Michael Worobey of the University of Arizona, their research has focused on the Huanan seafood market and the potential for live animals sold there—including species susceptible to SARS-like viruses—to have sparked the pandemic.

Worobey, like Andersen, did not respond to my requests for an interview or comments.[72] Several of the other co-authors on this market-theory research were among those who attended the February 1, 2020, meeting, including Holmes, Robert Garry, and Andrew Rambaut, and they also didn't grant interviews or provide comments.

Some of their research relies on analyses of the patient data that has been made available by Chinese authorities for the earliest cases in Wuhan—data that WHO officials have said was not fully shared and may contain significant gaps.[73, 74, 75] They also have examined a wide range of other kinds of publicly available data that indicates the Huanan seafood market was "the early epicenter of the COVID-19 pandemic."[76]

They made headlines in early 2022 when they posted a preprint research article[77] online that, before going through peer review, asserted the group's "analyses provide dispositive evidence for the emergence of SARS-CoV-2 via the live wildlife trade and identify the Huanan market as the unambiguous epicenter of the COVID-19 pandemic."

Worobey told the *New York Times* for a story about the preprint: "When you look at all of the evidence together, it's an extraordinarily clear picture that the pandemic started at the Huanan market."[78]

The *Times* covered the preprint as breaking news, posting the story on its website initially with just a few paragraphs and alerting readers: "This is a developing story." The *Times* tweeted: "New Research Points to Wuhan Market as Pandemic Origin" and "Breaking News: Two major scientific studies point to a market in Wuhan, China – not a lab in the same city – as the birthplace of the coronavirus pandemic."[79] The second scientific paper referenced in the tweet was a companion study[80] that Worobey co-authored.

Six months later, when the final peer-reviewed version of the main Huanan market paper was published in the journal *Science* in July 2022,[81] the preprint's language declaring "dispositive evidence" and "unambiguous epicenter" had been deleted.[82]

The version published in *Science* also added language that appears to acknowledge that it remains unknown how the virus got to the market, noting "there is insufficient evidence to define upstream events, and exact circumstances remain obscure." Still, the authors assessed that "our analyses indicate that the emergence of SARS-CoV-2 occurred through the live wildlife trade in China and show that the Huanan market was the epicenter of the COVID-19 pandemic."

Worobey, Andersen, Holmes, Garry, and Rambaut did not answer questions that I sent to them and their institutions' media relations teams asking why the bold language was removed from the final article.

On Twitter, Worobey has said the removal of the word "dispositive" was "a choice we made ourselves" in part because it was a legal term that was not best suited for a scientific audience, adding that the research team's results were "vastly strengthened" in the final paper.[83] Their paper included findings that the home locations of 155 of the earliest known Covid-19 cases were centered on the market "to an extent that could not be explained by chance."[84] Their paper also concluded that in the available data on early Covid-19 patients—which was provided during the WHO mission to China—those patients without a link to the market "resided significantly closer to the market than patients with a direct link to it."[85]

Koopmans, another of the paper's listed co-authors, told me by email that she thinks the significance of the wording change has been "overinterpreted."

"Of course here, the tone changed a bit in that it was less 'definitive,'" Koopmans said. "In my view, that is proper in science: as a scientist you hardly ever know anything for sure. That does not mean the level of doubt increased."

Koopmans, who did not grant an interview,[86] said by email: "I do think this is an important piece of work that provides strong evidence for introduction through the animal market system. Can I say 100% certain? No." She said further studies are needed to look for the origin of SARS-CoV-2 by tracing the farms and other sources of the animals sold in the Huanan market stalls where tests of surfaces detected the virus.

Because Koopmans was a member of the joint WHO–China study mission in early 2021 that deemed the lab origin of Covid-19 as "extremely unlikely,"[87] I was interested in her thoughts on some facts that have emerged since then, including the leaked 2018 DARPA research proposal that described plans to manipulate bat coronaviruses and also the safety concerns expressed by Ralph Baric and others about the Wuhan Institute of Virology's past use of biosafety level 2 labs for some coronavirus work.

"Your questions below are all about: what if something was going on that is hidden," Koopmans replied. "Concerns, proposed work that was not funded, things 'people may not have shared' all can be relevant but are not proof of anything. That becomes a lot of speculation and of course, I cannot know."

As of late 2022, testing of tens of thousands of animals[88] had still not found the natural source of the virus that became SARS-CoV-2.

Worobey has acknowledged this is an "evidentiary gap,"[89] attributing it in part to a lack of testing of the market's live SARS-CoV-2-susceptible animals before the facility was closed at the start of the outbreak, as well as a lack of testing at the farms that supplied the market,[90] which were also quickly closed and purged of their animals.[91] In ongoing commentary provided to news organizations and on Twitter, Worobey and some of the others in the research group aren't subtle about their opinions.

"Our two recent papers establish that a natural zoonotic origin is the only plausible scenario for the origin of the pandemic," Worobey said in a series of statements posted on Twitter in October 2022.[92]

"Conspiracy Theories about COVID-19 Help Nobody. The continued pushing of a 'lab-leak' theory is unsupported and dangerous," was the headline of an article that Worobey co-authored and published in the global affairs magazine *Foreign Policy*[93] in September 2022 the day after the *Lancet*'s Covid-19 commission released its report that called for further investigation of both the natural and lab-related hypotheses for the pandemic's origin.

"The COVID Lab Leak Theory Is Dead. Here's How We Know the Virus Came from a Wuhan Market," was the headline on the August 2022 article that Holmes wrote for the Conversation[94] in which he appears to cast continued calls for an investigation of the lab hypothesis as being xenophobic.

AROUND THE WORLD, SPURRED by the Covid-19 pandemic, a scientific building boom is underway with countries announcing plans to open even more new high-containment laboratories.

With more labs will come more risks.

The failure to conduct an independent probe of the coronavirus labs at the Wuhan Institute of Virology, as well as other research facilities in the city, shows the dangerous lack of independent and transparent international mechanisms for investigating laboratory safety issues in the United States and around the world.

Even more troubling, it once again reveals an ingrained culture of reluctance within the scientific community to investigate and police their own when it comes to conflicts between safety and science.

Like the mythical Pandora, whose curiosity compelled her to open the jar that unleashed the world's evil, every one of us is gambling on science's ability to govern itself.

There is currently little independent oversight of risky biological research around the world. In the United States, the government agencies entrusted with setting standards and overseeing safety have deeply conflicted interests: These same agencies also operate their own labs and often are funding or collaborating on the research with the same academic, private, and other government labs they are supposed to police.

We may never know whether the Covid-19 pandemic started in one of Wuhan's laboratories.

Even if it didn't, the broader dangers posed by the worldwide proliferation of these kinds of labs remain. Those risks underscore the critical need for stringent and enforced national and international lab standards and oversight, as well as a commitment to mandatory public transparency, to protect against future outbreaks.

In this moment, while the world is still mourning the millions of Covid-19-related deaths and the horror of the pandemic's catastrophic upheaval is still fresh, there is a chance to take action.

Ensuring the safety of this kind of research shouldn't be left up to scientists alone. We all face the consequences if—or when—people and systems fail.

We all have a stake in getting this right.

ACKNOWLEDGMENTS

When I started investigating laboratory accidents more than a decade ago, I was exploring a complex subject that was invisible to most people and rarely drew media attention. I never could have imagined there would eventually be such worldwide interest or that my reporting on the subject would lead to this book.

I want to thank the employees at the Centers for Disease Control and Prevention who, all those years ago, were the first to reach out to me about problems inside the agency's laboratories and make me aware of the urgent need for public scrutiny of the safety of biological research facilities. For obvious reasons, I can't acknowledge any of you by name. But my reporting on this topic—and ultimately this book—would never have happened if you hadn't had the courage to share your concerns, provide documentation, and help me expose dangerous conditions that others wanted to keep hidden.

This book also would not have happened if Howard Yoon, who would become my literary agent, hadn't reached out to me after reading one of my articles in *USA TODAY*. I especially want to thank Center Street's Alex Pappas for recognizing the importance of this reporting and going above and beyond to give me the time and space to cover this complex topic.

I am incredibly grateful for the scientists, biosafety experts, laboratory staff, and government watchdogs, many of whom are quoted in this book and others who asked not to be named, who have patiently shared their expertise. A special thank-you to Eric and Ellen Wedum, the son and daughter of Arnold Wedum, for sharing remembrances of their father. Thank you also to the families of lab workers sickened in the early days of Camp Detrick, especially Sherwood Davis's son Bruce and June Hope

Ellis's daughter Annie Whitehead, for helping me tell their stories. Thank you also to the archivists at several institutions cited throughout this book, especially to Jeff Karr of the American Society for Microbiology's archives for helping me find Arnold Wedum's papers in their collection.

I want to recognize the research assistance of Skylar Laird and Jessica Blake, now alumni of the Missouri School of Journalism, whose dogged tracking down of information and passion for public records is reflected within these pages. Thank you also to Sue Bencuya for fact-checking assistance on the manuscript.

I could not have done this book without the support of my colleagues and students at the Missouri School of Journalism, especially Dean David Kurpius, Associate Dean Fritz Cropp, Journalism Studies Faculty Chair Yong Volz, and Lawan Hamilton. Fritz, I will always be grateful for your encouragement.

This book builds on reporting I have done over the years at several news organizations. Thank you to my former colleagues at the *Atlanta Journal-Constitution*, especially Nancy Albritton, who was my editor when I covered the CDC beat. The biosafety reporting I did for many years on *USA TODAY*'s national investigative team would not have been possible without the support of former investigations editor John Hillkirk. Special thanks also to John Kelly, Nick Penzenstadler, and Tom Vanden Brook and the rest of the "Biolabs in Your Backyard" team.

It takes courage for news organizations to publish reporting that goes against the prevailing narrative. This was especially true for reporting that took the lab-leak hypothesis seriously early in the Covid-19 pandemic. Thank you to Tracy Weber at ProPublica for publishing my initial reporting in 2020, with Jessica Blake, revealing accidents with coronaviruses in Ralph Baric's UNC lab; and to Kristen DelGuzzi at *USA TODAY* for publishing my initial reporting on the secret February 1, 2020, meeting about Covid's origin and why the possibility of a lab accident shouldn't be dismissed.

Thank you to Marilyn W. Thompson and Christopher Leonard for your help navigating the book writing and publishing process. Thank you also to my former journalism professors at the University of Kansas, especially Tom Eblen and Paul Jess, and to my high school journalism instructor

John Hudnall, who all encouraged me to pursue a career in investigative reporting.

I was fortunate to have been raised in a family that loves books. Two of my aunts, Trish and Kathleen Ring, were teachers and reading specialists who nurtured my interest in writing, including by "publishing" my first books while I was a kid, binding them with cardboard covers. My mother, Jeanne Young, was a voracious reader who inspired me to always pursue the truth. I so wish she were here to read this.

I am deeply grateful for my family's understanding as I have been locked away completing this project. Thank you especially to Trish, Ted, David, Kerry, Kathy, and Jack for all your support.

Most importantly, I want to thank my amazing husband, Jeff Taylor. I could not have done this book without you. Thank you for patiently listening to me talk nonstop about labs, for reading early drafts, for encouraging me when I was exhausted, for taking care of EVERYTHING around our house so that I could stay focused, and for your willingness to give up a big chunk of our lives to this project. I am so lucky to have you in my life.

NOTES

Introduction: Covid-19, a Wuhan Lab—and a Horrifying Possibility

1 "China Opens First Bio Safety Level 4 Laboratory," AMEmbassy Beijing cable to Washington, January 19, 2018, https://www.washingtonpost.com/context /read-the-state-department-cable-that-launched-claims-that-coronavirus-escaped -from-chinese-lab/2b80aef2-f728-4c36-8875-3bf6aae1d272/?itid=lk_interstitial _manual_12. The document was released by the State Department in July 2020 after the *Washington Post* filed a Freedom of Information Act lawsuit. The existence of the cable had first been reported by *Washington Post* columnist Josh Rogin in April 2020: "State Department Cables Warned of Safety Issues at Wuhan Lab Studying Bat Coronaviruses," https://www.washingtonpost.com/opinions/2020/04/14 /state-department-cables-warned-safety-issues-wuhan-lab-studying-bat-coronaviruses/.

2 Vineet D. Menachery et al., "A SARS-like Cluster of Circulating Bat Corona-viruses Shows Potential for Human Emergence," *Nature Medicine* 21, no. 12 (November 2015): 1508–13, https://doi.org/10.1038/nm.3985.

3 Ben Hu et al., "Discovery of a Rich Gene Pool of Bat SARS-Related Corona-viruses Provides New Insights into the Origin of SARS Coronavirus," *PLoS Pathogens* 13, no. 11 (November 30, 2017): e1006698, https://doi.org/10.1371 /journal.ppat.1006698.

4 Shi Zhengli, "Reply to *Science* Magazine," *Science*, July 15, 2020, https://www.science .org/pb-assets/PDF/News%20PDFs/Shi%20Zhengli%20Q&A-1630433861.pdf.

5 "High-Containment Laboratories: National Strategy for Oversight Is Needed," U.S. Government Accountability Office, September 21, 2009, https://www.gao.gov /products/gao-09-574.

6 James W. LeDuc, email to Yuan Zhiming, "Suggestions," February 9, 2020, https://usrtk.org/wp-content/uploads/2022/04/UTMB-LeDuc-batch-1.pdf. Doc-ument obtained from the University of Texas Medical Branch through a public records request filed by U.S. Right to Know, a nonprofit consumer watchdog group that investigates biotechnology issues. 1813. See also: Shannon Murray, "Biosafety Expert Close to Wuhan Institute of Virology Urged Associates There to Address His Tough Questions about Lab Origin of SARS-CoV-2," U.S. Right to Know, December 2, 2021, https://usrtk.org/biohazards/biosafety-expert-close-to-wuhan

-institute-of-virology-urged-associates-there-to-address-his-tough-questions-about
-lab-origin-of-sars-cov-2/.

7 James Le Duc, through a spokesman, declined to be interviewed.

8 "2020 Annual Report of the Federal Select Agent Program," n.d., https://www
.selectagents.gov/resources/publications/docs/FSAP_Annual_Report_2020_508.pdf.

9 Yuan Zhiming did not respond to email requests for an interview.

10 James W. Le Duc and Yuan Zhiming, "Network for Safe and Secure Labs," *Science* 362, no. 6412 (October 19, 2018): 267, https://doi.org/10.1126/science.aav7120.

11 Le Duc and Yuan, "Network for Safe and Secure Labs."

12 Chris Buckley and Steven Lee Myers, "As New Coronavirus Spread, China's Old Habits Delayed Fight," *New York Times*, February 1, 2020, World, https://www
.nytimes.com/2020/02/01/world/asia/china-coronavirus.html.

13 Emily Feng and Amy Cheng, "Critics Say China Has Suppressed and Censored Information in Coronavirus Outbreak," *NPR*, February 8, 2020, https://www.npr
.org/sections/goatsandsoda/2020/02/08/803766743/critics-say-china-has-suppressed
-and-censored-information-in-coronavirus-outbrea.

14 "Novel Coronavirus (2019-NCoV) Situation Report – 20," World Health Organization, February 9, 2020, https://www.who.int/docs/default-source/coronaviruse
/situation-reports/20200209-sitrep-20-ncov.pdf?sfvrsn=6f80d1b9_4.

15 "Novel Coronavirus (2019-NCoV) Situation Report – 1." World Health Organization, January 21, 2020, https://www.who.int/docs/default-source/coronaviruse
/situation-reports/20200121-sitrep-1-2019-ncov.pdf?sfvrsn=20a99c10_4.

16 Y. Guan et al., "Isolation and Characterization of Viruses Related to the SARS Coronavirus from Animals in Southern China," *Science* 302, no. 5643 (October 10, 2003): 276–78, https://doi.org/10.1126/science.1087139. See also: David Cyranoski, "Bat Cave Solves Mystery of Deadly SARS Virus—and Suggests New Outbreak Could Occur," *Nature* 552, no. 7683 (December 1, 2017): 15–16, https://doi.org/10.1038/d41586
-017-07766-9.

17 Chaolin Huang et al., "Clinical Features of Patients Infected with 2019 Novel Coronavirus in Wuhan, China," *Lancet* 395, no. 10223 (February 15, 2020): 497–506. Published online January 24, 2020, https://doi.org/10.1016/S0140-6736(20)
30183-5.

18 Glenn Kessler, "Analysis | Timeline: How the Wuhan Lab-Leak Theory Suddenly Became Credible," *Washington Post*, May 25, 2021, https://www.washingtonpost
.com/politics/2021/05/25/timeline-how-wuhan-lab-leak-theory-suddenly-became
-credible/.

19 Tom Cotton (@SenTomCotton), Twitter Post and video, January 30, 2020, 11:45 a.m., https://twitter.com/SenTomCotton/status/1222923797503803392.

20 Kessler, "Analysis | Timeline."

21 Tom Cotton (@SenTomCotton), Twitter Post and video, January 30, 2020, 2:55 p.m., https://twitter.com/SenTomCotton/status/1222971592403226628.

22 "Zhengli Shi's Presentations at the NASEM U.S. China Dialogue Clean Draft v1.Docx," February 26, 2020, https://usrtk.org/wp-content/uploads/2022/04/UTMB
-LeDuc-batch-1.pdf. Documents obtained by U.S. Right to Know under a public records request filed with the University of Texas Medical Branch, 1626–30.

23 "Questions on nCoV in Wuhan lab.docx," February 9, 2020, https://usrtk.org/wp
   -content/uploads/2022/04/UTMB-LeDuc-batch-1.pdf. Documents obtained by
   U.S. Right to Know under a public records request filed with the University of
   Texas Medical Branch, 1814–16.

24 James W. LeDuc, email to David Franz, April 13, 2020, https://usrtk.org/wp-content
   /uploads/2022/04/UTMB-LeDuc-batch-1.pdf. Documents obtained by U.S. Right
   to Know under a public records request filed with the University of Texas Medical
   Branch, 806.

25 David Franz declined to be interviewed for this book.

26 Shi Zhengli did not respond to emails requesting an interview for this book.

27 Jane Qiu, "How China's 'Bat Woman' Hunted Down Viruses from SARS to the
   New Coronavirus," *Scientific American*, March 11, 2020, with updates on June 1,
   2020, https://www.scientificamerican.com/article/how-chinas-bat-woman-hunted
   -down-viruses-from-sars-to-the-new-coronavirus1/.

28 Qiu, "How China's 'Bat Woman' Hunted Down Viruses."

29 Yuan Zhiming, "Current Status and Future Challenges of High-Level Biosafety Laboratories in China," *Journal of Biosafety and Biosecurity* 1, no. 2 (September 1, 2019):
   123–27. Available online October 24, 2019, https://doi.org/10.1016/j.jobb.2019.09.005.

30 "China Opens First Bio Safety Level 4 Laboratory," AMEmbassy Beijing cable to
   Washington, January 19, 2018.

31 Shi Zhengli, "Reply to *Science* Magazine," *Science*, July 15, 2020, https://www.science
   .org/pb-assets/PDF/News%20PDFs/Shi%20Zhengli%20Q&A-1630433861.pdf.

32 Jon Cohen, "Wuhan Coronavirus Hunter Shi Zhengli Speaks Out," *Science*, July
   24, 2020, https://www.science.org/content/article/trump-owes-us-apology-chinese
   -scientist-center-covid-19-origin-theories-speaks-out.

33 Shi, "Reply to *Science* Magazine."

34 "Institute of Virology: Man-Made Coronavirus beyond Human Intelligence,"
   CGTN, April 18, 2020, https://news.cgtn.com/news/2020-04-18/Institute-of-Virology
   -Man-made-coronavirus-beyond-human-intelligence-PMUg5P6wTe/index.html.

35 Steven Lee Myers, "China Spins Tale That the U.S. Army Started the Coronavirus Epidemic," *New York Times*, March 13, 2020, World, https://www.nytimes
   .com/2020/03/13/world/asia/coronavirus-china-conspiracy-theory.html.

36 "US Urged to Release Health Info of Military Athletes Who Came to Wuhan in
   October 2019," *Global Times*, March 25, 2020, https://www.globaltimes.cn/content
   /1183658.shtml.

37 "EXPLAINER: China's Claims of Coronavirus on Frozen Foods," AP News,
   November 24, 2020, https://apnews.com/article/pandemics-beijing-global-trade
   -coronavirus-pandemic-china-28671d69256d84001a471876a6bc4077.

38 "WHO-Convened Global Study of the Origins of SARS-CoV-2 (Including
   Annexes)," World Health Organization, March 30, 2021, https://www.who.int
   /emergencies/diseases/novel-coronavirus-2019/origins-of-the-virus.

39 Kai Kupferschmidt, "'Compromise' WHO Report Resolves Little on Pandemic's Origins, but Details Probe's next Steps," *Science*, March 30, 2021, https://www.science
   .org/content/article/compromise-who-report-resolves-little-pandemic-s-origins-details
   -probe-s-next-steps.

40 "Joint Report - ANNEXES, WHO-Convened Global Study of Origins of SARS-CoV-2: China Part," World Health Organization, March 30, 2021, https://www.who .int/docs/default-source/coronaviruse/who-convened-global-study-of-origins-of-sars -cov-2-china-part-annexes.pdf. 130-133.

41 Peter Daszak (@PeterDaszak), Twitter Post, February 3, 2021, 2:30 a.m., https:// twitter.com/PeterDaszak/status/1356867745762181120.

42 Daszak and Shi did not respond to requests to be interviewed or provide comments for this book.

43 Anne Gulland, "UK Scientist with Links to Wuhan Lab 'Recuses Himself' from Inquiry into Covid Origins," *Telegraph*, June 22, 2021, https://www.telegraph.co .uk/global-health/science-and-disease/uk-scientist-centre-pandemic-origins-debate -removed-inquiry/.

44 Jon Cohen, "Prophet in Purgatory: EcoHealth Alliance's Peter Daszak Is Fighting Accusations That His Pandemic Prevention Work Helped Spark COVID-19," *Science*, November 17, 2021, https://www.science.org/content/article/we-ve-done-nothing -wrong-ecohealth-leader-fights-charges-his-research-helped-spark-covid-19.

45 Betsy McKay, "WSJ News Exclusive: Covid-19 Panel of Scientists Investigating Origins of Virus Is Disbanded," *Wall Street Journal*, September 25, 2021, Business, https://www.wsj.com/articles/covid-19-panel-of-scientists-investigating-origins-of -virus-is-disbanded-11632571202.

46 "COVID-19 Virtual Press Conference Transcript - 9 February 2021," World Health Organization, February 9, 2021, https://www.who.int/publications/m/item /covid-19-virtual-press-conference-transcript---9-february-2021. Video at: https:// www.youtube.com/watch?v=B0ZOTdEmco0.

47 In response to an interview request for this book, a WHO spokesperson said Peter Ben Embarek was "not available for interviews nor for written comments."

48 Alison Young and Nick Penzenstadler, "Inside America's Secretive Biolabs," *USA TODAY*, May 28, 2015, https://www.usatoday.com/story/news/2015/05/28/biolabs -pathogens-location-incidents/26587505/.

49 "Biolabs in Your Backyard, Digital Interactive Database," *USA TODAY*, May 28, 2015, https://www.usatoday.com/pages/interactives/biolabs/.

50 Jeremy Page and Drew Hinshaw, "China Refuses to Give WHO Raw Data on Early Covid-19 Cases," *Wall Street Journal*, February 12, 2021.

51 Stephanie Nebehay and John Miller, "Data Withheld from WHO Team Prob-ing COVID-19 Origins in China: Tedros," Reuters, March 20, 2021, https://www .reuters.com/article/us-health-coronavirus-who-china-report/data-withheld-from -who-team-probing-covid-19-origins-in-china-tedros-idUSKBN2BM26S.

52 "COVID-19 Virtual Press Conference Transcript - 15 July 2021," World Health Organization, July 15, 2021, https://www.who.int/publications/m/item/covid-19 -virtual-press-conference-transcript---15-july-2021.

53 "COVID-19 Virtual Press Conference Transcript - 15 July 2021."

54 Greg Heffer, "G7 Summit: World Leaders Discuss COVID Origins—as WHO Keeps Wuhan Lab Leak Theory 'Open,'" *Sky News*, June 13, 2021, https://news .sky.com/story/g7-summit-world-leaders-discuss-covid-origins-as-who-keeps-wuhan -lab-leak-theory-open-12331212.

55 "WHO Director-General's Opening Remarks at the Member State Information Session on Origins," World Health Organization, July 16, 2021, https://www.who.int /director-general/speeches/detail/who-director-general-s-opening-remarks-at-the -member-state-information-session-on-origins.

56 "Covid: China Rejects WHO Plan for Second Phase of Virus Origin Probe," BBC News, July 23, 2021, China, https://www.bbc.com/news/world-asia-china -57926368.

57 The White House, "Statement by President Joe Biden on the Investigation into the Origins of COVID-19," the White House, May 26, 2021, https://www.whitehouse .gov/briefing-room/statements-releases/2021/05/26/statement-by-president-joe-biden -on-the-investigation-into-the-origins-of-covid-19/.

58 "Declassified Assessment on COVID-19 Origins," Office of the Director of National Intelligence, October 29, 2021, https://www.dni.gov/index.php/newsroom/reports -publications/reports-publications-2021/item/2263-declassified-assessment-on -covid-19-origins.

59 House Energy and Commerce Committee Republicans, "The COVID-19 Origins Investigation," https://republicans-energycommerce.house.gov/the-covid-19-origins -investigation/.

60 "The Origins of Covid-19: An Investigation of the Wuhan Institute of Virology," House Foreign Affairs Committee Report Minority Staff, August 2021, https:// gop-foreignaffairs.house.gov/wp-content/uploads/2021/08/ORIGINS-OF -COVID-19-REPORT.pdf.

61 Maia Hibbett and Ryan Grim, "House Republicans Release Text of Redacted Fauci Emails on Covid Origins," the Intercept, January 12, 2022, https://theintercept .com/2022/01/12/covid-origins-fauci-redacted-emails/.

62 Jocelyn Kaiser, "NIH Says Grantee Failed to Report Experiment in Wuhan That Created a Bat Virus That Made Mice Sicker; EcoHealth Alliance Violated Terms of Grant, According to Letter to House Republicans," *Science*, October 21, 2021, https://www.science.org/content/article/nih-says-grantee-failed-report-experiment -wuhan-created-bat-virus-made-mice-sicker.

63 Reis Thebault, "In Latest Clash over Wuhan Lab, Fauci Tells Sen. Rand Paul: 'You Do Not Know What You're Talking About,'" *Washington Post*, July 20, 2021, https://www.washingtonpost.com/politics/2021/07/20/fauci-paul-wuhan-lab/.

64 Richard Horton, "Offline: COVID-19 as Culture War," *Lancet*, January 22, 2022, https://www.thelancet.com/action/showPdf?pii=S0140-6736%2822%2901585-9.

65 Senate Committee on Health, Education, Labor and Pensions, Minority Oversight Staff, "An Analysis of the Origins of the COVID-19 Pandemic Interim Report," October 2022, https://www.help.senate.gov/imo/media/doc/report_an_analysis_of_the _origins_of_covid-19_102722.pdf.

66 "Senator Murray Statement on Continuing Bipartisan Oversight Efforts Related to COVID-19 | The U.S. Senate Committee on Health, Education, Labor & Pensions," October 27, 2022, https://www.help.senate.gov/chair/newsroom/press/senator-murray -statement-on-continuing-bipartisan-oversight-efforts-related-to-covid-19.

67 "Preliminary Report for the Scientific Advisory Group for the Origins of Novel Pathogens (SAGO)," World Health Organization, June 9, 2022, https://www

.who.int/publications/m/item/scientific-advisory-group-on-the-origins-of-novel
-pathogens-report.

68 The WHO SAGO report includes the following note: "It is noted that three members of SAGO (Dr Vladimir Dedkov, Dr Carlos Morel, Professor Yungui Yang) do not agree with the inclusion of further studies evaluating the possibility of introduction of SARS-CoV-2 to the human population through a laboratory incident in this preliminary report due to the fact that from their viewpoint, there is no new scientific evidence to question the conclusion of the WHO-convened global study of origins of SARS-CoV-2: China Part mission report published in March 2021."

69 Jeffrey D. Sachs et al., "The *Lancet* Commission on Lessons for the Future from the COVID-19 Pandemic," *Lancet* 400, no. 10359 (October 8, 2022), https://doi.org/10.1016/S0140-6736(22)01585-9.

70 Sachs et al., "The *Lancet* Commission on Lessons."

71 "Preliminary Report for the Scientific Advisory Group for the Origins of Novel Pathogens (SAGO)," World Health Organization, June 9, 2022, https://www.who.int/publications/m/item/scientific-advisory-group-on-the-origins-of-novel-pathogens-report. 19.

72 "COVID-19 Virtual Press Conference Transcript - 9 February 2021," World Health Organization, February 9, 2021, https://www.who.int/publications/m/item/covid-19-virtual-press-conference-transcript---9-february-2021.

73 Smriti Mallapaty, "Closest Known Relatives of Virus behind COVID-19 Found in Laos," *Nature* 597, no. 7878 (September 24, 2021): 603, https://doi.org/10.1038/d41586-021-02596-2.

74 Angela Rasmussen and Michael Worobey, "Conspiracy Theories About COVID-19 Help Nobody," *Foreign Policy* (blog), https://foreignpolicy.com/2022/09/15/conspiracy-theories-covid-19-commission/.

And Edward C. Holmes, "The COVID Lab Leak Theory Is Dead. Here's How We Know the Virus Came from a Wuhan Market," the Conversation, http://theconversation.com/the-covid-lab-leak-theory-is-dead-heres-how-we-know-the-virus-came-from-a-wuhan-market-188163.

75 Michael Worobey et al., "The Huanan Seafood Wholesale Market in Wuhan Was the Early Epicenter of the COVID-19 Pandemic," *Science*, July 26, 2022, https://www.science.org/doi/10.1126/science.abp8715.

And Jonathan E. Pekar et al., "The Molecular Epidemiology of Multiple Zoonotic Origins of SARS-CoV-2," *Science*, July 26, 2022, https://doi.org/10.1126/science.abp8337.

Chapter 1: Martyrs to Science

1 Information in chapters 1 and 2 about Camp Detrick's workers who became infected from the base's laboratories is largely from archival materials that are part of what this book will refer to as the Wedum Binder. Unless otherwise noted, the names of infected workers came from documents in this binder, which is archived in the collection of the American Society of Microbiology's Center for the History of Microbiology/ASM Archives at the University of Maryland, Baltimore County. The archive has a large collection of documents donated by the family of Riley

Housewright, who was scientific director of the U.S. Army Biological Laboratories at Fort Detrick from 1956 to 1970. Among Housewright's papers is a large binder, titled "Occupational Laboratory Infections at Fort Detrick 1943–1970," that contains hundreds of pages of reports, lists, memos, and other records with synopsis information about worker infections that often include the workers' full names or initials. The cover page of the binder shows it was prepared by the Directorate of Industrial Health & Safety and under that it has the signature of "AG Wedum, M.D.," who was the base's safety director from 1946 to 1972. The binder also includes numerous published medical journal articles annotated in handwritten script with the names of the Detrick workers whose cases are described in the articles. Wedum's signature is on several of the documents and memos in the binder, and it appears that the annotations were made by him. Wedum's son, Eric, told the author that it had been his father's practice throughout his life to make handwritten annotations throughout records and journals. Eric Wedum said the signature and annotations on a sample of records from the archive look like his father's handwriting and resemble the kinds of notes he has made in other family records. Jeff Karr, the collection's archivist, said the binder was acquired from Housewright's home library in early 2003, shortly after his death.

2 Bruce Davis, son of Sherwood Davis, interviews with the author, January 20, 2022, and March 28, 2022.

3 Sidney Shalett, "U.S. Was Prepared to Combat Axis in Poison-Germ Warfare; Army Reveals That We Had Surpassed Foe in Research, with Britain and Canada Aiding—G.W. Merck Headed Study," *New York Times*, January 4, 1946, https://www .nytimes.com/1946/01/04/archives/us-was-prepared-to-combat-axis-in-poisongerm -warfare-army-reveals.html.

4 U.S. Army, Fort Detrick, "History," Archived by the Internet Archive Wayback Machine, https://web.archive.org/web/20210126063440/https://home.army.mil/detrick /index.php/about/history.

5 "NIE 18, 10 Jan 51, The Probability of Soviet Employment of Biological Weapons (BW) and Chemical Weapons (CW) in the Event of Attacks Upon the US," Series: National Intelligence Estimates and Related Reports and Correspondence, 1950–1985, 1950, Central Intelligence Agency, December 14, 1981, https://catalog .archives.gov/id/7326846.

6 Wedum Binder, "BRUCELLOSIS, 1. Laboratory-Acquired Acute Infection. Reprinted from the A.M.A. Archives of Internal Medicine, March 1959, Vol. 103, Pp. 381–397," March 1959, Center for the History of Microbiology/ASM Archives (CHOMA), Papers of Riley D. Housewright, University of Maryland Baltimore County. The cover page of this reprint of the journal article has the handwritten signature of "AG Wedum" and a note saying, "Don't give away. These reprints are scarce." The reprint is annotated with the names of patients described in the article. "William S. Davis," which is Sherwood Davis's full given name, is handwritten next to a case study in the journal article that begins: "A 45-year-old acutely ill Negro man was admitted, on Nov. 20, 1950, with a five-day history of chilliness, headache, and myalgia. As shown in Figure 7, his hospital course was characterized by..." Another typed document in the Wedum Binder lists the names of the sixty

people infected with brucellosis, including Davis, whose cases were included in the journal article.

7 Analysis by the author of cases detailed in the Wedum Binder.

8 Manuel S. Barbeito and Richard H. Kruse, "A History of the American Biological Safety Association," ABSA International, n.d., https://absa.org/about/hist01/.

9 "Arnold G. Wedum Distinguished Achievement Award," ABSA International, https://absa.org/awards/.

10 "Arnold Gerhard Wedum, Résumé," n.d., University of Montana Alumni Association.

11 Richard A. Puff, chief communications officer, University of Cincinnati College of Medicine, email to the author, November 2021.

12 Eric Wedum, son of Arnold and Bernice Wedum, interviews with the author, November 30, 2021, and August 31, 2022.

13 Arnold G. Wedum, "Disease Hazards in the Medical Research Laboratory," *Proceedings of the President's Conference on Occupational Safety* (Washington, DC: U.S. Department of Labor, Bureau of Labor Standards, June 23, 1964), https://tinyurl.com/4ju9jc77.

14 "Medical Aspects of Chemical and Biological Warfare," in *Textbook of Military Medicine* (Office of the Surgeon General, Department of the Army, United States of America, 1997), https://apps.dtic.mil/sti/pdfs/ADA398241.pdf.

15 *USAMRIID's Medical Management of Biological Casualties Handbook*, 9th ed. (Fort Detrick, MD: U.S. Army Medical Research Institute of Infectious Diseases, 2020), https://usamriid.health.mil/education/bluebookpdf/USAMRIID's%20Blue%20Book%209th%20edition%20-%20PDF%20format.pdf.

16 "Report of the W.B.C. Committee," February 19, 1942, National Academy of Sciences Archive.

17 "Medical Aspects of Chemical and Biological Warfare."

18 Special Report No. 185, Safety Program at Camp Detrick 1944 to 1953, Arnold G. Wedum, M.D., Safety Director, Cml C Biological Laboratories, 71.

19 A. G. Wedum, "The Detrick Experience as a Guide to the Probable Efficacy of P4 Microbiological Containment Facilities for Studies on Microbial Recombinant DNA Molecules," *Journal of the American Biological Safety Association* 1, no. 1 (April 1996): 7–25, https://doi.org/10.1177/109135059600100105.

20 "Biography Colonel Harold V. Ellingson, USAF MC," Office of Information Headquarters USAF Aerospace Medical Division, May 1965. Ohio State University archives.

21 Harold Ellingson, "Special Report #72, Accidental Laboratory Infections at a Biological Warfare Station," Camp Detrick, MD: Station Hospital, 1946.

22 Wedum Binder, "Occupational Infections at Fort Detrick 1944-1972 (List)," n.d., Center for the History of Microbiology/ASM Archives (CHOMA), University of Maryland Baltimore County.

23 Wedum Binder, A. G. Wedum, "Occupational Laboratory Infections at Fort Detrick 1943–1970; Statistical Summaries & Analyses, Published Case Reports," Directorate of Industrial Health and Safety, Fort Detrick, MD, n.d., Center for the History of Microbiology/ASM Archives (CHOMA), University of Maryland, Baltimore County.

24 Wedum Binder, A. G. Wedum and G. B. Phillips, "A Tabulation of Laboratory-Acquired Infections for Inclusion in the Survey of Laboratory Infections Compiled by the American Public Health Association's Committee on Laboratory Infections," Industrial Health and Safety Division, U.S. Army Biological Laboratories, Fort Detrick, Frederick, Maryland, August 1964, Center for the History of Microbiology/ASM Archives (CHOMA), University of Maryland, Baltimore County.

25 Analysis by the author of cases in the Wedum Binder.

26 Analysis by the author of names of infected workers contained in the Wedum Binder.

27 "Fort Detrick News," the *News*, August 18, 1967, https://newspaperarchive.com /news-aug-18-1967-p-6/.

28 "World War II Army Enlistment Records, Electronic Army Serial Number Merged File (Ruth A. Penfield)," n.d., U.S. National Archives & Records Administration, https://aad.archives.gov/aad/series-list.jsp?cat=WR26.

29 Wedum Binder, A. G. Wedum and G. B. Phillips, "A Tabulation of Laboratory-Acquired Infections."

30 United Press, "Missourians Helped Research Projects on Bacteria for War," *Jefferson City Daily Capital News*, January 8, 1946, https://newspaperarchive.com /jefferson-city-daily-capital-news-jan-08-1946-p-4/.

31 "Samuel J. Crumbine Banquet Honoring Cora M. Downs, Ph.D.," event program, Kansas Public Health Association, May 19, 1971, https://kuscholarworks.ku.edu /bitstream/handle/2271/830/kpha.crumbinemedal.1971.pdf?sequence=1&is Allowed=y.

32 K.U. News Bureau, University of Kansas news release, January 7, Kenneth Spencer Research Library, University of Kansas, Lawrence, Kansas. The news release does not provide a year, but the quotes provided in the news release match those in the United Press article published on January 8, 1946.

33 United Press, "Missourians Helped Research Projects."

34 "Brucellosis," Centers for Disease Control and Prevention, October 29, 2021, https://www.cdc.gov/brucellosis/index.html.

35 Analysis by the author of cases in the Wedum Binder.

36 "WAVE Rushed to Bethesda By Plane from Mexico," *Washington Evening Star*, September 9, 1945, https://newspaperarchive.com/washington-dc-washington-evening -star-sep-09-1945-p-2/. This short, three-paragraph article reported that Zarraga, who was described as a pharmacist mate second class, was flown back to Washington and admitted to the Naval Medical Center at Bethesda, Maryland. The article said the navy wouldn't disclose the nature of her illness, but that it was "contracted while she was attached to the Navy unit of the Special Projects Division of Chemical Warfare Service at Camp Detrick, Frederick. Md."

37 Wedum Binder, A. G. Wedum and G. B. Phillips, "A Tabulation of Laboratory-Acquired Infections."

38 Thomas E. Van Meter Jr. and Paul J. Kadull, "Laboratory-Acquired Tularemia in Vaccinated Individuals: A Report of 62 Cases," *Annals of Internal Medicine* 50, no. 3 (March 1959): 621–32.

39 Arnold G. Wedum, "Disease Hazards in the Medical Research Laboratory," *Proceedings of the President's Conference on Occupational Safety*, Washington, D.C.: U.S. Department of Labor, Bureau of Labor Standards, June 23, 1964, https://tinyurl.com/4ju9jc77.

40 R. Campbell Starr, "Army Chemical Corps Combats Hidden Hazards," Safety Standards, U.S. Department of Labor, February 1961, https://tinyurl.com/4prjbbfh.

41 A. G. Wedum, "The Detrick Experience as a Guide to the Probable Efficacy of P4 Microbiological Containment Facilities for Studies on Microbial Recombinant DNA Molecules," *Journal of the American Biological Safety Association* 1, no. 1 (April 1996): 7–25, https://doi.org/10.1177/109135059600100105.

42 Wedum Binder, A. G. Wedum, "Occupational Laboratory Infections at Fort Detrick, 1943–1970," Archives of the American Society for Microbiology, University of Maryland Baltimore County, Baltimore, MD.

43 "Medical Aspects of Chemical and Biological Warfare," in *Textbook of Military Medicine* (Office of the Surgeon General, Department of the Army, United States of America, 1997), https://apps.dtic.mil/sti/pdfs/ADA398241.pdf.

44 "Medical Aspects of Chemical and Biological Warfare."

45 Wedum Binder, Wedum and Phillips, "A Tabulation of Laboratory-Acquired Infections," and a February 1960 list of the names of sixty brucellosis patients featured in a reprint of a brucellosis journal article from the *Archives of Internal Medicine*. Records note that Kraft was hospitalized again for twenty-two days in 1955.

46 Stauffer Funeral Homes, "Mary Kraft Gorelick Obituary 2009," January 2009, https://www.staufferfuneralhome.com/obituaries/marykraft-gorelick.

47 Wedum Binder, Robert W. Trever, Leighton E. Cluff, Richard N. Peeler, and Ivan L. Bennett, "Brucellosis: I. Laboratory-Acquired Acute Infection," *AMA Archives of Internal Medicine* 103 (March 1959): 381–97.

48 Wedum Binder, Wedum and Phillips, "A Tabulation of Laboratory-Acquired Infections."

49 Wedum Binder, "Brucellosis: I. Laboratory-Acquired Acute Infection."

50 Bruce Davis, son of Sherwood Davis, interview with the author, March 28, 2022.

51 Wedum Binder, "A Tabulation of Laboratory-Acquired Infections."

52 Wedum Binder, "Brucellosis: I. Laboratory-Acquired Acute Infection."

53 Van Meter Jr. and Kadull, "Laboratory-Acquired Tularemia in Vaccinated Individuals: A Report of 62 Cases."

54 Analysis by the author of cases documented in the Wedum Binder.

55 Wedum Binder, Wedum and Phillips, "A Tabulation of Laboratory-Acquired Infections."

56 "Notice of Separation from the U.S. Naval Service," June Hope Ellis, January 25, 1946.

57 Annie Whitehead, daughter of June Hope Ellis DeYoung, interview with the author, June 6, 2022.

58 "Camp Detrick WAVE Is First Victim of Germ War Study," *Frederick Post*, January 25, 1946, https://newspaperarchive.com/frederick-news-post-jan-25-1946-p-1/. This

article, which features an interview with June Ellis while she was at Bethesda Naval Hospital, erroneously states that she was the first person sickened in the biowarfare program. In addition to the headline, the lede of the story—which did not have a byline—said that Ellis will "go down in history as America's first casualty in research in bacteriological warfare." Yet that wasn't accurate. Records from Wedum's safety division show dozens of lab-acquired infections before Ellis became infected and was diagnosed with brucellosis on March 31, 1945. Ellis eventually did go back to school, studying music education at Roosevelt University. She met her husband, Lynden DeYoung, at the university. As June DeYoung, she later taught music in the Gurnee (Illinois) public school system and in 1959 she was a featured performer in the role of Leonora in the Mid-West Opera Company's production of *Il Trovatore*, a flyer in her family's files shows. She died in 2016 at the age of ninety-three.

59 Wedum Binder, Calderon Howe et al., "Acute Brucellosis Among Laboratory Workers," *New England Journal of Medicine* 236, no. 20 (1947): 741–47. This journal article describes several Camp Detrick worker infections. According to other records in the Wedum Binder, June Ellis's case was used as "Case 3" in this paper.

60 Correspondence between June Hope Ellis and various Veterans Administration offices in Chicago, June 3, 1946–December 7, 1948. Provided to the author by Ellis's daughter, Annie Whitehead.

61 A. B. Chadwick, VA adjudication officer, letter from the Veterans Administration Regional Office in Chicago to June Hope Ellis, April 22, 1948.

62 Wedum Binder, A. G. Wedum and Paul Kadull, "Fact Sheet on Three Laboratory Occupational Deaths and a Plague Case at Fort Detrick, 1951, 1958, 1959, 1964," August 20, 1969, Center for the History of Microbiology/ASM Archives (CHOMA), University of Maryland-Baltimore County, Baltimore, MD.

63 Frederick News, "Brief Illness Is Fatal to Joel Willard, Well-Known Local Man Succumbs at Detrick Hospital," July 5, 1958, https://newspaperarchive.com/news-jul-05-1958-p-1/.

64 Wedum and Kadull, "Fact Sheet on Three Laboratory Occupational Deaths."

65 "Tydings Backs Detrick Restraints," *Frederick News-Post*, August 18, 1969, https://newspaperarchive.com/frederick-news-post-aug-18-1969-p-1/.

66 Mike Shanahan, Associated Press, "Germ Warfare Deaths Acknowledged by Army," *Fergus Falls Daily Journal*, September 20, 1975, https://newspaperarchive.com/fergus-falls-daily-journal-sep-20-1975-p-10/.

67 "Tydings Backs Detrick Restraints."

68 Wedum and Kadull, "Fact Sheet on Three Laboratory Occupational Deaths."

69 Wedum and Kadull. "Fact Sheet on Three Laboratory Occupational Deaths."

70 Rollie Atkinson, "Army Bares Three 'Cover Up' Deaths," *Frederick Post*, September 20, 1975, https://newspaperarchive.com/frederick-news-post-sep-20-1975-p-1/.

71 "Tydings Backs Detrick Restraints."

72 "Tydings Backs Detrick Restraints."

73 Camp Detrick became Fort Detrick in 1956. "Fort Detrick, Frederick, Maryland Fact Sheet," U.S. Army Corps of Engineers, February 2018, https://usace.contentdm.oclc.org/digital/api/collection/p16021coll11/id/5232/download.

74 Wedum Binder, Harold V. Ellingson, Paul J. Kadull, and Henry L. Bookwalter, "CUTANEOUS ANTHRAX Report of Twenty-Five Cases," reprinted from the *Journal of the American Medical Association* 131 (August 1946): 1105–08. Table 2 of the reprint, which summarizes medical observations on each of the twenty-five cases, contains handwritten annotations connecting the case numbers to the names of Detrick workers.

75 John W. Oliphant, Donald A. Gordon, Armon Meis, and R. R. Parker, "Q Fever in Laundry Workers, Presumably Transmitted from Contaminated Clothing," *American Journal of Epidemiology* 49, no. 1 (January 1949): 76–82, https://doi.org/10.1093/oxfordjournals.aje.a119261. (The journal was known as the *American Journal of Hygiene* at the time of publication.)

76 Edward A. Beeman, "Q Fever: An Epidemiological Note," *Public Health Reports (1896–1970)* 65, no. 3 (1950): 88, https://doi.org/10.2307/4587216.

Chapter 2: Invisible Mist

1 S. Edward Sulkin and Robert M. Pike, "Survey of Laboratory-Acquired Infections," *American Journal of Public Health and the Nations Health* 41, no. 7 (July 1951): 769–81, https://doi.org/10.2105/AJPH.41.7.769.

2 Sulkin and Pike, "Survey of Laboratory-Acquired Infections."

3 Morton Reitman and A. G. Wedum, "Microbiological Safety," *Public Health Reports* 71, no. 7 (July 1956): 659–65, https://www.ncbi.nlm.nih.gov/pmc/articles/PMC2031048/.

4 A. G. Wedum, "Control of Laboratory Airborne Infection," *Bacteriological Reviews* 25, no. 3 (1961): 210–16, https://www.ncbi.nlm.nih.gov/pmc/articles/PMC441094/.

5 Arnold G. Wedum, "Laboratory Safety in Research with Infectious Aerosols," *Public Health Reports* 79, no. 7 (July 1964): 619–33, https://www.ncbi.nlm.nih.gov/pmc/articles/PMC1915477/.

6 R. Campbell Starr, "Army Chemical Corps Combats Hidden Hazards," Safety Standards, U.S. Department of Labor, February 1961, https://tinyurl.com/4prjbbfh.

7 Wedum, "Laboratory Safety in Research with Infectious Aerosols."

8 Wedum, "Laboratory Safety in Research with Infectious Aerosols."

9 Morton Reitman and A. G. Wedum, "Microbiological Safety," *Public Health Reports (1896–1970)* 71, no. 7 (1956): 659, https://doi.org/10.2307/4589492.

10 K. R. Johansson and D. H. Ferris, "Photography of Airborne Particles during Bacteriological Plating Operations," *Journal of Infectious Diseases* 78, no. 3 (May 1, 1946): 238–52, https://doi.org/10.1093/infdis/78.3.238.

11 Morton Reitman, Milton A. Frank, Robert Alg, and Arnold G. Wedum, "Infectious Hazards of the High Speed Blendor and Their Elimination by a New Design," *Applied Microbiology* 1, no. 1 (January 1953): 14–17, https://doi.org/10.1128/am.1.1.14-17.1953.

12 Manuel S. Barbeito and Richard H. Kruse, "A History of the American Biological Safety Association," ABSA International, n.d., https://absa.org/about/hist01/.

13 Richard Kruse and Arnold G. Wedum, "Miscellaneous Publication 12: Recovery of Specific Microorganisms from Urine and Feces of Infected Animals," U.S.

Army Biological Laboratories, Fort Detrick, Maryland, November 1965, Defense Technical Information Center, Fort Belvoir, VA.

14 Wedum Binder, A. G. Wedum and G. B. Phillips, "A Tabulation of Laboratory-Acquired Infections."

15 The National Institute of Health did not change its name to the National Institutes of Health until 1948, https://www.nih.gov/about-nih/what-we-do/nih-almanac/chronology-events.

16 Robert J. Huebner, "Report of an Outbreak of Q Fever at the National Insitute of Health, II. Epidemiological Features," *American Journal of Public Health* 37 (April 1947): 431–40, https://www.ncbi.nlm.nih.gov/pmc/articles/PMC1623542/.

17 G. Briggs Phillips, "Technical Study 35: Microbiological Safety in U.S. and Foreign Laboratories," U.S. Army Chemical Corps Biological Laboratories, Fort Detrick, September 1961, Accession Number: AD0268635, Defense Technical Information Center, https://apps.dtic.mil/sti/citations/AD0268635.

18 I. Forest Huddleson and Myrtle Munger, "A Study of an Epidemic of Brucellosis Due to Brucella Melitensis," *American Journal of Public Health* 30 (August 1940): 944–54.

19 Associated Press, "Undulant Fever Fatal in Michigan, Newark, N.J. Student Dies, Forty Others Affected in State College," *New York Times*, February 5, 1939, https://www.nytimes.com/1939/02/05/archives/undulant-fever-fatal-in-michigan-newark-nj-student-dies-forty-other.html.

20 Phillips, "Technical Study 35."

21 Peter J. T. Morris, "The History of Chemical Laboratories: A Thematic Approach," *ChemTexts* 7, no. 3 (September 2021): 21, https://doi.org/10.1007/s40828-021-00146-x.

22 Arnold G. Wedum, "Bacteriological Safety," *American Journal of Public Health and the Nations Health* 43, no. 11 (November 1953): 1428–37, https://doi.org/10.2105/AJPH.43.11.1428.

23 D. Petts et al., "A Short History of Occupational Disease: 1. Laboratory-Acquired Infections," *Ulster Medical Journal* 90, no. 1 (2021): 28–31, https://www.ncbi.nlm.nih.gov/pmc/articles/PMC7907906/.

24 R. H. Kruse et al., "Biological Safety Cabinetry," *Clinical Microbiology Reviews* 4, no. 2 (April 1991): 207–41, https://doi.org/10.1128/CMR.4.2.207.

25 Kruse et al., "Biological Safety Cabinetry."

26 "Camp Detrick Scientists, Technicians Reunite," *Frederick News*, October 23, 1992, https://newspaperarchive.com/news-oct-23-1992-p-27/.

27 Theodore J. Cieslak and Mark G. Kortepeter, "A Brief History of Biocontainment," *Current Treatment Options in Infectious Diseases* 8, no. 4 (December 2016): 251–58, https://doi.org/10.1007/s40506-016-0096-2.

28 A. G. Wedum, "Control of Laboratory Airborne Infection," *Bacteriology Reviews* 25, no. 3 (1961): 210–16, https://www.ncbi.nlm.nih.gov/pmc/articles/PMC441094/.

29 Manuel S. Barbeito, Charles T. Matthews, and Larry A. Taylor, "Microbiological Laboratory Hazard of Bearded Men," *Applied Microbiology* 15, no. 4 (July 1967): 899–906.

30 Wedum, "Control of Laboratory Airborne Infection."

31 Arnold G. Wedum, "Special Report No. 185: Safety Program at Camp Detrick 1944 to 1953," Chemical Corps Biological Laboratories, Camp Detrick, July 1,

1953, Accession Number: AD0310671, Defense Technical Information Center, https://apps.dtic.mil/sti/citations/AD0310671.

32 Eric Wedum interview.

33 Ellen Wedum, daughter of Arnold and Bernice Wedum, interview with the author, December 12, 2021.

34 Eric Wedum interview.

35 Wedum, "Bacteriological Safety."

36 Wedum, "Control of Laboratory Airborne Infection."

37 Wedum, "Control of Laboratory Airborne Infection."

38 Starr, "Army Chemical Corps Combats Hidden Hazards."

39 Wedum, "Control of Laboratory Airborne Infection."

40 "Fort Detrick News," *Frederick News Post*, May 3, 1966, https://newspaperarchive .com/frederick-news-post-may-03-1966-p-3/.

41 Phillips, "Technical Study 35."

42 "Nixon Statement on Chemical and Biological Defense Policies and Programs," November 25, 1969, https://www.presidency.ucsb.edu/documents/remarks-announc ing-decisions-chemical-and-biological-defense-policies-and-programs.

43 A. G. Wedum, "Summary: Safety at Fort Detrick," May 1, 1970, Document contained in the Wedum Binder.

44 "Biological Safety at USAMRIID," https://web.archive.org/web/20220310015131 /https://www.usamriid.army.mil/biosafety/index.htm. In September 2022, USAMRIID removed the limited safety data it had posted for years on its website. USAMRIID spokesperson Caree Vander Linden said the removal was part of a project to update the website. "We received feedback that the information in its current format wasn't useful because there is no industry standard for comparison," she said in an October 13, 2022, email.

45 Eric Wedum interview.

46 W. Emmett Barkley, "In Celebration of Dr. Arnold G. Wedum's Legacy," *Journal of the American Biological Safety Association* 1, no. 1 (April 1996): 6, https://doi.org /10.1177/109135059600100104.

47 Barkley, "In Celebration of Dr. Arnold G. Wedum's Legacy."

48 Barkley, "In Celebration of Dr. Arnold G. Wedum's Legacy."

49 A. G. Wedum, "The Detrick Experience as a Guide to the Probable Efficacy of P4 Microbiological Containment Facilities for Studies on Microbial Recombinant DNA Molecules," *Journal of the American Biological Safety Association* 1, no. 1 (April 1996): 7–25, https://doi.org/10.1177/109135059600100105.

Chapter 3: The Leak

1 "2018 Annual Report of the Federal Select Agent Program," CDC USDA Federal Select Agent Program, n.d., https://www.selectagents.gov/resources/publications /annualreport/2018.htm.

2 CDC media relations statement emailed in response to questions from the author, March 31, 2022. "The 2018 flooding in the vicinity of USAMRIID was not included in the efforts listed in Table 9 of the 2018 FSAP Annual Report," the

statement said, adding that FSAP worked with USAMRIID once regulators were made aware of the situation.

3 Name redacted, Chief, DPW Environmental Management Division, "MEMO-RANDUM FOR RECORD, SUBJECT: June 7, 2018 Request to Continue Work Stoppage Involving Select Agents and Toxins at U.S. Army Medical Research Institute of Infectious Disease (USAMRIID)," Department of the Army U.S. Army Installation Management Command, Headquarters, United States Army Garrison, Fort Detrick, June 22, 2018. Obtained by the author under the federal Freedom of Information Act.

4 Anna Craig, inspector, "SWP-RD Report of Observations" at Fort Detrick—Area A (Steam Sterilization Plant), Maryland Department of the Environment, June 6, 2018. Obtained by the author under the Maryland Public Information Act.

5 "Limited Suspension of Registration, U.S. Army Medical Research Institute of Infectious Diseases," Federal Select Agent Program, June 28, 2018. Although USAMRIID and Fort Detrick, in public communications, characterized the May 17, 2018, leak as being a groundwater leak, the CDC's correspondence specifies that it involved both groundwater and leaking storage tanks.

6 Meeting of the Frederick Containment Lab Community Advisory Committee, July 17, 2018. Statements from Col. Scott Halter, Fort Detrick Garrison Commander, and Col. Gary Wheeler, USAMRIID commander, https://www.cityoffrederickmd.gov/Archive.aspx?AMID=69&Type=Recent.

7 "Environmental Assessment: Construction of Two Sterilization Facilities, Conversion and Abandonment of the Laboratory Sewer System, and Deactivation of the Steam Sterilization Plant," Prepared for United States Army Garrison, Fort Detrick, Frederick, MD, February 1997.

8 Wedum, "Special Report No. 185: Safety Program at Camp Detrick 1944 to 1953," 121.

9 Wedum Binder, "Occupational Laboratory Infections at Fort Detrick 1943–1970; Statistical Summaries & Analyses, Published Case Reports."

10 Wedum, "Special Report No. 185: Safety Program at Camp Detrick 1944 to 1953."

11 "Environmental Assessment, Construction of Two Sterilization Facilities, Conversion and Abandonment of the Laboratory Sewer System, and Deactivation of the Steam Sterilization Plant."

12 "Environmental Assessment, Construction of Two Sterilization Facilities, Conversion and Abandonment of the Laboratory Sewer System, and Deactivation of the Steam Sterilization Plant."

13 "Environmental Assessment Decommissioning and Demolition of Steam Sterilization Plant and Laboratory Sewer System U.S. Army Garrison Fort Detrick, Maryland," U.S. Army Corps of Engineers, November 2019, https://home.army.mil/detrick/application/files/3115/7385/0056/Draft_Fort_Detrick_SSP_and_LSS_FNSI_and_EA_November_2019.pdf.

14 "Environmental Assessment Decommissioning and Demolition of Steam Sterilization Plant and Laboratory Sewer System U.S. Army Garrison Fort Detrick,

Maryland." This 2019 environmental assessment doesn't detail what those microbes were.

15 "Environmental Assessment Decommissioning and Demolition of Steam Sterilization Plant and Laboratory Sewer System U.S. Army Garrison Fort Detrick, Maryland," U.S. Army Corps of Engineers.

16 "Types of Anthrax | CDC," November 19, 2020, https://www.cdc.gov/anthrax /basics/types/index.html.

17 Christopher K. Cote et al., "A Standard Method to Inactivate Bacillus Anthracis Spores to Sterility via Gamma Irradiation," edited by Janet L. Schottel, *Applied and Environmental Microbiology* 84, no. 12 (June 15, 2018): e00106–18, https://doi .org/10.1128/AEM.00106-18.

18 "Environmental Assessment Decommissioning and Demolition."

19 "Ceremony Marks Start of $30 Million Steam Sterilization Plant Project," July 22, 2008, https://www.army.mil/article/11092/ceremony_marks_start_of_30_million _steam_sterilization_plant_project.

20 "U.S. Army Corps of Engineers Baltimore District FY 2022 Forecast of Contracting Opportunities," September 30, 2021, https://www.nab.usace.army.mil/Portals /63/docs/BusinessWithUs/FCO/FY%2022%20%20FCO%20as%20of%201%20 Oct%2021.pdf?ver=zmjmglkjpiO8vC8n1Z0I2Q%3d%3d.

21 Alison Young, emails with Christopher Fincham, public affairs specialist, Baltimore District U.S. Army Corps of Engineers, Caree Vander Linden, USAMRIID public affairs officer, and Lanessa Hill, Fort Detrick spokesperson, March 22, 2022–May 5, 2022.

   Over several weeks, efforts were made to have Fincham, Vander Linden, or Hill explain what occurred with the "catastrophic" failure of the replacement SSP, which was called Building 8150. According to an Army Corps of Engineers contracting document (https://web.archive.org/web/20220420153405/https:// www.nab.usace.army.mil/Portals/63/docs/BusinessWithUs/FCO/FY%2022%20 %20FCO%20as%20of%201%20Oct%2021.pdf?ver=zmjmglkjpiO8vC8n 1Z0I2Q%3d%3d): "In 2016, the centralized plant experienced a catastrophic failure that resulted in total loss of the capability to treat the biomedical effluent. With the failure of Building 8150, the campus reverted to each facility having their own steam sterilization system. Building 375 resumed operation supporting the USAMRIID laboratories until 2018 when it also experienced a major system failure. The USAMRIID's BSL-3 and BSL-4 laboratories continue to operate today in a limited capacity under conditional system accreditation allowing temporary waste effluent treatment procedures approved by the Center [sic] for Disease Control (CDC). The conditional accreditation will expire when the new USAMRIID facility becomes operational. An accreditation from the CDC of the effluent treatment system is required prior to operating the new BSL-4 [sic] and BSL-4 laboratories." On April 20, 2022, Fincham provided an emailed statement saying: "In 2016, a flexible connection in the steam piping failed and was repaired in Building 8150. The failure occurred during testing of the system. The building was never used to process waste." The statement added that "the plant was not processing waste at that time, nor was it used to process waste at any other time." Because Fincham's statement did not jibe with what was in the contracting document—which indicated that labs were using it at the time of the catastrophic failure—I asked him to help reconcile the conflicting accounts. Fincham replied on May 5, 2022: "We can only speak to our USACE, Baltimore efforts and involvement, which does not include the day-to-day operation or management of facilities. USAMRIID would be better positioned to speak to the specifics..." But neither Vander Linden nor Hill, who were a part of the email string, responded to my questions.

22 "Fort Detrick, Frederick, Maryland Fact Sheet," U.S. Army Corps of Engineers, February 1, 2021, https://usace.contentdm.oclc.org/digital/api/collection/p16021coll11/id/5232/download.

23 Charles Hatfield, inspector, "NPDES Municipal Major Surface Water Inspection, Fort Detrick—Area C," Maryland Department of the Environment, June 6, 2018.

24 Hatfield, "NPDES Municipal Major Surface Water Inspection."

25 Hatfield, "NPDES Municipal Major Surface Water Inspection."

26 Hatfield, "NPDES Municipal Major Surface Water Inspection."

27 "2018 Annual Report of the Federal Select Agent Program," CDC USDA Federal Select Agent Program, n.d., https://www.selectagents.gov/resources/publications/annualreport/2018.htm.

28 Filippa Lentzos and Gregory Koblentz, "Fifty-Nine Labs around World Handle the Deadliest Pathogens—Only a Quarter Score High on Safety | Feature from King's College London," https://www.kcl.ac.uk/fifty-nine-labs-around-world-handle-the-deadliest-pathogens-only-a-quarter-score-high-on-safety.

29 "CDC LC Quick Learn: Recognize the Four Biosafety Levels," https://www.cdc.gov/training/quicklearns/biosafety/.

30 "Biosafety in Microbiological and Biomedical Laboratories (BMBL) 6th Edition | CDC Laboratory Portal | CDC," CDC, February 3, 2021, https://www.cdc.gov/labs/BMBL.html.

31 "Steam Sterilization Plant Fact Sheet," U.S. Army Corps of Engineers Baltimore District, https://www.nab.usace.army.mil/Portals/63/docs/Military/SSP/SSP_Fact Sheet_SSP.pdf.

32 "Steam Sterilization Plant Fact Sheet."

33 Federal biosafety expert with expertise in wastewater decontamination and treatment, who asked that they not be named, interview with the author, August 25, 2021.

34 "Environmental Assessment, Construction of Two Sterilization Facilities, Conversion and Abandonment of the Laboratory Sewer System, and Deactivation of the Steam Sterilization Plant," United States Army Garrison, Fort Detrick, Frederick, MD, February 1997.

35 Lanessa Hill (public affairs supervisor USAG Fort Detrick), email response to questions from author, February 4, 2022.

36 Lanessa Hill (public affairs supervisor USAG Fort Detrick), email response to questions from author, February 4, 2022.

37 Alison Young, email correspondence with USAMRIID spokesperson Caree Vander Linden and Fort Detrick spokesperson Lanessa Hill, April 7, 2022; April 26, 2022; May 17, 2022; and June 14, 2022.

38 Kimberly Darby, spokesperson, OSHA Office of Communications, email message to author, April 7, 2022.

39 Lanessa Hill (public affairs supervisor USAG Fort Detrick), text of talking points for employee briefings, provided in email response to questions from author, February 4, 2022.

40 Hill, text of talking points, email to the author, February 4, 2022.

41 When asked how many of the fifty-five people who went inside the SSP during the flooding period were not wearing Tyvek suits, nitrile gloves, boots, and PAPRs, army officials didn't directly answer the question. "All personnel wore the necessary PPE," said an army statement provided on June 30, 2022. Army officials did not respond to questions about how they defined "necessary" and whether that definition changed over time. Because the army's records and statements indicate that many of the workers who responded to the SSP during the first few days of the flooding event were not wearing the kind of respiratory and full-body protection that later would be called for in the talking points, the author sent an email on August 1, 2022, asking whether the army disputes this interpretation of the information. Public affairs officials did not reply.

42 Shelley C. Jorgensen, USAMRIID Responsible Official, letter to the Maryland Department of Health Office of Laboratory Emergency Preparedness and Response, June 1, 2018. The letter, sent to the department as formal notification of the evolving incident at Fort Detrick, states that an initial telephone notification was made to the office on May 24, 2018. It says USAMRIID notified CDC on May 17, 2018, held a teleconference with the agency on May 18, 2018, and received an inspection visit from the CDC on May 21–22, 2018. The letter was obtained by the author in response to a Maryland Public Information Act request.

43 "Public Health Security and Bioterrorism Preparedness and Response Act of 2002," June 12, 2002, https://www.govinfo.gov/content/pkg/PLAW-107publ188/pdf/PLAW-107publ188.pdf.

44 "History of FSAP and CDC | CDC," CDC, December 19, 2018, https://www.cdc.gov/cpr/dsat/history-fsap.htm.

45 "Civil Beat Law Center for the Public Interest, Inc. v. Centers for Disease Control & Prevention," The Civil Beat Law Center, https://www.civilbeatlawcenter.org/case/cdc/.

46 "2018 Annual Report of the Federal Select Agent Program," September 23, 2020, https://www.selectagents.gov/resources/publications/annualreport/2018.htm.

47 "Federal Select Agent Program," https://www.selectagents.gov/index.htm.

48 "Select Agents and Toxins List," Federal Select Agent Program, https://www.selectagents.gov/sat/list.htm.

49 "History | Federal Select Agent Program," Federal Select Agent Program, September 14, 2020, https://www.selectagents.gov/overview/history.htm.

50 "Amerithrax or Anthrax Investigation," Federal Bureau of Investigation, https://www.fbi.gov/history/famous-cases/amerithrax-or-anthrax-investigation.

51 "Justice Department and FBI Announce Formal Conclusion of Investigation into 2001 Anthrax Attacks," U.S. Department of Justice, February 19, 2010, https://

www.justice.gov/opa/pr/justice-department-and-fbi-announce-formal-conclusion
-investigation-2001-anthrax-attacks.

52 Stephen Engelberg, "New Evidence Adds Doubt to FBI's Case Against Anthrax
Suspect," ProPublica, https://www.propublica.org/article/new-evidence-disputes
-case-against-bruce-e-ivins.

53 Greg Gordon, Mike Wiser, and Stephen Engelberg, "FBI's Genetic Tests Didn't
Nail Anthrax Killer, GAO Says," *McClatchy Washington Bureau, PBS "Frontline"*
and ProPublica, December 19, 2014, https://www.mcclatchydc.com/news/nation
-world/national/national-security/article24777709.html.

54 David R. Franz, "Implementing the Select Agent Legislation: Perfect Record or
Wrong Metric?" *Health Security* 13, no. 4 (August 1, 2015): 290–94, https://www
.ncbi.nlm.nih.gov/pmc/articles/PMC4544819/.

55 "Samuel S. Edwin, Ph.D.," CDC, May 20, 2022, https://www.cdc.gov/cpr/aboutus
/leadership/samueledwin.htm.

56 Samuel Edwin, emailed statements to the author sent on June 24, 2022, and July
19, 2022.

57 Roger Andoh, CDC/ATSDR FOIA Officer, letter to the author in response to
FOIA Request # 22-01897-FOIA, July 28, 2022.

   In written responses to questions sent to the author by the CDC media office
on July 19, 2022, Dr. Samuel Edwin, director of the CDC's Division of Select
Agents and Toxins, indicated that an after-action review had been conducted to
determine how its inspection processes had missed serious containment issues at
the SSP. So on that same date, the author filed a FOIA request with the CDC
seeking a copy of the report of the review.

   Andoh, in his letter, said the CDC could not find any documents relating to
the FOIA request. The letter further said: "A search of our records failed to reveal
any documents pertaining to your request. Per the responsible program office, an
after-action review was conducted but no report was needed nor created to that
effect. FSAP created the Registration and Inspection of an Effluent Decontamination System policy and EDS Task Force to review decontamination system at registered entities (this is publicly available: https://www.selectagents.gov/regulations
/policy/effluent.htm). There were no containment issues as it relates to select agents
and toxins because agents and toxins are chemically treated with MicroChem Plus
or Bleach before leaving USAMRIID laboratories via the floor drain. Therefore,
there was no after-action report needed."

58 Federal Select Agent Program, "Policy Statement: Registration and Inspection of
an Effluent Decontamination System," August 6, 2018, https://www.selectagents
.gov/regulations/policy/effluent.htm.

59 Shelley C. Jorgensen, responsible official, USAMRIID, letter to Michele Piorek,
Office of Laboratory Emergency Preparedness and Response, Maryland Department of Health, June 1, 2018.

   And Samuel Edwin, emailed statement to the author sent on June 24, 2022.

   Accounts of what select agent research was allowed to resume after the
CDC's inspection differ. According to Jorgensen's letter: "After consultation with
CDC inspectors, USAMRIID resumed research activities with the exception of

biosafety level-3 and biosafety level-4 operations involving the use of select agents in non-human primates and their liquid waste, until appropriate waste treatment methods are implemented." According to Edwin's emailed statement: "The FSAP allowed for ongoing studies involving non-human primates to complete in high (BSL-3/ABSL-3) and maximum (BSL-4/ABSL-4) containment laboratories. No new studies were allowed to start while the SSP was in disrepair." On June 7, 2018, the CDC requested USAMRIID "continue its work stoppage" that the facility had voluntarily begun on May 18, 2018, Edwin said. CDC records show that on June 28, 2018, the select agent program formally imposed a "limited suspension" on USAMRIID select agent work in BSL-3 and BSL-4 labs that are "contributing liquid effluent" to the SSP.

60 Andy Horvitz, "PRESTO Precipitation Summary and Temperature Observations for the Washington, DC and Baltimore MD Area, May 2018," National Weather Service, https://www.weather.gov/media/publications/presto/2018may .pdf.

61 U.S. Army Garrison Fort Detrick Public Affairs statement in response to questions from the author, February 4, 2022.

Chapter 4: Nothing to See Here

1 Hatfield, "NPDES Municipal Major Surface Water Inspection," June 6, 2018.

2 Lanessa Hill, public affairs supervisor USAG Fort Detrick, email response to questions from author, February 4, 2022.

3 Fort Detrick, chief of DPW Environmental Management Division (name redacted), Memorandum for Record, June 22, 2018. Obtained by the author under the federal Freedom of Information Act. While Maryland Department of the Environment records list the estimated release as 2,000 gallons, which was what Fort Detrick initially reported, this later document says: "It is estimated the tank leaked approximately 3,000 gallons of chemically treated effluent onto a grassy area noted in Figure 1. It is assumed that some effluent may have flowed into a storm drain inlet located south of the leak area as denoted by the yellow arrow in Figure 1. This storm drain flows to Carroll Creek as shown in Figure 2."

4 Lanessa Hill, email response to questions from author.

5 Lanessa Hill, email response to questions from author.

6 Hatfield, "NPDES Municipal Major Surface Water Inspection," June 6, 2018.

7 Maryland Department of the Environment, "Telephone Report of Sewage Overflow," May 31, 2018.

8 Brad Metzger, district manager, compliance program, Maryland Department of the Environment, Water and Science Administration, email to Harry Hunsicker (program manager, compliance program, Water and Science Administration), et al., June 1, 2018. In the email, sent at 7:31 p.m. on a Friday, Metzger wrote: "Mark Lewis from Ft. Detrick called this incident in to our program yesterday May 31 at 11:00 AM. The telephone report, for reasons not yet determined, did not reach anyone in the Western Division. I had Frostburg and Hagerstown Staff search fax machines, mail boxes, and desks, etc. This afternoon and we did not find

the telephone report. Marks [sic] call today was to Charlie Hatfield for guidance on the 5 day written report. This call alerted us of the incident."

9 "Flooding to Fort Detrick Steam Sterilization Plant," Fort Detrick Media Advisory, Fort Detrick Public Affairs Office, May 31, 2018.

10 Fort Detrick, Memorandum for Record, June 22, 2018.

11 Rissah J. Watkins, Frederick County Health Department spokesperson, emailed statements from Barbara Brookmyer to the author, March 29–30, 2022.

12 Barbara Brookmyer, Frederick County Health Officer, email to the directors of the infectious disease outbreak and environmental health divisions of the Maryland Department of Health, and a Maryland Department of Environment official over federal facilities land restoration projects, May 31, 2018. Obtained by the author under the Maryland Public Information Act.

13 Barbara Brookmyer, email to Cliff Mitchell, director of the environmental health bureau at the Maryland Department of Health, June 14, 2018. Obtained by the author under the Maryland Public Information Act.

14 Fort Detrick's public affairs office, in a June 30, 2022, email to the author, said that because USAMRIID's testing had not detected pathogens in the area where the leak occurred, "the garrison and USAMRIID concluded there would be no value in further testing at additional locations on or off the installation." The statement noted that the Maryland Department of the Environment "did not direct further testing." Army officials did not address the author's questions about why copies of the testing records weren't provided to Brookmyer in response to her request.

15 Shelley C. Jorgensen, USAMRIID responsible official, letter to Michele Piorek, Maryland Department of Health, Office of Laboratory Emergency Preparedness and Response, June 1, 2018. This letter, obtained by the author under the Maryland Public Information Act from the files of state environmental records, was to serve as "formal written notification of an incident that took place" at the Fort Detrick SSP. The letter says that an initial telephone notification was made to the office on May 24, 2018.

16 "Title 10 Department of Health and Mental Hygiene, Subtitle 10 Laboratories, Chapter 11 Biological Agents Registry Program," Code of Maryland Regulations (C.O.M.A.R.) 10.10.11, https://health.maryland.gov/laboratories/docs/COMAR%2010.10.11%20(5.18.20).pdf.

17 Chase Cook, deputy director for media relations, Maryland Department of Health, email correspondence with the author, July 13, 2022.

18 Andy Owen, deputy director for media relations, Maryland Department of Health, email correspondence with the author, March 15–17, 2022.

19 Maryland Department of Environment, *NPDES Municipal Major Surface Water Inspection, Fort Detrick - Area C*, Charles Hatfield, June 6, 2018.

20 Maryland Department of the Environment, *SWP-RD Report of Observation*, Anna Craig (solid waste program inspector), June 6, 2018.

21 Shelley C. Jorgensen, responsible official, USAMRIID, letter to Michele Piorek, Office of Laboratory Emergency Preparedness and Response, Maryland Department of Health, June 1, 2018.

22 Joseph Gortva, email message to Charles Hatfield, Scott Boylan, and others, June 8, 2018.

23 Fort Detrick letter to the Frederick Containment Lab Community Advisory Committee, November 8, 2019. Obtained by the author under the Freedom of Information Act. The letter provided general information about testing, but no detailed results or methodology.

24 Jay Apperson, deputy communications director, Maryland Department of the Environment, email message to the author, April 12, 2022.

25 "Observed Precipitation," NOAA-National Weather Service, May 31 and June 1, 2018.

26 CDC media relations, email correspondence with the author, March 31, 2022.

27 Environmental Protection Agency, statements sent to the author by email from spokesman Roy Seneca, May 25, 2022.

28 US EPA, OLEM, "What Is EPCRA?" Overviews and Factsheets, July 24, 2013, https://www.epa.gov/epcra/what-epcra.

29 "USAMRIID Responses," email to the author, June 30, 2022. In response to questions about the rain that occurred prior to the testing, the statement said: "If any organisms had been present, the impact would be a dilutional effect, but there would be no effect on test performance."

30 Samuel S. Edwin, DSAT director, and Adis Dijab, national director, AgSAS, letter to USAMRIID, June 28, 2018, obtained by the author under the Freedom of Information Act.

31 Maj. Gen. (ret.) Barbara Holcomb, former Commanding General of Medical Research and Materiel Command and Senior Installation Commander of Fort Detrick July 2016–July 2019, emailed statement to the author, May 15, 2022.

32 Joseph J. Gortva, acting chief, environmental management division, Fort Detrick, "Hazardous Waste Determination and July 1st 2019 Hazardous Waste Spill at USAMRIID," August 1, 2019, letter to the Maryland Department of the Environment.

33 CDC Division of Select Agents and Toxins, Deputy Director for Public Health Service and Implementation Science (name redacted), "USAMRIID Biosafety Lapses." Letter to USAMRIID commander (name redacted), July 9, 2019. Obtained by the author under the Freedom of Information Act.

34 Shelley Jorgensen, Federal Select Agent Program Responsible Official at USAMRIID, email to Frederick County and Maryland state health officials, July 18, 2019. The email, obtained by the author under Maryland's state public records law, provides little information about this incident. It says it "took place inside Building 8150, Steam Sterilization Plant" and that the incident was outside of primary and secondary containment. It is unclear what material was spilled. The Building 8150 steam sterilization plant was not operational.

35 Randall Culpepper, deputy health officer/medical director, Frederick County Health Department, email string with other county and state health officials, July 19–July 27, 2019. At one point the individual on fever watch told health officials they were planning to travel out of state to attend a relative's funeral, but they intervened and told them they had to stay in the local area. The person, who

was being monitored since July 11, was "never actually being seen in person but simply told to self-monitor temp twice daily and if elevated to some unexplained level to contact CorpOHS. Since CorpOHS is closed on weekends, [redacted] was given the USAMRIID 24/7 manned phone number to call if temp elevated today or tomorrow," Culpepper wrote. "I plan to have a discussion with all parties involved on Monday (MDH, RIID, FCHD) to ensure there is a responsible and effective monitoring plan in place through the end of the 21 day monitoring period."

36 Federal Select Agent Program letter to USAMRIID, "Subject: Suspension of Registration, U.S. Army Medical Research Institute of Infectious Diseases (USAMRIID)," July 18, 2019.

37 Heather Mongilio, "Fort Detrick Lab Shut Down after Failed Safety Inspection; All Research Halted Indefinitely," *Frederick News Post*, August 2, 2019, https://www.fredericknewspost.com/news/health/fort-detrick-lab-shut-down-after-failed-safety-inspection-all-research-halted-indefinitely/article_767f3459-59c2-510f-9067-bb215db4396d.html.

38 City of Frederick Other Boards & Commissions Videos, Containment Lab Community Advisory Commitee meeting video, October, 8, 2019, https://cityoffrederick.granicus.com/ViewPublisher.php?view_id=25.

39 "The Containment Laboratory Community Advisory Committee (CLCAC) Eighth Annual Report: January 2018–December 2018," City of Frederick, Maryland, April 22, 2019, https://www.cityoffrederickmd.gov/DocumentCenter/View/12677/2018-Annual-Report---CLCAC-Frederick, https://www.cityoffrederickmd.gov/DocumentCenter/View/12677/2018-Annual-Report---CLCAC-Frederick.

40 "U.S. Census Bureau QuickFacts: Frederick County, Maryland," https://www.census.gov/quickfacts/frederickcountymaryland.

41 "Major Employers," City of Frederick, MD—Official Website, https://www.cityoffrederickmd.gov/160/Major-Employers?PREVIEW=YES&PREVIEW=YES.

42 "Fort Detrick | Base Overview & Info | MilitaryINSTALLATIONS," https://installations.militaryonesource.mil/in-depth-overview/fort-detrick.

43 "Brief Economic Facts Frederick County, Maryland," Maryland Department of Commerce, 2021, http://commerce.maryland.gov/Documents/ResearchDocument/FrederickBef.pdf.

44 "Environmental Assessment the Steam Sterilization Plant Replacement at Fort Detrick," U.S. Army Garrison Fort Detrick Directorate of Public Works—Environmental Division, August 2022, https://www.nab.usace.army.mil/Portals/63/Fort%20Detrick%20_SSP_EA_appendixA_Draft_Aug2022.pdf.

45 National Research Council of the National Academies, *Evaluation of the Health and Safety Risks of the New USAMRIID High-Containment Facilities at Fort Detrick, Maryland*, 2010, https://doi.org/10.17226/12871.

46 Containment Lab Community Advisory Committee meeting video, October 8, 2019.

47 "Member Information," Containment Lab Community Advisory Committee, City of Frederick, MD, https://www.cityoffrederickmd.gov/566/Members.

48 Containment Lab Community Advisory Committee meeting video, October 8, 2019.

49 An army spokesperson for Nunnally, who no longer works at Fort Detrick, said Nunnally was unavailable to answer questions about why the testing data was not provided.

50 There may not be many test results in the report. After months of questioning, the army eventually sent the author a statement on June 30, 2022. It said that only five swab samples were collected and tested at the SSP after the flooding and release incident. They wouldn't say how many water samples were tested.

51 "Test Sampling of Effluent Systems from USAMRIID Containment Laboratories Biological and Physical Challenge Results," U.S. Army Medical Research Institute of Infectious Diseases, June 20, 2018. Obtained by the author under FOIA.

52 Lanessa Hill, Caree Vander Linden, Lori Salvatore, and Chelsea Bauckman, "USAMRIID Responses," email to the author, June 30, 2022.

53 FOIA Office, U.S. Army Medical Research and Development Command, correspondence with the author about FOIA request FA-22-0020, May 20, 2022. In transmitting only one drain testing report when my FOIA request had asked for all reports over several years, the office said: "To provide some context, this record is a product from a lone recorded occurrence. Drain testing is not a routine process conducted at USAMRIID and therefore this record is the only resulting record."

54 "Biological Safety at USAMRIID," https://www.usamriid.army.mil/biosafety/index .htm.

55 The safety data was removed from the website in September 2022 as "part of an ongoing project to update the USAMRIID website," lab spokesperson Caree Vander Linden said in an October 13, 2022, email to the author. "We received feedback that the information in its current format wasn't useful because there is no industry standard for comparison. We are still considering how best to present safety-related information as part of the updated website content." She said the previously published information "is still accurate."

56 "USAMRIID Incidents in BSL-3 & 4 Laboratories: 2017, 2018, and 2019," archived by the Internet Archive Wayback Machine, March 19, 2022, https://www.usamriid .army.mil/Biosafety/Website%20chart%202017.2018.2019.pdf.

This chart was among the most recent lab safety data that USAMRIID had on its website, until the army took it down along with other safety data in September 2022.

57 In an emailed statement to the author on June 30, 2022, USAMRIID said: "There were no suspected lab-acquired infections in BSL-2 areas."

58 Internet Archive, Wayback Machine, USAMRIID incidents data, https://web .archive.org/web/20130412060753; http://www.usamriid.army.mil/biosafety/chart1 .pdf; https://web.archive.org/web/20161228081207; http://www.usamriid.army.mil /biosafety/Chart_2013-2015.pdf; https://web.archive.org/web/20170430212321; and https://www.usamriid.army.mil/biosafety/BarGraph_2016.pdf.

59 National Research Council, *Evaluation of the Health and Safety Risks of the New USAMRIID High-Containment Facilities at Fort Detrick, Maryland*, 2010, https:// doi.org/10.17226/12871.

60 National Research Council, *Evaluation of the Health and Safety Risks.*

61 "The Threat | Glanders," CDC, October 15, 2018, https://www.cdc.gov/glanders/bioterrorism/threat.html.

62 Arjun Srinivasan et al., "Glanders in a Military Research Microbiologist," *New England Journal of Medicine* 345, no. 4 (July 26, 2001): 256–58, https://www.nejm.org/doi/full/10.1056/nejm200107263450404.

63 "Laboratory-Acquired Human Glanders—Maryland, May 2000," Centers for Disease Control and Prevention, June 23, 2000, https://www.cdc.gov/mmwr/preview/mmwrhtml/mm4924a3.htm.

64 Robert Hawley, former chief of USAMRIID Safety and Radiation Protection Division, interview with the author, January 7, 2022.

65 Srinivasan et al., "Glanders in a Military Research Microbiologist."

66 Srinivasan et al., "Glanders in a Military Research Microbiologist."

67 National Research Council, *Evaluation of the Health and Safety Risks of the New USAMRIID High-Containment Facilities at Fort Detrick, Maryland*, 2010, 34, https://doi.org/10.17226/12871.

68 "The Fort Detrick Horror: A Closer Look at the US' Largest Biochemical Weapons Research Center," *Global Times*, May 29, 2020, https://web.archive.org/web/20210201132851/https://www.globaltimes.cn/content/1189967.shtml.

69 Zhao Lijian, Twitter post, March 12, 2020, https://twitter.com/zlj517/status/1238111898828066823.

70 Spokesperson Ministry of Public Affairs, Twitter post, March 29, 2021, https://twitter.com/mfa_china/status/1376489035271565313.

71 "Lack of Information Transparency at Fort Detrick Causes Concern," Xinhua News Agency, March 9, 2022, http://www.xinhuanet.com/english/20220309/ffb436eb1b0c45ef9e6e195ca2a41634/c.html.

Chapter 5: Lightning Strike

1 Justin S. Lee et al., "Analysis of the Initial Lot of the CDC 2019-Novel Coronavirus (2019-nCoV) Real-Time RT-PCR Diagnostic Panel," *PLOS ONE* 16, no. 12 (December 15, 2021): e0260487, https://doi.org/10.1371/journal.pone.0260487.

2 "CDC on Probation over Care of Animals: Director 'Appalled,' Says Steps Being Taken," *Atlanta Journal-Constitution*, November 17, 2006, main edition, A1. Archived by Factiva.

3 "Transmission of the Bacteria Which Cause Q Fever | CDC," Centers for Disease Control and Prevention, January 15, 2019, https://www.cdc.gov/qfever/transmission/index.html.

4 Sender and recipient names redacted. "Q Fever Lab," 1:23 p.m., May 25, 2007. Email obtained by the author under CDC FOIA request 07-00799. Emails about the Q fever incident, unearthed as part of a FOIA request for Building 18 incidents that I filed on June 22, 2007, when I was a reporter at the *Atlanta Journal-Constitution*, were not released until September 29, 2010—more than three years later and after I had moved to a position at *USA TODAY.*

5 Sender's name redacted. "Q-Lab Shut Down," 9:43 a.m., May 25, 2007. Email obtained by the author under the Freedom of Information Act.

6 "Q Fever Lab" email.

7 Alison Young, "CDC Action at Germ Lab Questioned; Duct Tape Used to Seal Door Inside Atlanta Facility after Possible Leak of Bioterror Bacteria Last Year," *Atlanta Journal-Constitution*, June 22, 2008, main edition, A1. Archived by Factiva.

8 Young, "CDC Action at Germ Lab Questioned."

9 CDC internal emails involving Casey Chosewood, director of the CDC Office of Health and Safety, July 17, 2008–July 23, 2008. Obtained by the author under the federal Freedom of Information Act.

10 Young, "CDC Action at Germ Lab Questioned."

11 Alison Young, "CDC Lab's Backup Power Fails During Storm," *Atlanta Journal-Constitution*, July 7, 2007, main edition, A1. Archived by Factiva.

12 Alison Young, "Outage Exposes Flaws at CDC Lab," *Atlanta Journal-Constitution*, July 20, 2007, first replate edition, A1. Archived by Factiva.

13 Young, "CDC Lab's Backup Power."

14 Young, "CDC Lab's Backup Power."

15 George Chandler, CDC director of buildings and facilities, email to several members of CDC leadership, "Ground Fault Incident," July 26, 2007.

16 Cory Schouten, "Who Files the Most FOIA Requests? It's Not Who You Think," *Columbia Journalism Review*, March 17, 2017, https://www.cjr.org/analysis/foia-report-media-journalists-business-mapper.php.

17 Young, "CDC Lab's Backup Power."

18 Katherine Norris, CDC/ATSDR FOIA Officer, Office of the Chief Information Officer, letter to the author transmitting records from FOIA Request 07-00799-FOIA, September 29, 2010.

19 Alison Young, "CDC Sits on Documents," *Atlanta Journal-Constitution*, April 26, 2009, main edition, B1. Archived by Factiva.

20 "Office of Enterprise Communications (CAU)," Centers for Disease Control and Prevention, April 4, 2006, https://www.cdc.gov/maso/pdf/OECfs.pdf.

21 Alison Young, "Exodus, Morale Shake CDC: Prominent Leaders Are Leaving the Agency in Droves, Restructuring Has Morale on the Decline, and Federal Funds Have Been Shifted. Current and Former Staff Say Someone Needs to Stop the Bleeding," *Atlanta Journal-Constitution*, September 10, 2006, main edition, A1. Archived by Factiva.

22 Young, "Exodus, Morale Shake CDC."

23 Alison Young, "E-Mails Outline CDC Backup Power Flaws: One Expert: Failure to Heed Warnings a 'Grave Breach of Responsibility,'" *Atlanta Journal-Constitution*, July 24, 2007, main edition, A1. Archived by Factiva.

24 A. G. Wedum and G. B. Phillips, "Criteria for Design of a Microbiological Research Laboratory," Army Biological Labs, Frederick, MD, January 29, 1964, https://apps.dtic.mil/sti/citations/AD0638419.

25 Internal CDC emails drafting a letter to the editor for publication in the *Atlanta Journal-Constitution*, July 20, 2007. Obtained by the author through CDC FOIA Request 07-00799-FOIA.

26 Alison Young, "CDC Safety: Germ Lab Outages Continue," *Atlanta Journal-Constitution*, July 13, 2008, main edition, A1. Archived by Factiva.

27 Alison Young, "Outage at CDC Lab Adds to Concerns," *Atlanta Journal-Constitution*, July 19, 2008, main edition, D1. Archived by Factiva.

28 "High-Containment Laboratories: National Strategy for Oversight Is Needed," U.S. Government Accountability Office, September 21, 2009, https://www.gao.gov /products/gao-09-574.

29 "High-Containment Laboratories," 1.

30 "High-Containment Laboratories," 71–72.

31 Alison Young, "Power, Airflow, Safety Issues Plague High-Tech CDC Labs," *USA TODAY*, July 9, 2015, https://www.usatoday.com/story/news/2015/07/09/new-cdc -lab-incidents-airflow/29920917/.

32 "Laboratory Infectious Agent Exposure Risk Assessment Tool." Reporting person's name redacted, Centers for Disease Control and Prevention, Fort Collins, CO, November 18, 2016. Obtained by the author under the Freedom of Information Act.

33 Alison Young, "Newly Disclosed CDC Biolab Failures 'Like a Screenplay for a Disaster Movie,'" *USA TODAY*, June 2, 2016, https://www.usatoday.com /story/news/2016/06/02/newly-disclosed-cdc-lab-incidents-fuel-concerns-safety -transparency/84978860/.

34 CDC emails involving multiple officials, February 13, 2009, https://www.document cloud.org/documents/2843223-Concerns-Within-CDC-About-Reporting-2009 -Decon.html.

35 Alison Young, "Airflow Problems Plague CDC Bioterror Lab," *USA TODAY*, June 12, 2012, archived by the Internet Archive Wayback Machine, https://web .archive.org/web/20160727000613/http://usatoday30.usatoday.com/news/nation /story/2012-06-13/cdc-bioterror-lab/55557704/1.

36 Young, "Airflow Problems."

37 "Incident Number IM3754407," Centers for Disease Control and Prevention, June 29, 2016. Obtained by the author under the Freedom of Information Act.

38 Mike Stobbe, "CDC Seeking $400 Million to Replace Lab for Deadliest Germs," AP News, February 23, 2018, https://apnews.com/article/a04e0e9ad22540b7b3d44 cb2e2b3bed4.

39 "CDC Congressional Budget Justification, FY 2023," Centers for Disease Control and Prevention, n.d., https://www.cdc.gov/budget/fy2023/congressional-justification .html, 396.

40 "CDC Congressional Budget Justification, FY 2023," 396.

41 "Roybal Building 18 High Containment Laboratory Upgrade and Continuity," CDC Office of Safety, Security, and Asset Management, Asset Management Services Office, January 8, 2018. Obtained by the author under the Freedom of Information Act.

Chapter 6: "Losing Credibility"

1 "CDC Lab Determines Possible Anthrax Exposures: Staff Provided Antibiotics /Monitoring," Centers for Disease Control and Prevention, June 19, 2014, https:// www.cdc.gov/media/releases/2014/s0619-anthrax.html.

2 Julie Steenhuysen, "UPDATE 3-U.S. CDC Says More Lab Workers May Have Been Exposed to Anthrax," Reuters, June 20, 2014, Healthcare, https://www.reuters.com/article/usa-anthrax-scare-idUSL2N0P118120140620.

3 "Report on the Potential Exposure to Anthrax," Centers for Disease Control and Prevention, July 11, 2014, https://www.cdc.gov/labs/pdf/Final_Anthrax_Report.pdf.

4 Alison Young, "Head of Troubled CDC Anthrax Lab Resigns," *USA TODAY*, July 23, 2014, https://www.usatoday.com/story/news/nation/2014/07/23/cdc-anthrax-lab-chief-resigns/13048413/.

5 "CDC Media Statement on Newly Discovered Smallpox Specimens," Centers for Disease Control and Prevention, July 8, 2014, https://www.cdc.gov/media/releases/2014/s0708-NIH.html.

6 House Energy and Commerce Committee Republicans, "Letter to GAO Regarding Federal Handling of Select Agents," May 19, 2015, https://republicans-energycommerce.house.gov/news/letter/letter-gao-regarding-federal-handling-select-agents/. Photographs of the boxes and specimen vials are included in attachments to the letter.

7 CDC Division of Select Agents and Toxins, "Joint CDC and FBI Investigation of Vials Labeled 'Variola' and Other Vials Discovered on the NIH Bethesda, MD Campus," August 8, 2014, https://osp.od.nih.gov/wp-content/uploads/Draft_Report_of_the_Blue_Ribbon_Panel_Supplement_to_Appendices_E_F.pdf.

8 CDC Division of Select Agents and Toxins, "Joint CDC and FBI Investigation."

9 Tom Frieden, interview with the author, May 6, 2022.

10 "CDC Director Releases After-Action Report on Recent Anthrax Incident; Highlights Steps to Improve Laboratory Quality and Safety," Centers for Disease Control and Prevention, July 11, 2014, https://www.cdc.gov/media/releases/2014/p0711-lab-safety.html.

11 Tom Frieden, "CDC Press Conference on Laboratory Quality and Safety after Recent Lab Incidents," Press Briefing Transcript, July 11, 2014, https://www.cdc.gov/media/releases/2014/t0711-lab-safety.html.

12 Thomas Frieden, "A Culture of Safety," July 15, 2014, email sent to All CDC and ATSDR workers. Obtained by the author.

13 Frieden email, July 15, 2014.

14 Tom Frieden, interview with the author, May 6, 2022.

15 Alison Young, "Sloppy Practices by CDC Scientist Cited in Lab Mishap," *USA TODAY*, August 15, 2014, https://www.usatoday.com/story/news/nation/2014/08/15/cdc-lab-mistake-avian-influenza-h5n1-strain/13110271/.

16 "Report on the Inadvertent Cross-Contamination and Shipment of a Laboratory Specimen with Influenza Virus H5N1," Centers for Disease Control and Prevention, August 15, 2014, https://www.cdc.gov/labs/pdf/InvestigationCDCH5N1contaminationeventAugust15.pdf.

17 Young, "Sloppy Practices."

18 "Clinic Lab Incidents—Selected Incidents," Centers for Disease Control and Prevention, prepared for CDC Director Tom Frieden in summer 2014. Obtained by the author under the federal Freedom of Information Act.

19 "Report on the Potential Exposure to Ebola Virus," Centers for Disease Control and Prevention, February 4, 2015, https://www.cdc.gov/labs/pdf/Investigation-into -Dec-22-2014-CDC-Ebola-event.pdf.

20 Natalie DiBlasio and Alison Young, "Lab Error at CDC May Have Caused Ebola Exposure," *USA TODAY*, December 24, 2014, https://www.usatoday.com/story /news/nation/2014/12/24/ebola-error-exposure-lab-atlanta/20878521/.

21 "CDC Announces the Formation of an External Laboratory Safety Workgroup," Centers for Disease Control and Prevention, July 24, 2014, https://www.cdc .gov/media/releases/2014/s0724-lab-workgroup.html. The members of the work group were Joseph Kanabrocki (work group chairperson), Associate Vice President for Research Safety and Professor of Microbiology, University of Chicago; Kenneth Berns (co-chair), Distinguished Professor Emeritus, Department of Molecular Genetics and Microbiology, College of Medicine, University of Florida, Gainesville; Debra Hunt, Assistant Professor, Director, Biological Safety, Occupational and Environmental Safety Office, Duke University/Duke University Health System; Thomas Inglesby, Chief Executive Officer and Director, University of Pittsburgh Medical Center for Health Security; Patricia Olinger, Director, Environmental Health and Safety Office, Emory University; Michael Pentella, Director, Bureau of Laboratory Sciences, Hinton State Laboratory Institute, Commonwealth of Massachusetts; David Relman, Professor of Medicine, Microbiology, and Immunology, Stanford University and Chief of Infectious Diseases, VA Palo Alto and Co-Director, Center for International Security and Cooperation (CISAC) and Senior Fellow, Freeman Spogli Institute for International Studies; Heather Sheeley, Corporate BioSafety Programme Lead, Public Health England; Fred Sparling, Professor of Medicine, School of Medicine, and Director, Southeast Regional Center of Excellence for Emerging Infections and Biodefense, University of North Carolina–Chapel Hill; Jill Taylor, Director, Wadsworth Center, New York State Department of Health; Domenica Zimmerman, Biosafety Officer, Director of the Environmental Health and Biosafety Regulations and Requirements Core in the Environmental Health and Safety, Biological and Chemical Safety Program, University of Texas Medical Branch.

22 "Recommendations of the Advisory Committee to the Director Concerning Laboratory Safety at CDC," Centers for Disease Control and Prevention, January 13, 2015, archived by the Internet Archive Wayback Machine, https://web.archive .org/web/20150322002958/https://www.cdc.gov/about/pdf/lab-safety/acd-lab -safety-recommendations-2015-01-16.pdf.

23 Alison Young, "Safety Experts Slam Lax Safety Practices at CDC Labs," *USA TODAY*, March 19, 2015, https://www.usatoday.com/story/news/2015/03/19/cdc -lab-safety-advisory-committee-report/25031285/.

24 "Laboratory Science & Safety | About | CDC," May 18, 2022, https://www.cdc .gov/about/lab-safety/index.html.

25 "Incident # 1793—Power Failure in Labs," Centers for Disease Control and Prevention, August 21, 2019. Obtained by the author under the federal FOIA.

26 Justin S. Lee et al., "Analysis of the Initial Lot of the CDC 2019-Novel Coronavirus (2019-nCoV) Real-Time RT-PCR Diagnostic Panel," *PLOS ONE* 16,

no. 12 (December 15, 2021): e0260487, https://doi.org/10.1371/journal.pone.026
0487.

27 David Willman, "Contamination at CDC Lab Delayed Rollout of Coronavirus Tests," *Washington Post*, April 18, 2020, https://www.washingtonpost.com
/investigations/contamination-at-cdc-lab-delayed-rollout-of-coronavirus-tests/2020
/04/18/fd7d3824-7139-11ea-aa80-c2470c6b2034_story.html.

28 Emily Anthes, "C.D.C. Virus Tests Were Contaminated and Poorly Designed,
Agency Says," *New York Times*, December 15, 2021, Health, https://www.nytimes
.com/2021/12/15/health/cdc-covid-tests-contaminated.html.

Chapter 7: Cloaked in Secrecy

1 Alison Young and Nick Penzenstadler, "Inside America's Secretive Biolabs," *USA
TODAY*, May 28, 2015, https://www.usatoday.com/story/news/2015/05/28/biolabs
-pathogens-location-incidents/26587505/.

2 "HIGH-CONTAINMENT BIOSAFETY LABORATORIES Preliminary Obser-
vations on the Oversight of the Proliferation of BSL-3 and BSL-4 Laboratories in the
United States," U.S. Government Accountability Office, October 4, 2007, https://
www.gao.gov/assets/gao-08-108t.pdf.

3 Nancy Kingsbury, "HIGH-CONTAINMENT LABORATORIES Recent Inci-
dents of Biosafety Lapses, Testimony Before the Subcommittee on Oversight and
Investigations, Committee on Energy and Commerce, House of Representatives,"
July 16, 2014, https://www.gao.gov/assets/gao-14-785t.pdf.

4 Lisa O. Monaco, assistant to the president for Homeland Security and Counter-
terrorism, and John P. Holdren, assistant to the president for Science and Technology, "Next Steps to Enhance Biosafety and Biosecurity in the United States,"
White House memo and attachments, October 29, 2015, archived by the Internet
Archive Wayback Machine, https://web.archive.org/web/20160212173736/https://
www.whitehouse.gov/sites/default/files/docs/10-2015_biosafety_and_biosecurity
_memo.pdf.

5 Monaco and Holdren, "Next Steps to Enhance Biosafety."

6 Justia Law, "Civil Beat Law Center for the Public Interest, Inc. v. Centers for Disease
Control & Prevention, No. 16-16960 (9th Cir. 2019)," https://law.justia.com/cases
/federal/appellate-courts/ca9/16-16960/16-16960-2019-07-10.html. Additional information at https://www.civilbeatlawcenter.org/case/cdc/.

7 Alison Young, "CDC Labs Repeatedly Faced Secret Sanctions for Mishandling
Bioterror Germs," *USA TODAY*, May 10, 2016, https://www.usatoday.com/story
/news/2016/05/10/cdc-lab-secret-sanctions/84163590/.

8 The research group at the CDC's Fort Collins facility was suspended from the
Federal Select Agent Program around 2007 and reinstated in 2010. At that time
Japanese encephalitis virus was listed as a select agent pathogen. It was removed
from the select agent list in 2012.

9 Young, "CDC Labs Repeatedly Faced Secret Sanctions."

10 Federal Select Agent Program letter to the National Animal Disease Center,
"Opportunity to show cause," July 23, 2020. Obtained by the author under the
FOIA.

11 Ted Petersen, environmental program supervisor, Iowa Department of Natural Resources, interview with the author, May 31, 2022.

12 Office of Communications, USDA Agricultural Research Service email to the author, June 8, 2022.

13 "2021 Global Health Security Index," NTI and Johns Hopkins Center for Health Security, December 2021, https://www.ghsindex.org/report-model/. The report benchmarks health security capacities in 195 countries, including on several indicators relating to government systems related to biosecurity as well as biosafety.

14 Tom Frieden, interview with the author, May 6, 2022.

15 Richard Pérez-Peña, "Agency Chief Is Fired after 7-Month-Old Dies in Day Care," *New York Times*, September 25, 2004, New York, https://www.nytimes.com /2004/09/25/nyregion/agency-chief-is-fired-after-7monthold-dies-in-day-care.html.

16 Alison Young, "Top U.S. Lab Regulator Replaced in Wake of Incidents with Bioterror Pathogens," *USA TODAY*, December 8, 2015, https://www.usatoday.com /story/news/2015/12/08/cdc-bioterror-lab-regulator-replaced/76976554/.

17 "CDC Generally Met Its Inspection Goals for the Federal Select Agent Program; However, Opportunities Exist to Strengthen Oversight (OEI-04-15-00430)," U.S. Department of Health & Human Services Office of Inspector General, May 2017, https://oig.hhs.gov/oei/reports/oei-04-15-00430.pdf.

18 "2021 Federal Select Agent Program Inspection Report Processing Annual Summary | Publications by Federal Select Agent Program | Resources," Federal Select Agent Program, July 13, 2022, https://www.selectagents.gov/resources/publications /inspection-summary2021.htm.

19 CDC Media Office, emailed response to questions from the author, September 16, 2022.

20 "2021 Annual Report of the Federal Select Agent Program | Publications by Federal Select Agent Program| Resources," Federal Select Agent Program, August 30, 2022, https://www.selectagents.gov/resources/publications/annualreport/2021.htm, 19.

21 Alison Young and Tom Vanden Brook, "Egregious Safety Failures at Army Lab Led to Anthrax Mistakes," *USA TODAY*, January 15, 2016, https://www.usatoday .com/story/news/nation/2016/01/15/military-bioterrorism-lab-safety/78752876/.

22 "Transcript: Department of Defense Press Briefing by Army Officials in the Pentagon Briefing Room on the Investigation into the Inadvertent Shipment from Dugway Proving Ground of Live Anthrax Spores," U.S. Department of Defense, January 15, 2016, https://www.defense.gov/News/Transcripts/Transcript/Article/643396 /department-of-defense-press-briefing-by-army-officials-in-the-pentagon-briefing/.

23 "AR 15-6 Investigation Report—Individual and Institutional Accountability for the Shipment of Viable Bacillus Anthracis from Dugway Proving Ground," U.S. Department of Defense, December 17, 2015, https://www.documentcloud.org /documents/2691592-Dugway-Proving-Ground-Anthrax-Shipment-AR-15-6.html.

24 "AR 15-6," 64.

25 "AR 15-6," 21.

26 Alison Young, "Army Lab Cited Eight Years Ago for Failing to Properly Kill Anthrax Samples," *USA TODAY*, June 12, 2015, https://www.usatoday.com/story /news/2015/06/12/dugway-live-anthrax-shipments/71093540/.

27 "AR 15-6," 22.

28 Young, "Army Lab Cited Eight Years Ago."

29 "AR 15-6," 62.

30 "AR 15-6," 63.

31 "AR 15-6," 87.

32 NRC Web, "Issued Significant Enforcement Actions," https://www.nrc.gov/about-nrc/regulatory/enforcement/current.html.

33 NRC Web, "Inspection of Medical, Industrial, and Academic Uses of Nuclear Materials," https://www.nrc.gov/materials/miau/inspection.html. Also "Inspection Reports" for Nuclear Power Reactors, https://www.nrc.gov/reactors/operating/oversight/listofrpts-body.html.

34 Ryan Ritterson et al., "A Call for a National Agency for Biorisk Management," *Health Security* 20, no. 2 (April 2022): 187–91, https://doi.org/10.1089/hs.2021.0163.

35 Stefano Bertuzzi did not grant an interview for this book. An expert tapped by ASM's public relations manager to provide an interview ultimately declined to be interviewed.

36 NIH Virtual Meeting and Listening Session: US Government Oversight Framework for Research Involving Enhanced Potential Pandemic Pathogens, National Institutes of Health, 2022, https://videocast.nih.gov/watch=45230.

37 Felicia Goodrum did not grant an interview.

38 Michael Imperiale, interview with the author, August 8, 2022.

39 David Gillum, interview with the author and written statement, August 3, 2022.

40 Gerald Parker, interview with the author, August 25, 2022.

Chapter 8: The Biolab Next Door

1 Alison Young and Nick Penzenstadler, "Inside America's Secretive Biolabs," *USA TODAY*, May 28, 2015, https://www.usatoday.com/story/news/2015/05/28/biolabs-pathogens-location-incidents/26587505/.

2 Lawrence Tsai, interview with the author, 2015.

3 "Officials: Rare Bacteria May Have Caused San Francisco Researcher's Death," Associated Press, May 3, 2012.

4 "City and County of San Francisco Certificate of Death, Richard Din," May 3, 2012. Obtained by the author through federal court filings.

5 Channing D. Sheets, Kathleen Harriman, Jennifer Zipprich, and Janice K. Louie, "Fatal Meningococcal Disease in a Laboratory Worker—California, 2012," *CDC Morbidity and Mortality Weekly Report*, September 5, 2014, https://www.cdc.gov/mmwr/preview/mmwrhtml/mm6335a2.htm.

6 "Epidemiologic Notes and Reports Laboratory-Acquired Meningococcemia—California and Massachusetts," *CDC Morbidity and Mortality Weekly Report*, January 25, 1991, https://www.cdc.gov/mmwr/preview/mmwrhtml/00001882.htm.

7 *Biosafety in Microbiological and Biomedical Laboratories (BMBL)* 6th ed., CDC Laboratory Portal, CDC, June 2020, https://www.cdc.gov/labs/BMBL.html.

8 *Biosafety in Microbiological and Biomedical Laboratories* 5th ed., December 2009, https://www.cdc.gov/labs/pdf/CDC-BiosafetymicrobiologicalBiomedicalLaboratories-2009-P.pdf.

9 Channing D. Sheets, "San Francisco VA Hospital Research Laboratory Inspection Report," Cal/OSHA, 2012.

10 "US Labor Department's OSHA Concludes Fatality Investigation at San Francisco VA Medical Center Research Laboratory, Issues Violation Notices," Occupational Safety and Health Administration, February 20, 2013, https://www.osha.gov/news/newsreleases/region9/02202013.

11 "US Labor Department's OSHA Concludes Fatality Investigation."

12 Statement from the San Francisco VA Health Care System to the author, August 9, 2022.

13 "High-Containment Laboratories: National Strategy for Oversight Is Needed," U.S. Government Accountability Office, September 21, 2009, https://www.gao.gov/products/gao-09-574.

14 A. Lynn Harding and Karen Brandt Byers, "Epidemiology of Laboratory-Associated Infections," in *Biological Safety: Principles and Practices*, 4th ed. (Hoboken, NJ: John Wiley & Sons, 2006).

15 Analysis by the author of annual reports to Congress from the Federal Select Agent Program for calendar years 2015–2021, which were obtained under the Freedom of Information Act.

16 Karen Brandt Byers and A. Lynn Harding, "Laboratory-Associated Infections," in *Biological Safety: Principles and Practices*, 5th ed. (Washington, DC: ASM Press, 2016).

17 "Fatal Laboratory-Acquired Infection with an Attenuated Yersinia Pestis Strain—Chicago, Illinois, 2009," *CDC Morbidity and Mortality Weekly Report*, February 25, 2011, https://www.cdc.gov/mmwr/preview/mmwrhtml/mm6007a1.htm.

18 Emma Graves Fitzsimmons, "Researcher Had Bacteria for Plague at His Death," *New York Times*, September 22, 2009, U.S., https://www.nytimes.com/2009/09/22/us/22chicago.html.

19 "Human Salmonella Typhimurium Infections Associated with Clinical and Teaching Microbiology Laboratories," CDC, January 17, 2012, https://www.cdc.gov/salmonella/2011/lab-exposure-1-17-2012.html.

20 Karen Byers, interview with the author, July 27, 2022.

21 Rocco Casagrande, interview with the author. August 2, 2022.

Chapter 9: The Many Lab Leaks of SARS-CoV-1

1 Eskild Petersen et al., "Comparing SARS-CoV-2 with SARS-CoV and Influenza Pandemics," *Lancet Infectious Diseases* 20, no. 9 (September 2020): e238–44, https://doi.org/10.1016/S1473-3099(20)30484-9.

2 Thomas G. Ksiazek et al., "A Novel Coronavirus Associated with Severe Acute Respiratory Syndrome," *New England Journal of Medicine* 348, no. 20 (May 15, 2003): 1953–66, https://doi.org/10.1056/NEJMoa030781.

3 "SARS Outbreak Contained Worldwide," World Health Organization, July 5, 2003, archived at the Internet Archive's Wayback Machine, https://web.archive.org/web/20041209200823; http://www.who.int/mediacentre/news/releases/2003/pr56/en/.

4 "SARS | Basics Factsheet | CDC," https://www.cdc.gov/sars/about/fs-sars.html.

5 "SARS (10 Years After)," Centers for Disease Control and Prevention, https://www.cdc.gov/dotw/sars/index.html.

6 "SARS: How a Global Epidemic Was Stopped," World Health Organization Western Pacific Region, 2006, https://apps.who.int/iris/bitstream/handle/10665/207501/9290612134_eng.pdf.

7 "SARS: How a Global Epidemic Was Stopped," 236.

8 Sonja Olsen, interview with the author, June 6, 2022.

9 "Biosafety and SARS Incident in Singapore September 2003—Report of the Review Panel on New SARS Case and Biosafety," Singapore Ministry of Health, 2003, National Archives of Singapore, https://www.nas.gov.sg/archivesonline/data/pdfdoc/20030923-MOH.pdf.

10 Sonja Olsen, interview with the author.

11 "Dr. Rollin, a CDC Disease Detective, Responds to the Ebola Outbreak," Centers for Disease Control and Prevention, July 16, 2018, http://1.usa.gov/1thhVi5.

12 Pierre Rollin, interview with the author, December 14, 2021.

13 Pierre Rollin, interview with the author.

14 Poh Lian Lim et al., "Laboratory-Acquired Severe Acute Respiratory Syndrome," *New England Journal of Medicine* 350, no. 17 (April 22, 2004): 1740–45, https://doi.org/10.1056/NEJMoa032565. This journal article about the Singapore lab infection case does not name the university or the institute housing the biosafety level 3 lab. However, the names of these institutions are disclosed in the earlier Singapore Ministry of Health report that is referenced in the journal article.

15 "Biosafety and SARS Incident in Singapore September 2003 Report of the Review Panel on New SARS Case and Biosafety," Singapore Ministry of Health, 2003, https://www.nas.gov.sg/archivesonline/data/pdfdoc/20030923-MOH.pdf.

16 "Biosafety and SARS Incident in Singapore September 2003," 15.

17 Sonja Olsen, interview with the author.

18 Pierre Rollin, interview with the author.

19 Lim et al., "Laboratory-Acquired Severe Acute Respiratory Syndrome."

20 "Biosafety and SARS Incident in Singapore September 2003," 13.

21 "SARS Case in Singapore Linked to Accidental Laboratory Contamination," World Health Organization, September 24, 2003, https://www.who.int/emergencies/disease-outbreak-news/item/2003_09_24-en.

22 "Taiwan Researcher Tests Positive for SARS after Laboratory Accident," Agence France Presse, December 17, 2003. Accessed through Factiva.

23 "A SARS Confirmed Case Infected in Research Laboratory in Taiwan," Taiwan Centers for Disease Control, December 17, 2003. Archived by the Internet Archive Wayback Machine on May 23, 2004, https://web.archive.org/web/20040523080929/http://203.65.72.83/En/dia/ShowPublication.ASP?RecNo=938.

24 "WHO: Severe Acute Respiratory Syndrome (SARS) in Taiwan, China," World Health Organization, December 17, 2003. Archived by the Internet Archive Wayback Machine on August 24, 2004, https://web.archive.org/web/20040803150502/http://www.who.int/csr/don/2003_12_17/en.

25 "Confirmed SARS Case in Research Laboratory in Taiwan—December 17 2003," Department of Health, Taiwan, R.O.C., December 17, 2003. Archived by the

Internet Archive Wayback Machine on August 24, 2004, https://web.archive.org/web/20040824025157/http://sars.doh.gov.tw/news/2003121701.html.

26 "A Report on the Laboratory-Acquired SARS Case in Taiwan," Center for Disease Control Department of Health, Taiwan, January 7, 2004, Archived by the Internet Archive Wayback Machine on August 3, 2004, https://web.archive.org/web/20040803094741/http://www.cdc.gov.tw/sarsen/.

27 "Audit Report for Laboratories of Biosafety Level 3 and Higher in Taiwan, 2007," *Taiwan Epidemiology Bulletin, Taiwan Centers for Disease Control* 24, no. 7 (July 25, 2008): 523–40, https://www.cdc.gov.tw/En/File/Get/53fRU0drzfunw22tKaDplw.

28 "A Report on the Laboratory-Acquired SARS Case in Taiwan."

29 Alice Hung, "Wrapup 1—Taiwan SARS Victim Wanted to Die at Home," Reuters, December 19, 2003. Archived through Factiva.

30 "SARS Contingency Committee Task Force Group Press Release—December 17 2003," Department of Health, Taiwan, R.O.C., December 17, 2003. Archived by the Internet Archive Wayback Machine on August 24, 2004, https://web.archive.org/web/20040824025459/http://sars.doh.gov.tw/news/2003121702.html.

31 "A Report on the Laboratory-Acquired SARS Case in Taiwan."

32 Li-Chi Hsieh, Wen-Chao Wu, and Shu-Hui Tseng, "Biological Select Agents and Toxins Management in Taiwan: From Past to Present," *Applied Biosafety* 26, no. 3 (September 1, 2021): 123–29, https://doi.org/10.1089/apb.19.0045.

33 Manny Mogato, "WHO Pushing for Lab Safety after Taiwan SARS Case," Reuters News, December 19, 2003. Archived by Factiva.

34 "WHO Post-Outbreak Biosafety Guidelines for Handling of SARS-CoV Specimens and Cultures," December 18, 2003, https://www.who.int/publications/m/item/who-post-outbreak-biosafety-guidelines-for-handling-of-sars-cov-specimens-and-cultures.

35 "China Takes Better Care of Collected SARS Specimens, Viral Strains," Xinhua News Agency, December 26, 2003. Archived by Factiva.

36 "China's Latest SARS Outbreak Has Been Contained, but Biosafety Concerns Remain—Update 7," World Health Organization, May 18, 2004, https://www.who.int/emergencies/disease-outbreak-news/item/2004_05_18a-en.

37 "Strengthening Lab Biosafety Important, Urgent Task: Health Official," Xinhua News Agency, July 8, 2004. Archived by Factiva.

38 "SARS: How a Global Epidemic Was Stopped," World Health Organization Western Pacific Region, 2006, 236, https://apps.who.int/iris/bitstream/handle/10665/207501/9290612134_eng.pdf.

39 "China Confirms SARS Infection in Another Previously Reported Case; Summary of Cases to Date—Update 5," World Health Organization, April 30, 2004, https://www.who.int/emergencies/disease-outbreak-news/item/2004_04_30-en.

40 Jim Yardley and Lawrence K. Altman, "China Is Scrambling to Curb SARS Cases after a Death," *New York Times*, April 24, 2004. Archived in Factiva.

41 "Strengthening Lab Biosafety Important, Urgent Task: Health Official," Xinhua News Agency, July 8, 2004. Archived by Factiva.

42 "China Reports Additional SARS Cases—Update," World Health Organization, April 23, 2004, https://www.who.int/emergencies/disease-outbreak-news/item/2004 _04_23-en.

43 "China Confirms SARS Infection in Another Previously Reported Case; Summary of Cases to Date—Update 5."

44 "Additional Patients in China under Investigation for SARS; WHO Team Travels to Beijing—Update 2," World Health Organization, April 26, 2004, https://www .who.int/emergencies/disease-outbreak-news/item/2004_04_26-en.

45 "SARS: How a Global Epidemic Was Stopped," World Health Organization Western Pacific Region, 2006, 236, https://apps.who.int/iris/bitstream/handle/10665 /207501/9290612134_eng.pdf.

46 "Investigation into China's Recent SARS Outbreak Yields Important Lessons for Global Public Health," World Health Organization, July 2, 2004. Archived by the Internet Archive Wayback Machine on December 4, 2004, https://web.archive .org/web/20041204113012/http://www.wpro.who.int/sars/docs/update/update _07022004.asp.

47 "SARS: How a Global Epidemic Was Stopped."

48 "SARS: How a Global Epidemic Was Stopped."

Chapter 10: Frozen in Time

1 Shanta M. Zimmer and Donald S. Burke, "Historical Perspective—Emergence of Influenza A (H1N1) Viruses," *New England Journal of Medicine* 361, no. 3 (July 16, 2009): 279–85, https://doi.org/10.1056/NEJMra0904322.

2 Michael B. Gregg, Alan R. Hinman, and Robert B. Craven, "The Russian Flu: Its History and Implications for This Year's Influenza Season," *JAMA* 240, no. 21 (November 17, 1978): 2260–63, https://doi.org/10.1001/jama.1978.03290210042022.

3 "H1N1 Virus Influenza," *World Health Organization Weekly Epidemiological Record*, no. 2 (January 13, 1978): 16–20, http://apps.who.int/iris/bitstream/handle/10665 /221680/WER5302_16-20.PDF.

4 Gregg, Hinman, and Craven, "The Russian Flu."

5 "Influenza—People's Republic of China, Taiwan, Philippines, United Kingdom, United States," *Morbidity and Mortality Weekly Report* 27, no. 3 (January 20, 1978): 8, https://stacks.cdc.gov/view/cdc/1584.

6 Gregg, Hinman, and Craven, "The Russian Flu."

7 Katsuhisa Nakajima, Ulrich Desselberger, and Peter Palese, "Recent Human Influenza A (H1N1) Viruses Are Closely Related Genetically to Strains Isolated in 1950," *Nature* 274, no. 5669 (July 1978): 334–39, https://doi.org/10.1038/274334a0.

8 R. G. Webster et al., "Evolution and Ecology of Influenza A Viruses," *Microbiological Reviews* 56, no. 1 (March 1992): 152–79, https://www.ncbi.nlm.nih.gov/pmc /articles/PMC372859/.

9 Michelle Rozo and Gigi Kwik Gronvall, "The Reemergent 1977 H1N1 Strain and the Gain-of-Function Debate," ed. Mark R. Denison, *mBio* 6, no. 4 (September 2015): e01013-15, https://doi.org/10.1128/mBio.01013-15.

10 H. C. Kung et al., "Influenza in China in 1977: Recurrence of Influenzavirus A Subtype H1N1," *Bulletin of the World Health Organization* 56, no. 6 (1978): 913–18.

11 Peter Palese, "Influenza: Old and New Threats," *Nature Medicine* 10, no. 12 (December 2004): S82–87, https://doi.org/10.1038/nm1141.

12 W. Graeme Laver and Robert G. Webster, "In Memoriam: Chu Chi Ming (1917–1998)," *Virology* 255, no. 1 (March 1999): 1, https://doi.org/10.1006/viro.1998.9551.

13 Rozo and Gronvall, "The Reemergent 1977 H1N1 Strain."

14 Amesh Adalja, interview with the author, April 28, 2022.

15 Amesh Adalja et al., "The Characteristics of Pandemic Pathogens," Johns Hopkins Bloomberg School of Public Health, Center for Health Security, May 2018, https://www.centerforhealthsecurity.org/our-work/pubs_archive/pubs-pdfs/2018/180510 -pandemic-pathogens-report.pdf.

Chapter 11: The Last Smallpox Death

1 "History of Smallpox," CDC, February 21, 2021, https://www.cdc.gov/smallpox /history/history.html.

2 "Smallpox," World Health Organization, https://www.who.int/health-topics /smallpox.

3 R. A. Shooter et al., "Report of the Investigation into the Cause of the 1978 Birmingham Smallpox Occurrence," 1980. Archived online by the U.S. National Library of Medicine, Bethesda, MD, https://www.nlm.nih.gov/nichsr/esmallpox /report_1978_london.pdf.

4 "Briton Becomes First to Die of Smallpox in Nearly a Year," *Washington Post*, September 12, 1978, https://www.washingtonpost.com/archive/politics/1978/09/12 /briton-becomes-first-to-die-of-smallpox-in-nearly-a-year/2f0d8ad4-0a37-4475 -962d-21a3c712c60c/.

5 BBC News, "How Smallpox Claimed Its Final Victim," August 10, 2018, Birmingham & Black Country, https://www.bbc.com/news/uk-england-birmingham -45101091.

6 Shooter, "Report of the Investigation," 62.

7 Shooter, "Report of the Investigation," 7.

8 William Stockton, "SMALLPDX IS NOT DEAD," *New York Times*, February 4, 1979, Archives, https://www.nytimes.com/1979/02/04/archives/smallpox-is-not -dead.html.

9 Shooter, "Report of the Investigation," 8.

10 "Variola Virus Repository Safety Inspections," World Health Organization, https:// www.who.int/activities/variola-virus-repository-safety-inspections.

11 Shooter, "Report of the Investigation," 190–91.

12 Shooter, "Report of the Investigation," 61.

13 "University Cleared of Smallpox Death," *Belfast Telegraph*, November 7, 1979, archived by the British Newspaper Archive, https://www.britishnewspaperarchive .co.uk/viewer/bl/0002318/19791107/045/0003.

14 Shooter, "Report of the Investigation," 58.

15 Shooter, "Report of the Investigation," 57.

16 Shooter, "Report of the Investigation," 57.

17 Shooter, "Report of the Investigation," 161.

18 Shooter, "Report of the Investigation," 98.

19 Shooter, "Report of the Investigation," 162.
20 Shooter, "Report of the Investigation," 163.
21 Shooter, "Report of the Investigation," 62.

Chapter 12: Anthrax Cloud

1 "Soviet Biological Warfare Threat, DST-1610F-057-86," Defense Intelligence Agency, 1986, archived by the National Security Archive at George Washington University, https://nsarchive2.gwu.edu/NSAEBB/NSAEBB61/Sverd26.pdf.
2 R. Jeffrey Smith, "Soviets Offer Account of '79 Anthrax Outbreak; U.S. Tied Incident to Biological Weapons," *Washington Post*, October 9, 1986, final edition. Archived by Factiva.
3 John H. Cushman Jr., "Russians Explain '79 Anthrax Cases," *New York Times*, April 14, 1988, Late City Final Edition. Archived by Factiva.
4 R. Jeffrey Smith and Philip J. Hilts, "Soviets Deny Lab Caused Anthrax Cases; Tainted Meat Blamed for 1979 Deaths," *Washington Post*, April 13, 1988. Archived by Factiva.
5 Smith and Hilts, "Soviets Deny."
6 Eliot Marshall, "Sverdlovsk: Anthrax Capital?: Soviet Doctors Answer Questions about an Unusual Anthrax Epidemic Once Thought to Have Been Triggered by a Leak from a Weapons Lab," *Science* 240, no. 4851 (April 22, 1988): 383–85, https://doi.org/10.1126/science.3358121.
7 Bryan Brumley, "US Officials Still Wary of Soviet Line on Anthrax Epidemic," Associated Press, April 16, 1988. Archived by Factiva.
8 Cushman, "Russians Explain."
9 Brumley, "US Officials Still Wary."
10 Smith and Hilts, "Soviets Deny."
11 Smith and Hilts, "Soviets Deny."
12 "Matthew S. Meselson Honored with the 2019 Future of Life Award for BWC Role," Belfer Center for Science and International Affairs, https://www.belfercenter.org/publication/matthew-s-meselson-honored-2019-future-life-award-bwc-role.
13 Marshall, "Sverdlovsk: Anthrax Capital?"
14 R. Jeffrey Smith, "Yeltsin Blames '79 Anthrax on Germ Warfare Efforts," *Washington Post*, June 16, 1992, https://www.washingtonpost.com/archive/politics/1992/06/16/yeltsin-blames-79-anthrax-on-germ-warfare-efforts/fea56f2d-bf9e-4787-b6ec-86bf190f3ddb/.
15 Smith, "Yeltsin Blames."
16 Faina A. Abramova, Lev M. Grinberg, Olga V. Yampolskaya, and David H. Walker, "Pathology of Inhalational Anthrax in 42 Cases from the Sverdlovsk Outbreak of 1979," *Proceedings of the National Academy of Sciences in the USA* 90 (March 1993): 2291–94, https://www.pnas.org/content/pnas/90/6/2291.full.pdf.
17 Matthew Meselson et al., "The Sverdlovsk Anthrax Outbreak of 1979," *Science* 266, no. 5188 (November 18, 1994): 1202–08, https://doi.org/10.1126/science.7973702.
18 Philip J. Hilts, "Deaths in 1979 Tied to Soviet Military," *New York Times*, November 18, 1994, World, https://www.nytimes.com/1994/11/18/world/deaths-in-1979-tied-to-soviet-military.html.

Chapter 13: The Plague from Pirbright

1 "10,528 Residents Test Positive for Brucellosis in Lanzhou after Brucella Leakage in Local Factory," *Global Times*, December 3, 2020, https://www.globaltimes.cn /content/1208864.shtml.

2 "Signs and Symptoms | Brucellosis," CDC, October 9, 2018, https://www.cdc.gov /brucellosis/symptoms/index.html.

3 "Announcement on the Handling of Brucella Antibody Positive Incidents of Lanzhou Veterinary Research Institute" (Google Translate), Health Commission of Lanzhou City, September 15, 2020, http://wjw.lanzhou.gov.cn/art/2020/9/15/art_4531_928158 .html.

4 "3.8 Mln USD Raised for Compensating NW China Brucella Cases," Xinhua News Agency, December 3, 2020, http://www.news.cn/english/2020-12/03/c_139561327 .htm.

5 "10,528 Residents Test Positive for Brucellosis in Lanzhou after Brucella Leakage in Local Factory," *Global Times*, December 3, 2020.

6 Jessie Yeung and Eric Cheung, "Bacterial Outbreak Infects Thousands after Factory Leak in China," CNN, September 17, 2020, https://www.cnn.com/2020/09/17 /asia/china-brucellosis-outbreak-intl-hnk/index.html.

7 Iain Anderson et al., "Foot and Mouth Disease 2007: A Review and Lessons Learned," presented to the Prime Minister and the Secretary of State for Environment, Food and Rural Affairs, March 11, 2008, https://www.gov.uk/government /publications/foot-and-mouth-disease-2007-a-review-and-lessons-learned.

8 Anderson, "Foot and Mouth Disease Review," 61.

9 Brian G. Spratt et al., "Independent Review of the Safety of UK Facilities Handling Foot-and-Mouth Disease Virus," August 31, 2007, https://webarchive .nationalarchives.gov.uk/ukgwa/20130822084033; http://www.defra.gov.uk/animalh /diseases/fmd/investigations/pdf/spratt_final.pdf.

10 "Final Report on Potential Breaches of Biosecurity at the Pirbright Site 2007," Health and Safety Executive (HSE), December 20, 2007, https://library-search .nics.gov.uk/cgi-bin/koha/tracklinks.pl?uri=http%3A%2F%2Flibrary2.nics.gov .uk%2Fpdf%2Fdard%2F2008%2FDVGI.pdf&biblionumber=97150.

11 Spratt, "Independent Review," 34.

12 Spratt, "Independent Review," 34.

13 HSE, "Final Report," 10.

14 Spratt, "Independent Review," 39.

15 Spratt, "Independent Review," 30.

16 Spratt, "Independent Review," 6.

17 Spratt, "Independent Review," 30–32.

18 "Foot and Mouth Disease," USDA Animal and Plant Health Inspection Service, https://www.aphis.usda.gov/aphis/ourfocus/animalhealth/animal-disease-infor mation/fmd/index.

19 HSE, "Final Report," 7.

20 "FMD 2007. Summary Epidemiology Report, Situation as at 10:00 Thursday 09 August, Day 6," Department for Environment, Food and Rural Affairs (Defra), August 9, 2007. Archived by the Internet Archive Wayback Machine, https://web

.archive.org/web/20080626042015; http://www.defra.gov.uk/footandmouth/pdf
/fmd-epireport090807.pdf.

21 Anderson, "Foot and Mouth Disease Review."
22 Anderson, "Foot and Mouth Disease Review," 104.
23 "DEFRA Issues Statement Regarding New Foot and Mouth Outbreak," Newsquest
    Media Group Newspapers, August 3, 2007. Archived by Factiva.
24 "British Govt Lab Says Not behind Disease Outbreak," Reuters, August 5, 2007,
    https://www.reuters.com/article/britain-cattle-laboratories/british-govt-lab-says-not
    -behind-disease-outbreak-idUSL0547342020070805.
25 Patrick Wintour and John Vidal, "Human Error May Have Led to Outbreak,"
    Guardian, August 5, 2007, UK news, https://www.theguardian.com/uk/2007/aug
    /06/footandmouth.ruralaffairs10.
26 "Farmers Speak of Their Devastation," *Irish Times*, August 8, 2007, https://www
    .irishtimes.com/news/farmers-speak-of-their-devastation-1.953274.
27 "FMD 2007. Summary Epidemiology Report, Situation as at 10:00 Thursday 09
    August, Day 6," Department for Environment, Food and Rural Affairs (Defra),
    August 9, 2007. Archived by the Internet Archive Wayback Machine, https://web
    .archive.org/web/20080626042015/http://www.defra.gov.uk/footandmouth/pdf
    /fmd-epireport090807.pdf.
28 Spratt, "Independent Review," 8.
29 Spratt, "Independent Review," 9.
30 Spratt, "Independent Review," 41.
31 Spratt, "Independent Review," 41.
32 HSE, "Final Report," 3.
33 HSE, "Final Report," 4.
34 Spratt, "Independent Review," 3.
35 Spratt, "Independent Review," 15.
36 Anderson, "Foot and Mouth Disease Review."
37 Anderson, "Foot and Mouth Disease Review," Appendix I. Two accidental releases
    occurred in Germany in 1977, the report says.
38 Nancy Kingsbury, "High-Containment Biosafety Laboratories—DHS Lacks Evi-
    dence to Conclude That Foot-and-Mouth Disease Research Can Be Done Safely on the
    U.S. Mainland, Testimony before the Subcommittee on Oversight and Investigations,
    Committee on Energy and Commerce, House of Representatives," U.S. Government
    Accountability Office, May 22, 2008, https://www.gao.gov/assets/gao-08-821t.pdf.
39 "DHS Report on Risks of Proposed Kansas Biocontainment Lab Is Incomplete,
    Says National Research Council," National Research Council, November 15, 2010,
    https://www8.nationalacademies.org/onpinews/newsitem.aspx?RecordID=13031.
40 "Site-Specific Biosafety and Biosecurity Mitigation Risk Assessment," U.S.
    Department of Homeland Security, October 2010. Archived by the Internet
    Archive Wayback Machine, https://web.archive.org/web/20160514173117/http://
    www.dhs.gov/xlibrary/assets/nbaf_ssra_final_report.pdf.
41 "Evaluation of a Site-Specific Risk Assessment for the Department of Home-
    land Security's Planned National Bio- and Agro-Defense Facility in Manhattan,

Kansas," National Research Council of the National Academies, 2010, https://www
.nationalacademies.org/our-work/evaluation-of-a-site-specific-risk-assessment-for-the
-department-of-homeland-securitys-planned-national-bio--and-agro-defense-facility
-in-manhattan-kansas.

42 "Evaluation of a Site-Specific Risk Assessment for the Department of Homeland Security's Planned National Bio- and Agro-Defense Facility in Manhattan, Kansas."

43 "Updated Site-Specific Biosafety and Biosecurity Mitigation Risk Assessment,
Volume II," U.S. Department of Homeland Security, February 2012. Archived by the
Internet Archive Wayback Machine, https://web.archive.org/web/20120712193226;
http://www.dhs.gov/xlibrary/assets/st/nbaf_updated_ssra_volume_ii.pdf.

44 "Evaluation of the Updated Site-Specific Risk Assessment for the National Bio-
and Agro-Defense Facility in Manhattan, Kansas," National Research Council,
2012, https://doi.org/10.17226/13418.

Chapter 14: "Time Bomb" in Louisiana

1 Chien Hung Wu et al., "Clinical Characteristics of Patients with Melioidosis
Treated in an Emergency Department," *Journal of Acute Medicine* 2, no. 1 (March
1, 2012): 13–18, https://doi.org/10.1016/j.jacme.2012.02.001.

2 W. Joost Wiersinga et al., "Melioidosis," *Nature Reviews Disease Primers* 4, no. 1
(February 1, 2018): 1–22, https://doi.org/10.1038/nrdp.2017.107.

3 "Serological Evidence of Burkholderia Pseudomallei Infection in U.S. Marines
Who Trained in Australia from 2012–2014: A Retrospective Analysis of Archived
Samples," Military Health System, July 1, 2019, https://health.mil/News/Articles
/2019/07/01/Burkholderia-pseudomallei-Infection.

4 Mark A. Koponen, Douglas Zlock, Darwin L. Palmer, and Toby L. Merlin, "Melioidosis: Forgotten, but Not Gone!" *Archives of Internal Medicine* 151, no. 3 (March
1, 1991): 605–08, https://doi.org/10.1001/archinte.1991.00400030135027.

5 Nittaya Khakhum, Itziar Chapartegui-González, and Alfredo G. Torres, "Combating the Great Mimicker: Latest Progress in the Development of Burkholderia
Pseudomallei Vaccines," *Expert Review of Vaccines* 19, no. 7 (July 2, 2020): 653–60,
https://doi.org/10.1080/14760584.2020.1791089.

6 Joan Stephenson, "Secrets of the 'Great Mimicker,'" *JAMA* 292, no. 15 (October
20, 2004): 1810, https://doi.org/10.1001/jama.292.15.1810-b.

7 Direk Limmathurotsakul et al., "Predicted Global Distribution of Burkholderia Pseudomallei and Burden of Melioidosis," *Nature Microbiology* 1, no. 1 (January 1, 2016):
15008, https://doi.org/10.1038/nmicrobiol.2015.8.

8 Allen C. Cheng and Bart J. Currie, "Melioidosis: Epidemiology, Pathophysiology,
and Management," *Clinical Microbiology Reviews* 18, no. 2 (April 2005): 383–416,
https://doi.org/10.1128/CMR.18.2.383-416.2005.

9 "2020 Annual Report of the Federal Select Agent Program," n.d., https://www
.selectagents.gov/resources/publications/docs/FSAP_Annual_Report_2020_508.pdf.

10 "Security Plan Guidance: Section 11(f)—Tier 1 Security | Compliance," Federal Select
Agent Program," September 16, 2020, https://www.selectagents.gov/compliance
/guidance/security-plan/section11f.htm.

11 "Security Plan Guidance: Section 11(f) – Tier 1 Security | Compliance," Federal Select Agent Program.

12 Andrew Lackner, Tulane National Primate Research Center director, interview with the author, February 2015.

13 Andrew Lackner, interview with the author.

14 "Emergency Response Report for TNPRC BPM Incident," U.S. Environmental Protection Agency Region 6, May 2015.

15 U.S. Department of Agriculture, Animal and Plant Health Inspection Service, Investigative and Enforcement Services, settlement agreement correspondence with Tulane National Primate Research Center, October 23, 2017. Obtained by the author under the Freedom of Information Act.

16 USDA correspondence with TNPRC, October 23, 2017.

17 USDA correspondence with TNPRC, October 23, 2017.

18 Alison Young, "Deadly Bacteria Release Sparks Concern at Louisiana Lab," *USA TODAY*, March 1, 2015, https://www.usatoday.com/story/news/2015/03/01/tulane-primate-bio-lab-bacteria-release/24137053/.

19 Katie Portacci, Tim Clouse, and Alejandro Rooney, "Burkholderia Pseudomallei Animal Health Risk Assessment" (Unredacted), U.S. Department of Agriculture Animal Plant Health Inspection Service. Obtained by the author through a Louisiana Public Records Act request.

20 Faimon A. Roberts III, "Tulane Was Slow to Notify Public Officials about Problem at Primate Center," NOLA.com, the *Advocate*, February 10, 2015, https://www.nola.com/news/communities/st_tammany/article_ff4fc9e8-69f2-58cc-8635-8731098aad1f.html.

21 Martin Enserink, "New Biodefense Splurge Creates Hotbeds, Shatters Dreams," *Science*, October 10, 2003, https://www.science.org/doi/pdf/10.1126/science.302.5643.206a.

22 "Biocontainment Research Facilities," NIH: National Institute of Allergy and Infectious Diseases, https://www.niaid.nih.gov/research/biocontainment-research-facilities.

23 "Regional BioSafety Lab Press Releases," Tulane National Primate Research Center, September 30, 2003, https://web.archive.org/web/20100612155536; http://www.tnprc.tulane.edu/rbl_press.html.

24 "Tulane Receives $13.6 Million for Biosafety Lab," Tulane National Primate Research Center (TNPRC) news release, September 30, 2003, https://web.archive.org/web/20100612155536; http://www.tnprc.tulane.edu/rbl_press.html. A footnote to the press release that TNPRC posted on its website noted that the original $13.6 million award was increased by NIH to $21 million.

25 "NIAID Funds Construction of Biosafety Laboratories," National Institutes of Health news release, September 30, 2003, https://web.archive.org/web/20100612155536; http://www.tnprc.tulane.edu/rbl_press.html.

26 TNPRC press release, September 30, 2003.

27 "Regional Biocontainment Laboratory," Tulane National Primate Research Center, April 9, 2019, https://tnprc.tulane.edu/regional-biosafety-laboratory.

28 "Biosafety Lab Dedicated," Tulane News, December 5, 2008, https://news.tulane.edu/news/biosafety-lab-dedicated.

29 TNPRC press release, September 30, 2003.

30 TNPRC press release, September 30, 2003.

31 Young, "Deadly Bacteria Release Sparks Concern at Louisiana Lab."

32 Department of Defense Contract HDTRA-14-C-0035, https://www.usaspending.gov/award/CONT_AWD_HDTRA114C0035_9700_-NONE-_-NONE-.

33 Tulane University School of Medicine, "Lisa Morici, PhD," https://medicine.tulane.edu/departments/microbiology-immunology-tips-mentor/faculty/lisa-morici-phd.

34 Morici and Roy did not respond to interview requests made to them and through the university's communications office.

35 Keith Brannon, "Breakthroughs and Beyond," *Tulane Med*, n.d., https://medicine.tulane.edu/sites/medicine.tulane.edu/files/pictures/TulaneMed_winter2019_reduced_save.pdf.

36 Young, "Deadly Bacteria Release Sparks Concern at Louisiana Lab."

37 "Entity Inspection Report: Tulane National Primate Research Center (CDC)" and related correspondence. Centers for Disease Control and Prevention, February 7, 2014. Obtained by the author under the federal Freedom of Information Act. The center's December 2013 inspection report, recently obtained under the Freedom of Information Act, cited the center for thirty violations. Some of the issues proved relevant to the Bp release, including citations for failing to have plans to adequately control access to areas with select agent pathogens to safeguard animals against intentional or accidental exposures, and having an inadequate response plan should an infection occur. At the time of the inspection, the center's occupational health program was listed as "currently under review."

38 "Emergency Response Report for TNPRC BPM Incident 18703 Three Rivers Road Covington, St. Tammany Parish, Louisiana," U.S. Environmental Protection Agency Region 6, May 2015.

39 Andrew Lackner, "CAB Update Jan 17, 2015," Tulane National Primate Research Center, https://web.archive.org/web/20151027130807; http://tulane.edu/tnprc/community-advisory-board/updates/cab-update-20150117.cfm.

40 Kim Chatelain, "Foreign Bacteria May Have Sickened Visiting USDA Scientist at Tulane Primate Center in Covington; Investigation Underway," *Times-Picayune*, NOLA com, February 8, 2015, https://www.nola.com/entertainment_life/health_fitness/article_dbf9861c-e8c6-543b-8738-01306dcae493.html.

41 "Ongoing Inquiry into Melioidosis Illness at Tulane Naitonal Research Center," Centers for Disease Control and Prevention media statement, February 7, 2015, https://www.cdc.gov/media/releases/2015/s0207-melioidosis.html.

42 Young, "Deadly Bacteria Release Sparks Concern at Louisiana Lab."

43 Alison Young, "Fifth Monkey Has Signs of Deadly Bacteria in Lab Mishap," *USA TODAY*, March 3, 2015, https://www.usatoday.com/story/news/2015/03/03/fifth-monkey-tulane-lab-incident/24344585/.

44 Alison Young, "CDC Seeks More Clues to Bioterror Lab Accident," *USA TODAY*, March 9, 2015, https://www.usatoday.com/story/news/2015/03/09/cdc-returns-to -tulane-primate-center/24672499/.

45 Young, "CDC Seeks More Clues to Bioterror Lab Accident."

46 Andrew Lackner, "CAB Update March 05, 2015," Tulane National Primate Research Center, https://web.archive.org/web/20151027130827; http://tulane.edu /tnprc/community-advisory-board/updates/cab-update-20150505.cfm.

47 Nathan E. Stone et al., "*Burkholderia Pseudomallei* in Soil, US Virgin Islands, 2019," *Emerging Infectious Diseases* 26, no. 11 (November 2020): 2773–75, https:// doi.org/10.3201/eid2611.191577.

48 Carina M. Hall et al., "*Burkholderia Pseudomallei*, the Causative Agent of Melioido- sis, Is Rare but Ecologically Established and Widely Dispersed in the Environment in Puerto Rico," *PLOS Neglected Tropical Diseases* 13, no. 9 (September 5, 2019): e0007727, https://doi.org/10.1371/journal.pntd.0007727.

49 "Melioidosis Locally Endemic in Areas of the Mississippi Gulf Coast after *Burkholde- ria Pseudomallei* Isolated in Soil and Water and Linked to Two Cases—Mississippi, 2020 and 2022," Centers for Disease Control and Prevention, July 27, 2022, https:// www.emergency.cdc.gov/han/2022/pdf/CDC_HAN_470.pdf. In its health alert, the CDC warned: "Once well-established in the soil, *B. pseudomallei* cannot feasibly be removed from the soil."

50 Lackner, "CAB Update," March 5, 2015.

51 Andrew Lackner, "CAB Update February 24, 2015," Tulane National Primate Research Center, https://web.archive.org/web/20150923110204; http://tulane.edu /tnprc/community-advisory-board/updates/cab-update-2015224.cfm.

52 Direk Limmathurotsakul et al., "*Burkholderia Pseudomallei* Is Spatially Distrib- uted in Soil in Northeast Thailand," *PLOS Neglected Tropical Diseases* 4, no. 6 (June 1, 2010): e694, https://doi.org/10.1371/journal.pntd.0000694.

53 Young, "Deadly Bacteria Release Sparks Concern at Louisiana Lab."

54 Alison Young, "Monkeys at Risk for Bioterror Bacteria Put Outdoors," *USA TODAY*, March 5, 2015, https://www.usatoday.com/story/news/2015/03/05/at-risk -monkeys-released-from-tulane-hospital/24471615/.

55 "Conclusion of Select Agent Inquiry into *Burkholderia pseudomallei* Release at Tulane National Primate Research Center," Centers for Disease Control and Preven- tion media statement, March 13, 2015, https://www.cdc.gov/media/releases/2015 /s0313-burkholderia-pseudomallei.html.

56 Alison Young, "Sloppy Lab Practice Cited in Bioterror Bacteria Release," *USA TODAY*, March 13, 2015, https://www.usatoday.com/story/news/2015/03/13/investigation -findings-tulane-lab-accident/70265838/.

57 Officials at the USDA, where Portacci was still employed, did not make her avail- able for an interview despite requests from the author. Lyndsay Cole, assistant director of public affairs, USDA Animal and Plant Health Inspection Service. Email exchange with the author, July 13–21, 2021.

58 Tim Clouse, retired USDA risk analyst, interview with the author, April 27, 2022.

59 On July 14, 2020, the author filed a FOIA request with the USDA seeking a copy of the risk assessment. The USDA provided a heavily redacted copy of the report

on February 26, 2021. While the vast majority of the details about Tulane's specific safety failures were redacted, the provided report included a few general references that indicated wastewater was a concern. In May 2021, the author filed a formal administrative appeal with the USDA of their excessive redactions. In October 2021, the USDA sent a letter upholding nearly all of their redactions. In April 2022 the author obtained an unredacted copy of the USDA risk assessment through a state public records request to the Louisiana Department of Agriculture and Forestry. In June 2022, with another state records request, the author obtained another copy of the full report from the Louisiana Department of Wildlife and Fisheries.

60 Tim Clouse, interview with the author, April 27, 2022.

61 Jeremy P. Schmidt, USDA/APHIS records specialist, email discussing FOIA request 2020-APHIS-05278-F, July 31, 2020. In this email, Schmidt wrote: "The APHIS FOIA office has completed its review and is proposing to release the entire document without any redactions."

62 Unidentified Tulane University official (name and title redacted), letter to Yvonne Marquez, Government Information Specialist, USDA/APHIS, October 2, 2020. Obtained by the author through a Freedom of Information Act request.

63 Tulane's letter cited federal statute 7 U.S.C. § 8401(h)(1). More information here: https://www.law.cornell.edu/uscode/text/7/8401 and here: https://www.govinfo.gov/content/pkg/PLAW-107publ188/pdf/PLAW-107publ188.pdf.

64 Katie Portacci, Tim Clouse, and Alejandro Rooney, "*Burkholderia pseudomallei* Animal Health Risk Assessment," USDA Animal and Plant Health Inspection Services, Veterinary Services, October 22, 2015. Obtained by the author under the Freedom of Information Act.

65 Portacci, Clouse, and Rooney, "*Burkholderia pseudomallei* Animal Health Risk Assessment."

66 Portacci, Clouse, and Rooney, "*Burkholderia pseudomallei* Animal Health Risk Assessment."

67 "Entity Inspection Report: Tulane National Primate Research Center (TNPRC)," Centers for Disease Control and Prevention, March 10, 2015. Obtained by the author under the federal Freedom of Information Act.

68 Eiko Yabuuchi et al., "Proposal of Burkholderia Gen. Nov. and Transfer of Seven Species of the Genus Pseudomonas Homology Group II to the New Genus, with the Type Species Burkholderia Cepacia (Palleroni and Holmes 1981) Comb. Nov.," *Microbiology and Immunology* 36, no. 12 (December 1992): 1251–75, https://doi.org/10.1111/j.1348-0421.1992.tb02129.x

69 Michael Strecker, email to the author, June 17, 2022.

70 USDA Animal and Plant Health Inspection Service, Investigative and Enforcement Services, "Settlement Agreement" and "Citation and Notification of Penalty," correspondence sent to Tulane National Primate Research Center, October 23, 2017. Obtained by the author under the FOIA.

71 Lyndsay Cole, assistant director of public affairs, USDA Animal and Plant Health Inspection Service, email correspondence with the author, June 30, 2022.

72 Michael Strecker, assistant vice president for communications, Tulane University, emailed statement to the author, July 28, 2021.

73 Jim LaCour, interview with the author, September 12, 2022.

74 Mark A. Alise, chief operations officer, Tulane National Primate Research Center, email and letter to the Louisiana Department of Environmental Quality, October 30, 2018.

75 Alise letter, October 30, 2018.

76 Charles Haas, interview with the author, April 14, 2022.

77 Alise letter, October 30, 2018.

78 Alise letter, October 30, 2018.

79 Dave Wagner, interview with the author, July 23, 2021.

80 Hall et al., "*Burkholderia Pseudomallei*, the Causative Agent of Melioidosis, Is Rare but Ecologically Established and Widely Dispersed in the Environment in Puerto Rico."

81 Stone et al., "*Burkholderia Pseudomallei* in Soil, US Virgin Islands, 2019."

82 Lourdes Iturralde, assistant secretary for environmental compliance at the Louisiana Department of Environmental Quality, letter to Mark A. Alise, chief operations officer, Tulane National Primate Research Center, July 28, 2021.

83 Tim Beckstrom, Louisiana DEQ, email to the author, May 4, 2022.

84 "TNPRC Regional Biocontainment Laboratory Upgrade for Capacity Building," Project Number 1G20AI167406-01. Award notice date September 23, 2021. National Institutes of Health RePORTER, https://reporter .nih.gov/project-details/10394502. After the author asked Tulane officials about this document and its statement that effluent decontamination capabilities are "desperately" needed, the text of the project narrative was removed from the NIH website. An archived version of the earlier record is available at https://web.archive .org/web/20220526184131; https://reporter.nih.gov/project-details/10394502.

85 Michael Strecker, email to the author, June 17, 2022.

86 CDC, emailed statement to the author, August 17, 2021.

Chapter 15: Engineered Microbes and Viral Ghosts

1 Andrea N. Ladd, biological safety officer and assistant director, EH&S, University of Wisconsin–Madison, "Template for Reporting Incidents Subject to the NIH Guidelines for Research Involving Recombinant or Synthetic Nucleic Acid Molecules to the National Institutes of Health Office of Science Policy (OSP)," University of Wisconsin–Madison, February 10, 2020.

Two versions of this NIH Guidelines report of the December 9, 2019, incident, one from NIH and the other from the university, were obtained by the author under public records laws. The report submitted to NIH by UW includes the following note: "*Confidential - do not release this information without written authorization of the University of Wisconsin–Madison." The version in NIH's files was further labeled in large type: "CONFIDENTIAL," but was released by federal officials without redactions. The version released by the university blacked out the name of the experiment's principal investigator, Yoshihiro Kawaoka. The university's justification: "Personally identifiable information regarding employees engaged in or employed in support of animal research. Under the balancing test inherent in Wisconsin's public records law, we have made the specific determination that the public interest in preventing harassment of staff and collaborators and protecting their safety outweighs the public interest in identifying the specific individuals involved with particular animals or research, or oversight of either."

2 Martin Enserink, "Scientists Brace for Media Storm Around Controversial Flu Studies," *ScienceInsider*, November 23, 2011, https://www.science.org/content /article/scientists-brace-media-storm-around-controversial-flu-studies.

3 Stephanie Sonnberg, Richard J. Webby, and Robert G. Webster, "2.1 Natural History of Highly Pathogenic Avian Influenza H5N1," *Virus Research* 178, no. 1 (December 5, 2013): 63–77, https://doi.org/10.1016/j.virusres.2013.05.009.

4 "Past Reported Global Human Cases with Highly Pathogenic Avian Influenza A(H5N1) (HPAI H5N1) by Country, 1997–2022 | Avian Influenza (Flu)," CDC, May 5, 2022, https://www.cdc.gov/flu/avianflu/chart-epi-curve-ah5n1.html.

5 "Human Infection with Avian Influenza A(H5) Viruses," World Health Organization Western Pacific Region, April 1, 2022, https://www.who.int/docs/default -source/wpro---documents/emergency/surveillance/avian-influenza/ai-20220401 .pdf.

6 "Past Examples of Possible Limited, Non-Sustained Person-to-Person Spread of Bird Flu | Avian Influenza (Flu)," CDC, March 24, 2022, https://www.cdc.gov /flu/avianflu/h5n1-human-infections.htm.

7 Jessica A. Belser et al., "A Guide for the Use of the Ferret Model for Influenza Virus Infection," *American Journal of Pathology* 190, no. 1 (January 1, 2020): 11–24, https://doi.org/10.1016/j.ajpath.2019.09.017.

8 Enserink, "Scientists Brace for Media Storm."

9 Sander Herfst et al., "Airborne Transmission of Influenza A/H5N1 Virus Between Ferrets," *Science* 336, no. 6088 (June 22, 2012): 1534–41, https://doi .org/10.1126/science.1213362.

10 Ed Yong, "Second Mutant Flu Paper Published," *Nature*, June 21, 2012, https:// doi.org/10.1038/nature.2012.10875.

11 Masaki Imai et al., "Experimental Adaptation of an Influenza H5 HA Confers Respiratory Droplet Transmission to a Reassortant H5 HA/H1N1 Virus in Ferrets," *Nature* 486, no. 7403 (June 2012): 420–28, https://doi.org/10.1038 /nature10831.

12 Masaki Imai et al., "Experimental Adaptation of an Influenza H5 HA."

13 Ron A. M. Fouchier et al., "Pause on Avian Flu Transmission Studies," *Nature* 481, no. 7382 (January 2012): 443, https://doi.org/10.1038/481443a.

14 Yoshihiro Kawaoka, "Flu Transmission Work Is Urgent," *Nature* 482, no. 7384 (February 2012): 155, https://doi.org/10.1038/nature10884.

15 Anthony S. Fauci, Gary J. Nabel, and Francis S. Collins, "A Flu Virus Risk Worth Taking," *Washington Post*, December 30, 2011, Opinions, https:// www.washingtonpost.com/opinions/a-flu-virus-risk-worth-taking/2011/12/30 /gIQAM9sNRP_story.html.

16 Marc Lipsitch and Barry R. Bloom, "Rethinking Biosafety in Research on Potential Pandemic Pathogens," *mBio* 3, no. 5 (October 9, 2012): e00360-12, https:// doi.org/10.1128/mBio.00360-12.

17 "National Science Advisory Board for Biosecurity—Findings and Recommendations," National Institutes of Health, March 29, 2012, https://www.nih.gov/sites/default/files/about-nih/nih-director/statements/collins/03302012_NSABB_Recommendations.pdf.

18 David Brown, "Scientists Asked to Withhold Details of Lab-Created Flu," *Washington Post*, December 21, 2011, FINAL edition, A01. Archived by Factiva.

19 Richard Ingham and Annie Hautefeuille, "Scientists Fight Back in 'Mutant Flu' Research Row," Agence France Presse, December 21, 2011. Archived by Factiva.

20 Brown, "Scientists Asked to Withhold Details," December 21, 2011.

21 Peter Palese, "Don't Censor Life-Saving Science," *Nature* 481, no. 7380 (January 2012): 115, https://doi.org/10.1038/481115a.

22 Terrence M. Tumpey et al., "Characterization of the Reconstructed 1918 Spanish Influenza Pandemic Virus," *Science (New York, N.Y.)* 310, no. 5745 (October 7, 2005): 77–80, https://doi.org/10.1126/science.1119392.

23 Centers for Disease Control and Prevention, "Researchers Reconstruct 1918 Pandemic Influenza Virus; Effort Designed to Advance Preparedness," October 5, 2005, https://www.cdc.gov/media/pressrel/r051005.htm.

24 "Ask a CDC Scientist: Dr. Terrence Tumpey and the Reconstruction of the 1918 Pandemic Virus | Pandemic Influenza (Flu) | CDC," November 29, 2018, https://www.cdc.gov/flu/pandemic-resources/1918-commemoration/special-features/ask-a-scientist-terrence-tumpey.htm.

25 Palese, "Don't Censor Life-Saving Science," January 2012.

26 Jamie Shreeve, "Why Revive a Deadly Flu Virus?" *New York Times*, January 29, 2006, Magazine, https://www.nytimes.com/2006/01/29/magazine/why-revive-a-deadly-flu-virus.html.

27 John Steinbruner, Elisa D. Harris, Nancy Gallagher, and Stacy M. Okutani, "Controlling Dangerous Pathogens: A Prototype Protective Oversight System," the Center for International and Security Studies at Maryland, University of Maryland, March 2007. Archived by the Internet Archive Wayback Machine, https://web.archive.org/web/20111201223542; http://www.cissm.umd.edu/papers/files/pathogens_project_monograph.pdf.

28 Steinbruner et al., "Controlling Dangerous Pathogens," March 2007.

29 "National Science Advisory Board for Biosecurity—Findings and Recommendations," National Institutes of Health, March 29, 2012, https://www.nih.gov/sites/default/files/about-nih/nih-director/statements/collins/03302012_NSABB_Recommendations.pdf.

30 Jim Turk, biological safety officer, University of Wisconsin–Madison, "NIH OBA Incident Report" of November 16, 2013, needlestick incident, November 19, 2013, https://www.documentcloud.org/documents/1698555-wi02.html, 373-377.

   The University of Wisconsin–Madison redacted portions of the description of the virus involved in the incident. The document described the needle as having "a reassortant virus on it, containing the HA from [redacted](H5N1) with the [redacted] mutation in the receptor binding site, and the rest of the genes from A/California/04/2009 (H1N1)."

31 Rebecca Moritz, University of Wisconsin lab safety official, "RE: H5N1 Lab exposer," email from Moritz to Thomas Haupt, Influenza Surveillance Coordinator/Research Scientist, Wisconsin Department of Health Services, November 18, 2013, 1:50 p.m. Moritz wrote: "The stick occurred when the individual was using a syringe to perform a procedure that could have easily been done without a needle. Long story short it was a miss use of sharps and poor handling. There were no eggs involved."

32 Dr. Jacqueline Corrigan-Curay, acting director, NIH Office of Biotechnology Policy, letter to Daniel Uhlrich, associate vice chancellor for research policy, University of Wisconsin–Madison, December 16, 2013, https://www.documentcloud .org/documents/1698555-wi02.html, 404–406.

33 Turk, "NIH OBA Incident Report," November 19, 2013.

34 Turk, "NIH OBA Incident Report," November 19, 2013. Also confirmed by the Public Health Madison & Dane County call intake log entries for November 16, 2013.

35 Thomas Haupt, Influenza Surveillance Coordinator/Research Scientist, Wisconsin Department of Health Services, "H5N1 Lab exposer," email to UW lab safety official Rebecca Moritz, copied to several state and CDC health officials, November 18, 2013, 11:06 a.m.

36 Turk, "NIH OBA Incident Report," November 19, 2013.

37 Dr. Amy P. Patterson, NIH associate director for science policy, and Sally Rockey, NIH deputy director for extramural research, letter to Martin Cadwallader, vice chancellor for research and dean of the graduate school, University of Wisconsin, December 17, 2013, https://www.documentcloud.org/documents/1698555-wi02 .html, 407–409.

38 Corrigan-Curay, letter to Uhlrich, December 16, 2013, 404–06.

39 Corrigan-Curray, letter to Uhlrich, December 16, 2013.

40 It is unclear how the miscommunication occurred. In response to my questions, UW spokesperson Kelly Tyrrell said in a November 4, 2022, email: "The Kawaoka lab believed it had access to a designated quarantine apartment and indicated this in the application to NIH." But UW provided no explanation for how the miscommunication happened, only how it was discovered. "In conversations with NIH, as indicated in the records you have, the miscommunication became apparent in subsequent follow-up and the university and lab immediately updated the Exposure Control Plan to reflect that high-risk exposures would result in quarantine in a dedicated hospital facility."

41 Patterson and Rockey, letter to Cadwallader, December 17, 2013.

42 Nick Penzenstadler, "Biolabs in Your Backyard," interactive, University of Wisconsin–Madison/Influenza Research Institute, USA TODAY, https://www.usatoday.com /pages/interactives/biolabs/#lab/WI02.

43 Patterson and Rockey, December 17, 2013.

44 Corrigan-Curray, letter to Uhlrich, December 16, 2013.

45 Jim Turk, University of Wisconsin biological safety officer, "NIH OBA Incident Report" of spill, November 9, 2013.

46 Daniel Uhlrich, University of Wisconsin–Madison associate vice chancellor for research policy, letter about the spill incident to Dr. Jacqueline Corrigan-Curay, acting director, NIH Office of Biotechnology Activities, December 20, 2013.

47 Patterson and Rockey, December 17, 2013.

48 Patterson and Rockey, December 17, 2013.

49 Patterson and Rockey, December 17, 2013.

50 Patterson and Rockey, December 17, 2013.

51 Dr. Sarah Van Orman, executive director University Health Services, and Dr. David Andes, University of Wisconsin professor of medicine and microbiology and chief of the division of infectious diseases, letter to Daniel Uhlrich, associate vice chancellor for research policy, graduate school, University of Wisconsin–Madison, December 20, 2013.

52 Van Orman and Andes, December 20, 2013.

53 Daniel Uhlrich, University of Wisconsin–Madison associate vice chancellor for research policy, letter to Dr. Jacqueline Corrigan-Curay, acting director NIH Office of Biotechnology Activities, December 20, 2013.

54 Dr. Jacqueline Corrigan-Curay, acting director, NIH Office of Biotechnology Activities, letter to Daniel Uhlrich, University of Wisconsin–Madison associate vice chancellor for research policy, December 24, 2013.

55 "Doing Diligence to Assess the Risks and Benefits of Life Sciences Gain-of-Function Research," whitehouse.gov, October 17, 2014, https://obamawhitehouse .archives.gov/blog/2014/10/17/doing-diligence-assess-risks-and-benefits-life-sciences -gain-function-research.

56 "NIH Lifts Funding Pause on Gain-of-Function Research," National Institutes of Health (NIH), December 18, 2017, https://www.nih.gov/about-nih/who-we-are/nih -director/statements/nih-lifts-funding-pause-gain-function-research.

57 "Gain of Function Research: A Symposium," National Academies, December 2014, https://www.nationalacademies.org/our-work/gain-of-function-research-a-symposium.

58 "Gain of Function Research: A Second Symposium," National Academies, March 10, 2016, https://www.nationalacademies.org/our-work/gain-of-function-research-a -second-symposium.

59 "Risk and Benefit Analysis of Gain of Function Research," Gryphon Scientific, April 2016, http://gryphonsci.wpengine.com/wp-content/uploads/2018/12/Risk-and -Benefit-Analysis-of-Gain-of-Function-Research-Final-Report-1.pdf.

60 "Recommendations for the Evaluation and Oversight of Proposed Gain-of-Function Research," National Science Advisory Board for Biosecurity, May 2016, https://osp .od.nih.gov/wp-content/uploads/2016/06/NSABB_Final_Report_Recommendations _Evaluation_Oversight_Proposed_Gain_of_Function_Research.pdf.

61 "Framework for Guiding Funding Decisions about Proposed Research Involving Enhanced Potential Pandemic Pathogens," U.S. Department of Health and Human Services, December 2017, https://www.phe.gov/s3/dualuse/Documents/p3co.pdf.

62 Jocelyn Kaiser, "EXCLUSIVE: Controversial Experiments That Could Make Bird Flu More Risky Poised to Resume," *Science*, February 8, 2019, https://www.science .org/content/article/exclusive-controversial-experiments-make-bird-flu-more-risky -poised-resume.

63 "Research Involving Enhanced Potential Pandemic Pathogens," National Institutes of Health (NIH), https://www.nih.gov/news-events/research-involving-potential -pandemic-pathogens.

64 Marc Lipsitch and Tom Inglesby, "Opinion | The U.S. Is Funding Dangerous Experiments It Doesn't Want You to Know About," *Washington Post*, February 27, 2019, https://www.washingtonpost.com/opinions/the-us-is-funding-dangerous-experiments-it-doesnt-want-you-to-know-about/2019/02/27/5f60e934-38ae-11e9-a2cd-307b06d0257b_story.html.

65 Ryan Bayha, director of strategic engagement, NIH Office of Science Policy, email to the author, September 2, 2022.

66 "NIH Commitment to Transparency on Research Involving Potential Pandemic Pathogens," National Institutes of Health, March 5, 2019, https://www.nih.gov/about-nih/who-we-are/nih-director/statements/nih-commitment-transparency-research-involving-potential-pandemic-pathogens.

67 "Framework for Guiding Funding Decisions about Proposed Research Involving Enhanced Potential Pandemic Pathogens," U.S. Department of Health and Human Services, 2017, https://www.phe.gov/s3/dualuse/Documents/P3CO.pdf.

68 HHS spokesperson, email to the author, August 19, 2022. Without providing details, the statement also said that the "HHS P3CO Review Group determined, in the case of this proposal, the research would be acceptable for HHS funding with recommended changes in the research plan to increase the potential benefits while decreasing risks."

69 Kelly Tyrrell, University of Wisconsin–Madison director of media relations and strategic communications, correspondence with the author in response to interview requests and written questions provided on July 22, 2022; August 3, 2022; October 27, 2022; and November 6, 2022.

70 "GoF Site Visit Interview Goals v2 - With Responses_Final," University of Wisconsin–Madison, July 5, 2015. This document labeled "final," which had been in development over several days, was circulated by UW's Amie Eisfeld, a research associate professor, to about a dozen UW officials involved in the safety of Kawaoka's labs, including Kawaoka; Tim Yoshino and Rebecca Moritz, the university's responsible official and alternate responsible official over select agent research; and Dr. Sarah Van Orman, executive director of University Health Services. Also on the email string was Doug Voegeli, who was a representative from Public Health Madison & Dane County and who had helped with answers to Gryphon's questions relating to local public health coordination. Eisfeld's email was sent after the group had held a meeting earlier that Sunday morning. The email and attached document were obtained by the author under a Wisconsin state public records request.

71 "GoF Site Visit Interview Goals v2."

72 "GoF Site Visit Interview Goals v2."

73 "GoF Site Visit Interview Goals v2."

74 Ladd, NIH incident report, February 10, 2020.

75 David Wahlberg, "A Safe Lab to Study Deadly Viruses? UW Researcher to Study Bird Flu at Specially Equipped Facility," *Capital Times & Wisconsin State Journal*, October 29, 2007. Archived by Factiva.

76 Ladd, NIH incident report, February 10, 2020.

77 Ryan Bayha, director of strategic engagement, NIH Office of Science Policy, email to the author, September 2, 2022. "The reassortant virus described in the incident report

is the same virus described in the 2012 *Nature* paper," Bayha confirmed, referring to this paper by Kawaoka's team: https://www.nature.com/articles/nature10831.

78 Bayha email, September 2, 2022.

79 Ryan Bayha, NIH Office of Science Policy, email to the author, August 5, 2022. According to Bayha, the incident occurred as part of NIH grant award 4R01AI06924, which was funded by the National Institute of Allergy and Infectious Diseases.

80 "Project Details: Transmissibility of Avian Influenza Viruses in Mammals, Project Number: 4R01AI069274-09," National Institutes of Health, n.d., https://reporter.nih.gov/search/x2YfCizmxkyxljH7zNTlRw/project-details/9121375.

81 Ladd, NIH incident report, February 10, 2020.

82 Ladd, NIH incident report, February 10, 2020.

83 Ladd, NIH incident report, February 10, 2020.

84 In response to state public records requests filed by the author in November 2021, officials at both Public Health Madison & Dane County, the local health department, and also at the Wisconsin Department of Health Services, the state health department, could find no record of the 2019 incident being reported to them. Officials at the state health department did not respond to repeated requests for comment on the apparent lack of reporting by UW and whether it is appropriate for UW to make decisions about discontinuing the quarantine of a lab worker potentially exposed to an enhanced avian influenza strain without consultation with local or state health officials.

85 "GoF Site Visit Interview Goals v2."

86 Kelly Tyrrell, University of Wisconsin–Madison director of media relations and strategic communications, emailed response to questions, November 16, 2022. "It remains the case that UW-Madison would immediately consult with university and local/state health officials in the event of an exposure or potential exposure," the statement added.

87 Morgan Finke, communications coordinator, Public Health Madison & Dane County, email response to questions from the author, August 10, 2022.

88 Finke, email response, August 10, 2022.

89 Ladd, NIH incident report, February 10, 2020.

90 "Incident Reporting—May 2019," Office of Science Policy (blog), https://osp.od.nih.gov/biotechnology/faqs-on-incident-reporting/.

91 Ryan Bayha, director of strategic engagement, NIH Office of Science Policy, emails to the author, August 5 and September 2, 2022.

92 Ladd, NIH incident report, February 10, 2020.

93 In a statement sent by Tyrrell on November 16, 2022, the university said: "The guidelines require overt or potential exposures to be immediately reported to the IBC. The incident was not an overt or potential exposure. However, UW's Select Agent Responsible Official called the IBC chair immediately following the incident to inform her. The chair sets the agenda for IBC meetings and set the discussion of the incident for the February 2020 meeting." As this book was finalized, UW had not responded to follow-up questions and a request to interview the IBC

chairperson or receive comment from them about why the incident wasn't brought to the full committee until February.

94 Bayha, August 5, 2022, and September 2, 2022.

95 Bayha, August 5, 2022.

96 Bayha, September 2, 2022.

97 Tyrrell, November 16, 2022.

98 Ryan Bayha, email to the author, December 2, 2022.

99 Bayha, August 5, 2022, and September 2, 2022.

100 HHS spokesperson, email to the author, August 19, 2022.

101 Tyrrell, November 16, 2022.

102 "Inspection Findings," CDC-Federal Select Agent Program, September 16–20, 2019. Two versions of this document were obtained by the author under the federal Freedom of Information Act. The most heavily redacted version was released in response to the author's initial FOIA request in October 2021. After the author filed an administrative appeal of the redactions in February 2022, the CDC provided what it called a "supplemental production" in July 2022 that released a slightly less redacted version of the record, disclosing, for instance, the part of the violation that noted it had been classified as "serious." The author's administrative appeal seeking the full record without redactions was still pending in November 2022.

103 Kelly Tyrrell, University of Wisconsin–Madison director of media relations and strategic communications, correspondence with the author, August 1, 2022.

104 Ladd, NIH incident report, February 10, 2020.

105 Ladd, NIH incident report, February 10, 2020.

106 Ladd, NIH incident report, February 10, 2020.

107 Bayha, correspondence with the author, August 5, 2022.

108 Tyrrell, November 30, 2022.

109 Michelle McKinney, Health Science Policy Analyst OSP, NIH, email to Andrea N. Ladd, University of Wisconsin–Madison biological safety officer, "RE: Incident Report Attached," March 27, 2020. Obtained by the author under the Freedom of Information Act.

110 Kelly Tyrrell, email to the author, August 1, 2022.

111 Tom Inglesby, interview with the author, July 27, 2022.

112 Tom Inglesby, "Horsepox and the Need for a New Norm, More Transparency, and Stronger Oversight for Experiments That Pose Pandemic Risks," *PLOS Pathogens* 14, no. 10 (October 4, 2018): e1007129, https://doi.org/10.1371/journal.ppat.1007129.

113 "Genomic Sequencing of SARS-CoV-2: A Guide to Implementation for Maximum Impact on Public Health," World Health Organization, January 8, 2021, https://www.who.int/publications-detail-redirect/9789240018440.

114 Kai Kupferschmidt, "How Canadian Researchers Reconstituted an Extinct Poxvirus for $100,000 Using Mail-Order DNA," *Science*, July 6, 2017, https://www.science.org/content/article/how-canadian-researchers-reconstituted-extinct-poxvirus-100000-using-mail-order-dna.

115 "WHO Advisory Committee on Variola Virus Research: Report of the Eighteenth Meeting," World Health Organization, November 2, 2016. Archived by the Internet Archive Wayback Machine, https://web.archive.org/web/20181105231226; https://www.who.int/csr/resources/publications/smallpox/18-ACVVR-Final.pdf?ua=1.

116 Ryan S. Noyce, Seth Lederman, and David H. Evans, "Construction of an Infectious Horsepox Virus Vaccine from Chemically Synthesized DNA Fragments," *PLOS One* 13, no. 1 (January 19, 2018): e0188453, https://doi.org/10.1371/journal.pone.0188453.

117 Ryan S. Noyce and David H. Evans, "Synthetic Horsepox Viruses and the Continuing Debate about Dual Use Research," *PLOS Pathogens* 14, no. 10 (October 4, 2018): e1007025, https://doi.org/10.1371/journal.ppat.1007025.

118 Noyce, Lederman, and Evans, "Construction of an Infectious Horsepox Virus Vaccine," January 19, 2018.

119 "Tonix Pharmaceuticals Presented Results from a Preclinical Study of TNX-801, a Potential Vaccine to Prevent Smallpox and Monkeypox, in a Poster Presentation at the 2020 American Society for Microbiology (ASM) Biothreats Conference," Tonix Pharmaceuticals Holding Corp, https://ir.tonixpharma.com/news-events/press-releases/detail/1186/tonix-pharmaceuticals-presented-results-from-a-preclinical.

120 "International Gene Synthesis Consortium," https://genesynthesisconsortium.org/.

121 Gregory D. Koblentz, "A Biotech Firm Made a Smallpox-like Virus on Purpose. Nobody Seems to Care," *Bulletin of the Atomic Scientists* (blog), February 21, 2020, https://thebulletin.org/2020/02/a-biotech-firm-made-a-smallpox-like-virus-on-purpose-nobody-seems-to-care/.

122 Kazunobu Kojima, emailed answers to questions from the author, June 6, 2022.

123 Jessica A. Bell and Jennifer B. Nuzzo, *2021 Global Health Security Index*, Nuclear Threat Initiative and Johns Hopkins Center for Health Security, 2021, https://www.ghsindex.org/report-model/.

124 Jaime Yassif, interview with the author, August 4, 2022.

125 Kojima, June 6, 2022.

126 "Joint Assessment Mechanism to Determine Pandemic Origins," NTI, n.d., https://www.nti.org/about/programs-projects/project/joint-assessment-mechanism-to-determine-pandemic-origins/.

127 Anthony S. Fauci, "Research on Highly Pathogenic H5N1 Influenza Virus: The Way Forward," *MBio* 3, no. 5 (October 9, 2012): e00359-12, https://doi.org/10.1128/mBio.00359-12.

128 Fauci, "Research on Highly Pathogenic H5N1."

Chapter 16: Chimeras

1 Baric, through UNC spokespeople, repeatedly declined interview requests from the author in 2020 and 2022.

2 Nell Greenfieldboyce, "How a Tilt Toward Safety Stopped a Scientist's Virus Research," NPR, November 7, 2014, https://www.wunc.org/2014-11-07/how-a-tilt-toward-safety-stopped-a-scientists-virus-research.

3 "Doing Diligence to Assess the Risks and Benefits of Life Sciences Gain-of-Function Research," whitehouse.gov, October 17, 2014, https://obamawhitehouse.archives.gov/blog/2014/10/17/doing-diligence-assess-risks-and-benefits-life-sciences-gain-function-research.

4 Ralph S. Baric and Mark R. Denison, "RE: Gain of Function Pause and Implications for Coronavirus Animal Model Development," November 12, 2014, https://osp.od.nih.gov/wp-content/uploads/2013/06/Gain_of_Function_Deliberative_Process_Written_Public_Comments.pdf, 28–32.

5 Baric and Denison, "RE: Gain of Function Pause."

6 Anton Zuiker, "Stalking SARS," *Endeavors*, UNC Research, September 1, 2003, https://endeavors.unc.edu/fall2003/baric.html.

7 "SARS: How a Global Epidemic Was Stopped," World Health Organization Western Pacific Region, 2006, https://apps.who.int/iris/bitstream/handle/10665/207501/9290612134_eng.pdf.

8 Zuiker, "Stalking SARS."

9 Baric and Denison, November 12, 2014.

10 Xing-Yi Ge et al., "Isolation and Characterization of a Bat SARS-like Coronavirus That Uses the ACE2 Receptor," *Nature* 503, no. 7477 (November 2013): 535–38, https://doi.org/10.1038/nature12711.

11 Rowan Jacobsen, " 'We Never Created a Supervirus.' Ralph Baric Explains Gain-of-Function Research," *MIT Technology Review*, July 26, 2021, https://www.technologyreview.com/2021/07/26/1030043/gain-of-function-research-coronavirus-ralph-baric-vaccines/.

12 Jacobsen, " 'We Never Created a Supervirus.' "

13 Vineet D. Menachery et al., "A SARS-like Cluster of Circulating Bat Coronaviruses Shows Potential for Human Emergence," *Nature Medicine* 21, no. 12 (November 2015): 1508–13, https://doi.org/10.1038/nm.3985. The acknowledgments section of the paper notes: "Experiments with the full-length and chimeric SHC014 recombinant viruses were initiated and performed before the GOF research funding pause and have since been reviewed and approved for continued study by the NIH."

14 Declan Butler, "Engineered Bat Virus Stirs Debate over Risky Research," *Nature*, November 12, 2015, https://doi.org/10.1038/nature.2015.18787.

15 Boyd Yount et al., "Reverse Genetics with a Full-Length Infectious CDNA of Severe Acute Respiratory Syndrome Coronavirus," *Proceedings of the National Academy of Sciences* 100, no. 22 (October 28, 2003): 12995–13000, https://doi.org/10.1073/pnas.1735582100.

16 Menachery et al., "A SARS-like Cluster of Circulating Bat Coronaviruses."

17 Zhengli Shi and Zhihong Hu, "A Review of Studies on Animal Reservoirs of the SARS Coronavirus," *Virus Research* 133, no. 1 (April 2008): 74–87, https://doi.org/10.1016/j.virusres.2007.03.012.

18 UNC Gillings School of Global Public Health, "New SARS-like Virus Can Jump Directly from Bats to Humans, No Treatment Available," November 9, 2015, https://sph.unc.edu/sph-news/new-sars-like-virus-can-jump-directly-from-bats-to-humans-no-treatment-available/.

19 "New SARS-like Virus Can Jump Directly from Bats to Humans."

20 Butler, "Engineered Bat Virus," November 12, 2015.

21 Helen Branswell, "SARS-like Virus in Bats Shows Potential to Infect Humans, Study Finds," *STAT*, November 9, 2015, https://www.statnews.com/2015/11/09/sars -like-virus-bats-shows-potential-infect-humans-study-finds/.

22 Menachery et al., "A SARS-like Cluster of Circulating Bat Coronaviruses," November 2015.

23 Menachery et al., "A SARS-like Cluster of Circulating Bat Coronaviruses," November 2015.

24 Alison Young and Jessica Blake, "Near Misses at UNC Chapel Hill's High-Security Lab Illustrate Risk of Accidents with Coronaviruses," ProPublica, August 17, 2020, https://www.propublica.org/article/near-misses-at-unc-chapel-hills-high-security -lab-illustrate-risk-of-accidents-with-coronaviruses.

25 Daniel Eisenman, UNC-Chapel Hill biological safety officer, letter to Ryan Bayha, senior analyst for biosecurity and biosafety policy, NIH Office of Science Policy, "RE: Mouse Bite Involving a Mouse Infected with Mouse Adapted SARS CoV," February 15, 2016. The author obtained copies of this letter from the university and from NIH under state and federal public records requirements. The university used white-out to make all references to SARS, MERS, and 1918 influenza disappear from the version it released. The version later released by NIH included the references to the viruses.

26 Eisenman, February 15, 2016.

27 Young and Blake, "Near Misses at UNC Chapel Hill's High-Security Lab."

28 Young and Blake, "Near Misses at UNC Chapel Hill's High-Security Lab."

29 "FW: PO Response Needed (by COB Today 8/19/2020) Biosafety at UNC," August 19–21, 2020, https://www.documentcloud.org/documents/21182763-pages -from-nih_foia_153-160.

30 "FW: PO Response Needed (by COB Today 8/19/2020) Biosafety at UNC," August 19–21, 2020, https://www.documentcloud.org/documents/21182763-pages -from-nih_foia_153-160.

31 Mara Hvistendahl and Sharon Lerner, "FBI Sought Documents Related to U.S.-Funded Coronavirus Research in China," the Intercept, January 20, 2022, https:// theintercept.com/2022/01/20/coronavirus-research-china-ecohealth-fbi/.

32 Alison Young and Jessica Blake, "Here Are Six Accidents UNC Researchers Had with Lab-Created Coronaviruses," ProPublica, August 17, 2020, https://www .propublica.org/article/here-are-six-accidents-unc-researchers-had-with-lab-created -coronaviruses.

33 Garry Coulson, biosafety officer, University of North Carolina at Chapel Hill, email to NIH officials, "RE: NIH Incident Report—Preliminary," April 22, 2020. Obtained by the author under a public records request.

34 Derek Kemp, email transmitting the pdf of records, "RE: Request for University of North Carolina-Chapel Hill IBC Records," July 20, 2020.

35 "FAQs About IBC Meetings and Minutes," Office of Science Policy (blog), https://osp .od.nih.gov/biotechnology/faqs-about-ibc-meetings-and-minutes/.

36 Allan C. Shipp, director of outreach, NIH Program on Biosecurity and Biosafety Policy, memo to Institutional Biosafety Committee (IBC) Chairs, Biological Safety Officers, and Contacts for IBCs, November 21, 2014, archived by the Internet Archive Wayback Machine, https://web.archive.org/web/20150512181822/https://osp.od.nih.gov/sites/default/files/resources/2014%20Memo%20on%20Access%20to%20IBC%20Meeting%20Minutes%20and%20Other%20Documentation.pdf.

37 "Dr. Ralph Baric Receives O. Max Gardner Award for Coronavirus Research," UNC Gillings School of Global Public Health, October 12, 2021, https://sph.unc.edu/sph-news/dr-ralph-baric-receives-o-max-gardner-award-for-coronavirus-research/.

38 *2022 Annual Meeting: Presentation Ceremony for Members Elected in 2021*, National Academy of Sciences, April 29, 2022, 5:20–5:45, http://www.nasonline.org/about-nas/events/annual-meeting/nas159/2021-ceremony.html.

39 Menachery et al., "A SARS-like Cluster of Circulating Bat Coronaviruses," November 2015.

40 Ben Hu et al., "Discovery of a Rich Gene Pool of Bat SARS-Related Coronaviruses Provides New Insights into the Origin of SARS Coronavirus," *PLoS Pathogens* 13, no. 11 (November 30, 2017): e1006698, https://doi.org/10.1371/journal.ppat.1006698.

41 Hu et al., "Discovery of a Rich Gene Pool of Bat SARS-Related Coronaviruses."

42 "SARS-CoV-2 and NIAID-Supported Bat Coronavirus Research | An Analysis: Evolutionary Distance of SARS-CoV-2 and Bat Coronaviruses Studied Under the NIH-Supported Research Grant to EcoHealth Alliance," NIH National Institute of Allergy and Infectious Diseases, October 20, 2021, https://www.niaid.nih.gov/diseases-conditions/coronavirus-bat-research.

43 Lei-Ping Zeng et al., "Bat Severe Acute Respiratory Syndrome-Like Coronavirus WIV1 Encodes an Extra Accessory Protein, ORFX, Involved in Modulation of the Host Immune Response," ed. S. Perlman, *Journal of Virology* 90, no. 14 (July 15, 2016): 6573–82, https://doi.org/10.1128/JVI.03079-15.

44 Boyd Yount, Kristopher M. Curtis, and Ralph S. Baric, "Strategy for Systematic Assembly of Large RNA and DNA Genomes: Transmissible Gastroenteritis Virus Model," *Journal of Virology* 74, no. 22 (November 15, 2000): 10600–611, https://doi.org/10.1128/JVI.74.22.10600-10611.2000.

45 Zeng et al., "Bat Severe Acute Respiratory Syndrome-Like Coronavirus WIV1 Encodes an Extra Accessory Protein, ORFX, Involved in Modulation of the Host Immune Response."

   And Hua Guo et al., "Evolutionary Arms Race between Virus and Host Drives Genetic Diversity in Bat Severe Acute Respiratory Syndrome-Related Coronavirus Spike Genes," ed. Julie K. Pfeiffer, *Journal of Virology* 94, no. 20 (September 29, 2020): e00902-20, https://doi.org/10.1128/JVI.00902-20.

46 Donald G. McNeil Jr., "How I Learned to Stop Worrying and Love the Lab-Leak Theory,*" *Medium* (blog), May 25, 2021, https://donaldgmcneiljr1954.medium.com/how-i-learned-to-stop-worrying-and-love-the-lab-leak-theory-f4f88446b04d.

47 *W. Ian Lipkin—What We Need to Know About Coronavirus*, 2020, https://www.youtube.com/watch?v=W28lG6jZyCs.

48 Kristian G. Andersen et al., "The Proximal Origin of SARS-CoV-2," *Nature Medicine*, March 17, 2020, https://doi.org/10.1038/s41591-020-0820-9.

49 W. Ian Lipkin, email to the author, August 23, 2022.

50 "Prof. Ian Lipkin Brings Science to Hollywood's Contagion | Columbia Public Health," August 27, 2011, https://www.publichealth.columbia.edu/public-health-now /news/prof-ian-lipkin-brings-science-hollywoods-contagion.

51 W. Ian Lipkin, "Biocontainment in Gain-of-Function Infectious Disease Research," *mBio* 3, no. 5 (November 2012): e00290–12, https://doi.org/10.1128/mBio.00290-12.

52 David Cyranoski, "Inside the Chinese Lab Poised to Study World's Most Dangerous Pathogens," *Nature* 542, no. 7642 (February 1, 2017): 399–400, https://doi .org/10.1038/nature.2017.21487.

53 Rowan Jacobsen, " 'We Never Created a Supervirus.' "

54 "WHO-Convened Global Study of Origins of SARS-CoV-2: China Part," https:// www.who.int/publications-detail-redirect/who-convened-global-study-of-origins -of-sars-cov-2-china-part.

55 Peter Ben Embarek, COVID-19 Virtual Press conference transcript, February 9, 2021, https://www.who.int/publications/m/item/covid-19-virtual-press-conference -transcript---9-february-2021.

56 "Joint Report: ANNEXES, WHO-Convened Global Study of Origins of SARS-CoV-2: China Part," World Health Organization, March 30, 2021, 131.

57 "Joint Statement on the WHO-Convened COVID-19 Origins Study," United States Department of State, March 30, 2021, https://www.state.gov/joint-statement-on-the -who-convened-covid-19-origins-study/.

58 Associated Press, "The WHO's Chief Says It Was Premature to Rule Out a Lab Leak as the Pandemic's Origin," NPR, July 15, 2021, Shots - Health News, https:// www.npr.org/2021/07/15/1016436749/who-chief-wuhan-lab-covid-19-origin -premature-tedros.

59 Adam Taylor, Emily Rauhala, and Martin Selsoe Sorensen, "In New Documentary, WHO Scientist Says Chinese Officials Pressured Investigation to Drop Lab-Leak Hypothesis," *Washington Post*, August 12, 2021, https://www.washingtonpost.com /world/2021/08/12/who-origins-embarek/.

60 "Virus Origin/Origins of the SARS-CoV-2 Virus," WHO, https://www.who.int /emergencies/diseases/novel-coronavirus-2019/origins-of-the-virus.

61 "WHO-Convened Global Study of Origins of SARS-CoV-2: China Part," March 30, 2021, https://www.who.int/publications-detail-redirect/who-convened-global -study-of-origins-of-sars-cov-2-china-part.

62 Jesse D. Bloom et al., "Investigate the Origins of COVID-19," ed. Jennifer Sills, *Science* 372, no. 6543 (May 14, 2021): 694, https://doi.org/10.1126/science.abj0016.

63 Jacobsen, " 'We Never Created a Supervirus.' "

64 Shi Zhengli, "Reply to *Science* Magazine."

65 Amy Qin and Chris Buckley, "A Top Virologist in China, at Center of a Pandemic Storm, Speaks Out," *New York Times*, June 14, 2021, World, https://www .nytimes.com/2021/06/14/world/asia/china-covid-wuhan-lab-leak.html.

66 *Lab Leak or Natural Origin? Scientists Discuss How the #COVID19 Pandemic Began*, Facebook Live video discussion on pandemic origins sponsored by *Science* magazine,

September 30, 2021, https://www.facebook.com/ScienceMagazine/videos/lab-leak-or
-natural-origin-scientists-discuss-how-the-covid19-pandemic-began/2941880282
717315/.

67 "Curriculum Vitae, Linfa (Lin-Fa) Wang," n.d., https://globalhealth.duke.edu/sites
/default/files/cv/cv-linfa-wang-220202.pdf.

68 *Lab Leak or Natural Origin?*

69 *Lab Leak or Natural Origin?*

70 Michael Worobey et al., "The Huanan Seafood Wholesale Market in Wuhan Was
the Early Epicenter of the COVID-19 Pandemic," *Science*, July 26, 2022, https://
www.science.org/doi/10.1126/science.abp8715.

71 *Lab Leak or Natural Origin?*

72 "China Didn't Warn Public of Likely Pandemic for 6 Key Days," Associated
Press, April 20, 2021, https://apnews.com/article/virus-outbreak-health-ap-top
-news-international-news-china-clamps-down-68a9e1b91de4ffc166acd6012
d82c2f9.

73 Nectar Gan, Caitlin Hu, and Ivan Watson, "China Imposes Restrictions on
Research into Origins of Coronavirus," CNN, April 16, 2020, https://www.cnn
.com/2020/04/12/asia/china-coronavirus-research-restrictions-intl-hnk/index.html.

74 Gan, Hu, and Watson, "China Imposes Restrictions."

75 Dake Kang, Maria Cheng, and Sam McNeil, "China Clamps Down in Hidden
Hunt for Coronavirus Origins," Associated Press, December 30, 2020, https://
apnews.com/article/united-nations-coronavirus-pandemic-china-only-on-ap-bats
-24fbadc58cee3a40bca2ddf7a14d2955.

76 Xiaodong Wang, "Progress Continues in Coronavirus Trace," *China Daily*, January 26, 2020, https://www.chinadaily.com.cn/a/202001/26/WS5e2d3124a310128
2172734dd.html.

77 Daniel R. Lucey and Kristen Kent, "With Evidence against the Origin of
COVID-19 Being the Seafood Market in December, a Call to Share and Discuss All Data at the 73rd World Health Assembly in May," Science Speaks blog,
Infectious Disease Society of America, April 27, 2020, https://www.idsociety.org
/science-speaks-blog/2020/with-evidence-against-the-origin-of-covid-19-being-the
-seafood-market-in-december-a--call-to-share-and-discuss-all-data-at-the-73rd
-world-health-assembly-in-may/.

78 Jeremy Page and Natasha Khan, "On the Ground in Wuhan, Signs of China Stall-
ing Probe of Coronavirus Origins," *Wall Street Journal*, May 12, 2020, World,
https://www.wsj.com/articles/china-stalls-global-search-for-coronavirus-origins
-wuhan-markets-investigation-11589300842.

79 "Wuhan's Huanan Seafood Market a Victim of COVID-19: CDC Director," *Global Times*, May 26, 2020, https://www.globaltimes.cn/content/1189506
.shtml.

80 Since then, researchers from the Institut Pasteur and the National University of
Laos have identified in Laos bat viruses that are slightly closer relatives of the
Covid-19 virus. These newly discovered viruses are up to 96.8 percent identical to
the SARS-CoV-2 virus. (RaTG13 is a 96.2 percent match.) https://www.nature.com
/articles/s41586-022-04532-4.

81 Peng Zhou et al., "A Pneumonia Outbreak Associated with a New Coronavirus of Probable Bat Origin," *Nature* 579, no. 7798 (March 2020): 270–73, https://doi .org/10.1038/s41586-020-2012-7.

82 Xing-Yi Ge et al., "Coexistence of Multiple Coronaviruses in Several Bat Colonies in an Abandoned Mineshaft," *Virologica Sinica* 31, no. 1 (February 1, 2016): 31– 40, https://doi.org/10.1007/s12250-016-3713-9.

83 Over time, the members of DRASTIC split into two groups. In the original group, the acronym stood for Decentralized Radical Autonomous Search Team Investigating COVID-19: https://drasticresearch.org/. Many members later formed a different group called DRASTIC Science, with their acronym standing for Dedicated Research and Scientific Team Investigating Covid-19: https://drasticscience.com/.

84 Monali C. Rahalkar and Rahul A. Bahulikar, "Lethal Pneumonia Cases in Mojiang Miners (2012) and the Mineshaft Could Provide Important Clues to the Origin of SARS-CoV-2," *Frontiers in Public Health* 8 (2020), https://www.frontiersin.org /articles/10.3389/fpubh.2020.581569.

85 DRASTIC Research, "Rossana Segreto," https://drasticresearch.org/tag/rossana -segreto/.

86 Paul Farhi and Jeremy Barr, "The Media Called the 'Lab Leak' Story a 'Conspiracy Theory.' Now It's Prompted Corrections—and Serious New Reporting," *Washington Post*, June 10, 2021, https://www.washingtonpost.com/lifestyle/media/the-media -called-the-lab-leak-story-a-conspiracy-theory-now-its-prompted-corrections--and-seri ous-new-reporting/2021/06/10/c93972e6-c7b2-11eb-a11b-6c6191ccd599_story.html.

87 Antonio Regalado, "Curious Coincidence: Sleuths," *MIT Technology Review Curious Coincidence* podcast, https://www.technologyreview.com/supertopic/curious -coincidence/.

88 The Seeker, Twitter post, May 18, 2020, with updated archived link on October 8, 2020, https://twitter.com/TheSeeker268/status/1314253565922168832.

89 Jeremy Page, Betsy McKay, and Drew Hinshaw, "The Wuhan Lab Leak Question: A Disused Chinese Mine Takes Center Stage," *Wall Street Journal*, May 24, 2021, https://www.wsj.com/articles/wuhan-lab-leak-question-chinese-mine-covid-pandemic -11621871125.

90 Page, McKay, and Hinshaw, "The Wuhan Lab Leak Question."

91 Peng Zhou et al., "Addendum: A Pneumonia Outbreak Associated with a New Coronavirus of Probable Bat Origin," *Nature* 588, no. 7836 (December 2020): E6, https://doi.org/10.1038/s41586-020-2951-z.

92 The addendum said that the virus "was renamed RaTG13 in our Article to reflect the bat species, the location and the sampling year." It also noted that the virus was previously described in a 2016 paper, which it cited.

93 Jane Qiu, "How China's 'Bat Woman' Hunted Down Viruses from SARS to the New Coronavirus," *Scientific American*, March 11, 2020, https://www.scientific american.com/article/how-chinas-bat-woman-hunted-down-viruses-from-sars -to-the-new-coronavirus1/.

94 "Joint Report: ANNEXES, WHO-Convened Global Study of Origins of SARS-CoV-2: China Part," World Health Organization, March 30, 2021, 131.

95 Jane Qiu, "Meet the Scientist at the Center of the Covid Lab Leak Controversy," *MIT Technology Review*, February 9, 2022, https://www.technologyreview.com/2022/02/09/1044985/shi-zhengli-covid-lab-leak-wuhan/.

96 "Declassified Assessment on COVID-19 Origins," Office of the Director of National Intelligence, October 29, 2021, https://www.dni.gov/index.php/newsroom/reports-publications/reports-publications-2021/item/2263-declassified-assessment-on-covid-19-origins.

97 Shi Zhengli, "Reply to *Science* Magazine."

98 Qiu, "Meet the Scientist."

99 Katie Bo Williams, Zachary Cohen, and Natasha Bertrand, "Exclusive: Intel Agencies Scour Reams of Genetic Data from Wuhan Lab in Covid Origins Hunt," CNN, August 5, 2021, https://www.cnn.com/2021/08/05/politics/covid-origins-genetic-data-wuhan-lab/index.html.

100 "Joint Report: ANNEXES, WHO-Convened Global Study of Origins of SARS-CoV-2: China Part," World Health Organization, March 30, 2021, 132.

101 Michael R. Gordon, Warren P. Strobel, and Drew Hinshaw, "WSJ News Exclusive | Intelligence on Sick Staff at Wuhan Lab Fuels Debate on Covid-19 Origin," *Wall Street Journal*, May 23, 2021, World, https://www.wsj.com/articles/intelligence-on-sick-staff-at-wuhan-lab-fuels-debate-on-covid-19-origin-11621796228.

102 Joint Report: ANNEXES, WHO-Convened Global Study, 132.

103 "Fact Sheet: Activity at the Wuhan Institute of Virology," United States Department of State, January 15, 2021, https://2017-2021.state.gov/fact-sheet-activity-at-the-wuhan-institute-of-virology/.

104 "Statement by President Joe Biden on the Investigation into the Origins of COVID-19," the White House, May 26, 2021, https://www.whitehouse.gov/briefing-room/statements-releases/2021/05/26/statement-by-president-joe-biden-on-the-investigation-into-the-origins-of-covid-19/.

105 "Unclassified Summary of Assessment on Covid-19 Origins," Office of the Director of National Intelligence, August 26, 2021, https://www.dni.gov/index.php/newsroom/reports-publications/reports-publications-2021/item/2236-unclassified-summary-of-assessment-on-covid-19-origins.

106 "Declassified Assessment on COVID-19 Origins," Office of the Director of National Intelligence, October 29, 2021, https://www.dni.gov/index.php/newsroom/reports-publications/reports-publications-2021/item/2263-declassified-assessment-on-covid-19-origins.

107 DRASTIC Research, "DRASTIC Analysis of the DEFUSE Documents," September 20, 2021, https://drasticresearch.org/2021/09/20/1583/.

108 Sharon Lerner and Maia Hibbett, "Leaked Grant Proposal Details High-Risk Coronavirus Research," the Intercept, September 23, 2021, https://theintercept.com/2021/09/23/coronavirus-research-grant-darpa/.

109 Bryan A. Johnson et al., "Loss of Furin Cleavage Site Attenuates SARS-CoV-2 Pathogenesis," *Nature* 591, no. 7849 (March 2021): 293–99, https://doi.org/10.1038/s41586-021-03237-4.

110 B. Coutard et al., "The Spike Glycoprotein of the New Coronavirus 2019-nCoV Contains a Furin-like Cleavage Site Absent in CoV of the Same Clade," *Antiviral Research* 176 (April 2020): 104742, https://doi.org/10.1016/j.antiviral.2020.104742.

111 "PROPOSAL: VOLUME I , Project DEFUSE: Defusing the Threats of Bat-Borne Coronaviruses," March 27, 2018, https://www.documentcloud.org/documents /21066966-defuse-proposal.

112 EcoHealth president Peter Daszak has said the proposal wasn't funded. Tabatha Thompson, chief of communications, DARPA, in an email to the author on August 29, 2022, said: "In accordance with U.S. Federal Acquisition Regulations, we are not at liberty to divulge who may have or may not have submitted a proposal in response to any of the agency's solicitations. Further, information contained within bids is considered proprietary and can only be released by the bidder. That being said, DARPA has never funded directly, nor indirectly as a subcontractor, any activity associated with the EcoHealth Alliance."

113 Neil L. Harrison and Jeffrey D. Sachs, "Did US Biotechnology Help to Create COVID-19?" Project Syndicate, May 27, 2022, https://www.project-syndicate .org/onpoint/did-us-technology-help-create-covid-19-in-china-by-neil-l-harrison-and -jeffrey-d-sachs-2022-05.

114 Daniel Engber and Adam Federman, "The Lab-Leak Debate Just Got Even Messier," the *Atlantic*, September 25, 2021, https://www.theatlantic.com/science/archive /2021/09/lab-leak-pandemic-origins-even-messier/620209/.

115 Jesse Bloom, interview with the author, July 17, 2022.

116 David Baltimore Q&A, "The Debate over Origins of SARS-CoV-2," California Institute of Technology, June 22, 2021, https://www.caltech.edu/about/news/the -debate-over-origins-of-sars-cov-2.

117 Sharon Lerner and Mara Hvistendahl, "Peter Daszak Answers Critics and Defends Coronavirus Research," the Intercept, March 11, 2022, https://theintercept.com /2022/03/11/covid-nih-ecohealth-peter-daszak-interview/.

118 Michael Worobey did not respond to multiple requests for an interview or comments made by the author in July, August, October, and November 2022, directly to him and through the University of Arizona's communications office.

119 *Lab Leak or Natural Origin?*

120 Edward C. Holmes et al., "The Origins of SARS-CoV-2: A Critical Review," *Cell* 184, no. 19 (September 16, 2021): 4848–56, https://doi.org/10.1016/j.cell.2021.08.017.

121 "The Origins of SARS-CoV-2: A Critical Review."

122 *Lab Leak or Natural Origin?*

123 *Lab Leak or Natural Origin?*

124 Edward C. Holmes, "The COVID Lab Leak Theory Is Dead. Here's How We Know the Virus Came from a Wuhan Market," the Conversation, http://theconver sation.com/the-covid-lab-leak-theory-is-dead-heres-how-we-know-the-virus-came -from-a-wuhan-market-188163.

125 Kristian G. Andersen, Twitter post, August 4, 2022, 5:20 p.m., https://twitter.com /K_G_Andersen/status/1555302663008399360.

126 Kristian G. Andersen, Twitter post, August 20, 2022, 5:51 a.m., https://twitter.com/k_g _andersen/status/1560927423499313152?s=11&t=C9rVWu_9Kpw41ElqMWRpzA.

127 Kristian G. Andersen, Twitter post, April 3, 2022, 8:10 p.m., https://twitter
.com/K_G_Andersen/status/1510771778511024128.

128 Kristian G. Andersen, Twitter post, August 5, 2022, 4:43 p.m., https://twitter
.com/K_G_Andersen/status/1555655721336729600.

Chapter 17: Secret Meetings

1 Alison Young, "'I Remember It Very Well': Dr. Fauci Describes a Secret 2020
Meeting to Talk about COVID Origins," *USA TODAY*, June 17, 2021, https://
www.usatoday.com/story/opinion/2021/06/17/covid-19-fauci-lab-leaks-wuhan
-china-origins/7737494002/.

2 Farrar did not respond to requests from the author for an interview or comments
for this book.

3 Greg Folkers of NIH/NIAID email to Jennifer Routh (part of the NIH/NIAID
communications team) and Anthony Fauci, and copied to several others, January 27, 2020, https://usrtk.org/wp-content/uploads/2022/08/Talking-Points-for
-NIAID-Director-Dr.-Fauci.pdf. This email, obtained by U.S. Right to Know from
the House Committee on Oversight and Reform, indicates that in the days prior
to the February 1, 2020, meeting, there was general awareness among some at
NIH that NIAID had been funding work with coronaviruses in China, including
research by the Wuhan Institute of Virology. In this January 27, 2020, email, the
funding relationship is described in terms relating to expertise that the agency
could tap into when talking about coronaviruses. The email says in part: "when
talking about CoV (not necessarily in this venue) we have on our team (Vincent
and folks we fund, Peter Daszak, Ralph Baric, Ian Lipkin, etc.) probably the
world's experts non-human coronaviruses...NIAID has funded Peter's group for
coronavirus work in China for the past 5 years...Collaborators include Wuhan
Institute of Virology (currently working on the nCoV), and Ralph Baric..."

4 Kristian G. Andersen, email to Anthony Fauci, copied to Jeremy Farrar, January
31, 2020, 10:32 p.m. Obtained from the NIH through a Freedom of Information Act lawsuit by Buzzfeed News. https://www.documentcloud.org/documents
/20793561-leopold-nih-foia-anthony-fauci-emails 3187.

5 Andersen email to Fauci, January 31, 2020.

6 Holmes did not respond to multiple emails from the author sent in 2021 and 2022
requesting an interview, answers to questions, or any comments. Eventually, in
November 2022, in response to the author's continued requests, a spokesperson for
the University of Sydney sent an email saying that Holmes was unavailable for an
interview.

7 Jonathan Shaw, "The SARS Scare—A Cautionary Tale of Emerging Disease Caught
in the Act," *Harvard Magazine*, March–April 2007, https://www.harvardmagazine
.com/2007/03/the-sars-scare.html.

8 Jeremy Farrar with Anjana Ahuja, *Spike: The Virus vs the People—The Inside Story*
(London: Profile Books Ltd, 2021), 60.

9 Farrar and Ahuja do not name the paper.

10 Farrar and Ahuja, *Spike*, 61.

11 Farrar and Ahuja, *Spike*, 59.

12 Anthony Fauci, interview with the author, June 16, 2021.

13 BuzzFeed News, emails of Anthony Fauci January–June 2020 obtained through a FOIA lawsuit, June 2021, https://www.documentcloud.org/documents/20793561 -leopold-nih-foia-anthony-fauci-emails, 3169.

14 Natalie Bettendorf and Jason Leopold, "Anthony Fauci's Emails Reveal the Pressure That Fell on One Man," *BuzzFeed News*, June 1, 2021, https://www.buzzfeednews .com/article/nataliebettendorf/fauci-emails-covid-response.

15 Francis Collins declined through a spokesperson to be interviewed for this book.

16 Yasmeen Abutaleb and Shane Harris, "Trump Administration's Hunt for Pandemic 'Lab Leak' Went Down Many Paths and Came up with No Smoking Gun," *Washington Post*, June 15, 2021, https://www.washingtonpost.com/national-security/us -intelligence-wuhan-lab-coronavirus-origin/2021/06/15/2fc2425e-ca24-11eb-afd0 -9726f7ec0ba6_story.html.

17 Young, " 'I Remember It Very Well.' "

18 BuzzFeed News, emails, https://www.documentcloud.org/documents/20793561 -leopold-nih-foia-anthony-fauci-emails, 3125–3135.

19 U.S. Rep. James Comer, Ranking Member, House Committee on Oversight and Reform, and U.S. Rep. Jim Jordan, Ranking Member, House Committee on the Judiciary, letter to HHS Secretary Xavier Becerra, with a twelve-page attachment containing images of the redacted emails and excerpts of notes that were hand transcribed during the *in camera* review by committee staff, January 11, 2022, https:// republicans-oversight.house.gov/wp-content/uploads/2022/01/Letter-Re.-Feb -1-Emails-011122.pdf.

20 Jimmy Tobias, Twitter thread, November 22, 2022, https://twitter.com/jamesc tobias/status/1595096888373649414. In this thread, Tobias shared links to two baches of records released through his FOIA lawsuit: Fauci-Farrar emails, https:// www.documentcloud.org/documents/23316400-farrar-fauci-comms and Fauci-Andersen emails, https://www.documentcloud.org/documents/23316408-fauci -andersen-comms-unredacted. Additional information about Tobias's lawsuit, filed by The FOIA Project: https://foiaproject.org/case_detail/?title=on&style=foia &case_id=34675.

21 Michael Farzan declined to be interviewed.

22 Comer and Jordan, *in camera* review of redacted emails and unredacted emails released in response to Jimmy Tobias's FOIA lawsuit.

23 Comer and Jordan, *in camera* review of redacted emails.

24 Comer and Jordan, *in camera* review of redacted emails.

25 Emails released by Tobias's FOIA lawsuit.

26 Comer and Jordan, *in camera* review of redacted emails.

27 Comer and Jordan, *in camera* review of redacted emails and unredacted emails released in response to Jimmy Tobias's FOIA lawsuit.

28 Comer and Jordan, *in camera* review of redacted emails and unredacted emails released in response to Jimmy Tobias's FOIA lawsuit.

29 Jeremy Farrar, Kristian Andersen, Edward Holmes, Robert Garry, Ron Fouchier, Christian Drosten, and Andrew Rambaut declined to be interviewed or did not respond to interview requests.

30 Anthony Fauci, interview with the author, June 16, 2021.

31 Comer and Jordan, *in camera* review of redacted emails and unredacted emails released in response to Jimmy Tobias's FOIA lawsuit.

32 Kristian G. Andersen, email to Peter Daszak and several other scientists, "Re: URGENT: Please review by NOON if at all possible…" February 4, 2020. Obtained through open records requests filed by U.S. Right to Know. https://usrtk.org/wp-content/uploads/2020/12/NASEM_Andersen-Email_Baric-1.pdf.

33 Marcia McNutt, president of the National Academy of Sciences; John L. Anderson, president of the National Academy of Engineering; and Victor J. Dzau, president of the National Academy of Medicine, "NASEM Response to OSTP Re Coronavirus_February 6, 2020," February 6, 2020, https://www.nationalacademies.org/news/2020/02/national-academies-provide-rapid-response-to-white-house-on-coronavirus-data-needs#&gid=1&pid=1.

34 Andersen et al., "The Proximal Origin of SARS-CoV-2."

35 "The Proximal Origin of SARS-CoV-2—Overview of Attention for Article Published in *Nature Medicine*, March 2020," Altmetric, https://www.altmetric.com/details/77676422.

36 Young, "'I Remember It Very Well.'"

37 James Gorman and Carl Zimmer, "Scientist Opens Up About His Early Email to Fauci on Virus Origins," *New York Times*, June 14, 2021, Science, https://www.nytimes.com/2021/06/14/science/covid-lab-leak-fauci-kristian-andersen.html.

38 BuzzFeed News, emails, https://www.documentcloud.org/documents/20793561-leopold-nih-foia-anthony-fauci-emails, 2951–2952.

39 Fauci-Farrar emails released under Jimmy Tobias's FOIA lawsuit, 92–93.

40 Holmes did not respond to emails from the author sent in June 2021 and also in July, August, and November 2022 requesting an interview, answers to questions, or any comments. Eventually, in November 2022, in response to the author's continued requests, a spokesperson for the University of Sydney sent an email saying that Holmes was unavailable for an interview.

41 This Week in Virology, "TWiV 940: Eddie Holmes in on Viral Origins," September 28, 2022, https://www.microbe.tv/twiv/twiv-940/.

42 "TWiV 940: Eddie Holmes in on Viral Origins."

43 Kristian G. Andersen et al., "The Proximal Origin of SARS-CoV-2," *Virological*, February 16, 2020, https://virological.org/t/the-proximal-origin-of-sars-cov-2/398/1.

44 BuzzFeed News, emails, https://www.documentcloud.org/documents/20793561-leopold-nih-foia-anthony-fauci-emails, 2401. Email from Kristian Andersen on March 6, 2020.

45 Andrea Bellemare, "No, the New Coronavirus Wasn't Created in a Lab, Scientists Say | CBC News," CBC, March 24, 2020, https://www.cbc.ca/news/science/coronavirus-wasnt-created-in-lab-no-signs-genetic-engineering-1.5508735.

46 Kate Holland, "Sorry, Conspiracy Theorists. Study Concludes COVID-19 'Is Not a Laboratory Construct,'" *ABC News*, March 27, 2022, https://abcnews.go.com/US/conspiracy-theorists-study-concludes-covid-19-laboratory-construct/story?id=69827832.

47 "No, the Coronavirus Wasn't Made in a Lab. A Genetic Analysis Shows It's from Nature," *Science News*, March 26, 2020, https://www.sciencenews.org/article /coronavirus-covid-19-not-human-made-lab-genetic-analysis-nature.

48 Francis Collins, "Genomic Study Points to Natural Origin of COVID-19," NIH Director's Blog, March 26, 2020, https://directorsblog.nih.gov/2020/03/26/genomic -research-points-to-natural-origin-of-covid-19/.

49 Comer and Jordan, *in camera* review of redacted emails.

50 Mediaite, "Bret Baier: Sources 'Confident' Coronavirus Started in Wuhan Lab," April 16, 2020, https://www.mediaite.com/tv/foxs-bret-baier-sources-increasingly -confident-coronavirus-outbreak-started-in-wuhan-lab/. The report quotes Baier as emphasizing "there is no one who's saying this was a bio-weapon . . . They're saying it occurred naturally because China was trying to show that they could be as good or better than the U.S. in handling viruses, discovering viruses, and that this was a botched effort to contain this and it got out to the population."

51 Comer and Jordan, *in camera* review of redacted emails.

52 Comer and Jordan, *in camera* review of redacted emails.

53 "Statement by Anthony S. Fauci, M.D. | NIH: National Institute of Allergy and Infectious Diseases," August 22, 2022, https://www.niaid.nih.gov/news-events /statement-anthony-s-fauci-md.

54 Sheryl Gay Stolberg, "Francis Collins, a Former N.I.H. Director, Will Fill in as a Science Adviser to Biden," *New York Times*, February 17, 2022, U.S., https://www .nytimes.com/2022/02/17/us/politics/biden-francis-collins-nih.html.

55 Peter Daszak email to several scientists who had agreed to sign the letter, "RE A Statement in support of the scientists, public health and medical profession- als of China," February 6, 2020, https://usrtk.org/wp-content/uploads/2020/11 /The_Lancet_Emails_Daszak-2.6.20.pdf. Obtained by U.S. Right to Know.

56 Peter Daszak email exchange with Ralph Baric, "No Need for You to Sign the 'State- ment' Ralph!!" February 6, 2020, https://usrtk.org/wp-content/uploads/2021/02 /Baric_Daszak_email.pdf. Obtained by U.S. Right to Know.

57 Linfa Wang declined to be interviewed for this book or to provide any comments or additional context about the conversation that Peter Daszak references in this email.

58 Peter Daszak email exchange with Ralph Baric.

59 "PROPOSAL: VOLUME I , Project DEFUSE: Defusing the Threats of Bat-Borne Coronaviruses," March 27, 2018, https://www.documentcloud.org/documents/2106 6966-defuse-proposal.

60 Peter Daszak email exchange with Ralph Baric.

61 Charles Calisher et al., "Statement in Support of the Scientists, Public Health Professionals, and Medical Professionals of China Combatting COVID-19," *Lan- cet* 395, no. 10226 (March 7, 2020): e42–43, https://doi.org/10.1016/S0140-6736 (20)30418-9.

62 Parliamentlive.TV, "House of Commons Science and Technology Committee," December 15, 2021, https://parliamentlive.tv/event/index/7a2dfe49-3cbe-49be-97ee -3d33183cab15.

63 Daszak did not respond to requests for comment, including about Horton's statements during the committee meeting.

64 Parliamentlive.TV, "House of Commons Science and Technology Committee."

65 Kristian G. Andersen, Twitter Post, January 20, 2022, 5:55 p.m., https://twitter.com/K_G_Andersen/status/1484298570190635009.

66 *Encuentro con Jeffrey Sachs*, 2022, June 14, 2022, https://www.youtube.com/watch?v=7rRBuX4U0DU and https://web.archive.org/web/20220630143856/https://gatecenter.org/en/ndp-encuentro-jeffrey-sachs, 12:25.

67 Richard Ebright, Twitter post, May 31, 2021, https://twitter.com/r_h_ebright/status/1399240387043155971.

68 Parise Adadi et al., "Open Letter #4: Call for a Comprehensive Investigation of the Origin of SARS-CoV-2, If Possible with Chinese Government Participation," June 2021, https://www.researchgate.net/publication/352799874_Open_Letter_4_Call_for_a_Comprehensive_Investigation_of_the_Origin_of_SARS-CoV-2_if_Possible_with_Chinese_Government_Participation.

69 Neil L. Harrison and Jeffrey D. Sachs, "A Call for an Independent Inquiry into the Origin of the SARS-CoV-2 Virus," *Proceedings of the National Academy of Sciences* 119, no. 21 (May 24, 2022): e2202769119, https://doi.org/10.1073/pnas.2202769119.

70 Alison Young, "Deleted COVID-19 Genetic Fingerprints Show It's Still Possible to Dig for Lab Leak Evidence," *USA TODAY*, June 24, 2021, https://www.usatoday.com/story/opinion/2021/06/24/covid-19-lab-leak-investigation-deleted-genetic-fingerprints-show-its-possible-dig-lab-leak-ev/7778194002/.

71 Jeffrey D. Sachs et al., "The *Lancet* Commission on Lessons for the Future from the COVID-19 Pandemic," *Lancet* 400, no. 10359 (September 14, 2022), https://doi.org/10.1016/S0140-6736(22)01585-9.

72 Michael Worobey did not respond to multiple requests for an interview or comments made by the author in July, August, October, and November 2022, directly to him and through the University of Arizona's communications office.

73 Jeremy Page and Drew Hinshaw, "China Refuses to Give WHO Raw Data on Early Covid-19 Cases," *Wall Street Journal*, February 12, 2021, https://www.wsj.com/articles/china-refuses-to-give-who-raw-data-on-early-covid-19-cases-11613150580.

74 Stephanie Nebehay and John Miller, "Data Withheld from WHO Team Probing COVID-19 Origins in China: Tedros," Reuters, March 20, 2021, https://www.reuters.com/article/us-health-coronavirus-who-china-report/data-withheld-from-who-team-probing-covid-19-origins-in-china-tedros-idUSKBN2BM26S.

75 "Preliminary Report for the Scientific Advisory Group for the Origins of Novel Pathogens (SAGO)," World Health Organization, June 9, 2022, https://www.who.int/publications/m/item/scientific-advisory-group-on-the-origins-of-novel-pathogens-report. 16-17.

76 Michael Worobey et al., "The Huanan Seafood Wholesale Market in Wuhan Was the Early Epicenter of the COVID-19 Pandemic," *Science*, July 26, 2022, https://www.science.org/doi/10.1126/science.abp8715.

77 Michael Worobey et al., "The Huanan Market Was the Epicenter of SARS-CoV-2 Emergence," *Zenodo*, February 26, 2022, https://doi.org/10.5281/zenodo.6299600.

78 Carl Zimmer and Benjamin Mueller, "New Research Points to Wuhan Market as Pandemic Origin," *New York Times*, February 26, 2022, https://www.nytimes.com/interactive/2022/02/26/science/covid-virus-wuhan-origins.html. The preprint was covered as breaking news, with the early versions of the story consisting of only a few paragraphs, including Worobey's quote, and noting, "This is a developing story." https://web.archive.org/web/20220226192514/https://www.nytimes.com/interactive/2022/02/26/science/covid-virus-wuhan-origins.html.

79 Archive of tweets from the *New York Times* Twitter account on February 26, 2022, Internet Archive Wayback Machine, https://web.archive.org/web/20220226210418/https://twitter.com/nytimes.

80 Jonathan E. Pekar et al., "The Molecular Epidemiology of Multiple Zoonotic Origins of SARS-CoV-2," *Science* 377, no. 6609 (August 26, 2022): 960–66, https://doi.org/10.1126/science.abp8337.

81 Worobey et al., "The Huanan Seafood Wholesale Market."

82 Matthew Wright, a spokesman for the *Science* family of journals, said in a November 2, 2022, email to the author that editors don't comment on the review process for individual articles. "Speaking in general terms, however, it is standard practice for our editors to remove superlative adjectives during the editorial process."

83 Michael Worobey, Twitter post at 3:45 a.m. on October 27, 2022, https://twitter.com/MichaelWorobey/status/1585538074464747520. The post was in response to questions being asked by journalists from *Vanity Fair* and ProPublica.

84 Worobey Twitter post at 3:45 a.m. on October 27, 2022.

85 Worobey et al., "The Huanan Seafood Wholesale Market."

86 In her November 2, 2022, email to the author, Koopmans said that because a "substantial part of the underlying data" used in the Worobey paper was derived from the 2021 joint WHO–China mission, in which she was a participant, the Worobey team sought her input on "the data, their line of reasoning, and the draft text. I provided my views and comments." In the email, Koopmans also said: "The moment a real new piece of information would be shared that could point to a lab, I would urgently press for follow up. I just have not seen them, which is why the lab hypothesis in my assessment ranks much lower than a natural zoonotic origin." Koopmans did not grant an interview and in a November 18, 2022, email did not directly answer follow-up questions from the author, including questions about whether the joint WHO–China team studying Covid-19's origin discussed the safety of WIV's work with novel bat coronaviruses at biosafety level 2 and whether the leaked 2018 DARPA research proposal involving the WIV was a piece of evidence worth investigating.

87 "COVID-19 Virtual Press Conference Transcript - 9 February 2021," World Health Organization, February 9, 2021, https://www.who.int/publications/m/item/covid-19-virtual-press-conference-transcript---9-february-2021.

88 "Preliminary Report for the Scientific Advisory Group for the Origins of Novel Pathogens (SAGO)," World Health Organization, June 9, 2022, 17–19.

89 Worobey Twitter post at 3:45 a.m. on October 27, 2022.

90 Worobey et al., "The Huanan Seafood Wholesale Market in Wuhan Was the Early Epicenter of the COVID-19 Pandemic," Supplementary Materials.

91 Michael Standaert and Eva Dou, "In Search for Coronavirus Origins, Hubei Caves and Wildlife Farms Draw New Scrutiny," *Washington Post*, October 11, 2021, https://www.washingtonpost.com/world/asia_pacific/china-covid-bats-caves-hubei/2021/10/10/082eb8b6-1c32-11ec-bea8-308ea134594f_story.html.

92 Worobey Twitter post at 3:45 a.m. on October 27, 2022.

93 Angela Rasmussen and Michael Worobey, "Conspiracy Theories About COVID-19 Help Nobody," *Foreign Policy*, September 15, 2022, https://foreignpolicy.com/2022/09/15/conspiracy-theories-covid-19-commission/.

94 Edward C. Holmes, "The COVID Lab Leak Theory Is Dead. Here's How We Know the Virus Came from a Wuhan Market," the Conversation, August 14, 2022, http://theconversation.com/the-covid-lab-leak-theory-is-dead-heres-how-we-know-the-virus-came-from-a-wuhan-market-188163.

INDEX

Abramova, Faina, 133
ABSA International, 22, 100,
    107
Adalja, Amesh, 124–125
aerosol-generating equipment,
    183
aerosolized particles, 9, 12, 21–23, 73,
    102–105, 133–134
Agharkar Research Institute, 214
Agricultural Bioterrorism Protection Act
    of 2002, 163
Alise, Mark, 166
American Association for the
    Advancement of Science,
    132
American Biological Safety Association,
    22, 100, 107
American Society for
    Microbiology, 99
American Society for Virology, 99
Ames, Iowa, 92
Andersen, Kristian, 221–223, 227–231,
    235, 237
Anhui Medical University, 120
animal holding rooms, cleanup process
    for, 38–39
anthrax infections, 15–18, 34–35,
    133–134
Atha, Ken, 104
Atlanta Journal-Constitution, 65
Auchincloss, Hugh, 188
avian influenza accident. *See* H5N1 avian
    influenza

bacteria. *See also individual bacteria by
    name*
    aerosolized, 9, 12
    containment of, 23–24
Baier, Bret, 232
Baldwin, Agnes, 22
Baltimore, David, 219–220
Baric, Ralph. *See also* University of North
    Carolina laboratories
    concerns on Wuhan's bat virus
        research, 208
    creating hybrid viruses,
        198–201
    Daszak and, 233–234
    elected into National Academy of
        Sciences, 204
    MIT Technology Review interview,
        209
    pushing back against federal funding
        pause, 197–198
    on SARS-CoV-2 origin,
        209–210
Barkley, W. Emmett, 30
Bartonsville, Maryland, 3
bat coronaviruses. *See* coronavirus
    chimeras
Bedson, Henry, 127–128
Bertuzzi, Stefano, 99
Bethesda Naval Hospital, 14
Biden, Joe, xx, 217
Biland, David, 139
bio-defense research, USAMRIID's labs
    are world's largest, 36–37

315